FREEDOM WITHOUT PERMISSION

FREEDOM WITHOUT PERMISSION

Bodies and Space in the Arab Revolutions

FRANCES S. HASSO AND ZAKIA SALIME, *editors*

Duke University Press · Durham and London · 2016

© 2016 DUKE UNIVERSITY PRESS
All rights reserved

Designed by Courtney Leigh Baker
Typeset in Trade Gothic and Arno Pro by Graphic Composition, Inc.,
Bogart, Georgia

Library of Congress Cataloging-in-Publication Data
Names: Hasso, Frances Susan, editor. | Salime, Zakia, editor.
Title: Freedom without permission : bodies and space in the Arab revolutions /
    Frances S. Hasso and Zakia Salime, editors.
Description: Durham : Duke University Press, 2016. | Includes bibliographical
    references and index.
Identifiers: LCCN 2016016046
ISBN 9780822362210 (hardcover : alk. paper)
ISBN 9780822362418 (pbk. : alk. paper)
ISBN 9780822373728 (ebook)
Subjects: LCSH: Sex role—Arab countries—History—21st century. | Arab Spring,
    2010–
Classification: LCC HQ1075.5.A65 F74 2016 | DDC 305.30917/4927—dc23
LC record available at https://lccn.loc.gov/2016016046

COVER ART: European Pressphoto Agency b.v. / Alamy Stock Photo

To all those who struggle for a just world and dignified lives.
And to those who teach us to think, imagine, and act anew.

CONTENTS

ACKNOWLEDGMENTS

Like all collaborative projects, this book would not have been possible without a wide range of support from many individuals and programs. Many of the ideas in the book were hammered out at the Geographies of Gender in the Arab Revolutions workshop at the Nasher Museum of Art at Duke University in December 2013. We are incredibly grateful to the scholars who participated in the workshop as presenters and interlocutors for their comments, provocations, and energy: Lamia Benyoussef, Courtney Berger, Laurel Bradley, Elyse Crystall, Susanne Dahlgren, Karina Eileraas, Susana Galán, Banu Gökarıksel, M. Ali Kadivar, Cybelle McFadden, Ali Mian, Alyssa Miller, Jessica Namakkal, Nora Fisher Onar, Sonali Pahwa, Tamar Shirinian, Louis Yako, and Nadia Yaqub.

We appreciate Banu Gökarıksel for her insights on each chapter and for ultimately writing the final chapter of the book. Endless thanks go to Sonali, Lamia, Susanne, Susana, Karina, and Banu for their patience and efficiency during the very productive process of writing, revising, and editing their chapters. We hope they are as proud of the book as we are.

Courtney Berger, our editor at Duke University Press, supported this project when it was still germinating and at every stage thereafter and offered productive criticism that facilitated its completion. The incisive feedback and support of three anonymous reviewers energized us and pushed the project to the next level.

We are grateful to Elizabeth Ault, Susana Galán, Susanne Dahlgren, and Jamal Dillman-Hasso for critical readings of drafts of the introduction and to Jamal for preparing the consolidated bibliography.

We thank Marialana Weitzel, Keri Majikes, Kim Carlisle, Sheila Devis, and the staff of the Nasher Museum for administrative assistance they provided at different stages. Special thanks to the calm Sandra Korn at Duke

University Press, who was crucial in helping us move the book to production.

We appreciate the Duke University sponsors who funded the workshop and volume and made the project possible: Program in Women's Studies (Director's Discretionary Fund and Charlotte Bunch Endowment), Islamic Studies Center (Carnegie Transcultural Islam Project), Office of the Dean of Trinity College of Arts and Sciences, Franklin Humanities Institute, International Comparative Studies Program, and Middle East Studies Center.

Last but not least, we thank our family members for their emotional support!

Introduction FRANCES S. HASSO AND ZAKIA SALIME

This book examines the gendered and sexual dimensions of the 2011 Arab revolutions and uprisings, with specific attention to conjunctures between bodies and spaces. It does so by incorporating the language and insights of activists and revolutionaries who themselves worked with theoretical assumptions as they imagined and produced different futures. The revolutions, a sequence of related nonviolent political ruptures of world-historical significance, were initiated by Tunisians who forced their long-time autocratic president to step down on 14 January, inspiring activists with equality, justice, and democracy agendas around the world. The Revolution in Tunisia was followed by large-scale mobilizations and revolts in Egypt, Yemen, Bahrain, Morocco, and Syria, as well as upheavals in every Arab country. Millions rose against militarized, securitized, and unaccountable states, Western imperialism, poverty, and national and transnational forms of economic extraction. The revolutions occurred in places where majorities struggled to be free from repression and degradation and in many cases feed families and access clean water—in short, to live dignified lives. Ruling governments in every Arab country fearfully consolidated as millions chanted in Arabic, "Al-sha'b yurid isqat al-nizam!"—The people want the fall of the regime! In Arabic *nizam* denotes "order," "regime," and "system"; thus the resounding collective demand challenged many orders and systems and was not read simply as a call to rearrange ruling seats. The valences of this chant differed among and within countries, over time, and in many cases between revolutionaries and activists as gendered, sexualized, ideological, and class tensions came to the fore.

Despite calling these revolutions "Arab," we recognize ethnic terrains and borders to be contested, identifications and solidarities to be multiple, and antecedents to be plural and layered. Nouns such as *spring, revolution,* and *uprising* continue to be debated as descriptions of the cataclysmic events that began in December 2010 in Tunisia. The "Spring of Equality" and the "Amazigh Spring," coined in the Maghreb, stressed gender struggle, challenged the universalism of *Arab*, and insisted on forms of community and solidarity based on multiple identifications. Any descriptive term is inflected by its genealogies and meaning layers and further complicated by different languages. These are multisited struggles with many historical precursors. Their conclusions have not been written. They are ongoing "process[es] of becoming" that are being "pushed" to their "limits."[1] They continuously generate rereading and reevaluation, sometimes distorted by presentist cynicism and despair.

Disagreements emerged as state-sponsored repression and violence intensified, ruling classes reasserted themselves, exhaustion set in, precarious economic conditions worsened, and ideological and strategic differences emerged among activists. After the first flush of revolutionary fervor, the meanings of slogans such as *social justice, freedom,* and *human dignity* were questioned. Who deserves dignity? How capacious is the freedom and social justice being struggled for? How does respect for ethnic, religious, and ideological differences play within these demands? What is the ideal national community? What is the appropriate role of policing and military power in postcolonial states? Multiple answers, imaginaries, and anxieties emerged.

Tensions and disagreements were often inscribed on and worked through gendered and sexual embodiments and symbolism. Even at the level of language, were girls, women, and nonconformists included in *the people*? Does *regime* refer only to governments, or does it include other controlling systems that require felling? Why did conflict so often take sexualized forms on men's and women's bodies? These questions became especially important as competing masculinisms—for example of anarchist football fans, legislators, police and military forces, established oppositions, kings and presidents, clerics, Islamist formations, and Western and regional interventionist forces—asserted themselves in every setting. Though divided by ideology, positionality, and priorities, women and girls burst seams, categories, and rules designed to hold in their bodies, voices, and minds. Just as repressive governments can no longer assume that the universal postcolonial subject will accept the indignities and injustices imposed by governments, security forces, and class elites, everyone was put on notice that neither would girls and women. The revolutions publicly disputed gender and sexual orders in novel, unauthorized, and often shocking ways, even as a range of forces actively worked to reassert order and respectability boundaries. This is a permanent legacy that will continue to roil sexual and gendered orders in the region.

This book is the outcome of a collaborative research project initiated in a late 2012 call for papers to examine spatialized gender and sexual dynamics and symbolism in the revolutions under the title Geographies of Gender in the Arab Revolutions. We held an intensive two-day workshop at the Duke University Nasher Museum of Art in December 2013 with authors of accepted papers, an interlocutor in feminist geography, and a cross-disciplinary group of scholars, including PhD students, from the Durham and Chapel Hill area in North Carolina. We incorporated a tour and discussion of an art exhibit, *Lines of Control: Partition as a Productive Space*, which was evocative in its focus on "psychological and physical" borders, violence, and spatial policing and transgression, themes that emerge throughout the volume.[2] The authors use interpretive methodologies to reflect on spatial, embodied, and gendered dimensions of revolutions and uprisings in Bahrain, Egypt, Morocco, Saudi Arabia, Tunisia, and Yemen. The final chapter offers a comparative study of the Gezi uprising in Istanbul and an analytical coda to the volume.

The authors in this book make four major interventions in analyzing these multiscalar revolutions. First, rather than relying on social science definitions of *revolution* as transformed states and overthrown leaders, we use the term to broadly capture affective, intimate, embodied, institutional, and spatial registers of upheaval and transgression. Thus *revolution* in this volume includes "civilpolitics," intimate politics, interstitial politics, and heterotopia. Revolution occurred at the levels of identification, imagination, aesthetics, and emotion. Its sites were proximal and virtual, in bedrooms, on blogs, and on streets. We illustrate how revolution generated emancipatory and repressive possibilities, including fleeting wins, memories that cannot be forgotten, spaces that will never be the same, and permanent loss and destruction. We are particularly attentive to words and their spatial and political significance. Such words include *hirak* and *harakiyya* (movement), *tkoulisse* (backroom discussions), *madaniyya* (civility), *fawda* (chaos), *passe partout* (she goes everywhere), *ghazwat* (invasion), and *saha* and *midan* (square or space). The revolutions notably inaugurated forms of solidarity and identification. But they also produced emancipatory disidentifications that were overt in a manner rarely seen before.

Activists condemned and criticized not only sovereign forms of power such as security forces, ruling governments, and Western imperialism but also totalizing institutions, sensibilities, and ideologies that stress belonging and foreclose nonconformity and plurality.

This relates to the second intervention. The authors disrupt taken-for-granted understandings of place and space and are particularly interested in the nexus of bodies and spatiality as activists engaged in world-challenging and world-making. Indeed the body is not merely a surface or casement of the individual. It is a material space of multiple dimensions that irrupts and interrupts normative orders and activates competing ones through imagination, symbolism, and enactment. Bodies are central to anxiety about difference and depictions of boundaries perceived as impermeable or dangerous, as indicated by infection, invasion, and contamination metaphors. Each chapter indicates how embodiments, gender codes, and spatiality persistently informed each other. The book shows how a range of contentions were prominently worked out through and on bodies, which themselves are scales and locations of individual life, subjectivity, and voice, as well as sites of inscription and expression.[3] In the revolutions and uprisings, bodies and subjectivities were formed and transformed as they congregated in public squares and cafés, on blogs using anonymizing handles, on Facebook chats with chosen interlocutors, and in secret meetings, thus well beyond what Hannah Arendt called "a space of appearance."[4] People slept, dined, and held open discussions in streets and squares and on front stoops in mixed age, class, and ideological groups. Bodily encounters in physical spaces generated new sensibilities and alliances across sexual differences that challenged taken-for-granted divisions. But they also produced conflicts that reinforced or produced new iterations of partitioning.

In a third analytical intervention, we highlight the dilemmas that continue to be posed by ideological conflict, sexual difference, and class inequality, which are embodied, inscribed in a variety of spaces, and not easily overcome by mass protest. Indeed these sources of inequality and difference were central to strategies of policing and control by governments. But they were also important on the street and among activists and revolutionaries. Thus even as the authors in this volume argue for the dramatic and everyday making and contesting of spaces through symbolic and bodily transgressions, they also demonstrate the "sticky" and embodied aspects of difference and inequality that limited the horizons of the inclusive pluralities that emerged in every revolution and uprising. Solidarities across difference and redefinitions of space in these revolutions and uprisings were often restricted by various forms of policing and moral control, which were persistently structured by gendered and sexual master narratives and anxieties.

Fourth, consistent with a wealth of feminist scholarship, this book undermines the public/private dichotomization of metaphoric and physical spaces, bodies, and social relations. Such boundaries are historical and ideological, constituting rather than simply describing a cleanly divided social world. Moreover they are freighted with gendered assumptions as women so often come to be associated with the body, nature, reproduction, intimacy, emotion, family life, the home, and the sexual, as if these ever exist outside of discourse, politics, economy, and revolution. Or as if boys and men too are not embodied, reproductive, sexual, emotional, intimate, and produced by and implicated in homes and families. The world of the selfie, the iPhone, YouTube, Facebook, and personal blogging makes distinctions between public and private even more difficult, as demonstrated in every chapter. Nevertheless one of the most striking features of the revolutions and uprisings was the centrality of the public square and its massive nonviolent occupation by men and women from diverse walks of life. Women and girls widely and insistently claimed cities, streets, neighborhoods, and cyberspace in a historically unprecedented manner. They protested in the light of day and the dark of night, creating new relationships to space and to others, building new sensibilities and communities across difference. The bodies, voices, and ideas of boys and girls, men and women converged in unity, poetry, song, discussion, and ideological conflict in cyberspace, cemeteries, and malls and on sidewalks, streets, roundabouts, and squares. But people also connected and argued in bedrooms, cars, and kitchens. This book shows, however, that the public square "eventfulness" of the uprisings, which made them globally legible and consumable as media "spectacle,"[5] often concealed the quotidian, dispersed, embodied, and less visible dimensions of especially sexual and gendered dynamics in multiple sites, including the "private," virtual, and discursive.

Some definitional points are in order regarding the words *place* and *space* in this book. Tahrir Square in Cairo, the Pearl Roundabout in Manama, the revolution squares in Aden, the moving automobile on streets in Jeddah, Gezi Park in Istanbul, Rabat's Aquarium Theater, alleys, front stoops, neighborhood barricades, bedrooms, and kitchens are spaces and places. Space refers to *arrangements* and *interactions* (e.g., between hu-man bodies, animals, nature, sound, the visual, the digital, built environ-ments) at multiple scales, not all of them material. For example, blogs and Facebook pages may be considered distributed kinds of "squares." Places are more grounded and specific, "the lived and dynamic location where different people, social agents or powerful actors come together in unpre-dictable and even shifting ways." Place enables us to account for the "inter-section between worlds and selves" and involves "emotion, imagination, perception, and memory."[6]

Spaces and places are similar, however, in being patterned by institu-tionalized inequalities, ideology, and behavioral scripts, shaping how users inhabit them and encounter others. They are also similar in being *made*, redefined, and "reclaimed."[7] As these authors discuss, these makings and remakings occur through use (everyday and extraordinary encounters; bar-riers and checkpoints), memory (of massacres, street battles, sexual as-saults, major mobilizations), representation (graffiti, aesthetics, poems, songs, sartorial practices), and Facebook and Twitter wars. This dynamism, emergence, and multiplicity is difficult to control. On the other hand, as indicated by our third intervention, boundaries and hierarchies are often *weighty*, reinforced by powerful ideologies, sensibilities, and institutions that may reconstitute to effectively respond to challenges.

Valences and Circuits of Revolution

This volume considers revolution at multiple scales that include digital cir-cuits and platforms, imagination, institutions, language, embodied prac-tices, and physical spaces. The authors richly demonstrate that the revo-lutions and uprisings fit uneasily within any totalizing ideology, strategy, theory, or method. As Asef Bayat argues, the "Arab uprisings occurred at a time on the global stage when the idea of revolution had dissipated. The decline of the key grand ideologies—revolutionary nationalism, Marxism-Leninism, and Islamism—had left the protagonists with no revolutionary utopia to imagine."[8] For us this multiplicity of sites and scales, and the ap-parent open-endedness and dynamism, shatter classic definitions of revo-lution. Leaders were compelled to step down in Tunisia, Libya, Egypt, and Yemen, for better or worse. Whether or not the revolutions successfully overturned regimes, their languages of "dignity" and "freedom," and the processes they inaugurated, interpellated multiple subjectivities. Their outcomes cannot be measured by traditional means. In Bahrain, for example, while the Pearl Revolution did not overthrow the Khalifa regime, Frances Hasso argues that it has transformed space, thinking, relationships, and society in multiple ways. Creative activism by the Southern Movement articulated new "civil" forms of life in southern Yemen, argues Susanne Dahlgren. Lamia Benyoussef demonstrates spatial and imaginative inaugurations and transgressions since 2011 in Tunisia, including that of "freedom that does not require permission."

These massive mobilizations widely used the slogan "Liberty, dignity and social justice." To adapt Chantal Mouffe's analysis of radical democracy, they articulated subject positions and identities of political freedom, respect for embodied forms of life, economic redistribution, and pluralistic frames of belonging.[9] We recognize with Wendy Brown that "freedom is neither a philosophical absolute nor a tangible entity but a relational and contextual practice that takes shape in opposition to whatever is locally and ideologically conceived as unfreedom." It is not possessed, universal, pure, or ever fully achieved.[10] Moreover, while freedom, in Nikolas Rose's words, is "infused with relations of power, entails specific modes of subjectification and is necessarily a thing of this world, inescapably sullied by the marks of the mundane," this does not mean it is "a sham or liberty an illusion; rather it opens up the possibility of freedom as neither a state of being nor a constitutional form but as a politics of life."[11] Indeed freedom from a variety of subordinations was explicit in these revolutions and uprisings. As unfashionable as it seems in some theoretical circles, we take such desires seriously, even as the multiple meanings of freedom and its limits were widely understood, including by activists.

The revolutions have been marked, Farhad Khosrokhavar argues, by "the pursuit of freedom through cultural creativity . . . mobilizing people through a new symbolism expressed in rage, irony, 'theatrality,' and dramatization, but also with sarcasm towards the dictator and his family and elite and derision of power holders."[12] Zakia Salime points to the emergence of "aesthetic citizenship" marked by embodied, symbolic, and artistic performances of everyday hybrid languages, orality, national identity, and belonging. The Syrian intellectual-activist Samar Yazbek argues that the revolutions radically challenged a binary between intellectual and activist so that "writing is now for everyone."[13] Rather than "denying these insurgencies the term 'revolution,'" Hamid Dabashi contends, "we are now forced to reconsider the concept and understand it anew."[14]

The digital revolution remains key to mobilizing, innovative organizing, and creative expression in the revolutions and uprisings, which, after all, erupted to challenge authoritarian governments. As indicated in many of these chapters, girls and women in the region were major drivers of digital activism, constituting 30 to 33 percent of active tweeters in the 2011 Tunisian and Egyptian revolutions.[15] Digital technologies fundamentally shifted activism and civic engagement from at least 2010 and were especially important in initiating a domino effect when they were used to bring "the details of social mobilization—and success—against the strongmen of Tunisia and Egypt."[16] Mobile phones facilitated mobilization during the crisis periods of the revolutions, "when physical spaces for public conversation and debate closed down."[17] Individual and choreographed acts of defiance posted on many virtual platforms proliferated in every country, including Saudi Arabia, the focus of Susana Galán's chapter.

The digital revolution is double-edged, however, and coexists with "old" media, an adjective we understand as historically relative. Between the mid-1990s and mid-2000s Arabic satellite television technology was heralded as offering new opportunities for free expression and political mobilization, until regime and corporate interests shut down these possibilities. Similarly, even as they offer opportunities for revolutionary and feminist mobilization, expression, and creativity, Facebook, Twitter, Microsoft, YouTube, and Vodafone are corporate circuits designed to make money for CEOs and shareholders. The economic value of these corporations is produced by unpaid users. They are equally available to state and international security forces and imperialistic, sectarian, misogynist, and racist actors,[18] as illustrated in a number of chapters, including by Hasso and Benyoussef. Benyoussef argues that in Tunisia and its diaspora, even as Facebook "paved the way for novel" and emancipatory expression, it also turned into a tool to express conservative, misogynistic, homophobic, or racist sentiments. Moreover "traditional" media, including state-controlled television and radio stations and newspapers, continue to distribute their messages and arguably have far more impact and reach than social media. Nevertheless, as Gillian Rose explains, the "capture of space" by hegemonic systems is always partial, with multiple and diverse openings for individual and collective forms of resistance.[19]

As the chapters by Galán, Sonali Pahwa, and Karina Eileraas indicate, blogs have been crucial to new forms of activism by girls and women in the region. Unlike Facebook, Twitter, and YouTube, blog platforms may be open-source (e.g., Wordpress) or corporate-controlled. A blog may be set by its owner to be open or limited to a chosen audience. Personal blogs have become part of "the virtual agora" in the region,[20] facilitating continuums of intimacy and publicness conducive to girls' and women's authorship and community. Personal blogs have become sites of solidarity, trust, dissensus, and disidentification beyond proximal relations.[21] Even before 2011 Hoda Elsadda argued that Egyptian women literary bloggers produced a "literary counterpublic" that challenged public/private and intimate/formal dichotomies and the gendered restrictions of primarily male literary and political salons.[22] Pahwa contends that personal blogs, initially dismissed as a feminine genre, created "intimate publics" and spaces of alterity. Largely writing in English to avoid censorship, Saudi women bloggers found protection in what Galán calls "camouflage" operations that use "familiar and informal language" to open up "interstitial" spaces for conversation and feminist critique. The Egyptian feminist activist Aliaa Elmahdy, Eileraas argues, used her blog to stage disidentification and expanded forms of belonging and community.

Spatial Body Politics

Linda Zerilli defines politics as a "world-building practice of publicly articulating matters of common concern," in the process inaugurating freedom practices with others in space. From this perspective, politics is about being "out of order" in relation to dominant understandings of where particular bodies and ideas belong.[23] For Jacques Rancière politics refers to enacted and collectively shared moments of emancipatory rupture in dominant logics of hierarchical separation and control, which he calls "police." Rancière describes the "essence of politics" as enactment of "dissensus" for emancipation goals. Politics in this reading "makes visible that which had no reason to be seen, it lodges one world into another." It does not emerge from preconstituted subject positions or identitarian categories (e.g., worker, woman, feminist, Shi'a). Nor is it attached to spheres, spaces, or institutions deemed "proper" for politics.[24] Police, in contrast, does not recognize "particular categories of people as subjects qualified to speak" or "understand the claims of social subordinates as speech." Politics enacts "equality" without requiring the poor, stateless, or noncitizen to be categorized as fully rights-bearing.[25] Rancière's definition of politics relies on "opening up new spaces" to disrupt the partitioning of thinking and life.[26] Feminist geographers similarly understand politics to include "out of place" embodiments, such as when black, pregnant, disabled, poor, homeless, or otherwise nondominant or nonconforming people enter hegemonic spaces.[27]

Coming together in protest across differences in urban spaces was central to the revolts in the region. This required "participants to accept social differences that are often used to divide them" and "building coalitions of young and old, poor and middle class, women with hijabs and without, migrants, refugees, adherents of different religions and sects, people from the slums as well as the posh areas."[28] This emancipatory coming together of difference to rupture the status quo is close to "politics" as defined by Rancière, albeit Ehsani's "coalition" indicates less ephemerality. If we take Engin Isin seriously, however, the city is a "force field that operates as a difference machine." It actively "assembles (groups), generates, distributes, and differentiates differences, incorporates them within strategies and technologies, and elicits, interpellates, adjures, and incites them."[29] This limits the possibilities of emancipatory assemblage across difference. Pahwa directs our attention away from iconic revolutionary figures and public squares in her discussion of the "digital homes" made by Egyptian women bloggers. For Aliaa Elmahdy, the focus of the chapter by Eileraas, actual streets in Cairo were dangerous for nude protest. Indeed they were often dangerous for clothed women and men. Thus Elmahdy's embodied performance protest was facilitated by the selfie and hosted on her blog.

Benyoussef, Dahlgren, Galán, Salime, and Hasso in this volume also highlight the significance of presence and absence, visibility and invisibility, inclusion and exclusion of different kinds of bodies and voices. Benyoussef examines how competing "mythscapes" of belonging and community in revolutionary and postrevolutionary Tunisia depended on fundamental exclusions and elisions. Dahlgren contrasts public with being hidden, silenced, and marginalized rather than private in southern Yemen, recognizing agencies in homosocial spaces and intimacies in street corners and revolution squares. Salime discusses Moroccan 20 February activists' articulation of spatial metaphors such as *kawlassa* and *tkoulisse* (deriving from the French *coulisse*) to highlight ideological, gendered, and ethnic exclusions at the "backstage" of the movement's general assemblies despite stated commitments to pluralism, inclusiveness, and transparency. Hasso shows that gendered, classed, and racialized partitions in how bodies inhabit and circulate in space in Bahrain were artifacts of ideological struggle at particular historical moments, with dominant images of gender segregation and black-robed women hiding as much as they revealed.

Spatial thinking is central to organization, mobilization, and conceptualizations of status quos and their transformation.[30] The term *hirak*, used in southern Yemen to describe the Southern Movement, signaled a politics of *movement* that encouraged mixed-gender activism on street corners, in offices, and in home spaces (Dahlgren). Moroccan activists used a similar term, *harakiyya*, to refer to the 20 February Movement (Salime). Both imply the open-ended putting of dynamics *in the plural* into motion, differing from the goals of traditional social movements and revolutionary projects. Spatial conceptualizations also have gendered registers and implications even if these are not acknowledged or explicit.[31] For example, resistance discourse typically challenges "up" (usually the state) and is less likely to consider gendered and sexualized forms of inequality on lower scales.

Many events described in this book illustrate the significance of embodied spatial strategies in the revolutions and uprisings, including the occupations of the Pearl Roundabout in Manama, Bardo Square in Tunis, and the revolution squares in Aden; the climbing of the clock tower in Tunis; the Freeze events in Rabat and the "standing man" protest in Istanbul's Gezi Park; and the nude performance protests in Egypt and Tunisia. While nationalist movements, anticolonial movements, Islamist organizations, political parties, and unions usually organize themselves hierarchically, the revolutions and uprisings challenged these dynamics. Malek Sghiri notes that Tunisian revolutionary activists quickly developed an awareness of the benefits of fluidity rather than hierarchal chains of command: "My union background made me argue for at least some degree of organization, but I gradually came to realize that the secret to our success was partly down to our chaotic state, or rather, the number and variety of leaders and the absence of a domineering centralizing command that would stifle initiative and hinder immediate responses to a rapidly developing situation on the ground."[32] The 2008 strike by Gafsa miners in Tunisia offered a precursor to such activist decentralization.[33]

These dynamics challenge Miriyam Aouragh's claim that the Arab revolutions were marked by Leninist "democratic centralism," which she defines as "independent organizations" coexisting with a "vanguard."[34] Rather Dahlgren, Hasso, Salime, and Eileraas show that tension sometimes emerged with organized oppositions, political parties, and established feminist organizations and activists. While it's true that social transformation projects find their surest grounds in shared struggles, memories, and proximal relations in a variety of spaces,[35] such grounded confrontation historically privileges the young, physically able, willing, armed, and masculine. Decentralization and dispersals of authority, facilitated by digital technology, produced intimate politics on multiple scales and allowed girls and women to make new spaces, in contrast to their frequent exclusion and minoritization in classically hierarchical organizations and forms of resistance.

Bodies Out of Order

All spaces are structured by ideological assumptions and experienced situationally and interpreted subjectively.[36] This book attends to the microphysics of gendered bodies and voices in the revolutions, which Sara Mourad contends "brought back attention to the body as a political medium."[37] After posts and images of his self-immolation in front of a woman municipal police officer in Sidi Bouzid in December 2010 went viral, the Tunisian vegetable seller Mohamed Bouazizi was simplistically read to represent humiliated Muslim or Arab masculinity,[38] a position not easily attached to women's bodies and subjectivities. Khaled Fahmy calls the Egyptian revolution a "revolution of the body" (*thawrat al-jasad*) in his consideration of the case of Samira Ibrahim, who insistently challenged her arrest and subjection to a "virginity" exam by the Egyptian military in March 2011.[39] Women's bodies in the Arab revolutions have been "sites of dissent and revolution," argues Sherine Hafez, even as they "are disciplined and regulated through discourses of patriarchy, Islamism and secular modern masculinity."[40]

Feminist scholars of the Middle East challenge understandings of "public" space as masculine and attached to power and "private" space as feminine and without power. They also highlight the sociopolitical processes that produce where and when particular kinds of bodies, practices, and voices belong.[41] In her studies of Cairo, Farha Ghannam argues that a framework of a fixed public "world of men" against a private "world of women" "fails to account for the continuous struggle to define the boundaries" and the centrality of this struggle with kin boys, men, and older women in the production of gender inequality.[42] Scholars of Yemen have contested definitions of the "domestic" as feminine, "privilege-deprived," and segregated and highlighted women's agency and generational differences in women's mobility "maps" in urban gender-segregated Yemen.[43] Paul Amar has shown that well before 2011 the security state's "thug" appellation to working-class and poor men in Cairo was facilitated by middle- and upper-class forms of feminism invested in state control and respectability in public space.[44]

Nevertheless there is deep and wide evidence of masculine privilege in access to and experiences of urban space in the modern world, although class status, racialization, dress, and temporality modify this claim. Space is "elastic" and experienced differently by women and men, at night and in daytime. Experiences are further structured by visible sexual or ethnic signifiers of minority status.[45] Doreen Massey, drawing on the work of Elizabeth Wilson, writes that European city culture developed in relation to men, and women were historically seen to threaten metropolis culture and order because they were freer from patriarchal constraints associated with living in familial and less anonymous settings. European cities were historically seen as "a realm of uncontrolled and chaotic sexual license, and the rigid control of women in cities has been felt necessary to avert this danger."[46] Studying contemporary European urban life, Hille Koskela argues that "an essential part of women's socializations turns out to be spatial," in the sense of being cultivated to learn mobility limits in relation to home.[47]

In the 1970s Fatima Mernissi contended that Moroccan city streets were considered male spaces in which "only prostitutes and insane women wandered freely."[48] Thirty years later Fatima Sadiqi and Moha Ennaji found that while many Moroccan city streets remain an "aggressive domain" for women's voices and bodies, such exclusions had been effectively challenged by feminists in the 1990s and 2000s.[49] Anouk de Koning found that in early twenty-first-century Cairo the mobility trajectories of upper-middle-class women were "crucially determined by class-based inequalities and distinctions." Yet their experiences were universal in that streets were considered spaces "for men to inhabit . . . spend time, observe and interact with passers-by, comment and flirt." Women, in contrast, were required to be on their way to a destination and subject to a male gaze.[50] Despite the fact that cities are often "described as hostile and dangerous for women," they offer women "fascinating freedoms and possibilities."[51] These possibilities and freedoms may be the very reasons cities are sometimes made inhospitable to women. An evaluation of cities as unsafe for women assumes that less urban locations are inclusive and welcoming. Many educated Palestinian women who moved to the mixed metropolitan cities of Haifa and Jaffa, for example, experienced them as offering "a space of choice" in comparison to the kin-based restrictions the women face in villages and smaller towns.[52]

Police and politics as understood by Rancière correspond in many ways with feminist understandings of embodiment, subjectivity, and space as co-constituted and socially defined and redefined rather than natural or static. Feminist scholars, however, more deeply consider how embodied alterity, interlocking positionalities, and unconscious desires, what Mernissi calls "psychological needs,"[53] have staying power. Liz Bondi and Joyce Davidson stress, for example, that while not fixed, gender identities and places are not "freely chosen or easily transformed. Instead the dynamic interplay between space, place, and sexualized embodiments is subject to inertia and 'stickiness.'"[54] *Stickiness* refers to obdurate subordinations connected to particular bodies, spaces, and times.[55] It follows that although spaces and places that reproduce dominance can be "breached" by subversive actions, the effects of such breaches are "uncertain and contestable."[56] These limits have certainly been true in the Arab uprisings, where the purveyors of policing are not only state agents. While Ultras soccer fans in Egypt challenge the control of neighborhoods and streets by agents of the security state, for example, they also exclude girls and women from "fun" and resistance mobilizations.[57] Moralizing and sexualizing gendered policing quickly became essential to a range of repressive players aiming to take back liberated and liberating spaces in the revolutions and uprisings, as discussed in a number of chapters. In response to the Pearl Revolution in Bahrain, existing sectarian partitions intensified and often took sexualized forms (Hasso). In October 2011 and March 2013, respectively, the young Egyptian and Tunisian feminists Aliaa Elmahdy and Amina Tyler provoked solidarity as well as violent and misogynistic, trivializing, and Islamophobic responses when they posted protest images of themselves naked (Eileraas). Both body activists dramatically breached partition lines given the unlimited pings and reverberations of the digital world, but responses largely proved their points.

How much unity is possible after euphoria at the scene of rupture has dissipated, particularly when those invested in particular hierarchies have much to lose? A number of chapters indicate that inequality is sticky and ideological and positional differences are difficult to negotiate or dissolve. Beyond frissons of solidarity and recognition, it is unclear under what conditions doing politics together across difference can more than temporarily supersede policing sensibilities and practices, including by activists with competing desires, interests, and notions of emancipation. The violent outcomes of many of these revolts have tempered assumptions that even radical and massive ruptures in public squares and streets can easily overturn or erase historical patterns of repression, inequality, and ideological disagreement, including in everyday embodied relations. Such sticky divisions often became bases to reconsolidate lines of control.

Massey argues that every space includes elements of order and chaos. *Order* because all phenomena are caused and thus explicable, and organized systems by definition aim to arrange things and bodies in relation to each other. *Chaos* is intrinsic because any configuration, interaction, or movement always has potential for "unintended consequences."[58] In 2011 a phrase that rhymed the Arabic word *thawra* with *fawda*, or *revolution* with *chaos*, was used repeatedly by authoritarian leaders desperate to maintain "law and order" in Egypt (Mubarak), Tunisia (Ben Ali), Libya (Qaddafi), Yemen (Saleh), and Syria (Asad), even as the regimes were significant sources of violence and economic and political suffering.[59] The significance of regime-produced order and chaos rhetoric in the region, which preexists 2011, powerfully resonated with the twenty scholars who participated in the Geographies of Gender in the Arab Revolutions workshop, the precursor to this book. As feminist scholars we immediately recognized that chaos is often symbolized by and linked to fears of women's sexuality and boundary-crossing enactments.

The *thawra-fawda* phrase indicates the importance of competing spatial imaginaries of power distribution. Beyond this the words evoke layers of historical meaning related to gender, sexuality, and alterity. Nonconforming subjectivities and unruly bodies are often cast as "the antithesis of the rational modern progressive and civilised subject, disciplined and obedient." Citizens are told that "these bodies respond favourably to a strong and dominant government which seeks to impose order on chaos."[60] Repressive governments in the region have historically constituted themselves as protectors of women and ethnic and religious minorities, and thus better than the spectral alternative, previously represented as post-2003 Iraq.[61] More recently present-day Syria and Libya have been added to the mix.

Leaders who used such language in fact enunciated, even promised, that revolution would translate into negative chaos: destruction and a terrifying loss of predictability and control in daily life. In contrast to Massey's opposition between order and chaos, repressive postcolonial governments often used resources that include state and informal violence to reinforce their preferred order. They promised their people that "the absence of an oppressive state would give free rein to sectarian and communal chaos in society"; they assured that law, prisons, security services, and organized violence were ready to respond to popular resistance; and they encouraged "fear of Imperialist-Zionist-Western attempts" to violate national sovereignty if their rule is undermined.[62] Thus potential and real chaos in its negative valence has been intrinsic to the order they sustain.

Chaos discourse and fear of chaos thread through revolutionary and counterrevolutionary dynamics and remain relevant beyond Arab settings. The opposite of chaos in such discourse is "security" and "stability." The chaos feared by Western powers, economic elites, and authoritarian governments anxious not to lose their geopolitical and economic footing or control differs from the fear of average people that precarious life will be made more unbearable by war, sectarianism, and dislocation. These very governments have a history of building and funding security formations accountable only to them, supporting sectarian and socially conservative formations to undermine leftist and democratic challenges, consolidating wealth and resources to maintain political, personal, and family power, and restricting expression and political association.

A contrasting revolutionary slogan emerged from Jordan and went viral in the Arab feminist Facebook and blogosphere in 2011: "Sawt al-mar'a thawra"—The voice of women is a revolution.[63] Its evocative power comes from the play on and rhyme with an Islamic hadith whose provenance is suspect, "Sawt al-mar'a 'awra" (The voice of women is defective). The word 'awra expresses equivalence between women's voices and sexualized body parts. In this reading women's voices should be silent in the company of unrelated men, and a woman's body parts should be hidden from all men except her husband to avoid sexual disorder (*fitna*). This power to produce disorder comes from the purported ability of women's bodies and voices to enthrall men and destabilize the hegemonic ordering of bodies in space. The feminist slogan that emerged in 2011 defied this understanding by affirmatively declaring women's voices to be irrepressible sources of positive disorder. The Arab revolutions have in many cases led to increased sectarianism, ethnic and ideological violence, territorial divisions, rape and sexual assault, foreign interventions, disfranchisement, and dislocation. As already indicated, the foundations of these violent dynamics were in many cases decades in the making, embedded in authoritarian systems and colonial and imperial relations. In many situations nonviolent and widely inclusive revolutionary projects have become militarized. This volume invites us to connect the Arab revolutions with chaos in the positive sense, whereby dominant distributions of subordination are ruptured and rearranged more fairly in a variety of realms.

Chapter Summaries

Given the degree to which the revolutions were embedded in national histories of resistance and explicitly developed in relation to each other, the chapters are organized chronologically according to empirical focus. In chapter 1 Sonali Pahwa investigates the relationship between digital and political repertoires in Egypt, with a focus on women's personal blogs that emerged before the 2011 revolution. She shows that the intimate publics generated by these blogs were not simply sites of debate about revolution but were staging grounds for entirely new political enactments that include identification and disidentification. She frames activist women's personal blogs as "intimate" rather than "private sites of re-forming a social self." The centrality of gender performance in these blogs indicates a productive relationship between gendered affects and political subjectivities in digital publics. Pahwa argues that the politics of the blogs was not merely sentimental; they challenged the dominant scripts of national politics, reconfigured proximity and distance to intimates, and challenged a public/private dichotomy. Women's blogs countered a hegemonic dramaturgy of revolution with a beginning and an end and offered alternative theaters of sentiment and politics.

In chapter 2 Lamia Benyoussef explores competing "mythscapes" in Tunisia in the immediate prerevolutionary period, during the revolution, and since by examining music, poetry, visual culture, Facebook projects, and activist campaigns on the streets. She shows that prerevolutionary cultural material anticipated and reflected the sharp class, cultural, and ideological tensions that continue in Tunisia. The mythscapes produced in these different historical moments relied on very different forms of Tunisian and transnational affiliations, historical reference points, and gendered imaginaries and projects. Benyoussef demonstrates that intense collective anxieties about belonging and authenticity thread through the embodied experiences and metaphors examined. The 14 January Revolution, moreover, inaugurated forms of Tunisian feminist activism that boldly occupy and transform a variety of spaces and differentiate themselves from alliance with the patriarchal state feminism of Bourguiba and Ben Ali and the gender complementarity logic of conservatives.

Susanne Dahlgren analyzes the southern Yemeni revolution, which created new spaces in the city and reconstituted gendered subjectivities and practices, in chapter 3. Revolution squares all over Aden became sites of organizing, street-corner universities, and havens of embodied forms of care and comfort. As the Southern Revolution mobilized women, young people, and the poor, it produced widespread conviction that women should be reintegrated into public space, as was the case during the postcolonial socialist republic in the South (1967–90). The activities of the Southern Movement are part of what Dahlgren terms "civilpolitics," an imaginary of state power that is subservient and accountable to civil rather than military, tribal, and clerical forces.

In chapter 4 Frances S. Hasso explores spatialized embodied and sectarian dynamics in Bahrain's 14 February or Pearl Revolution. She argues that gendered, sexualized, and racializing dynamics worked through each other as long-standing conflict between the majority of citizens and the Khalifa rulers intensified. She calls this the sex-sect-police nexus. Hasso's chapter emphasizes that the Pearl Revolution ruptured the gendered arrangements of bodies and voices in space and triggered sexualization as a racializing state technique. The Pearl Revolution also led to a rise in women-led confrontational street politics not necessarily authorized by Bahraini opposition men. These have produced sublimated tensions not captured by images of orderly gender-segregated marches.

Zakia Salime considers the 20 February Movement in Morocco in chapter 5. She argues that the movement represents an inaugurative moment that set into motion new political, cultural, and gendered dynamics, interrupting the conceptualization of politics, gender, and citizenship around already given identities and modalities of mobilization. By forging new modes of political engagement and discursive spaces, the movement liberated multiple possibilities for the co-imbrication of sex, gender, culture, and politics in Morocco. She examines these inaugurations by studying discursive, performative, and artistic spaces initiated or expanded by 20 February, which she terms forms of "aesthetic citizenship." She also shows that feminist enunciations have taken a "sexual turn" on the protest scene and beyond.

In chapter 6 Susana Galán explores the Women2Drive campaign and digital activism that challenges restrictions on women's mobility and inhabitations of space in Saudi Arabia. She argues that the driving campaign is an example of cautious interstitial gender politics that nevertheless creates radical languages and communities of resistance. Galán examines cars as products, surfaces, interiorities, and vehicles of mobility. Due to gendered regulation of public spaces, blogs and other virtual media represent some of the few available outlets for women to express themselves and enact politics. It is by expressing "individual sentiment" in blogs that sensibilities become shared. By constituting alternative realities, activist bloggers enact a virtual heterotopia where less restrictive futures can be imagined and staged in the present.

Karina Eileraas analyzes the Egyptian Aliaa Elmahdy's nude blogging in chapter 7, arguing that this activism may be read as a performance of rage against the status quo. Elmahdy brought sex to Tahrir Square on her own terms, injecting herself into the geopolitical scene as a gendered and sexualized subject, activist, and artist. Her "body-that-feels" surrenders full control, magnifies vulnerability, and exposes her to potential sexual harassment and violence in real time and space. Conversely her "cyber body" seduces a voyeuristic audience while performing in the time and space of her choosing. Elmahdy, Eileraas argues, transforms "the photographic field into a space of possibility by writing herself into history as a political and sexual agent."

In the concluding chapter Banu Gökarıksel uses the analytical tools of feminist geography to reflect on the implications of the overall project, as well as to examine gendered-spatial dimensions in iconic representations of the 2013 Taksim Gezi Park protests in Istanbul. Her analysis reveals the gendered and sexual politics at work in the images and accounts that have come to represent the Gezi protests. Some of these images rely on established norms, symbols, and roles, but others challenge dominant understandings of femininity and masculinity. Her analysis traces two themes that link the Gezi uprising to other cases examined in the volume. The first focuses on the body as an intimately political site at the experiential and representational levels. The second explores the crisscrossing of the public/private divide and the domestication of so-called public space during the revolutions and uprisings.

NOTES

1. Malek Sghiri, "Greetings to the Dawn: Living through the Bittersweet Revolution (Tunisia)," in *Diaries of an Unfinished Revolution*, edited by Layla Al-Zubaidi, Matthew Cassel, and Nemonie Craven Roderick, translated by Robin Moger and Georgina Collins (New York: Penguin Books, 2013), 44.

2. Nasher Museum of Art at Duke University, "Lines of Control: Partition as a Productive Space," September 19, 2013–February 2, 2014," http://nasher.duke.edu/exhibitions/lines-of-control/.

3. Linda McDowell, *Gender, Identity and Place: Understanding Feminist Geographies* (Minneapolis: University of Minnesota Press, 1999), 34, 40.

4. In Mustafa Dikeç, "Space as a Mode of Political Thinking," *Geoforum* 43, no. 4 (2012): 672.

5. Rosalba Icaza and Rolando Vázquez, "Social Struggles as Epistemic Struggles," *Development and Change* 44, no. 3 (2013): 668; Nishant Shah, "Citizen Action in the Time of the Network," *Development and Change* 44, no. 3 (2013): 667.

6. Amy Mills, "Critical Place Studies and Middle East Histories: Power, Politics, and Social Change," *History Compass* 10, no. 10 (2012): 779.

7. Nada Shabout, "Whose Space Is It?," *International Journal of Middle East Studies* 46, no. 1 (2014): 165; Kaveh Ehsani, "Radical Democratic Politics and Public Space," *International Journal of Middle East Studies* 46, no. 1 (2014): 159.

8. Asef Bayat, "The Arab Spring and Its Surprises," *Development and Change* 44, no. 3 (2013): 599.

9. Chantal Mouffe, *The Return of the Political* (New York: Verso, 2005), 35, 56–57, 70.

10. Wendy Brown, *States of Injury: Power and Freedom in Late Modernity* (Princeton, NJ: Princeton University Press, 1995), 9, 24.

11. Nikolas Rose, *Powers of Freedom: Reframing Political Thought* (Cambridge: Cambridge University Press, 1999), 94–95.

12. Farhad Khosrokhavar, *The New Arab Revolutions That Shook the World* (Boulder: Paradigm, 2012), 1–2.

13. Samar Yazbek, introduction to *Diaries of an Unfinished Revolution: Voices from Tunisia to Damascus*, edited by Layla Al-Zubaidi, Matthew Cassel, and Nemonie Craven Roderick, translated by Robin Moger and Georgina Collins (New York: Penguin Books, 2013), 1–2, 6.

14. Hamid Dabashi, *The Arab Spring: The End of Postcolonialism* (London: Zed Books, 2012), 5.

15. Philip N. Howard and Muzammil M. Hussain, *Democracy's Fourth Wave? Digital Media and the Arab Spring* (New York: Oxford University Press, 2013), 48.

16. Kees Biekart and Alan Fowler, "Transforming Activisms 2010+: Exploring Ways and Waves," *Development and Change* 44, no. 3 (2013): 528, 529; Howard and Hussain, *Democracy's Fourth Wave?*, 22.

17. Howard and Hussain, *Democracy's Fourth Wave?*, 5, 19, 20, 22–23; Khosrokhavar, *The New Arab Revolutions That Shook the World*, 41, 42.

18. For example, Miriyam Aouragh, "Framing the Internet in the Arab Revolutions: Myth Meets Modernity," *Cinema Journal* 52, no. 1 (2012): 152–55.

19. Liz Bondi and Joyce Davidson, "Situating Gender," in *A Companion to Feminist Geography*, edited by Lise Nelson and Joni Seager (Malden, MA: Blackwell, 2005), 20–25; Gillian Rose, *Feminism and Geography: The Limits of Geographical Knowledge* (Minneapolis: University of Minnesota Press, 1993), 137–60.

20. Khosrokhavar, *The New Arab Revolutions That Shook the World*, 79.

21. Fereshteh Nouraie-Simone, "Wings of Freedom: Iranian Women, Identity, and Cyberspace," in *On Shifting Ground: Muslim Women in the Global Era*, edited by Fereshteh Nouraie-Simone (New York: Feminist Press at the City University of New York, 2005), 61–79; George Weyman, "Speaking the Unspeakable: Personal Blogs in Egypt," *Arab Media and Society* 3 (Fall 2007), http://www.arabmediasociety.com/?article=425.

22. Hoda Elsadda, "Arab Women Bloggers: The Emergence of Literary Counterpublics," *Middle East Journal of Culture and Communication* 3, no. 3 (2010): 314–15, 317–18.

23. Linda M. G. Zerilli, *Feminism and the Abyss of Freedom* (Chicago: University of Chicago Press, 2005), 22–28, 9.

24. Jacques Rancière, "The Thinking of Dissensus: Politics and Aesthetics," in *Reading Rancière: Critical Dissensus*, edited by Paul Bowman and Richard Stamp (London: Continuum, 2011), 1–17; Jacques Rancière, "Politics and Aesthetics: An Interview," *Angelaki: Journal of the Theoretical Humanities* 8, no. 2 (2003): 192, 201; Jacques Rancière, "Ten Theses on Politics," *Theory and Event* 5, no. 3 (2001): 1, 11–13, http://muse.jhu.edu/journals/theory_and_event/v005/5.3ranciere.html; Joseph J. Tanke, *Rancière: An Introduction, Philosophy, Politics, Aesthetics* (London: Continuum, 2011).

25. Andrew Schaap, "Enacting the Right to Have Rights: Jacques Rancière's Critique of Hannah Arendt," *European Journal of Political Theory* 10, no. 1 (2011): 30, 23, 24.

26. Dikeç, "Space as a Mode of Political Thinking," 673, 674.

27. McDowell, *Gender, Identity and Place*, 34–70.

28. Ehsani, "Radical Democratic Politics and Public Space," 159.

29. Engin F. Isin, "Engaging, Being, Political," *Political Geography* 24, no. 3 (2005): 375.

30. For example, Dikeç, "Space as a Mode of Political Thinking," 669.

31. One of the few scholarly examinations of spatiality in the Arab revolutions is Salwa Ismail's comparative analysis of revolutionary dynamics in Cairo and Damascus, "Urban Subalterns in the Arab Revolutions: Cairo and Damascus in Comparative Perspective," *Comparative Studies in Society and History* 55, no. 4 (2013): 865–94. Although its subject is men, it is not concerned with issues of gender and sexuality. Ismail found that the

"infrastructures of protest lay in the micro-processes of everyday life that developed at the quarter level, in community forms of organization and in popular youth's modes of action and interaction with state government" (878). Revolutionary consciousness and activity emerged from "spatially grounded hostility," dynamics, and history (873, 874). With regard to Cairo, a focus on Midan Tahrir, the "tech generation," young middle-class icons, and the "cultured," she argues, elided daily violent battles between police and poor and working-class residents, especially boys and men, in the "informal" neighborhoods of Cairo (865, 869, 871, 873). In Damascus subaltern urbanites were spatially and ideo-logically divided and in conflict because the regime fosters control through sect-based co-optation as well as "clientalization and exclusion" in distributing resources such as neighborhood-based housing (884, 885, 889, 890).

32. Sghiri, "Greetings to the Dawn," 29.

33. Khosrokhavar, *The New Arab Revolutions That Shook the World*, 29.

34. Aouragh, "Framing the Internet in the Arab Revolutions," 151. Democratic central-ism is classically used to describe the structure of a proletarian vanguard party, as first developed in the Russian Revolution and widely applied by top-down leftist movements in the Arab world.

35. Sghiri, "Greetings to the Dawn," 21, 27, 34, 41.

36. Anna J. Secor, "The Veil and Urban Space in Istanbul: Women's Dress, Mobility and Islamic Knowledge," *Gender, Place and Culture: A Journal of Feminist Geography* 9, no. 1 (2002): 5–22; Hille Koskela, "Urban Space in Plural: Elastic, Tamed, Suppressed," in *A Companion to Feminist Geography*, edited by Lise Nelson and Joni Seager (Malden, MA: Blackwell, 2005), 257–70.

37. Sara Mourad, "The Naked Body of Alia: Gender, Citizenship, and the Egyptian Body Politic," *Journal of Communication Inquiry* 38, no. 1 (2014): 63, 67, 74.

38. Paul Amar, "Middle East Masculinity Studies: Discourses of 'Men in Crisis,' Indus-tries of Gender in Revolution," *Journal of Middle East Women's Studies* 7, no. 3 (2011): 38.

39. Khaled Fahmy, "Revolution of the Body" (Arabic), *Jadaliyya*, May 2012, http://arabic.jadaliyya.com/pages/index/5489/%D8%AB%D9%88%D8%B1%D8%A9-%D8%A7%D9%84%D8%AC%D8%B3%D8%AF.

40. Sherine Hafez, "The Revolution Shall Not Pass through Women's Bodies: Egypt, Uprising and Gender Politics," *Journal of North African Studies* 19, no. 2 (2014): 175.

41. Leslie P. Peirce, *The Imperial Harem: Women and Sovereignty in the Ottoman Empire* (Oxford: Oxford University Press, 1993). Pierre Bourdieu of course has analyzed gender in relation to built environments, especially home spaces, in Algeria. For a review of the debates in Western feminist scholarship on spatiality, see Don Mitchell, "Feminism and Cultural Change: Geographies of Gender," in *Cultural Geography: A Critical Introduction* (Malden, MA: Blackwell, 2000), 199–229. Also see the superb book by McDowell, *Gender, Identity and Place*.

42. Farha Ghannam, *Remaking the Modern: Space, Relocation, and the Politics of Identity in a Global Cairo* (Berkeley: University of California Press, 2002), 89–92.

43. Gabriele Vom Bruck, "A House Turned Inside Out: Inhabiting Space in a Yemeni City," *Journal of Material Culture* 2, no. 2 (1997): 141; Toni Kotnik, "The Mirrored Public: Architecture and Gender Relationship in Yemen," *Space and Culture* 8, no. 4 (2005):

472–83; Susanne Dahlgren, "Morphologies of Social Flows: Segregation, Time, and the Public Sphere," in *Gendering Urban Space in the Middle East, South Asia, and Africa*, edited by Martina Rieker and Kamran Asdar Ali (New York: Palgrave Macmillan, 2008), 45–70.

44. Paul Amar, *The Security Archipelago: Human-Security States, Sexuality Politics, and the End of Neoliberalism* (Durham, NC: Duke University Press, 2013), esp. 210–33.

45. Koskela, "Urban Space in Plural," 257–58, 259.

46. Doreen Massey, "Politics and Space/Time," in *Place and the Politics of Identity*, edited by Michael Keith and Steve Pile (London: Routledge, 1993), 149–50.

47. Koskela, "Urban Space in Plural," 257.

48. Fatima Mernissi, *Beyond the Veil: Male-Female Dynamics in Modern Muslim Society* (Bloomington: Indiana University Press, 1987), 142–43.

49. Fatima Sadiqi and Moha Ennaji, "The Feminization of Public Space: Women's Activism, the Family Law, and Social Change in Morocco," *Journal of Middle East Women's Studies* 2, no. 2 (2006): 91–92.

50. Anouk de Koning, "Gender, Public Space and Social Segregation in Cairo: Of Taxi Drivers, Prostitutes and Professional Women," *Antipode: A Radical Journal of Geography* 41, no. 3 (2009): 535, 547.

51. Koskela, "Urban Space in Plural," 263.

52. Hanna Herzog, "Mixed Cities as a Place of Choice: The Palestinian Women's Perspective," in *Mixed Towns, Trapped Communities: Historical Narratives, Spatial Dynamics, Gender Relations and Cultural Encounters in Palestinian-Israeli Towns*, edited by Dan Rabinowitz and Daniel Monterescu (Burlington, VT: Ashgate, 2007), 243–44, 249.

53. Mernissi, *Beyond the Veil*, viii.

54. Bondi and Davidson, "Situating Gender," 16.

55. Also see on "congealing," Geraldine Pratt and Susan Hanson, "Geography and the Construction of Difference," *Gender, Place and Culture: A Journal of Feminist Geography* 1, no. 1 (1994): 19–22, 25–26.

56. Bondi and Davidson, "Situating Gender," 23.

57. Hasso is involved in a research project on the Ultras.

58. Massey, "Politics and Space/Time," 156, 157.

59. These two videos illustrate the use by rulers of the chaos/revolution discourse as well as its undermining by activists: Mohamedbaolo, "Thawra.mp4," 15 March 2011, YouTube, https://www.youtube.com/watch?v=Aoo0fI3CzwY; Abu Ziad, "Revolution-Chaos" (Arabic), 16 March 2011, YouTube, https://www.youtube.com/watch?v=nvEn4Mbs6IU. In RT Arabic, "Ali Abdullah Saleh: What Happened in Yemen Was Chaos, Not Revolution" (Arabic), 25 March 2013, YouTube, https://www.youtube.com/watch?v=r6-ylug1b3Q, Saleh, deposed ruler of Yemen, uses the word *chaos* a number of times in an interview with Russian television. Saleh argues that these are *not revolutions* but chaos.

60. Hafez, "The Revolution Shall Not Pass through Women's Bodies," 178.

61. For example, Fatima el-Issawi, "The Arab Spring and the Challenge of Minority Rights: Will the Arab Revolutions Overcome the Legacy of the Past?," *European View* 10, no. 2 (2011): 250, 257.

62. Khosrokhavar, *The New Arab Revolutions That Shook the World*, 8–9.

63. An image of the *sawt al-mar'a thawra* poster is available at http://www.aljabha.org /?i=66387. See Yqeen, "A Woman's Voice Is a Revolution, Not *'awra*" (Arabic), YouTube, 10 September 2012, https://www.youtube.com/watch?v=jgqoAo6GCWs. The post-July 2013 uses of this slogan by Islamist women in Egypt during street demonstrations against the military government illustrate the instability of language and make evident that women's bodies and voices may revolt against the repressive order of militarism but not necessarily seek to undermine unequal gendered and sexual forms of spatial order.

1 POLITICS IN THE DIGITAL BOUDOIR Sentimentality and the Transformation of Civil Debate in Egyptian Women's Blogs

SONALI PAHWA

The blog had a scarlet border and was dotted with hand-drawn flowers and adorned with a self-portrait. A spray of curly hair announced a surprisingly conventional performance of femininity for a political dissident. Mona's blog, *Maat's Bits & Pieces* (named after an Egyptian goddess), began in 2006 as an autobiographical blog, with regular posts about her life as a university student, her feelings, and even her love life. The posts grew increasingly politicized after the murder of Khaled Said in June 2010, and particularly after Egypt's 2011 uprising. Mona became a committed activist who founded the movement against military trials for civilians in post-revolution Egypt and established a separate blog for that project in March 2011. Her autobiographical blog was widely read and cited, with political posts maintaining an emotionally charged voice that resonated with accounts of torture and wrongful detention in her other blog. The intimate publics that these blogs invoked seemed iconic of a moment of revolutionary politics in which affective recognition of political sentiments modeled political recognition.[1]

Autobiographical blogs like *Maat* maintained their popularity as sites of debate about political transformation after the uprising. Most of these blogs were written, intriguingly, by middle-class women in their twenties. Their intimate publics were sites of debate about the revolution, as well as staging grounds for entirely new political repertoires. This chapter investigates the relationship between digital and political repertoires in Egypt, with a focus on women's blogs as theaters for the transformation of autobiographical performance into a repertoire of debate about national politics. These blogs are less well known outside Egypt than contemporaneous movements for women's rights. The growing presence of women at protests in the aftermath of the 2011 uprisings, and some horrific instances of sexual harassment, fueled an exponential rise in antiharassment activist groups that by 2012 included HarassMap (established in 2010), Operation Anti-Sexual Harassment/Assault, Basma, and Shuft al-Taharrush.[2] Nor did personal blogs claim the highest profile in digital activism. Rather reportage centered on the *We Are All Khaled Said* Facebook page, later revealed to be established by the male activist Wael Ghonim, who was credited with launching a "Facebook revolution."[3] Less visibly and without heroic accolades, the women bloggers of whom I write created spaces for reflecting on revolutionary times, using them to incubate new forms of writing about political sentiments. I argue that these were also sites of performing gendered roles and relations for an audience of anonymous readers. The centrality of gender performance in blogs with activist content indicates a productive relationship between gendered affects and political subjectivities in Egyptian digital publics.

Examining the digital practices of women bloggers as affective repertoires, I trace the emergence of a politics that is not merely sentimental but redistributes roles within the sphere of national political activism. By using digital space to reconfigure proximity and distance to their intimates, these bloggers turned a conventional genre of women's "personal" blogs into a space for enacting potentially political affects, like anger and sadness. Their "intervention in the visible and the sayable" was not just discursive but also performative.[4] Blogs were sites for rehearsing new roles and relationships for civic-minded women. The feelings that these women performed in their blog writing shaped their personas no less than the content of their writing. Bringing formerly private affects into the digital publics of personal blogs reframed the figure of the sentimental woman as a political actor rather than a passive national icon.

I situate the lives and writings of three socially and politically critical Egyptian women bloggers within a digital landscape and cityscape, examining the kinds of place the blogs generated. These were practiced places that combined registers of talk among intimates and debate about national politics.[5] The authors set the stage for empathetic forms of relation with readers in dramatic scenes where heightened emotions crystallized political conflicts. The blogs served as theaters for affective politics that accommodated roles outside the rationalist discourse usually found in newspaper and television debates on Egyptian politics. Even after the 2011 revolution the cast of characters in those hegemonic publics remained defined by a masculinist nationalism. As countersites in which real cultural landscapes were "simultaneously represented, contested, and inverted,"[6] the women's blogs accommodated experimental practices from across the "real" sites that bloggers inhabited. Their digital repertoires rehearsed the embodiment of a political actor who stood outside the habitus of norma- tive politics—for example, by writing revolutionary dramas as personal stories. The dialectic between gender and genre in women's blogs shaped a digital heterotopia in which empathetic recognition was the norm. The bloggers' gendered and political disidentifications with mainstream po- litical debate played out on the same stage.

The three bloggers at the center of this chapter exemplify the intersec- tions of gendered and political disidentification in revolutionary Egypt: Mona the antimilitary activist, Fatma the feminist researcher, and Eman the literary blogger and sometime feminist organizer, all defined their blogs as "personal" but used them to engage in debates on revolutionary and gen- der politics. What does it mean, then, to call a blog "personal"? Through content analysis and analysis of interviews conducted with the bloggers in 2011, I examine their productions of personalized political space in every- day dramatic digital performances. Through a more limited analysis of au- dience using interviews and blog-post comments, I interpret the uptake of blog discourse and the mapping of blog communities as part of the social geography that emerged in revolutionary Egypt.

The Personal, Political, and Gendered in Blog Genres

Gender was a significant marker of genre in the Egyptian blogosphere and literary establishment. While male columnists and commentators dominated mainstream media, bloggers with names like Wahda Misriyya (An Egyptian Woman) and Bint Misriyya (An Egyptian Girl) wrote lyri- cal prose that was distinct from the learned style of media commentators considered to be authorities. The women's writing was also recognizably different from prose by male bloggers like Alaa Abdel Fattah, Wael Ab- bas, and Karim Amer, who gained fame in Egypt for publishing exposés of police abuse that got them jailed by the Mubarak regime.[7] By contrast to the sensationalist style used by men bloggers, a smaller number of women political bloggers such as Zeinobia and Baheyya (who did not disclose their real names) used more distant prose to report horrific events such as the murder of Khaled Said in June 2010.[8] While male bloggers' bold writing showed that they did not fear state violence and imprisonment, the genre of the personal blog staged the rhythms of quieter sanctuaries and protected lives.

In 2008 Cairo's Shorouk publishing house collated selected posts of three personal bloggers, all women, into books that became best sellers. Rehab Bassam, Ghada Mahmoud, and Ghada Abdel Aal became instant literary celebrities and won critical praise for posts that were now read as "short stories."[9] Abdel Aal's blog *I Want to Get Married* was even turned into a prime-time Ramadan television serial in 2010. Although the personal blog genre accounted for a substantial portion of Egypt's digital real estate (47.5 percent of the Egyptian blogosphere in 2007),[10] the attention given to female bloggers sealed its gendered identity as a women's genre. The bloggers I write about rose to prominence shortly after these pioneers and adopted aspects of their lyrical, intimate style of writing.

The revolutionary upheaval of 2011 reshaped the boundaries between personal and political blog genres in many ways. Bloggers of all stripes made forays into explicitly political discourse. For instance, Bint Misriyya in March 2011 posted lengthy, argumentative pieces, such as "The Army Must Go,"[11] in contrast to her usual mix of succinct sociopolitical commentary and film reviews. The collective emotional tenor of Egypt's politicized blogosphere shifted, as Susana Galán notes, from frustration and resignation to a higher pitch of hope and fear.[12] The sentimental drama of revolution that played out on television screens was refracted through the blogosphere in a minor key, in accordance with the minoritarian history of the blog genre.

Prerevolution Egypt had seen an efflorescence of blogs on Islam, literature, feminism, and minority identities.[13] Even high-profile activist blogs, like that of the 6 April Movement, spoke from marginal subject positions. An emphasis on first-person experience marked blog posts about the Egyptian revolution as a staging of personal feelings more than nationalist sentiment. Lasto Adri's post "My Country, My Dream" described her trembling disbelief at living what seemed like a dream on 6 February 2011.[14] The bloggers' idiosyncratic voices maintained a discursive space outside a larger media public. Their impersonal online selves were means of disidentification, inaugurating different social relations in counterpublic space.[15]

Their expressions of emotion reoriented the discourse on nationalist sentiment in television broadcasts. Most significantly, the blogs I examine incorporated vocabulary from media debates on national politics into the intimate register of the personal post.

Digital publics pose new questions for theorists of publics and counterpublics, particularly when they invert flows of discourse from private to public spheres. For instance, Nancy Fraser argues that civil societies for elite white women in the nineteenth-century United States "creatively used the heretofore quintessentially 'private' idioms of domesticity and motherhood precisely as springboards for public activity."[16] I find the opposite in Egyptian blogs, which recontextualized mainstream media debates into worlds of intimate reflection. Like many digital publics, these blogs modeled modes of communication on friendship more than stranger sociality.[17] Bloggers exchanged authoritative distance from their interlocutors for empathetic proximity. Approaching their digital practices as a repertoire of transposable dispositions (as in performance) allowed women bloggers to articulate a spatially fluid conception of politics that challenged a public/private division. The bloggers' practices generated repertoires of dissent that were unabashedly gendered, potentially disruptive, and imaginatively transformative of the spaces and languages of normative politics.

Intimate Publics of Independent Women

The intimacy of blog communities was a foundational aspect of the blog's reputation as a safe space for women's public voices. The pioneering blogger Eman told me that in the early days (ca. 2005–6), when the Egyptian blogosphere itself numbered only thirty or forty blogs, bloggers read each other's posts and encouraged each other. A mix of men and women populated the blogosphere, and some female bloggers complained that men's posts were granted an automatic authority and were more widely cited than their own. However, a piece of folk wisdom I heard repeated in Cairo's writerly circles, perpetuated perhaps by Shorouk's publications,[18] was that blogs were a women's genre. The relative informality of short-form blog writing, coupled with its use for writing emotion, gave it a gendered association for many journalists and novelists.[19]

But this gendered association did not seem to bother women bloggers, who came to own it on their terms. In 2005 a group of them formed an aggregator site called *Kalam Banat* (Girls' Talk), which linked about thirty blogs by young women, and facilitated conversation via the comments field of their own blogs. A friendly, supportive community welcomed newcomers and those who returned to this intimate public. When Rehab Bassam, whose blog had been published by Shorouk, returned to post after a year's absence, members of Girls' Talk welcomed her back with conspiratorial pleasure. "I've missed you, rascal!" wrote Dina El Hawary.[20] Dina wrote a post of her own the same day, and several old blog friends posted comments such as "Keep going ya didoo please don't disappear :)."[21] A paratext of friendly conversation surrounded the monologues of blog posts, creating a matrix of support for their voices.

A personal space within a supportive community, the blog offered a site of independence for Cairene women without their own spaces. These professional women in their twenties lived with their parents, in accordance with social restrictions against setting up an adult household before they married. Their social and professional lives outside the home occupied scattered sites that came together in their social media homes. On a Facebook page or a blog they could consolidate different spaces of their lives, familial and professional, and reconcile the relationships of girlhood and adulthood. Some women told me they used social media for "going out," for example, to meet with friends from university days who tended to stay home after they married. "I see what my friends are up to on Facebook, say 'Hello, it's been a while,' or use the chat feature," said Lobna, a twenty-three-year-old news photographer. For Cairene women who had less access to urban recreational space than did their male peers, the blog or social media page served, as it did for activists, as "an alternative urban hub."[22] They frequently spoke of it as a home space as well. "When I hear my brother return home, I'll write to him on Facebook from my room! Isn't that silly?" smiled Lobna. Her digital home was a space that grounded her identities as adventurous photographer and dutiful daughter. It afforded her a relative privacy within the family home in which she could reconstruct a world that combined her different social roles.

The privacy of a digital home enabled other women to recalibrate intimacies. Eman, who described her family as conservative, said she avoided Facebook because it reflected a social world from which she dissociated herself after a political awakening in her college years. "When I speak to old friends on Facebook now, we end up arguing because we're different," she explained. "Here you'll find the kind of reactionary people who said,

'We are sorry, Mr. President' after the revolution." Eman's digital world was formed by anonymous intimacies. She used to call in to a favorite talk show on Radio Cairo and made friends with the hosts, and nowadays she has developed similar virtual friendships on Twitter, where she finds people to be "more revolutionary" than in her social world.

The pleasure of intimate conversation with relative strangers was also among the reasons Eman started her blog in 2005. The blogosphere, then known only to well-educated young Egyptians (particularly those working in engineering and information technology), opened the way to an alternative circle of intimates. "I liked leaving my narrow world, at home with the other kids, and going to my blog," Eman said. The persona she developed in her blog conversations was an intimate one, and she resisted taking on the role of a public figure. When her blog became well known, however, she found the "noise" of constant comments aggravating. "It's a home. I don't want it to be a wide world. I'd rather it was just so," she said, drawing her hands close together. A home-like blog allowed Eman to experiment with emotional performance, as we shall see, and she cherished it as a space of alterity. In contrast to a closed counterpublic, unavailable to public discourse,[23] the personal blog enabled a circuit of intimacy. Since blog interlocutors were linked in a circuit of friendship, the bloggers' emotional performances were spared evaluation by a spectatorial public, as in Lauren Berlant's model of affective recognition.[24] The networked digital home instead allowed Eman to put an everyday self and its repertoire on display. In this "outing" she shaped a role that was independent and yet tethered to a web of supportive intimates.

The poetics of space in these Egyptian women's blogs (and other digital homes) were intimate but not private sites of re-forming a social self. They staged new publics in a mode of rehearsal, such as blog conversations that modeled television debates. The intersubjective space created by blog comments and conversations resembled the German women's salons of an earlier era, "within which new forms of *sociability and intimacy* could develop among members of an emergent civil society."[25] Indeed practices of intimacy and civility were intertwined in blog conversations as they accommodated a wider range of interactions than the women's salon. Egyptian bloggers typically alternated between personal musings and political commentary. Whimsical conversations between blog friends about their feelings similarly shared space with more measured, civil debates about matters like women's rights, both within comments sections and across blogs. In these negotiations of intimacy and civility within the same space, the blogger developed a unique digital persona.

Yet there remained gaps between the roles a blogger embodied in different forms of interaction, as dramatized in blog posts about painful conflicts with friends and family. In such examples the blogger drew readers into her intimate conflicts by writing in a voice of heightened affect. The gap between her dispassionate intellectual voice and more dramatic performances highlighted gaps between norms of public discourse and the affective potential of digital writing. The experimental repertoires of women bloggers in my study ruptured divides between public and private voice by performatively transforming space through shifts in voice.

Affective Performance and Subject Formation in the Digital Self

Eman and Fatma were young women drawn to blogs as spaces in which to write alternative stories of their apparently exemplary lives as successful professionals. After reading several whimsical posts about her life and moods on Eman's blog *Lasto Adri* (I Don't Know), its title borrowed from a poem sung by Abdel Halim Hafez, I was surprised to find the author was a serious young engineer. She had begun to write the blog while still a university student. It provided her a connection with days when writing was as much a part of her life as engineering. "I don't want to forget that I was happy or sad . . . leaving aside concerns with politics or any issue—I just *write*," she told me. Eman's professional life left her less than fulfilled, and she found blogging, as well as translating articles and blog posts for Global Voices and Meedan.net, to be a satisfying complement. Writing across genres on her blog (and elsewhere in the digital landscape) allowed her to combine her personal and professional roles into something more dynamic.

Blogging also allowed Eman to develop a distinctive voice. In the early days she had admired the male bloggers Ahmed Gharbeia and Ramy Karam for the elegant formal Arabic with which they flexibly voiced both political commentary and humorous posts, such as Karam's 2009 poem about swine flu as a sign of larger social disease in Egypt.[26] She modeled her writing on theirs and worked hard to master the grammar of formal Arabic. "But then I learned that I'm learning about myself, not just about language," she told me. The medium of formal Arabic enabled her to write about serious matters at the same time as it gave a poetic quality to her everyday stories and descriptions. She thus claimed a discursive authority on par with male bloggers. But Eman also insisted on her right to use the blog as an open space. She was not interested in being a voice of authority on social and political matters. Rather she considered each post to be an abstract composition, "a message in a bottle," to be interpreted as the reader liked. An example from May 2011 asks, "A question that puzzles me: do we grow up when we bear concerns, or bear concerns when we grow up?" These fragments of writing, united by an authorial voice, were elements of her varied virtual persona.

A major tag for Eman's blog posts was "Feelings" (written in English). Crafting impersonal "messages" out of her emotions, she invited others to inhabit her shifting subject positions as "virtual synesthetic perspectives."[27] Eman received several responses, for instance, to a post on 20 October 2012 in which she wrote, "Happiness is not a decision, sometimes moods simply change and there's nothing you can do." Most commenters simply agreed, though one argued for a more scientific perspective on emotions. The interactive space of the blog enabled a dialectic of recognition between reader and blogger, without either easily objectifying the other's emotions in gendered terms. Thus Eman's blog attracted many comments from men who appreciated engaging with a poetic repertoire of emotion that was not markedly feminine. The fact that these readers could have civil conversations with the blogger on the subject of feelings, and other avowedly personal matters, marked the blog as more than a space for intimates. It was an intimate public where strangers developed a repertoire of debate modeled loosely on friendly conversation.

As Eman won a loyal following, she began to record some of her popular posts as podcasts. She read writings posted a year or more previously, embodying her blog persona in a changing voice. An August 2013 podcast about sadness staged the writer's idiosyncratic view that negative emotions were productive: "How often has sadness summoned up the artist in you? And how often has pain stimulated the creativity in you? As for the mundane . . . not-feeling just creates a walking shadow . . . who longs for nothing and belongs to nothing."[28]

The "message in a bottle" posts had catalyzed a confidently embodied performing subject. Eman's podcast readings drew the most numerous and enthusiastic comments of any of her posts. Interpreted as dramatic monologues by an appreciative audience, these performances staged a polemical feminine subject. Nevertheless she commanded her own space and invited appreciation for her opinionated statements on their own terms. She kept her more overtly political questions for a separate group blog, as we shall see. In her personal blog her voice was whimsical, opinionated, and articulate. Like a salon hostess, she conversed without anger or being argumentative.

In another personal blog Eman's age peer and blog friend Fatma staged a one-woman show that narrated the everyday frustrations and failures of her professional identity as a feminist researcher. Unlike Eman, Fatma used her blog to bring together her roles as a middle-class daughter and a socially critical activist. She staged her home as a contentious place in her dramatic posts. After studying for a master's degree in human rights, Fatma had developed an extensive academic knowledge of feminism, but bringing the lessons of her feminist identity into the family home produced several conflicts. And the quiet, determined young woman believed it was her duty to stage such uncomfortable moments for the benefit of others. "If you're a feminist, you must talk about the violence and oppression in your life. That's why you write! So people passing through the same experience will learn from your struggle." Fatma often dropped the armor of her academic vocabulary of feminism in her blog posts to make them more accessible to friends and strangers.

Fatma's unembellished writing staged the uncomfortable position of a feminist in a socially conservative home. "I believe that women's toughest struggles are in their personal lives," she began one blog post. Her blog writings were chiefly about her personal life. Here she reenacted debates in a vulnerable voice, showing how often she acted out of weakness when confronted with social expectations. In the post just mentioned, which detailed the recent end of her romantic relationship, Fatma expressed anger at herself for seeking security in a lover. Writing alternately in the voices of disillusionment and her formerly romantic self, she staged as an external monologue a conversation she would have liked to have with friends. She wished women friends would discuss more openly problems in their romantic relationships. Her own confessions were deeply personal: "I just wanted a man . . . who would be my alternate world, far from the family, which could not accept me as I was."[29] But she gamely put them up on her blog to invite empathetic recognition from other women.

Sometimes Fatma's posts rehearsed conversations that were all but impossible offline. For these she used the language of her higher education, English, rather than the language she used at home or with family. She also used English when she was angry with friends and wanted to change the terms of their conversation. Recounting a painful instance of sexual harassment in English because it would have felt too shameful in Arabic, she analyzed the sexualized curse word *labwa* (lioness) that a man on the street had called out to her.[30] Her silent fury during the event acquired a composed form in her blog post, which calmly dissected why the man equated an independent woman with an animal that "is sexually very active . . . is [a] breadwinner, . . . hunts the animals." Reenacting the painful incident on her blog and in English helped her overcome the shame of the insult by assuming the role of scholarly analyst. She ended the post by noting that it felt like an achievement: "I am astonished that I am discussing this in public. I am adopting a new strategy to get the private public."

In 2011 Fatma decided to stop wearing hijab (Islamic headscarf) after fourteen years, explaining that she had become unconvinced it was a religious duty. The recent revolution in Egypt gave her the final spur she needed to act on her bold new belief. But she could not find sympathy for her decision and her identity as an Islamic feminist. She wrote in English about her uncomfortable position: "I want to say that what struck me [was] the polarization of the Egyptian society. On [one] side the conservative powers, which includes my family, my extended family, neighbors, and many others categories of the Egyptian society, and on the other hand the progressive powers which includes the Human rights defenders, academics and journalists who constitute my social cycle. I hated [the] unstopping nagging and the covert threats of my family and I hated the extra warm congratulations of my progressive friends."[31]

Fatma's angry posts in English received comments only from foreign academics, who engaged with her politics rather than her emotions. Her friends and local readers remained silent, giving her privacy in her pain, she said. She had wanted to initiate a conversation with them but settled for having her experience recognized. Fatma's confessional blog attracted few comments in general, even though it was well known among bloggers and in feminist circles. She told me that friends warned her about exposing herself to shame. "When I write about a relationship, or sexuality, my friends say I'm performing an emotional striptease," she said. Rehearsing her own anger gave her a sense of dignity, while putting naked emotions at the center of her blog conversations in a way that made readers uncomfortable. It was difficult for her to know if they did actually empathize with her, as she hoped.

Responses to Eman's and Fatma's respective writings about sadness and shame showed that gentler emotions found their way into a public circuit of discourse and affirmation more easily than others. And yet the blog served in both cases to generate conversational repertoires centered on the blogger's emotions. Readers entered into an intimate public where they encountered the blogger as a friend and related to her moods and positions but only secondarily to her social identity. Meanwhile the blogger had carved out a social space that was relatively independent of her professional and familial lives. The intimate public of the blog emerged as a social circuit shaped by discourse as well as affective recognition.

Bloggers' use of emotions constituted more than an experiment with discourse. I argue that their sentimental calibrations of proximity and distance were also a kind of dramatic performance. Their blog performances attracted appreciative and sympathetic audiences. Mobilizing these audiences as participatory publics for political purposes proved to be a project for group rather than individual blogs, however. When some of Egypt's best-known women bloggers planned campaigns around particular issues, they joined forces with blog friends to create a space for solidarity. Here too they found it expedient to sentimentalize their positions in order to contest constraints of hegemonic political discourse. As the bloggers oriented their spaces toward wider audiences of strangers, affective recognition became a means to political recognition, not an end in itself. As we will see in the following examples, they found the repertoires developed on their personal blogs well suited to consolidating new political identities and relations, especially after the revolution.

From Solo to Ensemble Performance:
Blog Networks as New Political Space

Friendship among bloggers often took the form of emotional support and affirmative comments on the writings of others. Moreover bloggers recognized political allies among their blog friends. The combination of friendship and political alliance launched several projects. Early in her blogging career Eman found that several other young professional women shared her concerns about gender politics. So she joined hands with four other Egyptian bloggers in 2006 to create a space of discussion about gender roles online. "I used to talk to a blogger called Shaimaa and told her I was angry. My father would always say no when I wanted to go out because girls don't go out in our family. So I had the idea of pulling all the girls together on one day, online, to say how we're tired of things. We did this together and invited three other bloggers who were also girls." The four women blogged one day under the slogan "Kolena Laila" (We Are All Laila),[32] choosing for their collective tag the name of the activist young protagonist in the path-breaking 1964 film *Al-Bab al-maftuh* (The Open Door). "We wanted to show that our individual stories are not isolated cases," Eman wrote.[33]

Simply demonstrating the volume of young middle-class women's discontent with their social position was a political intervention as far as the organizers were concerned. Their performative gesture generated a substantial discursive movement, however. Over three years the annual event of simultaneous blogging about the frustrations of middle-class young women called We Are All Laila expanded into a week-long event that featured participants from eighteen Arab countries. Each blogger spoke from her digital home, with the temporal simultaneity of speech and the signature tag of the campaign materializing a virtual public space of women's dissent. The blog posts written for the campaign received an unexpectedly warm welcome from readers, who asked to join by writing blog posts about their own views and experiences of gender oppression the next time. The event turned into an enduring political space, with its own aggregator website and a fond place in the memory of participants.

A remarkable feature of the space was its emergence as gender mixed. The initial blog posts for Laila gained a healthy response from men, who appreciated seeing the constraints of gender roles from the perspectives of women. Men could imagine themselves in the place of angry women, expanding the category of those who identified as Laila. For instance, Sara received responses from men and women on the Baniadmeen blog to a post about sexual harassment she ironically titled "We Are Sorry."[34] The post describes the different reactions of three friends when one of them is touched inappropriately on a tram. She staged the confusion and shame of the moment with long ellipses, multiple question marks, and bursts of disbelieving "hahahaha" to evoke what could not be put in words. Among the fifteen sympathetic comments, one from a man called Micheal said, "I put myself in your place and realized how humiliating it would be to have people touch my body in public just because I was female." Sara's reconstruction of the scene of harassment within a collective blogging project helped to generate empathy. Staging the experience of three friends invited readers of all genders to embody imaginatively the role of a supportive friend and witness.

The campaign tag "We Are All Laila" encouraged readers to move from blog to blog and see how stories resonated across a social landscape. From the beginning the idea of a space to talk about harassment attracted objections. Typically critics objected to the project as maligning Egyptian men.[35] A mission statement from the organizers after the first edition clarified the politics of We Are All Laila: "If it can be called a campaign at all, it is not one against men, but against the culture and inherited social traditions from which both men and women suffer." Nor was it intended to disrupt the solidarity of the emerging blogosphere, in which different political campaigns offered mutual support. Eman and Shaimaa wrote that their aim was not to create blocs among the bloggers but "to take advantage of the free space of dialogue that the blog allows, and also because we have some credibility here as bloggers whom you already know."[36]

In order to encourage the expressions of support seen in comments to the early editions of Laila, the organizers decided in the second year to ask young men to participate in blogging, and later to help organize the event as well. Eman mentioned that not all the male bloggers participating in the project supported the program. But consensus was not the point. "It doesn't matter if you're with or against us," she told me. "The important thing is social discussion so people listen to each other." Yet the project was founded on the experiences of women and did privilege their voices in the discussion. We Are All Laila displayed some of the fertile contradictions of a discourse public that "selects participants by criteria of shared social space . . . , habitus, topical concerns, intergeneric references, and circulating intelligible forms."[37] The repertoires of its writers were embedded in a gendered habitus in that the protagonists of their digital dramaturgies were clearly female. Yet the participation of men in an event focused on gender analysis and critique foregrounded its importance as an intimate public where men and women "listened to each other."

Eventually, however, the therapeutic quality of blogging about painful instances of harassment made Laila a personal project for its organizers.

Eman said that she had begun the project for herself and female friends, and once it helped her overcome her own anxieties she found herself less interested in sustaining it. Still she believed it should go forward under new leadership. "But something like this needs funding and support," she explained. "And if the funding comes from outside the country, you open the door to accusations of serving foreign agendas. So I got tired and gave it up." The process of turning anger and shame into therapeutic blog performances had been more productive for her than the effort of creating an enduring public space for feminist conversations. Thus the Laila project ended after three years. Its legacy was that it helped Eman and other feminist bloggers develop a repertoire of arguments and stances that served them well in future debates.

Blog conversations also served as rehearsal space for developing repertoires of debate on the meaning of politics after revolution. Fatma was concerned that feminist projects were being pushed to one side in revolutionary political organizing, and she picked arguments on her blog that sought to return to center stage the problem of the revolutionary's gendered persona. In February 2011, for example, Fatma recalled a conversation with her friend and fellow blogger Maha, who expressed surprise at seeing women in Islamic headscarves leading protests in Cairo. Fatma considered herself an Islamic feminist and disagreed with her friend's belief about the incompatibility of faith and feminism. So she restaged their conversation via a blog post. She cited Maha's statement and dissected the prejudice of feminists who deemed hijab a constraint on a woman's agency. Maha accepted the challenge and wrote back in her blog about the gender beliefs at large among religious Muslim women, many of whom did not espouse Fatma's feminist beliefs and indeed accepted a secondary position to men.[38]

Staging the debate across blogs allowed Fatma to foreground what she considered a problematic relationship of revolutionary political to feminist projects in Egypt. She rewrote a friendly conversation as a civil debate on this topic in formal, scholarly language. Transposing marginal debates into the formal register of civil debate was a signature move of Egyptian bloggers writing about revolutionary politics. Yet feminist bloggers remained largely outside the dominant repertoire in the revolutionary blogosphere, which was shaped by the claims-based discourse of human rights organizations. In this context bloggers like Fatma were often described as advocates of "special interests" rather than advocates of the common good. Arguments between bloggers on the question of what constituted the common good in national politics point to the precarious future of blogs as sites of civil debate after the 2011 revolution.

"Sitting at the Table" versus the Personal Blog

Fatma's friend Maha, an MA student of international human rights, maintained a bilingual blog with a tag line in English: "Impressionistic diary about coffee, love, lyrical writing." While she once blogged to share poetry and short stories, her posts after the 2011 revolution were predominantly about human rights cases. Maha called herself a feminist and mentioned that the most shared post on her blog was about women's rights in the new Egyptian Constitution. But when I met her in December 2011, she expressed mixed feelings about using the blogosphere for feminist projects after the revolution. "We feminists in our twenties are trying to position ourselves as a pressure group, but we have not sat down at a table to negotiate our rights," she told me. "So if we didn't have a blogosphere, there would be nothing expressing our views." Even so, Maha did not believe useful conversations about women's rights could happen in the blogosphere. She insisted these must take place in civil society, as part of larger political debates.

Maha rarely wrote on her personal blog after the revolution, focusing her energies instead on street activism and online debates on human rights. She created a YouTube account for testimonies about human rights abuse and contributed posts to the political site *Al-Hiwar al-mutamaddin* (Civil Debate).[39] She believed it was more important to participate as a woman in new debates on civil society than to demonstrate ways in which women were excluded from these debates. "I don't agree with women's protests, like the tiny one on March 8, 2011," she told me, referring to an International Women's Day protest in Cairo that had been attacked by men. "Women activists need to position themselves within a public agenda."

For Maha a public agenda meant arguing for the rights of the socially excluded or alienated. For instance, she focused her blog activism in 2011 on supporting Maikel Nabil, an iconoclastic blogger who was both pro-Israel and an atheist, and had been recently imprisoned for his scathing criticism of the Egyptian Army. While she worked to frame his case "within a public agenda," she did not feel able to engage in similar online activism for feminist purposes. The time for rehearsing feminist debates online was over, she believed, and it was now expedient to organize on the ground and gain wider currency for women's questions in civil society: "You know, these activists all know each other and speak to each other online. We have to go offline to reach others, do a grassroots campaign in the countryside and elsewhere."

The Laila bloggers' strategy of gaining support by inviting empathy declined after 2010, given revolutionary and postrevolutionary contexts where discourse on rights and civil society was on the rise. The tenuous position of women's politicized personal blogs at this time pointed to tension between quests for affective and civil recognition. While emotional writing was the norm during the days of revolution, political bloggers later began to play the role of responsible commentators by speaking and writing more formally.

In the aftermath of the uprising certain hypotheses about blogs as training grounds for civil society acquired the reputation of proven fact. Early analysts of the Egyptian blogosphere posited its potential as "an alternative urban hub . . . acting as an interface between events in the street and the Internet."[40] The blogosphere was considered an incubator of civil society discourse, since "online forums and networks involve kinds of participation which articulate well with the process of accountable politics — criticism, negotiation, argument."[41] But the blog repertoires of Egyptian women were often as sentimental as they were "civil" in the civil society sense. Maha was among a number of bloggers who shifted from blog writing to civil society activism in 2011, in the spirit of moving from rehearsal of new subjectivity to public enactments. Like Maha's personal blog, which became a record of her activism, Mona's blog *Maat* also became predominantly political.

As the postrevolution blogosphere began to mirror the sphere of mainstream politics, feminists such as Fatma grew concerned about the narrowing of spaces for alternative debate. Feminism undeniably took a backseat to other revolutionary concerns, but the repertoires of women bloggers arguably transformed civil society politics in other ways. Mona, the high-profile leader of the No Military Trials for Civilians campaign, had decided not to join the Women's Day protest on 8 March 2011. But her personal blog foregrounded sexualized abuse at other protests. On 9 March, for example, *Maat* featured an eyewitness account by the journalist Rasha al-Ezab of how the army had forcibly dispersed a sit-in in Tahrir that day. She wrote that soldiers had threatened her with sexual torture, which they were openly inflicting on men. They also abused other female protesters, including a young woman from the South who just happened to be in the square. She "faced the dirtiest of insults, and cried for hours."[42] Al-Ezab's depiction of women's vulnerability in revolutionary contexts used a trope of defiled innocence to assert the right of protesters to gather in public without being molested. Her theatrical staging of women's vulnerability was an appeal to conventional sentiments about women's virtue, particularly that of the young provincial visitor, in order to make a powerful point about the injustice of army brutality.

Throughout the political upheavals of 2011 Egyptian activists deployed "sentimental models of affective recognition to establish political grounds for imagining survival."[43] A famous example of this is the activism that followed the 17 December 2011 assault by soldiers on a woman physician in Tahrir, referred to as *sitt al-banat* in Arabic and "the girl in the blue bra" in English. This event provoked the largest women's march Cairo had ever seen.[44] The chant "The girls of Egypt are a red line" and the "protection" provided by a male human chain staged female honor in a way that feminists like Maha considered patriarchal. In other instances, however, female activists deployed sentiment critically and radically.

Mona's own blog posts deployed sentimental politics against the grain. As she became an increasingly prominent activist, often interviewed by television networks and filmed marching at the head of demonstrations, she frequently evoked her younger persona on her personal blog. A post titled "My Self That Has Passed" voiced nostalgia for her old life now that the revolution had transformed the rhythm of her days.[45] And her political posts on the blog were written as passionate appeals to friends. She voiced her anger against the military regime for human rights violations in personal terms, writing "Shame on you, Dr Mamdouh!" to the military prosecutor who summoned Rasha al-Ezab for writing an exposé of torture by the military.[46] Such bursts of anger seemed to heighten the ethical power of Mona's activist persona. This was especially the case when she played the role of an Antigone-like sister to call for the rights of her imprisoned brother and other male activists.

Mona's emotional outbursts had the effect of making political concerns immediate to her social media followers. They constructed new proximities within publics. She also addressed other bloggers in the voice of a friend, bringing discourse among those who were now public figures back into the register of conversation among peers. One of her blog posts in October 2012, for instance, criticized the Facebook page that led calls for the 2011 protests but refused to publicize the recent death in police custody of a working-class protester, Essam Atta: "I am gravely disappointed with the Facebook page *We Are All Khaled Said*, disappointed because I naïvely imagined that the similarity between the story of Essam Atta's murder and that of Khaled Said would lead the page to adopt his case without hesitation. . . . Essam's case brought out the worst in all of us . . . our greater sympathy with people who look like us, and our doubts about people with more modest circumstances than our own."[47] What if the man killed in police custody had not been Atta, whom the *We Are All Khaled Said* page administrators called a thug, but her own brother Alaa Abdel Fattah, Mona asked rhetorically? Alaa was a well-known blogger and a brave activist. His stints of imprisonment, most recently in 2013–14, were a cause célèbre in Egypt's activist circles. His friends resurrected the Twitter hashtag #FreeAlaa with considerable success on these occasions. Mona spoke in the voice of a loyal sister to put a more obscure victim's situation on par with her brother's, reminding revolutionaries of their ethical proximity to comrades of varied backgrounds and of their mutual obligations as part of a community. Her sisterly anger and uncompromising voice showed the discourse of *We Are All Khaled Said* to be narrowly liberal. Her idealistic persona gave her considerable ethical authority in the blogosphere, even though her youth and gender excluded her from the negotiating tables of political parties.

In 2011, when revolution transformed the space of Egyptian politics into a theater of rousing nationalist songs, protest footage, and scandalous violations, bloggers' repertoires of sentiment enabled them to intervene against injustice by staging solidarity through intimacy with those imprisoned or tortured. However, activists found it difficult to appeal to the emotions of political authorities and those of a wider media public without evoking conservatively gendered icons, such as the virtuous woman and the dutiful sister. Even the quintessential alternative digital space, the *We Are All Khaled Said* Facebook page, had become a stage of mainstream national politics in which middle-class martyrs were fetishized to the exclusion of others. In this context women who blogged for activist purposes were either pushed into mainstream norms of civil debate or excluded from political conversations altogether.

Sustaining Feminist Repertoires of Dissent and Disidentification

After the return to military rule feminist bloggers shared with other Egyptian activists the quandary of preserving their repertoires of dissent in oppressive times. Their blogs no longer had the high profile achieved with the shift in the "distribution of the sensible" during the waves of uprising. After General Abdel Fattah al-Sisi banned protests in 2013, masses of street activists were detained without charge, including many prominent women. But digital dissent largely eluded the arm of the regenerated police state. While blogs declined in popularity, the digital landscape continued to blossom. Satirical memes and videos about al-Sisi online circulated widely by 2015,[48] in contrast to the fawning respect the president received from television anchors. At first glance there was a sharp separation between critical digital politics, limited safely to Facebook pages and YouTube videos, and the world of young activists who faced kidnapping and torture.[49] Digital dissent did, however, keep alive verbal repertoires that filtered into other spaces. Feminist bloggers could claim credit for introducing into public discourse styles of storytelling that had previously been seen as personal and thus shameful.

My speculative conclusion on how digital repertoires came to permeate offline practice builds on the example of a post on Eman's blog several years ago. It was a podcast modeled on a talk show, centering on a single professional woman's path to activism. The way Eman transposed her voice as a blogger onto that of the talk show host illustrates how digital actors "suggested, rehearsed, and articulated" counterpublics in anticipatory gestures.[50] Eman showed how conversation on her blog could model new kinds of women's voices by rehearsing unheard stories and disregarded feelings. The success of her podcasts emboldened her to experiment with radio-style interviews during the second edition of We Are All Laila in 2009. Eman's interviews with the Egyptian political bloggers Zeinobia and Shahinaz Abdel Salam and the Iraqi blogger Haydar Fadil built on the television talk show persona of a charming female host (or hosts, as in MBC's *The View*–style show *Kalam nawaʿim*). Eman infused the generic role with her distinctive voice to rehearse a talk show genre in which women were hailed not as glamour girls or maternal figures but as inspiring friends.

With brief musical interludes, Eman's podcast interviews staged intimate conversations with peers whom she presented as pioneers. Eman began her interview with Shahinaz, an Alexandrian activist and author of the political blog *Wahda misriyya* (An Egyptian Woman),[51] by saying, "She's not just an Egyptian, but she has a voice that can be different." Shahinaz went on to narrate how she came to be an activist while training as an engineer by describing her lifelong independent streak, beginning with stories about small rebellions against her prescribed role at home, then forays into activism at university.

Eman's friendly questions elicited stories about the prejudice Shahinaz had faced while marching with men, and the women laughed together at a particularly absurd edict by an obscure sheikh encouraging polygyny. Even at work, Shahinaz reported, she found male colleagues arguing that she had, for instance, taken the place of a man on a sought-after business trip. In this biographical telling, her participation in the 2005 anti-Mubarak protests seemed a suitable culmination of an adventurous youth. Shahinaz's social and political rebellions were narrated in an intimate register in Eman's interview, staging a sympathetic, everyday persona rather than an abstract portrait of the activist or, more controversially, female revolutionary. At the same time, it allowed for more than a celebratory narrative. "When anyone in my family sees me speaking on television at a protest, being critical, they phone me and fight with me," Shahinaz revealed. Eman's faux radio show made room for unconventional women's feelings, such as the hurt caused by an unsupportive family and disgust at conservative colleagues. It integrated an activist's stories (commonly seen in blogs) with the conventions of the talk show success story, channeling the sentimental appeal of each to present the female engineer-activist as an everyday hero.

I speculate that the storytelling style of women's personal blogs, and comparable confessional genres in Egyptian digital media, created appealing characters that could easily be transposed into mainstream media. The voices of characters such as Shahinaz resonated with the vibrant currents of affect associated with digital genres. As such, they drew audiences in by different linguistic and affective paths and opened up identification with women's concerns. Staging gender through voice and affect proved to be a powerful way to gain male allies for feminist causes, and affective discourse promised to serve mainstream political causes as well.

Conclusion

Bloggers in Egypt drew a genre distinction between so-called personal and political blogs, but I argue that the former shaped politics as well. Particularly in a period of revolutions and uprisings, women's personal blogs offered a space for reframing the performance of citizenship. These alternative theaters of sentimental repertoire countered hegemonic narratives of revolution as a cathartic process that began and ended in the streets. The gendering of Egyptian personal blogs from their early years as a women's genre transformed somewhat with a rise in activism across genres. As affective recognition became a powerful means of gaining legitimacy for demands for rights, the dramaturgy of sentiment in personal blogs adapted to a range of revolutionary concerns. Egyptians of different genders identified with the virtualized emotions and positions rehearsed in personal blogs. At the same time, women bloggers performed their virtual personas strategically, using sentiment to calibrate gendered voice when they engaged in political debate online. These virtual performances of self and the digital spaces that enabled the fine-tuning of political voice remained sites of transformation beyond the dramatic narrative arc of revolution.

Icons of the Egyptian revolution, such as the martyr Khaled Said, became protagonists in a story that concluded with the downfall of the Mubarak regime. In 2011 several Egyptian activists were lauded as heroes of a moment whose mission had been accomplished. Digital spaces such as blogs gave them a place to continue rehearsing repertoires of dissent as the revolution unfolded and encountered setbacks. I argue that these spaces preserved forms of revolutionary social relations across gender and class lines. As a site for the practice of virtual and potentially transformative social roles, the "women's genre" of the personal blog was part of a reconstitution of the public sphere, in which a revised "apportionment of parts and positions" foreshadowed the possibility of new political actors.[52]

NOTES

1. Lauren Berlant and Jay Prosser, "Life Writing and Intimate Publics: A Conversation with Lauren Berlant," *Biography* 34, no. 1 (2011): 184.

2. Vickie Langohr, "Women's Rights Movements during Political Transitions: Activism against Public Sexual Violence in Egypt," *International Journal of Middle East Studies* 47, no. 1 (2015): 131–35.

3. Among a plethora of news articles in English forwarding this claim, see Jose Antonio Vargas, "Spring Awakening: How an Egyptian Revolution Began on Facebook," *New York Times*, 17 February 2012, http://www.nytimes.com/2012/02/19/books/review/how-an-egyptian-revolution-began-on-facebook.html?_r=0.

4. Jacques Rancière, *The Politics of Aesthetics: The Distribution of the Sensible*, translated by Gabriel Rockhill (London: Continuum, 2004), 37.

5. On "practiced places," see Michel de Certeau, *The Practice of Everyday Life*, translated by Steven Rendall (Berkeley: University of California Press, 1984), 96.

6. Michel Foucault and Jay Moskowitz, "Of Other Spaces," *Diacritics* 16, no. 1 (1986): 24.

7. Marc Lynch, "Blogging the New Arab Public," *Arab Media and Society*, February 2007, http://www.arabmediasociety.com/articles/downloads/20070312155027_AMS1_Marc_Lynch.pdf.

8. Zeinobia's post on Said's murder is "For Khalid, for His Family and for Egypt 'Graphic,'" *Egyptian Chronicles*, 10 June 2010, http://egyptianchronicles.blogspot.com/2010/06/for-khalid-for-his-family-and-for-egypt.html.

9. For example, Ahmed Bahgat, "Sanduq al-dunya," *Al-ahram*, 13 February 2008, http://www.ahram.org.eg/Archive/2008/2/13/AMOD5.HTM.

10. Mansour Mohamed, "Is Blogging a Bursting Bubble?," *Daily News Egypt*, 3 November 2007, accessed 15 October 2011, www.thedailynewsegypt.com. Also cited in Wael Salah Fahmi, "Bloggers' Street Movement and the Right to the City: (Re)Claiming Cairo's Real and Virtual 'Spaces of Freedom,'" *Environment and Urbanization* 21, no. 1 (2009): 93.

11. Bint Misriyya, "The Army Must Go" (Arabic), March 2011, http://www.bentmasreya.net/2011/03/blog-post_23.html.

12. Susana Galán, "'Today I Have Seen Angels in Shape of Humans': An Emotional History of the Egyptian Revolution through the Narratives of Female Personal Bloggers," *Journal of International Women's Studies* 13, no. 5 (2012): 17–30.

13. For Egypt this is documented in Ahmed Naji, *Al-mudawwanat min al-Bust ila al-Twit* (Blogs from Posting to Tweeting) (Cairo: Arab Network for Human Rights Information, 2010). The congruence between digital discourse and the politics of minor and subaltern social groups has long been noted. Iranian émigrés in California formed their transnational communities online (Alexanian) at the same time as social and political rebels within Iran took advantage of a relatively unpoliced blogosphere to challenge linguistic (Doostdar) and gendered (Amir-Ebrahimi) norms of public discourse. Janet A. Alexanian, "Publicly Intimate Online: Iranian Web Logs in Southern California," *Comparative Studies of South Asia, Africa, and the Middle East* 26, no. 2 (2006): 134–45; Alireza Doostdar, "The Vulgar Spirit of Blogging: On Language, Culture, and Power in Persian Weblogestan," *American Anthropologist* 106, no. 4 (2001): 651–62; Masserat Amir-Ebrahimi, "Transgression in Narration: The Lives of Iranian Women in Cyberspace," *Journal of Middle East Women's Studies* 4, no. 3 (2008): 89–118.

14. Lasto Adri, "My Country, My Dream," accessed 1 November 2013, http://lastoadri.com/blog/archives/2589/. This website has since disappeared from the web and web archive. Only the Arabic Lasto Adri blog exists at this writing (http://lasto-adri.blogspot

.com/, accessed 6 March 2016); the last post on the Arabic site is from 12 July 2010, announcing the shift of the blog to "a new home."

15. José E. Muñoz, *Disidentifications: Queers of Color and the Performance of Politics* (Minneapolis: University of Minnesota Press, 1999), 178, 5.

16. Nancy Fraser, "Rethinking the Public Sphere: A Contribution to the Critique of Actually Existing Democracy," *Social Text*, no. 25/26 (1990): 61.

17. For example, Ilana Gershon, *The Breakup 2.0: Disconnecting over New Media* (Ithaca: Cornell University Press, 2010).

18. The three titles by Ghada Abdel Aal, Ghada Mohamed Mahmoud, and Rehab Bassam are no longer on the publisher Shorouk's website; nor is a news article from 2008 on the *Albawaba* news site that notes the books were best sellers at a prominent Maadi bookstore that year. For reference to Rehab Bassam and Ghada Abdel Aal's blog-to-books, see mlynxqualey, "Where Have All the Egyptian (Literature) Blogs Gone?," *Arabic Literature (In English)*, 8 August 2010, http://arablit.org/2010/08/08/where-have-all-the-egyptian -literature-blogs-gone/. For an interview with Rehab Bassam, see Caroline Rooney, "'In Less Than Five Years': Rehab Bassam Interviewed by Caroline Rooney, Dar Al-Shorouk, Nasr City, Cairo, April 2010," *Journal of Postcolonial Writing* 47, no. 4 (August 2011): 467–76. Ghada Abdel Aal's book was translated and published in English: *I Want to Get Married! One Wannabe Bride's Misadventures with Handsome Houdinis, Technicolor Grooms, Morality Police, and Other Mr. Not Quite Rights*, translated by Nora El Tahawy (Austin: University of Texas Press, 2010).

19. Hoda Elsadda, "Arab Women Bloggers: The Emergence of Literary Counterpublics," *Middle East Journal of Culture and Communication* 3, no. 3 (2010): 312–32.

20. Dina El Hawary, comment (Arabic), 23 September 2012, http://hadouta.blogspot .com/2012/09/blog-post_23.html?showComment=1348413100736#c8305303735226 513870. El Hawary is responding to a post on Girls' Talk (*Huwadit*), "Like the Breeze That Leaves a Moist Trace" (Arabic), 23 September 2012, http://hadouta.blogspot.com/2012 /09/blog-post_23.html?showComment=1348413100736#c8305303735226513870.

21. Dina El Hawary, "A Bit of Reality . . . a Lot of Imagination" (Arabic), *Confusion* post (Arabic), 30 September 2012, http://dinahawary.blogspot.com/2012/09/blog-post.html. Comment on post, 1 October 2012, http://dinahawary.blogspot.com/2012/09/blog-post .html?showComment=1349074781653#c5100970275131508154.

22. Fahmi, "Bloggers' Street Movement and the Right to the City," 106.

23. Michael Warner, "Publics and Counterpublics," *Public Culture* 14, no. 1 (2002): 79.

24. Berlant and Prosser, "Life Writing and Intimate Publics," 181.

25. Seyla Benhabib, "The Pariah and Her Shadow: Hannah Arendt's Biography of Rahel Varnhagen," *Political Theory* 23, no. 1 (1995): 17.

26. The post, now deleted, was on Karam's blog *Beyond Normal*, which is still partly visible at http://beyondnormal.blogspot.com.

27. Brian Massumi, *Parables for the Virtual: Movement, Affect, Sensation* (Durham, NC: Duke University Press, 2002), 35.

28. For example, "Alien and Not Alien," podcast, 11 August 2013, accessed 1 November 2013, http://lastoadri.com/blog/archives/3479/.

29. Fatma, "Safha wa intahit" (A Chapter That Ended), *Brownie*, 22 April 2012, http://atbrownies.blogspot.com/2012/04/blog-post_22.html.

30. Fatma, "Women, Sexuality, and Name Calling," *Brownie*, 23 January 2010, http://atbrownies.blogspot.com/2010_01_01_archive.html.

31. Fatma, "The Latest Decision: Taking the Veil Off," *Brownie*, 19 June 2011, http://atbrownies.blogspot.com/2011/06/latest-decision-taking-veil-off.html.

32. English translations of selected posts from the group blog can be accessed at http://kolenalaila.com/en/.

33. "Kolena Laila 2006: 2nd Statement," *Kolena Laila*, 12 September 2006, http://kolenalaila.com/blog/archives/27.

34. "We Are Sorry," *Baniadmeen* (Human Beings), 30 December 2009, http://baniadmeen.blogspot.com/2009/12/blog-post_30.html.

35. "Responses," *Kolena Laila*, 8 September 2006, http://kolenalaila.com/blog/archives/24. The blog administrator gathered these critical comments in a separate section, including, for example, "Rad ʿala Kolena Laila" (A Response to We Are All Laila), on the blog *ʿAadi Baʾa* (Just Normal), http://ody911.blogspot.com/2006/09/blog-post.html.

36. "Kolena Laila 2006: Thani Marra Klakit" (We Are All Leila 2006: Second Take), *Kolena Laila*, 12 September 2006, http://kolenalaila.com/blog/archives/27#idc-container.

37. Warner, "Publics and Counterpublics," 75.

38. Maha Al Aswad, "Back to the Old Feminist Debate: Hijab and the Egyptian Revolution," *Maha Al Aswad*, 14 February 2011, http://mahaalaswad.wordpress.com/2011/02/14/back-to-the-old-feminist-debate-hijab-and-the-egyptian-revolution/.

39. Maha Al Aswad, "Masr al-thawra wa masr al-intikhabat: Khawatir ʿala al-mawdhuʿ al-hali" (Egypt of Revolution and Egypt of Elections: Thoughts on the Current Situation), 3 December 2011, http://www.ahewar.org/debat/show.art.asp?aid=285886.

40. Fahmi, "Bloggers' Street Movement and the Right to the City," 106.

41. Lynch, "Blogging the New Arab Public," 8.

42. "Rasha al-Ezab tihki ʿan.. silkhana al-jaysh fi al-tahrir.. al-mathaf al-masri sabiqan" (Rasha al-Ezab Speaks about the Army's Abattoir . . . Formerly the Egyptian Museum), *Maat's Bits & Pieces*, 11 March 2011, http://ma3t.blogspot.com/2011/03/blog-post_11.html.

43. Berlant and Prosser, "Life Writing and Intimate Publics," 184.

44. Glen Johnson and Luke Harding, "Egyptian Women Protest in Cairo against Brutal Treatment," *Guardian*, 20 December 2011, http://www.theguardian.com/world/2011/dec/20/egyptian-women-protest-cairo-treatment.

45. "Nafsi allati madhat" (My Self That Passed), *Maat's Bits & Pieces*, 15 June 2011, http://ma3t.blogspot.com/2011/06/blog-post_19.html.

46. "ʿAyb ya duktur Mamduh" (Shame, Dr. Mamduh), *Maat's Bits & Pieces*, 19 June 2011, http://ma3t.blogspot.com/2011/06/blog-post_19.html.

47. Translated by the author. "Law kan ʿIsam ʿAtta ʿAlaʾ ʿAbd al-Fattah" (If Essam ʿAtta Were Alaa Abdel Fattah), *Maat's Bits & Pieces*, 28 October 2012, http://ma3t.blogspot.com/2012/10/blog-post_28.html.

48. For instance, this video in the YouTube series Alsh Khana: Alshakhanah Alshangy (Alshangy's Funhouse), 8 June 2015, https://www.youtube.com/watch?v=vDl-wTXJwB4.

49. In May and June 2015 Egyptian rights groups such as the Association for Freedom of Thought and Expression and Alkarama, as well as Human Rights Watch, documented dozens of disappearances. Their reports are cited briefly in Erin Cunningham and Heba Habib, "Egyptian Groups: Government Has Been Kidnapping Students, Activists," *Washington Post*, 13 June 2015, http://www.washingtonpost.com/world/middle_east/in-egypt-activists-document-a-surge-of-forced-disappearances/2015/06/12/75274570-0dff-11e5-a0fe-dccfea4653ee_story.html.

50. Muñoz, *Disidentifications*, 179.

51. Accessed 1 November 2013, http://lastoadri.com/blog/archives/2728/.

52. Rancière, *The Politics of Aesthetics*, 12.

2 GENDER AND THE FRACTURED MYTHSCAPES OF NATIONAL IDENTITY IN REVOLUTIONARY TUNISIA

LAMIA BENYOUSSEF

Tunisia's 2011 Revolution remade the country and triggered the most far-reaching changes in Arab imaginations and politics since the end of colonialism. The revolution began on 17 December 2010 with the self-immolation of Mohamed Bouazizi, a vegetable seller in the poor southern town of Sidi Bouzid. Until 14 January 2011, when President Zine al Abidine Ben Ali was forced to resign, social media narrated Bouazizi as an unemployed college graduate who killed himself because he was humiliated by a slap from Faida Hamdi, a municipal woman police officer to whom he had allegedly refused to pay a bribe to keep his scale weights. It turned out that Bouazizi had not completed high school, his first name was Tareq, and there was no evidence that he was slapped. The early days of the Tunisian revolution were embedded in this gendered account of humiliated masculinity, joblessness, and an oppressive state. Hundreds of thousands of unemployed young people identified with the story as the revolt spread to the South and interior regions.

After the departure of Ben Ali, Islamists returned from exile in Europe and organized for the National Constituent Assembly elections held on 27 October 2011. The Islamist Ennahda Party won the largest proportion of seats, although not a majority. Its leaders struck a strategic alliance with two centrist political parties, the Congress for the Republic, led by Moncef Marzouki, and the Democratic Forum for Labor and Liberties (Ettakatul), led by Mustapha Ben Jaafar. Hamadi Jebali of Ennahda was appointed prime minister, Marzouki as interim president, and Ben Jaafar as president of the Assembly. Although the Constituent Assembly was legally mandated to write a new constitution within a year and then step down, the ruling coalition, known as the Troika, refused to dissolve it, sparking numerous protests, especially after the assassination of the trade union leader Chokri Belaid on 6 February 2013 and the Popular Front parliamentarian Muhammad Brahmi on 25 July 2013.[1]

The Salafist trend, whose adherents largely came from outside Tunisia, particularly Europe, increasingly gained ground. President Beji Caid Essebsi declared a state of emergency in response to Salafist attacks against the Bardo Museum and Western tourists in Sousse in 2015.[2] The increase in terrorist attacks in Tunisia; the lack of transparency in investigating the killing of Belaid and Brahmi; the massacres of Tunisian soldiers in Kasserine, Goubellat, Jendouba, Rawad, Oued Ellil, and Kef operations; and the effects of the civil war in Libya are only some of the ways the Tunisian revolution is ongoing.[3] Tunisians continue to struggle with class inequality, resource maldistribution, and ideological fissures that to some degree had been sublimated in the previous authoritarian context. Authenticity discourse dominates the postrevolutionary symbolic landscape among Tunisians on the left and right of the spectrum, reflecting fractures and anxieties about identity, belonging, and the nature of the ideal community. These fractures and anxieties are often expressed on and through bodies and biological metaphors and animated by gendered and sexual signs.

In this chapter I use music, satire, cartoons, and videos as discursive texts to analyze key revolutionary and postrevolutionary moments in Tunisia. These texts express four ideal-type narratives, each relying on and reproducing a "mythscape" with its own historical reference points, identifications, elisions, and sexual and gendered imaginaries and sensibilities.[4] The *populist* narrative is redistributive in its class politics, but not necessarily inviting to women as full citizen-subjects. The *pluralist* narrative is anti-imperial, democratic, and class conscious, drawing on leftist and cosmopolitan idioms, solidarities, and identifications, but not necessarily gender-aware. The *secularist* narrative defends the Bourguibist legacy and is advocated by, among others, Tunisian women who benefited from state-led women's rights projects and fear the socially conservative possibilities of democracy.[5] The *Islamist* narrative reproduces conservative gender and sexual imaginaries. I show that storytelling, ideology, and imagination are crucial to understanding revolutionary Tunisia. But I also demonstrate the continuing primacy of embodied solidarities and conflicts in physical places. The mythscapes examined symbolically exceed the boundaries of colonial and postcolonial frames of reference even as they are never outside of those frames.

In the remainder of this chapter I discuss my positionality in relation to the Tunisian revolution in the spirit of feminist reflexivity on knowledge and power. I illustrate how feminine subject positions, including emasculation, came to stand in for national trouble and betrayal in a 2011 amateur street-level performance by boys and men. The impact of this performance, part of a *populist revolutionary mythscape*, was multiplied through Facebook, its intended audience. I then explore the aesthetic and affective dimensions of the *pluralistic revolutionary mythscape* in mobilization music that circulated on cyber circuits before and after the revolution. This music insistently articulated transnational cosmopolitan forms of identification and belonging, although its gender messages were not necessarily inclusive of girls and women as revolutionary and national subjects. I discuss *Islamist mythscapes* produced in Tunisian hip-hop, folk, and rap music but also enacted symbolically and physically on streets, in clock towers, and in squares. The musical texts I examine denounce injustice and express Islamic solidarity across time and geographic borders, but often include explicitly antifeminist and misogynist messages. I call attention to queer productions of time and space in a number of politically and culturally charged moments. I examine the sexual and gendered compositions of *secularist mythscapes*, which I argue are expressed through class and racial elisions, and I discuss activist enactments in public spaces that destabilize taken-for-granted equivalencies between gendered-sexual bodies, space, and socioeconomic status.

Reflections on a Postcolonial Feminist Positionality

I am a Tunisian-born woman academic teaching in the U.S. Deep South. Before 2011 I did not identify as a political activist, join a political party, or participate in the Tunisian opposition. My uncle Nejib Ben Youssef was assassinated by the Bourguiba regime on 26 January 1978, during labor protests that escalated into a massive general strike. Hundreds were killed, wounded, and imprisoned in an event that came to be called Black Thursday. After that time members of my family, including myself, did not feel Tunisian because we believed that the leaders of the Tunisian syndicalist movement were complicit in the massacre. The Tunisian revolution offered many families like mine symbolic repatriation.

Ideologically I am neither a Bourguibist nor an apologist for Islamists. I see myself as a Tunisiast and as such take issue with a simplistic Western understanding of Tunisia as divided between an Arabophone Islamist proletariat and a Western-educated Francophone elite. Such a vision occludes the fact that Islamists are an integral part of the new Tunisian capitalist bourgeoisie, with ties to England, the United States, and rich countries of the Gulf. It is largely the children of the poor who participate in dangerous clandestine immigration to Europe or jihadism in Syria and Iraq. Both Islamists and secularists are part of the post-Bourguiba elite that studied in Western universities. Moreover a secular/nonsecular binary is not particularly useful for understanding ideological trends and attached mythscapes in Tunisia because it misses how the main divisions are between different kinds of Muslim subjectivities and ideals of belonging. It also misrecognizes the vernacular nature of the term *secular*.[6] I do not claim to have objective knowledge of Tunisia, because knowledge is never impartial and is always imbricated in relations of power. While there is no way to remove the influence of my educational privilege, I am reflexively aware of it.[7]

When the Revolution broke out in late December 2010 it coincided with the beginning of winter break in the United States, allowing me to closely follow the revolution unfolding in my home country before the *New York Times* covered the events. Although I was not on the ground or exposed to rape and bullets, I was full of fear. As I circulated videos of riots and funerals in Kasserine, Tala, and Kef, I was aware that I might be arrested as a result when I returned to Tunisia. In the first phase of the revolution, relaying messages through Facebook became an underground railway of solidarity. Perhaps the scariest experience was when an eighteen-year-old cousin in Tunisia I was chatting with suddenly told me he had to end the conversation because it was his turn to take a baton and join the neighborhood protection committee. Having seen videos of butchered Tunisians, I was afraid the chat room exchange would be our last conversation until I saw the green light indicating he was back online.

In the professional setting I inhabit, the most difficult moment during the revolution was when I was told by a senior colleague with little knowledge of the region, "Finally the Middle East is going to know democracy and have a constitution as we did in the West with the Magna Carta in 1215." I struggled with distorted temporal imaginaries, limited knowledge, and selective historical memory. As a woman in the U.S. academy, I am expected to play native informant, explaining ongoing events back home according to a Eurocentric narrative of Arab masculine honor and humiliation.[8] Just as it became unsafe for women to circulate at night in postrevolutionary Tunisia, it is often unsafe for Muslim and Arab women faculty in the North American academy to mention the 340 BCE Constitution of Carthage or that a tiny Muslim country like Tunisia abolished slavery in 1846, before the United States or France did so in its colonies. Such counterhegemonic knowledge and subaltern experiences are too often understood as "uncivil," perhaps even grounds to terminate a faculty contract, as suggested by the 2014 case of Steven Salaita at the University of Illinois.[9]

The Gender of National Betrayal in a Populist Mythscape

Immediately following Ben Ali's forced departure, dozens of home-made videos were posted on Facebook from all parts of Tunisia mocking the president's televised speech of 13 January and denouncing the vanity and ruthlessness of his wife, Leila Trabelsi, and her clan. These satirical videos used a mishmash of Tunisian, eastern, "Arab," and U.S. pop culture references. One of these videos, *Leila Trabelsi Seduces Ben Ali and Murad Juha Protects the Neighbourhood*, was posted on Facebook on 17 January 2011 by a neighborhood watch group in Menzel Bourguiba in Tunis.[10] The video shows a forty-something man sequentially impersonating in Arabic President Ben Ali, Leila Ben Ali, and a cowboy. The main character opens and ends his speech with Islamic religious formulations, although the last thing we hear is the national anthem sung by other men "onstage" and in the audience. The stage is a neighborhood sidewalk after dark, with large Tunisian flags in the background. About six male teenagers and young men surround the main actor, carrying props and occasionally helping him with his lines.

The most arresting feature of this video is its presentation of Tunisian national identity as a drag performance wherein different kinds of femininity represent sources of trouble. In the sequence the main character plays a henpecked Ben Ali, who in a nasal voice and Sahelian accent apologizes to the Tunisian people for his emasculation and sobs during his speech for having been fooled by his spouse and her family. In the second scene the voice is in falsetto and speaks the uneducated Tunisian Arabic of Leila Ben Ali, who wears a generous smear of red lipstick and a sequined dress and furs. She is a cruel sorceress who knows the current price of chameleons and cares only about her family.

In the third and final scene, the longest in the fourteen-minute video, the amateur actor retires through a back door and reappears in a cowboy hat, identifying himself as Murad Juha, a forty-five-year-old salt-of-the-earth resident of the town of Menzel Bourguiba. He reveals his exact location—9 April 1938 Avenue, a street named after Tunisia's Martyrs' Day—and vows to protect the women and children of his hometown, the Tunisian flag, and the people from snipers, who continued to terrorize Tunisians in the days after Ben Ali had stepped down. Juha carries "white weapons," some of which stand against the metal door that serves as a backdrop, including shovels, an axe, and sticks. He promises that his people are willing to "die on/for this flag," whose corner he grabs and gestures with to a small audience (we only hear) and the intended digital audience. Juha recites a satirical poem criticizing Ben Ali in the Tunisian dialect of popular poetry: "It is not I who toppled you, but the generation of young people you once described as the hair gel and low-hanging pants generation, the Facebook people." He then threatens to eat the snipers raw with his bare teeth if they dare come closer to Menzel Bourguiba.

The many voices Murad Juha performs produce relations and geographies that transcend his immediate surroundings into a dialogic auditory interaction with Tunisians in and outside Tunisia.[11] The nickname of the trickster Juha in the title of the video invites us to think of national identity as a performance and a political trick since in Arab folklore, Juha appears as both a wise man and a fool. In this apparently thoroughly male production, state tyranny is transposed to women characters. Because fear of rape and people's talk limits the mobility of girls and women in the evening and prevents them from participating in the actual performance, girls and women enter the dialogic space only as viewers, commenters, and sharers on Facebook. The demonization of Leila Trabelsi recalls the negative personification of Hamdi, the policewoman accused of slapping Bouazizi and supposedly compelling him to burn himself to death.

As indicated in this example and others in the chapter, while digital media have paved the way for novel expressions of gender, sexual, racial, and social emancipation, they are equally available for enacting conservative, misogynistic, homophobic, or racist sentiments. Indeed the cyber world is often a space where difference is maintained rather than suspended and where anxieties about otherness are rechanneled and refashioned rather than eradicated.[12] The populist local and national solidarities expressed in the *Leila Trabelsi* video coexisted with the cosmopolitan mythscape expressed in a genre of revolutionary music.

Pluralistic Transnational Mythscapes and Identifications

Beginning in 2010 and intensifying in January and February 2011 hundreds of videos of *musique engagée* appeared on Tunisian blogs, YouTube, Dailymotion.com, and personal Facebook pages. This revolutionary music had strong affective and mobilizing power, although it differed in the inclusions, gender sensibilities, and politics it imagined. A strand of this music was pluralistic and strikingly multiethnic. The mythscape it produced drew on anticolonial and antiracist traditions to articulate leftist border-crossing identifications and political critique.

On the night of 13 January 2011, before Ben Ali stepped down, government television propaganda showed the return of calm to the streets of Tunis. In response Tunisian activists, emboldened by fear of government retaliation and the killing of young men in Kasserine, Tala, Le Kram, and Sidi Bouzid, used their Facebook pages to post songs associated with protest music from Mai 68, Woodstock, the American civil rights movement, Central and Latin American revolutionary movements, and the Arab world. Songs included Charles Aznavour's "Les Comédiens," Lise Médini's "Deux chants révolutionnaires," Richie Havens's "Freedom," Joe Cocker's "With a Little Help from My Friends," Tracy Chapman's "Revolution Song," and Nathalie Cardone's "Che Guevara." The music of Bob Marley, Sheikh Imam, Marcel Khalife, May Nasr, Amel Hamrouni, and Hedi Guella was also widely circulated.

This pluralistic mythscape included the words and performances of Amel Mathluthi's "Kelmti Hurra" (My Word Is Free), which she sang on Avenue Habib Bourguiba on 14 January 2011, near the Tunisian Ministry of the Interior, during a massive gathering insistently calling on Ben Ali to "degage!"[13] Although Mathluthi's song had been banned from Tunisian airwaves before Ben Ali fell, Tunisian youth were familiar with it from a widely circulated YouTube video of a performance at the Bastille on 13 July 2008, which Mathluthi dedicated to all oppressed people around the world, mentioning Tunisians, Palestinians, Iraqis, Africans, and "the people who are free yet oppressed."[14] The lyrics encouraged the "free" to rise against fear (my translation):

I am those who are free and unafraid
I am the secrets that will not die
I am the voice of those who will not cave in
I am meaning amid chaos
I am the right of the oppressed
That is sold by the dogs
Who are robbing the people of their bread.

Mathluthi's first album, *Kelmti Hurra*, was released in January 2012 to mark the first anniversary of the Tunisian revolution. She dedicated her Arabic rendition of the Joan Baez song "Here's to You" to Bouazizi, linking the Tunisian revolution with transnational radical struggles. "My Word Is free" helped create a shared imaginative space of freedom that does not require permission and after the revolution served as an ironic backdrop in satirical critiques of the Troika alliance.

Many revolutionary songs originated in Palestinian or North African Jewish resistance music. The popular anthem of the revolution, "Raji' li bladi" (I Am Returning to My Country), revised a Palestinian nationalist song to express alienation, exile, and a desire to "return," as I argue elsewhere.[15] A refrain insists that the "light of the revolution remains alive in my heart" and challenges the "traitors, collaborators, and reactionaries." A repeated clause announces the symbolic "return" of marginalized southern Tunisians to economic inclusion and full citizenship. The music intertextually links the fates of Tunisia and Palestine: just as the departure of the British brought Zionism to its full fruition for Palestinians, liberation from French colonial rule relied on violence and exclusions in secular independent Tunisia. The lyrics "There on the battle ground, men we shall be! Do not be sad, O Mother, O Sisters" cast Tunisian women in the roles of weeping mothers and sisters for male heroes, despite their centrality to the revolution. Echoing the male-centered Tunisian nationalist literature of the colonial period,[16] the promise of liberation in the song seems to exclude sisters and mothers.

This strand of world music, I argue, served as a space for the "marking and articulation" of a pluralistic and cosmopolitan Tunisian identity in and outside Tunisia, conjuring "feelings of deep attachment to place."[17] The songs, which were widely posted on Facebook, inspired feelings of excitement, fear, displacement, and belonging. For me as a Tunisian cyber activist living in the diaspora, they elicited a desire to return. Tunisians everywhere felt they were part of something larger than themselves as they contributed to the traffic of information and songs. The music allowed us to inhabit the homelessness of the diasporic North African Jew, Palestinian, and *pied noir*, but also histories and experiences of subordinated groups who are not "Eastern," "Arab," or Tunisian. The music bound younger and older Tunisians into a project of struggle and introduced young people to knowledge about parents and grandparents who may have been involved in student and labor movements in the 1960s and 1970s.

Beyond music, Tunisian cyber activists widely used handles such as Volcain, Voltaire Averroès, Che Guevara, and Sofienne David to identify with global histories of subordination and struggle.[18] The articulations of cosmopolitan identifications opposed the binarisms and exclusions of Eastern and Western orthodoxies. In this transnational mythscape a cyber handle that combines Voltaire (the French Enlightenment philosopher and playwright) and Averroès (Ibn Rushd, the Cordoba-born Muslim philosopher) located Tunisian postrevolutionary identity in the unacknowledged interstices between Eastern and Western philosophy. A name combination like Sofienne David rewrites Jews and "infidels" (*kuffar*) into a cosmopolitan identity that includes Abu Sofian, the leader of the Quraysh tribe of Mecca who fought Muhammad before accepting Islam. These transnational and transhistorical mythscapes of pluralistic "brotherhood" often did not include women, however, reflecting a larger tension in leftist and "Third Worldist" revolutionary discourse. Islamist revolutionary music produced an explicitly misogynist masculinist mythscape.

*The Corruption of Secular Time
and Women in Islamist Mythscapes*

The Tunisian revolution was accompanied by a hip-hop, folk, and rap music scene created by male artists like Bendir Man, El Général, Psyco M, and Balti.[19] These artists denounced injustice and oppression (including of veiled women), government corruption, the pro-Zionism of the Ben Ali government, and secularism. Their music articulated a mythscape of purist authenticity, a particular Islamic solidarity across borders and time, and conservative and repressive gender and sexual politics.

Psyco's well-known Arabic rap song "Manipulation" is a lengthy pedagogical performance of almost fifteen minutes.[20] The YouTube rendition from November 2010 relies on extensive archival historical images. The words and images evoke the Ottoman Empire as an ideal. The song presents modern secularism, particularly as established in Turkey by the "traitor" Atatürk, as well as the Arab nation-state and women's liberation, as aspects of a Euro-Zionist-Christian conspiracy against Muslims that began with the First World War, "when General Allenby entered Jerusalem" and proclaimed, "Now is the end of the Crusades." Psyco M frames Arab nationalist leaders as part of a colonial, anti-Islamic project: "The flag of my country is not red and white with a star and a moon. . . . My flag has a glorious history. . . . [It] is the *tawhid* flag. . . ."[21] My home is from the Gulf to the Atlantic." Muslims, he mourns, "used to have one God, they used to be brothers in Islam," but now they are divided and scattered by nationalism, secularism, and atheism into Tunisians, Algerians, and Egyptians. He condemns the personal status laws that replaced Islamic shariʿa, as well as liberated women, unveiled women, and Egyptian cinema. The song pours anger on the Tunisian reformer Tahar al Haddad, artists Sawsen Maalij and Nouri Bouzid, feminists Huda Shaʿrawi and Olfa Youssef, and artists believed to be gay such as the Tunisian singer Chemseddine Bacha for destroying the moral fabric of the Muslim *umma*.

Balti's 2011 YouTube rap performance, "Passe Partout," translated as "She Goes Everywhere," created a major controversy because, with over 285,000 hits on YouTube alone, the video presented all Tunisian women as prostitutes and linked political and social reform to morally cleansing the country and policing women's sexuality, mobility, and behavior.[22] This misogynistic performance was delivered in French and the Arabic dialect of Tunisia. The approximately four-and-a-half-minute video is composed with what are likely images from Facebook, many of them used repeatedly, of light-skinned, dressed-up women posing at parties, at home, at the beach, dancing, with alcohol, with other women, and with men. These still images are interspersed with advertising images of women selling perfume and other products, as well as images of food dishes, jewels, and cars.

In the lyrics Balti decries the levity and materialism of the modern Tunisian young woman, who likes fashion, miniskirts, dresses, stiletto shoes, "ice cream," bikinis, brand names, money, jewels, big cars, camera lights, and one-night stands, or "taking a bridegroom every night." She goes to night clubs in Tunis, Hammamet, and Sousse, dances on tables, drinks champagne and white wine, and takes pictures with famous people and posts them on Facebook. She likes dating rich men who own Hummers and BMWs. From a modest social background, Balti's Tunisian girl "slips out of her skin" like a snake to ape Western women and Tunisian women above her social class.

The video, which, beginning at 3:04, includes an image of a veiled older woman cleaning a floor and an image of a working-class man painting or cleaning a wall, opposes the materialism of the unveiled modern girl who goes where she likes and consumes what she wants to the sacrifices of her modest veiled mother, who is happy with the little she can prepare at home. This binary reproduces the Mother/Goddess versus Whore dichotomy found in the current Maghrebi popular imaginary and Francophone Maghrebi nationalist literature of the 1950s and 1960s. As was the case for many male nationalist North African writers and reformers in an earlier period, in these modern masculinist Islamist mythscapes, the good Tunisian woman should be a selfless sacrificing mother, not an equal citizen, mobile subject, or sexual agent. If U.S. male rappers are said to demean women by using misogynistic lyrics and objectifying their bodies to prove they are authentic gangsters,[23] conservative Tunisian male rappers, most of whom come from modest social backgrounds, use misogynistic rhetoric coated in religious language to prove to themselves and others that they matter in a society that increasingly tells them they are irrelevant.

The popularity of Tunisian rap accompanied a surge of graffiti in English, French, and Arabic. Although such graffiti is a nice change from the sexual obscenities one usually encountered before the revolution, it can echo racist language and imagery, as illustrated by an image photographed in June 2015 in Tunis (figure 2.1). This graffiti redeploys the slurs "thug" and "nigga" and the phrase "life for life" (or "an eye for an eye") against the Tunisian police, represented as subhuman. This racialized language differs from "traditional" Tunisian racism, which fetishizes blackness, as seen in the portrait of the healer or sorceress in Bouzid's film *Man of Ashes*.[24]

While it is true that Tunisian rap is a means of political dissent, much of it is also part of a mythscape that produces Islamist and masculinist forms of community invested in control of women's bodies and behavior. In the transnational male imaginary produced in these revolutionary rap songs, Tunisian women artists, intellectuals, and everyday young women who do not veil are condemned as inauthentic (*mutafassikhat*) and immoral (*fasidat*). The songs allow marginalized lower-class men to inscribe themselves as the central figures in Tunisian Muslim identity. The masculinist and misogynistic worldview produced in these audiovisual performances,

FIGURE 2.1. "Thug," Al Manar I, Tunis, 29 June 2015. Photograph by Lamia Benyoussef.

while presumably expressing the subject positions of alienated poor and working-class boys and men, can also be racist.

Islamist mythscapes are difficult to understand solely at ideational, psychological, or discursive levels. These audiovisual mythscapes worked through embodied enactments and sartorial practices in different spaces to articulate certain notions of temporality and place. On 22 January 2011 a bearded Tunisian expatriate wearing a leather jacket, gloves, a red and white checkered keffiyeh around his neck, and an Islamic skull cap stood in front of the Tunisian Embassy in London during a demonstration. He was flanked by other young male Salafists carrying signs in Arabic and French and black flags with Arabic writing. Using a microphone, he directed his rhetoric largely at the staff of the embassy, threatening them by declaring that he and his friends were "back" after being oppressed by the Ben Ali regime. In Tunisian Arabic mixed with occasional English and French, he announced the bringing of sharіʿa law and Islam to Tunisia. He insulted Mohamed Ghannouchi, the Tunisian prime minister who took power after Ben Ali's departure, the Tunisian diplomatic corps in the building, and all secularist Tunisians: "You are hypocrites, profligate and closer to unbelief than Islam!" He commanded a Tunisian woman embassy employee at a window to wear a veil and continued:

> We are inviting you to follow the righteous path! Until you follow the Quran and the Sunna, no salvation, no success and no prosperity shall be in Tunisia. You have been fooled by Sarkozy, Obama, and the tyrannical and doomed West! Sarkozy is the biggest apostate. That profligate is also a killer. You are not Muslims until you are governed by that which God had ordained. Ben Ali is gone, and now what did you do? Create democratic parties? Democracy is unbelief. . . . There is no salvation for you if you do not follow the holy shariʿa law, the Sunna of the Messenger of God, may peace be on him, and the caliphate. Even the national anthem, my brothers, is a *kufr* [blasphemy]![25]

Although the design and colors of the modern Tunisian flag hark to the Ottoman Caliphate period, the speaker rewrote the red flag of Tunisia as a French gift: "The French gave you a red flag! And for it you are dying!" Following his speech antinationalist green flags were posted on conservative religious blogs to oppose the red Tunisian flag. The Salafist identity he performed was ironically produced through modern symbols of "Muslim" identity in the West: beards, skullcaps, red-checkered scarves, hijabs, and black tawhid flags stating, "There is no God but God and Muhammad is his Prophet." The event was designed for multiple audiences: those at the demonstration, embassy personnel, and an unbounded digital audience. The medieval language reminded thousands of Tunisians who commented on this video of the archaic Arabic used in Ramadan religious TV series and films about the early days of Islam, such as Mustapha Akkad's 1976 film *Muhammad, the Messenger of God*, which recounts Muhammad's persecution by his Quraysh tribe, his exodus from Mecca, and crucial early Muslim battles.[26]

This approach to time became clear in performances of non-Salafist Islamists in Tunis. When the exiled Ennahda leader Rached Ghannouchi returned to Tunis on 31 January 2011 he was welcomed at Carthage International Airport by Islamist partisans who sang "Talaʿa al badru ʿalayna" (The Full Moon Rose over Us), reportedly chanted by Medina residents upon the arrival of the Prophet Muhammad to their city in 622.[27] In the mythscape of these disciples the song symbolized a return to Islamic enlightenment for Tunisians after decades of exile, alienation, and ignorance during the authoritarian secular rule of Bourguiba and then Ben Ali. To quote the opening lines (my translation):

The full moon rose over us
From the valley of farewells
Gratitude we must show
Where the call is to God
O you, the Emissary chosen from us
You came with commandments to be followed
You came and ennobled this city of Medina
Welcome, you the best of Messengers.

In this mythscape the Tunis of 2011 is symbolically reborn through intertextual references to three historical moments known to all Tunisian Muslims: Medina in 622 CE, when Muhammad first entered after his exodus from Mecca; Muhammad's 630 conquest of Mecca after his tribe broke a 628 treaty; and the "opening" or Islamization of Ifriqiyaa when ʿUqba Ibn Nafiʿ founded the Great Mosque of Kairouan in 670. In August 2013, Rached Ghannouchi positively compared the pro-Ennahda Kasbah sit-in participants to the Muslim armies that conquered Mecca in 630.[28]

On 25 March 2012 Tunisian artists participated in a planned parade on Habib Bourguiba Avenue that competed with an event organized by Salafists calling for application of shariʿa law. Whereas women occupied a preeminent position in the artists' parade, they were essentially absent from the Salafist demonstration.[29] The competing mythscapes were reflected in contrasting sartorial practices in the same space and time. Men and women artists wore bright, carnivalesque colors with masks and clown face-paint, while Salafists wore somber colors. When male shariʿa supporters climbed the 7 November Clock Tower and waved the black flag of the caliphate they desired, dozens of satirical and critical images and video postings appeared on Facebook and YouTube describing this event as the Razzia, or Conquest of the Clock, as in episode 12 of the satirical television series *Khubzulugia* (Breadology). The episode and a 2012 video commenting on the clock tower incident are titled *Ghazwat al Mungala*,[30] invoking for most Muslims temporal and spatial configurations located at the dawn of Islam. The narrator in the video suggests that the Salafist Conquest of the Clock on 25 March 2012, which may also be translated as "invasion of the clock," aims to divide Tunisians from each other at the direction of outside forces, as indicated by a puppet master's manipulating figures (2:15). He also suggests that the Salafist desire to turn Tunisian modernity back to the dawn of Islam is itself carnivalesque theater, no different from the International Art Day celebration organized by Tunisian artists.

In *Getting Medieval*, Carolyn Dinshaw defines the "queer historical impulse" as "making connections across time between, on the one hand, lives, texts, and other cultural phenomena left out of sexual categories back then and, on the other, those left out of current sexual categories now."[31] In more recent work Dinshaw explains that the "queer historical impulse" refers not only to "gay" or "homosexual" dynamics but also to "forms of desirous, embodied being that are out of sync with the ordinarily linear measurements of everyday life that engage heterogeneous temporalities." She is interested in "asynchrony," or "how different time frames or temporal systems collide in a single moment of now." The Tunisian Islamists who dressed, acted, and spoke like characters out of medieval Muslim hagiographies live in secular time and suffer from contemporary problems and crises. Rather than being marooned in the past, we can use Dinshaw's concept of queer historical time to understand their "desire to build another kind of world."[32] The asynchrony of Tunisian Islamists' practices points to years of alienation and subjugation under Ben Ali but also in European contexts where Salafism seems to thrive among migrants.

However authentic and traditional Salafists and statist Islamists claim to be, their symbolics and rhetoric are as messily hybrid and modern as the pluralist mythscapes that rely on leftist and Third-Worldist social justice imaginaries. Moreover Islamist mythscapes require their own forgetting. While leftists more or less acknowledge the plight of the Youssefists in the early 1960s, the hundreds of Tunisians killed by Bourguiba's army on 26 January 1978 (Black Thursday), and the Bread Riots of 1984, with few exceptions the history of torture and persecution of students and leftist activists in Bourguiba's prisons in the late 1960s and 1970s remains unknown to most Tunisians.[33] Many believe that only Islamists were victims of the authoritarian secular state.

Embodiment and Elisions in Secularist Mythscapes

Secularist mythscapes produced their own sexual and gendered exclusions, which were often classed and racialized. After independence an urban bourgeoisie from Tunis and the Sahel (Mediterranean Coast) ruled Tunisia. In contrast Islamists who came to power after the 2011 revolution are likely to be supported by people from lower social classes and rural, southern and western interior regions that were neglected by the postcolonial state. They are also more likely to be what some urban bourgeoisie privately describe with the racial term *azroug*, or "blue people."

Veils and beards were coded as "sectarian" and banned in government and academic institutions under the postcolonial governments of Bourguiba and Ben Ali. After 11 September 2001 veils and beards became visible gendered markers of identity that signaled opposition to Ben Ali and the West. After the January 2011 revolution, the Ennahda Party and other Islamist actors marketed Islamic identity as commodity spectacle with veils, *niqabs*, *jilbabs*, *babouches*, religious books, and so on. Pious and often lower-class and rural Tunisian women who wore the facial veil were empowered to challenge secularist restrictions on "Islamic" dress, while feminists who did not wear this clothing worried about its imposition.[34]

The battle between two forms of feminine embodiment and sartorial practice came to a head on International Women's Day, 8 March 2011, when an Islamist demonstration countered a march by the Tunisian Association of Democratic Women. Dozens of women affiliated with Hizb ut-Tahrir, a far-right Islamist party, marched in downtown Tunis to demand the right of women to wear hair and facial veils and men to wear beards in workplaces.[35] Secularist cyber activists responded with satirical political cartoons inspired by Hollywood science-fiction movies. A cartoon captioned "Sauvez notre pays des ninjas warriors: OVNI: Objet voilé non identifié" (Save our country from the Ninja Warriors: NIVO: Non-identified veiled object) depicts a woman wearing a black niqab and robe as a ninja warrior character.[36] Her body is round and looks like a spaceship, indicating the degree to which many Tunisians see the ideological agenda of Islamists as an alien cultural invasion. However, most men and women interested in practices of embodied piety are not "outsiders" or returnees to Tunisia.

While the facial veil is rejected as a foreign import in this secularist mythscape, the rejection is enunciated from a hybrid privileged location since the ninja warrior figure originates in Japanese and American video games, which are not accessible to all Tunisian youth. Contrasting themselves with the "backwardness" of returning Tunisians affiliated with Ennahda and Hizb ut-Tahrir, Tunisian secularists place themselves in the futuristic time of Western progress and modernity as if to highlight the gap between them and the anachronistic time the Muslim Sisters wished to inhabit on Women's International Day.

In addition to representing women who wear face veils as aliens, the secularist mythscape depicts Islamist men as infectious threats, as indicated by a disturbing 2011 political cartoon captioned "The Muslim Brothers, or the viruses that threaten Tunisia's project of modernity."[37] A tiny bearded and armed Islamist man wearing red shoes and an Afghani-type hat is located in the bottom right corner of the cartoon. A bald, frightened-looking, olive-skinned Tunisian man at the bottom left is in the effeminate position of seeking protection from the admired white-looking scientist studying the Eastern virus under a microscope, looking for what ails the nation. The virus is represented in the scientist's thought bubble by identical images of armed and bearded Islamist men. The bald man asks the scientist, "Doctor! Why are you silent? You are scaring us! What is this bacterium circulating in Tunisia? Is it very dangerous? Is it contagious? Answer me!" To which the physician replies, "What a strange thing! This is the dumb Islamist bacterium. It is not indigenous to Tunisia. It originates in Afghanistan and the Gulf countries. This is a dangerous bacterium that affects the brain! May God protect us all!" In the same way the French racialized Tunisians in *Princess Tam Tam* with a French man in blackface wearing Arab drag ("Tahar") in colonial society,[38] the small and nefarious Afghan figure in the bottom right corner states, "You are wrong! We are viruses, not bacteria." The Afghani character indicates his potential to annihilate when he suggests that the Islamist threat to Tunisia is viral and difficult to eradicate.

By mixing images from the Japanese anime world with archival footage of events that took place in Tunisia after the revolution, the secularist producer of the *Ghazwat al Mungala* video invoked for satirical purposes a mishmash of imaginary spaces and mythical temporalities, including American comics and the fantasy world order of Japanese anime in its secular and progressive time. In the first scene of *Ghazwat* the viewer sees the familiar anime character Captain Khobza, who emerged in summer 2011. He wears the Tunisian red *chechia* (fez), the black mask of Zorro, and the tight costume of a superhero with the Arabic letter "kh."[39] His name means "loaf of bread" in the Tunisian Arabic dialect he speaks. As in nationalist literature and visual culture in French colonial Tunisia, the agent of progress and modernity in postrevolutionary Tunisia remains the Tunisian man in the secularist mythspace. The outspoken hero supports the cause of

FIGURE 2.2. Screenshot from "Ghazwat al Mungaala: Min Khubzulugia, Halaqa 12," YouTube, 1 April 2012, http://www.youtube.com/watch?v=K1_qPiCrjNI.

those who lost their lives in the struggle for bread and dignity and is a foil to the selfish *khobziste*, a Tunisian word that compounds the Arabic word for *bread* with the French suffix -*ist* to refer to self-preserving individuals who take no sides in political disputes.

In the second scene of the *Ghazwat* video, an authoritative voice in standard Arabic establishes a filial connection between the Tunisian Captain Khobza, who inhabits the panoptical time of progress and modernity, and Japanese anime characters born in Tokyo, such as Sasuki, Voltron, and Captain Majed (the Arabic name of Captain Tsubasa). The affinity between modern Japan and modern Tunisia is reinforced in the third scene, which shows the map of Tunisia with English and Japanese labels for Tunisian cities (figure 2.2). The exclusion of Arabic suggests a shift in the way secular leftists imagine Tunisia's national identity. Rather than evoking the myth of Tunisia's Punic personality, situated between Phoenicia (East) and Rome (West),[40] this mythscape evokes a postrevolutionary Tunisian "super-breadist" located between the United States (Superman) and Japan (Captain Tsubasa).

As indicated by the narration in this video, many leftist Tunisians came to view the return of exiled Ennahda leaders from France and England and the establishment of the Islamist-dominated government as colonization by a foreign power, a "colonial government," according to feminist scholar

Olfa Youssef.[41] In early 2013 the Tunisian poet and reporter Ahmed ʿUmar Zaʿbar published on Facebook a parody of "The Full Moon Rose over Us" titled "Ignorance Rose over Us from the Valleys of the Riffraff." Rejecting the Islamist narrative of the enlightened reopening of Tunisia, the parody cautioned against ignorance, treachery, misogyny, and hunger for power concealed by false piety:

> Ignorance rose over us from the valleys of the riffraff,
> The Salafist rose upon us wearing religion as a mask,
> He imposed tyranny upon us and viewed females as a thing,
> He saw the victory we accomplished as marriage and intercourse,
> You who are full of muck—what is mind but light?
> But the darkness of the bearded hates the brightness of light.
> You who have been implanted among us with treacherous words
>   you came,
> You came to ruin the city and turn the world upside down,
> You brought us ignominy and the barbarism of the riffraff.
> So many years you dwelled in caves that the compass you lost.
> You sanctified our murder as if beasts from the bushes you were.
> In the Land of Islam a disease has compromised the spine.
> Ignorance rose upon us to say farewell to science.
> The ignorant pretends to be wise while religion he buys and sells.
> Have patience, they say, it is an obligation, but no need for patience
>   anymore.
> Followers of our Prophet they are not.
> What are they but a mere headache?[42]

In language that recalls French Orientalist discourse, the poet presents the new invaders as oversexed Arab warmongers who are violent, greedy, and oppressive to women. A video of the poem captions the spoken words over moving images of the Qatari Hamad Bin Khalifa Al Thani, Saudi Prince Saud al Faisal, Barack Obama, Hillary Clinton, Joseph Biden, Yusuf Qaradawi of the Muslim Brotherhood, and Salafist figures. In this reading the riffraff are bearded Islamists, Gulf countries, the Arab League, religious clerics (seen as servants of Western imperialism), the U.S. government, and Western reporters, all coming from outside to destroy Tunisia. However accurate its critique of Western and regional elites, the parody also reflects class and cultural divisions among Tunisians, since *riffraff* connotes lower-class people. After two bloody terrorist attacks in 2015, many

Tunisians concluded that fanaticism, barbarism, and terrorism are not produced solely on foreign ground.

As I have demonstrated, gendered and sexual symbolism is central to revolutionary and postrevolutionary ideological struggles in Tunisia, but these conflicts are invariably worked out on multiple scales, including embodied practices in physical spaces. New forms of radical and inclusive activism in postrevolutionary Tunisia have destabilized taken-for-granted ideological equations between gendered-sexual bodies and space.

Claiming Public Space

The ideological fissures of postrevolutionary Tunisia are enacted in physical space and cyberspace, as indicated by the clock tower scaling and International Women's Day battles. Men's and women's status, behavior, and sartorial practices in public spaces were central representational sites in these battles.

No place is more iconic and crucial to collective memory in Tunisia than Habib Bourguiba Avenue, which remains the main thoroughfare for protests and marches. All leaders since the late nineteenth century have attempted to resignify this avenue in their image. When the French colonized Tunisia in 1881, the street was referred to in Arabic as Bab Bhar (the Door to the Sea). The French marked it as theirs by building on the east side of the Medina the French Consulate (1890–92), the Cathedral of Saint Vincent de Paul (1897), and the Municipal Theater (1920). After World War I the street was renamed Avenue Jules-Ferry for the founder of French colonial education in Africa. When the Allies defeated the Axis Powers in Tunisia, native soldiers who fought with the Free French Forces of Charles de Gaulle marched in segregated regiments on this avenue in the victory parade of U.S., French, and British troops on 20 May 1943. Soon after Tunisia became independent in 1956, the street was renamed Avenue Habib Bourguiba after the self-proclaimed "Father of the Nation." After General Ben Ali's 1987 coup d'état, when he summoned physicians to declare Bourguiba incompetent to rule, he built 7 November 1987 Square at the end of the avenue. After the revolution the square was renamed 14 January 2011 Square.

The avenue remains a battleground.[43] Tunisian feminists took to this artery on International Women's Day in 2011, 2012, and 2013. They would not give up rights acquired through the Personal Status Code Bourguiba

FIGURE 2.3.
"Révolution
tunisienne" by
Carlos Latuff;
originally published
22 January 2011,
Nawaat.org.

enacted in 1957. In the early months of 2011 people spontaneously participated in street cleaning on Habib Bourguiba Avenue and the Kasbah
to accompany their demands for the dissolution of the Constitutional
Democratic Rally (RCD) Party and Mohamed Ghannouchi's Troika government.[44] In one of the street-cleaning videos a young man declares, "My
brother, we are cleaning the country. Just as we cleansed it from the germs
that used to occupy it, now we are going to rid the country of the legacy
they left behind."[45] This public border-crossing of class, gender, and status
differences is superbly captured in a cartoon posted on the Tunisian website Nawaat.org.[46] In the image (figure 2.3) a muscular young man wearing
jeans and sneakers and caped in a Tunisian flag sweeps—a menial activity

of women at home and lower-class men on the streets—the entire country of Ben Ali's RCD Party.

During the country's anticolonial struggle, Tunisian nationalists opposing French acculturation policies encouraged women to wear the *sefsari*, a white or off-white nylon or silk cloth worn like a robe. The sefsari fell out of use in postcolonial Tunisia because of Bourguiba's antiveiling policies. It made a remarkable comeback after the 2011 revolution to counter Islamic niqab fashion. Between 8 March 2012 and April 2012 dozens of women wearing black face veils associated with the Hizb ut-Tahrir Party again marched in downtown Tunis with banners calling for freedom to wear the veil at work and in universities. Some Tunisian women responded with sefsari-wearing demonstrations, combining the white robe with the traditional red wool chechia usually worn by men, on which was pinned a red ribbon depicting the Tunisian flag.

The killing of Chokri Belaid, a labor activist and leftist, in February 2013 outside his home convulsed Tunisia and transformed the landscape of national politics. It was the first political assassination in Tunisia since the murder of the syndicalist leader Farhat Hached in 1952 by the Red Hand, a secret terrorist organization of right-wing French settlers suspected of working with the French colonial authorities. Over a million people from all over Tunisia and many political affiliations attended Belaid's funeral procession.[47] Challenging a division where women mourn the dead person at home while men take the body to the cemetery, Belaid's wife, Basma Khalfawi, a lawyer, accompanied the funeral procession with her daughter, Nayruz, along with thousands of Tunisian women.[48] They marched with National Guard protection from the home of Belaid's parents in Djebel Djeloud to his resting place in the Djellaz Cemetery. On the day he was killed and during his funeral procession, Khalfawi made the victory sign with her fingers and ululated with other women.[49] In one of the most vivid scenes of the Arab revolutions, women (notably with their hair uncovered) helped carry Belaid's coffin, by social practice a prerogative of men in Muslim and Tunisian funeral rites.[50] When the Ennahda minister of religious affairs Noureddine Khadimi condemned the participation of women in the procession as un-Islamic, many Tunisian observers saw this as another example of the distorted priorities of a leadership whose primary concern was that living women entered a cemetery.

Mbarka Brahmi, the wife of the leftist Muhammad Brahmi, slain on 25 July 2013, carried a flag and gave a political speech at her husband's funeral in Djellaz.[51] She also rode in the military vehicle that carried the coffin to the cemetery and relocated the *farq*, the third day after death, which Muslims usually mark at home, to the protest space in Bardo Square known as *i'tisam al rahil* (sit-in of departure).[52] The sit-in was launched in front of the National Constituent Assembly in Tunis after Brahmi's assassination.[53] The protesters called for the dissolution of the assembly and its replacement with a temporary government of Tunisian technocrats to address the threat of terrorism and the economic crisis. Ramadan 2013, which began on 9 July, was unusual because thousands of families broke the fast with friends, strangers, and poor people who ate at the Bardo sit-in every night. Participants also observed the twenty-seventh night of Ramadan, the Eid prayer, and the Eid ceremony in Bardo Square. Partisans of the Islamist government set up a rival sit-in in the Kasbah of the Old City and occasionally counterprotested at Bardo.[54] On the fortieth day after Brahmi's death opposition forces organized a huge demonstration to demand the dissolution of the government, contest new travel restrictions forbidding Tunisian women younger than thirty-five from traveling without a father's or husband's permission, and challenge Ennahda's nomination of conservative figures to head the Ministry of the Interior and the Ministry of Education.[55] On 28 September 2013 the Islamist-led government agreed to a plan to step down, allowing the formation of an interim government until the next election.

Conclusion

Aesthetics, political discourse, and embodied forms of activism in Tunisia indicate the coexistence of competing mythscapes, each with gendered and sexual registers. Tensions between these strands intensified and came to a head after the 2011 revolution, even as beliefs shifted in response to events, knowledge, and analysis. For pluralists, revolutionary sensibilities incorporated new forms of inclusion, redistribution, and social justice, although these mythscapes did not always recognize women as subjects of history or revolution. Feminists working within this frame pushed its boundaries wider, allying with neither authoritarian state feminism nor the moralizing gender-sexual repressive logics of Islamists and other conservatives.

Tunisians, like many postcolonial subjects, are often imprisoned by colonial oppositional frames that perpetuate their own forms of remembering, forgetting, and domination. Although secularists often preach tolerance and inclusion, their caricatures of Ennahda leaders and Islamists were at times dehumanizing and inflected by class anxieties. Defining Islamists as permanent outsiders is akin to the discourse of the Christian right on Islam in Europe and North America. Similarly Islamists often condemn sexual and gender nonconformity and articulate a purist mythscape whose temporality is similar to the anti-Semitic discourse of nineteenth-century colonial France, which targeted Jews and Muslims. The current Islamist dream of retrieving a pure and untainted early Muslim community originates in French scientific racism about "l'homo Islamicus."[56]

Across ideological divisions, anxieties about national identity and life itself are often expressed in gendered and sexual representations and enactments. The secularists, for example, often locate Tunisian identity in the myths of Kahena, the warrior queen of the Berbers who resisted the Arabs, and Elissa, founder of Carthage and queen of the Amazons.[57] The Islamists, in contrast, locate Tunisian identity in Medina Islam, the veil, and the stories of Muhammad's wives and daughters. Each mythscape forgets and remembers for its purposes. Much historical scholarship remains to be done.

NOTES

1. For details about the assassination of Belaid and Brahmi, see "Tunisia: Chokri Belaid Assassination Prompts Protests," BBC News, 6 February 2013, http://www.bbc.com/news /world-21349719; Carlotta Gall, "Second Opposition Leader Assassinated in Tunisia," New York Times, 24 July 2013, http://www.nytimes.com/2013/07/26/world/middleeast /second-opposition-leader-killed-in-tunisia.html?pagewanted=all. At this writing, the assassinations are unresolved. Their families have accused the Ennahda Party and their Salafi acolytes of orchestrating the murders. Ennahda, in turn, has accused Nidaa Tunis and their RCD adherents of the murders. On 30 October 2014, Al Jazeera broadcast a controversial documentary claiming that Basma Khalfawi and Belaid were divorced and Khalfawi's lover ordered the murder. The Belaid family sued the Qatari satellite channel. See Sarra Hlaoui, "Affaire Belaïd: Le coupable parfait d'Al Jazeera," Business News, 31 October 2014, http://www.businessnews.com.tn/la-boite-noire-dal-jazeera-un-documentaire -rocambolesque-et-tendancieux,520,50750,3.

2. Eric Cunningham, "Tunisia Rampage Raises New Fears about Reach of Islamic State Groups," Washington Post, 19 March 2015, http://www.washingtonpost.com/world/tunisia -vows-to-fight-back-after-brutal-attack-on-renowned-tunis-museum/2015/03/19 /6663f968-cdb6-11e4-8730-4f473416e759_story.html; Hugh Naylor, "Witnesses Recall the Horror of Terrorist Attack on Tunisian Beach," Washington Post, 27 June 2015, http://www .washingtonpost.com/world/africa/tourists-recount-horror-of-terror-attack-on-the

-beach/2015/06/27/49209f2e-1c4d-11e5-bed8-1093ee58dad0_story.html; Eric Goldstein, "Tunisia: Emergency Shouldn't Trump Rights," Human Rights Watch, 7 July 2015, https://www.hrw.org/news/2015/07/07/tunisia-emergency-shouldnt-trump-rights.

3. On the massacre of soldiers, see Khaled Boumiza, "Moncef Marzouki amnistie les terroristes et enterre leurs victimes," *Tunisie Secret*, 14 July 2014, http://www.tunisie-secret.com/Moncef-Marzouki-amnistie-les-terroristes-et-enterre-leurs-victimes_a967.html; Nabil Ben Yahmed, "Les amnistiès de Moncef Marzouki Frappent encore l'armée et Rashid Ammar rompt le silence," *Tunisie Secret*, 6 November 2014, http://www.tunisie-secret.com/Les-amnisties-de-Moncef-Marzouki-frappent-encore-l-armee-et-Rachid-Ammar-rompt-le-silence_a1158.html.

4. Andy Bennett uses the term *mythscape* to theorize the "relationship between space and place" in an age of digital music scenes. Bennett argues that a mythscape emerges when "decontextualized images and information are recontextualized by audiences into new ways of thinking about and imagining places." Andy Bennett, "Music, Media and Urban Mythscapes: A Study of the 'Canterbury Sound,'" *Media, Culture and Society* 24, no. 1 (2002): 88, 89.

5. The exceptional liberation of Tunisian women is a state myth used in particular by ousted president Ben Ali to conceal his poor record on human rights. The Personal Status Code may have granted women exceptional rights in the 1950s, when it was promulgated, but not today, when Tunisian women still face legal discrimination in inheritance, employment, and domestic violence, as documented by the Association of Tunisian Women Democrats. For further information on this subject, see the ATFD website, https://www.facebook.com/femmesdemocrates?fref=ts.

6. See Sindre Bangstad's insightful discussion of secularism in "Contesting Secularism/s: Secularism and Islam in the Work of Talal Asad," *Anthropological Theory* 9, no. 2 (2009): 188–208. There is no pure Anglo-Saxon or French model of secularism. Although France understands itself as a country that restricts religion to the private sphere, a 1905 law separating church and state recognizes Catholicism, Calvinism, Lutheranism, and Judaism as official religions in the Alsace region. When Muslims living in the Alsace-Moselle applied for state-funded schools like members of other religions, they were reminded that France is a secular country. The debate over women's reproductive rights in the United States and the Supreme Court decision in favor of the craft store Hobby Lobby, which denies employees contraception coverage on religious grounds, demonstrate that U.S. secularism is not neutral of religion and is contested. See Giles Fraser, "France's Much Vaunted Secularism Is Not the Neutral Space It Claims to Be," *Guardian*, 16 January 2015, http://www.theguardian.com/commentisfree/belief/2015/jan/16/france-much-vaunted-secularism-not-neutral-space-claims-to-be; Ariane de Vogue, "Hobby Lobby Wins Contraceptive Ruling in Supreme Court," ABC News, 30 June 2014, http://abcnews.go.com/Politics/hobby-lobby-wins-contraceptive-ruling-supreme-court/story?id=24364311.

7. Kim V. L. England, "Getting Personal: Reflexivity, Positionality, and Feminist Research," *Professional Geographer* 46, no. 1 (1994): 250.

8. For example, Elizabeth Day, "The Slap That Sparked a Revolution," *Guardian*, 14 May 2011, http://www.theguardian.com/world/2011/may/15/arab-spring-tunisia-the-slap.

9. For details on the Steven Salaita case, see Richard Laugesen, "Chancellor Decrees Faculty at Illinois Are Subject to Civility Test; Trustees Back Her to the Hilt," CFA Illinois, 22 August 2014, http://cfaillinois.org/2014/08/22/chancellor-decrees-faculty-at-illinois -are-subject-to-civility-test-trustees-back-her-to-the-hilt; Scott Jaschik, "Out of a Job," *Inside Higher Ed*, 6 August 2014, https://www.insidehighered.com/news/2014/08/06 /u-illinois-apparently-revokes-job-offer-controversial-scholar; Colleen Flaherty, "Salaita Speaks Out," *Inside Higher Ed*, 10 September 2014, https://www.insidehighered.com/news /2014/09/10/steven-salaita-speaks-out-about-lost-job-offer-illinois.

10. *Leila Trabelsi tutih bi Ben 'Ali wa murad juha yahmi alhuma*, Facebook, 17 January 2011, https://www.facebook.com/photo.php?v=134539096610250.

11. Mikhail Bakhtin, *The Dialogic Imagination: Four Essays* (Austin: University of Texas Press, 1992), 279–80.

12. Lisa Nakamura, *Cybertypes: Race, Ethnicity and Identity on the Internet* (New York: Routledge, 2002), 10, 59–60.

13. Aigledecarthage5, "Amel Mathluthi: Kelmti hura (Live: Rue Habib Bourguiba)," YouTube, 24 January 2011, http://www.youtube.com/watch?v=tT460cZhqkI.

14. K4r10, "Amel Mathluthi Live à Bastille," 13 July 2008, YouTube, https://www .youtube.com/watch?v=iBqV4mVg2Hs. All translations in this chapter are mine.

15. Lamia Ben Youssef Zayzafoon, "Is It the End of State Feminism? Tunisian Women during and after the Revolution," in *The Arab Revolutions in Context: Civil Society and Democracy in a Changing Middle East*, edited by Benjamin Isakhan, Fethi Mansouri, and Sharam Akbarzadeh (Carlton: Melbourne University Publishing, 2012), 58. The Tunisian revolution song is a remake of a Palestinian song of exile: Ellouzi Abdallah, "Raje3 raje3," YouTube, 27 March 2011, https://www.youtube.com/watch?v=CPjfcQwHS-0.

16. See my discussion of the patriarchal images of the Tunisian woman in the national- ist literature of President Habib Bourguiba and the social reformer Tahar al Haddad in *The Production of the Muslim Woman: Negotiating Text, History, and Ideology* (Lanham, MD: Lexington Books, 2005), 95–134.

17. Ray Hudson, "Regions and Place: Music, Identity, and Place," *Progress in Human Geography* 30, no. 5 (2006): 626.

18. On her Facebook page the Tunisian feminist activist Raja Ben Slama dismisses such virtual identities as "cyber-niqabs," duplicitous undercover activism without social responsibility. Her analogy of face veiling problematically echoes French colonial rhetoric of the veil as a cowardly method of resistance during the Algerian Revolution.

19. Bendir Man originally performed in a June 2010 concert in Montreal. Bendir Man's song "Ammar 404," about state censorship of the Internet, went viral between 17 Decem- ber 2010 and 14 January 2011. See Schizoblog, "Bendir Man: Ammar 404 en Premiere Mo- dial @ Montréal," YouTube, 27 June 2010, http://www.youtube.com/watch?v=mwGxNyy -kEk. After he was detained for questioning on 6 January 2011 by the Ben Ali secret police and then released, El Général wrote a song released on 10 January about his detention and the plight of Tunisian people under the regime: Michelangelo Severgnini, "El Général, the Voice of Tunisia, English Subtitles," YouTube, 10 January 2011, http://www.youtube .com/watch?v=IeGlJ7OouRo.

20. Still Foued, "Psyco M: Manipulation 2011.mp4," YouTube, 18 November 2010, http://www.youtube.com/watch?v=d_R5wjUXYX8.

21. The tawhid flag is the black and white banner that reinforces the concept of mono-theism in Islam. Today it is used primarily by Islamic fundamentalist and militant groups.

22. Ezzeddine Sassi, "Balti: Passe partout avec le clip," YouTube, 26 May 2011, https://www.youtube.com/watch?v=42Y79YjaSPk.

23. For further information, see Denean T. Sharpley-Whiting, *Pimps Up, Ho's Down: Hip Hop's Hold on Young Black Women* (New York: New York University Press, 2007); Ronald Weitzer and Charis E. Kubrin, "Misogyny in Rap Music: A Content Analysis of Prevalence and Meanings," *Men and Masculinities* 12, no. 1 (2009): 3–29.

24. Nouri Bouzid, *Man of Ashes* (Seattle: Arab Film Distribution, 1986), VHS.

25. Shariah4Tunisia, "Tunisian Calls for Shari'a (Khilafah) Part 1/2" (Arabic), You-Tube, 22 January 2011, http://www.youtube.com/watch?v=7r3z_woxxUk; Shariah4Tuni-sia, "Tunisian Calls for Shari'a (Khilafah) Part 2/2" (Arabic), YouTube, 22 January 2011, http://www.youtube.com/watch?v=OBAtx3waqRU.

26. See excerpt of Mustapha Akkad's film: MrRotate7, "[Al Risala] Ruddaha 'Alaya In istata'at ya aba jahl," YouTube, 4 December 2010, http://www.youtube.com/watch?v=p_U9s3fDBTo. *Al Risala* (Arabic) (London: Filmco International Productions, 1976).

27. "Tala'a al badru 'Alayna/Rashid al-Ghannushi," YouTube, 12 September 2012, https://www.youtube.com/watch?v=zH3IzmEVSI4.

28. "Tashbih al-Ghannushi li-mudhaharat Ennahda bi 'fath mecca' yuthir ghadhab attunisiyyin" (Rached al-Ghannouchi's Comparison of Ennadha's Demonstration to Muhammad's Opening of Mecca Causes Anger among Tunisians), *Al Ra'y*, 5 August 2013, http://www.alrai.com/article/600216.html.

29. For a story and photos, see Ahmed Ellali, "Several Thousand Salafists Demonstrate for Islamic Law, Attack Dramatists in Tunis," *Tunisialive*, 25 March 2012, http://www.tunisia-live.net/2012/03/25/several-thousand-salafists-demonstrate-for-islamic-law-attack-dramatists-in-tunis/.

30. EtsSoussouna, "Ghazwat al Mungaala: Min khubzulugia, halaqa 12," YouTube, 1 April 2012, accessed 11 December 2014, http://www.youtube.com/watch?v=K1_qPiCrjNI (video is not available for viewing in the United States).

31. Carolyn Dinshaw, *Getting Medieval: Sexualities and Communities, Pre- and Postmod-ern* (Durham, NC: Duke University Press, 1999), 1.

32. Carolyn Dinshaw, *How Soon Is Now? Medieval Texts, Amateur Readers, and the Queerness of Time* (Durham, NC: Duke University Press, 2012), 4, 5, 6, 34.

33. On the Youssefists, see "Marzouki décore des militants nationalistes et yousséfistes," *La Presse de Tunisie*, 23 March 2013, http://www.lapresse.tn/23012016/64436/marzouki-decore-des-militants-nationalistes-et-youssefistes.html. On Black Thursday, see Syrine Guediche, "Rappelons-nous la journée du 'jeudi noir,' 26 janvier 1978," *Tunisie Numérique*, 26 January 2012, http://www.tunisienumerique.com/rappellons-nous-la-journee-du-26-janvier-1978-le-jeudi-noir/99336. On the Bread Riots, see Yüsra N. M'Hiri, "Tunisie-Histoire: Il y a 30 ans mourait Fadel Sassi, martyr des 'émeutes de pain,'" *Kapitalis*, 4 January 2014, http://www.kapitalis.com/politique/19975-tunisie-histoire-il-y-a

-30-ans-mourait-fadhel-sassi-martyr-des-emeutes-du-pain.html. For some exceptions, see ʿAmira Aleya Sghaier, *Bourguiba: Le despote* (Tunis: Maghreb International Presse et Editions, 2011).

34. Houda Trabelsi, "Hijab Regains Popularity in Tunisia," *Magharebia*, 24 February 2011, http://magharebia.com/en_GB/articles/awi/features/2011/02/24/feature-04; Ons Bouali, "Hijab, niqab et autres draps venus d'ailleurs," *Nawaat*, 25 April 2011, http://nawaat .org/portail/2011/04/25/hijab-niqab-et-autres-draps-venus-dailleurs/.

35. Monia Ghanmi, "Tunis tatasadda lil-radicaliyya," *Magharebia*, 12 April 2012, http:// magharebia.com/ar/articles/awi/features/2011/04/12/feature-03.

36. "Sauvez notre pays des ninjas warriors: OVNI: Objet voilé non identifiè," 28 April 2011, accessed 7 September 2013, https://www.facebook.com/photo.php?fbid= 10150558877675058&set=a.10150307387720058.565038.362301210057&type=1&theater.

37. Anis Ben Hmida, cartoon, 9 May 2011, http://www.facebook.com/photo.php ?fbid=152339871499786&set=0.107497095989248&type=1&theater#!/photo.php?fbid =152339641499809&set=0.107497095989248&type=1&theater&pid=304462&id= 100001713224880.

38. *Princess Tam Tam*, directed by Edmond T. Greville (New York: Kino International, 1935).

39. Ghaith J., "Captain Khobza, La Star Politique de l'été en Tunisie," *Tixup*, 26 June 2011, www.tixup.com/internet/6200-captain-50bza-la-star-politique-de-l'ete-en-tunisie .html.

40. Zayzafoon, *The Production of the Muslim Woman*, 118.

41. Commenting on the funeral of the slain Belaid, she wrote on her Facebook page the same day, "1 million and 400,000 people walked Chokri Belaid to his last home. We will out, God Willing, this colonial government. Long Glory to Tunisia" (8 February 2013, https://www.facebook.com/#!/OlfaTounes). Youssef also implies the government is responsible for Belaid's killing, using language that recalls the 1952 killing of the nationalist and syndicalist leader Farhat Hached by the French.

42. Ahmed ʿUmar Zaʿbar, "Kalimat Ahmad ʿumar Zaʿbar, shaʿir wa iʿlami tunsi," You-Tube, 21 January 2013, http://www.youtube.com/watch?v=UsDGTd43Dbo, my translation.

43. Synda Tagine and Monia Ben Hammadi, "Tunisie: Manifestation du 9 Avril. Le régime policier marque un retour fracassant," *Business News*, 9 April 2012, http://www .businessnews.com.tn/tunisie-manifestations-du-9-avril—le-regime-policier-marque -un-retour-fracassant,519,30424,1; Asma Smadhi, "Activists Call for Greater Protection of Women's Rights in Draft Constitution," *Tunisialive*, 2 July 2013, http://www.tunisia-live .net/2013/07/02/governments-commitment-to-womens-rights-called-into-question/.

44. NiD Hal, "Nettoyage de l'Avenue H. Bourguiba, les jeunes donnent l'exemple," You-Tube, 13 February 2011, http://www.youtube.com/watch?v=Hs0030GvO-k; Marwaforem, "Tunisie 2011: Kasbah Mars 2011," YouTube, 5 March 2011, http://www.youtube.com /watch?v=QnMTAafVrxY.

45. NiD Hal, "Nettoyage de l'Avenue H. Bourguiba, les jeunes donnent l'exemple."

46. This website is run by Sami Ben Gharbia, a longtime opponent of Ben Ali.

47. Paul Owen, "Tunisia: Police Fire Tear Gas at Chokri Belaid's Funeral—As It Happened," *Guardian*, 8 February 2013, http://www.theguardian.com/world/middle-east-live/2013/feb/08/tunisia-turmoil-funeral-general-strike-live.

48. "Chokri Belaïd et sa fille escortés par les militaires," *Tixup*, 8 February 2013, http://www.tixup.com/galeries-de-photos/26021-chokri-belaid-et-sa-fille-escortes-par-les-militaires.html.

49. Zeineb Farhat, "Des Femmes libres face aux hommes en colère!," *Opinion Internationale*, 18 February 2013, http://www.opinion-internationale.com/2013/02/18/des-femmes-libres-face-aux-hommes-en-colere-2_15874.html.

50. According to Hatem Kalai, president of the Audio-Visual Association of Beja Lovers, the presence of related women at funerals is not unheard of in the Beja area, which gave dozens of martyrs to the revolution. And if the deceased was martyred or is a young woman, women may participate in the funeral procession (personal conversation with Hatem Kalai, 27 February 2014).

51. "Après la mort de Chokri Belaïd, la Tunisie en attente," *Slate Afrique*, 8 February 2013, http://www.slateafrique.com/616625/tunisie-3eme-journee-de-deuil-pour-chokri-belaid; Tuniscope, "Discours de Mbarka Brahmi au Jellez" (Arabic), YouTube, 27 July 2013, http://www.youtube.com/watch?v=cV1yUfE5P4I.

52. "Funérailles émouvantes de Brahmi: Des milliers au Jellaz, des millions devant la télé," *Leaders*, 27 July 2013, http://www.leaders.com.tn/article/funerailles-emouvantes-de-brahmi-des-milliers-au-jellaz-des-millions-devant-la-tele?id=11934.

53. For scenes at the sit-in, see Wassim B.A., "Sit-in Bardo, Tunisie," YouTube, 27 July 2013, https://www.youtube.com/watch?v=w_uUvTqz-Yg; Tunisia Live, "Bardo Sit-in Sunday, July 28, 2013," YouTube, 28 July 2013, https://www.youtube.com/watch?v=AR86eF8weKQ.

54. For protests and clashes at the Bardo sit-in, see Tarek Amara, "Tunisian Army Seals Off Bardo Square after Protests," *BDlive*, 29 July2013, http://www.bdlive.co.za/africa/africannews/2013/07/29/tunisian-army-seals-off-bardo-square-after-protests.

55. "Tunisie: Restrictions arbitraires à la liberté de voyager," *Human Rights Watch* 10 July 2013, https://www.hrw.org/fr/news/2015/07/10/tunisie-restrictions-arbitraires-la-liberte-de-voyager; "Tunisie: Manifestation pour demander le départ du gouvernement," *La Croix*, 7 September 2013, http://www.la-croix.com/Actualite/Monde/Tunisie-manifestation-pour-reclamer-le-depart-du-gouvernement-2013-09-07-1009901.

56. In *Études d'histoire religieuse* (1857; Saint-Amand: Gallimard, 1992), 187, for example, the French philologist Ernest Renan asserts there is only one Islam and it existed in the lifetime of Muhammad, Abu Bakr, Omar, and Ali. In this reading mystical Islam, Umayyad Islam, Abbasid Islam, the Western Caliphate of Spain, and Persian Islam are corruptions of the "original" Arabian Semitic form.

57. Oualid Chine, "Les Tunisiennes sont supérieurs aux Tunisiens," *Mag14*, 6 July 2 012, http://www.mag14.com/encre-noire/47-encre-noire/737-les-tunisiennes-sont-superieures-aux-tunisiens.html.

3 MAKING INTIMATE "CIVILPOLITICS" IN SOUTHERN YEMEN

SUSANNE DAHLGREN

No one can be expected to imagine new things; but one can expect people . . .
to exercise fantasy so as to round out the full living reality on the basis of what
they know.
—Antonio Gramsci, letter to Tatiana Schucht, 1927

The Republic of Yemen is one of the core countries involved in the 2011
Arab uprisings. But Yemenis in the southern provinces had additional
long-standing grievances against the regime that coalesced in 2007 and
gained momentum in 2011 as the Southern Revolution, a "peaceful revolution" that demands regional sovereignty based on a return to pre-unity
state borders. Informed by ethnographic fieldwork in the southern Yemeni
city of Aden since 1988, in what was then the People's Democratic Republic
of Yemen (PDRY), and almost every year since (most recently in spring
2013), in this chapter I discuss the formation of new gendered subjectivities and practices and the redefinition of public spaces in the Southern
Revolution. I examine struggles over sovereignty, space, and boundaries
as cultural practices.[1] The Southern Revolution, which includes the Southern Movement (Hirak, literally "movement") and multiple independent
informal projects, constitutes civil forms of life and belonging under militarized forms of insecurity.[2] It actively produces a "social imaginary" that
challenges power structures and relations through inclusive and demili-

tarized language, symbolism, and embodied practices.[3] It makes a future sovereign southern state imaginatively possible on multiple scales, including the "square," through what I term *civilpolitics*, inspired by the concept *geopolitics*, to capture the enacting of civility in space.[4] In this imaginary, revolutionaries and activists expect national authority in the future ideal state to be subservient and accountable to independent democratic organizations rather than a platform for the military, tribes, or the clergy, and for state apparatuses to focus on meeting the needs of people.[5] Through civilpolitics southern revolutionaries enact collective ownership of public spaces and produce new forms of intimacy that rely on mutual care and inclusion, particularly of girls and women.

The Southern Revolution carved out free and pluralistic physical and communicative spaces in a hostile, violent, and malfunctioning environment, producing a counterhegemonic reality.[6] The Southern Revolution invents the present and future, to use Gramsci's words, "on the basis of what [revolutionaries] know," but also through imagination, storytelling, and embodied practices in physical spaces. Since 2011 informal independent activities and projects have mushroomed in southern Yemen, including one-person community-based initiatives, youth groups focused on community improvement projects, and intellectual gatherings. The activities include restoring historical buildings, cleaning residential areas, and preserving historical knowledge of the city by transmitting it to younger generations.[7] These projects join men and women of all age groups and social strata and rely on social media such as Facebook, WhatsApp, and Twitter for communication and mobilization.

The civil state advocated by the Southern Revolution harkens to and yet differs from the PDRY that in May 1990 was unified with the Yemen Arab Republic (North Yemen) to form the Republic of Yemen.[8] The PDRY, centered in the city of Aden, had been governed by the Yemeni Socialist Party, which continues to exist in northern and southern Yemen. The northern faction of the Yemeni Socialist Party is committed to Yemeni unity, while the southern faction supports the Southern Revolution.[9] The Southern Revolution aims to re-create a society that once was, but in an iteration that meets the requirements of the present, including support for freedom of expression and democratic transparency in government. Since unity in 1990, southerners argue, the Sana'a regime has marginalized them, looted their land and resources, and excluded their people from the military and civil service. Activists in the Southern Revolution do not believe the Sanaʿa-based government represents them.

Partitions

There are similarities between the Southern Revolution and the Yemeni Youth Revolution that began in January 2011 in larger cities in the North and South to demand an end to the regime of President ʿAli ʿAbdullah Saleh. Both subscribe to peaceful unarmed resistance but have been brutally confronted by state violence that has left hundreds of civilians dead. Both rely on individual initiatives and decentralized, nonhierarchical networks. People in the North converged in urban "change (*taghyir*) squares" established by the 2011 Youth Revolution, whereas in the South revolutionaries constituted "revolution squares" (*sahat al-thawra*). The change squares were radical in opening up parallel spaces for northern women and men who had never been politically active on a large scale.[10] Indeed on 15 April 2011 President Saleh rhetorically targeted thousands of protesters on the streets of the northern capital of Sanaʿa who were demanding his ouster. He called on Yemenis to support "freedom, security, and stability, and reject chaos," which he blamed on "bandits." He accused protesters of being "apostates" and "liars" and called on the opposition to "reject the mixing of sexes as it is forbidden by Islam. The mixing of sexes is forbidden in the Al-Jamiʿa Street!"[11] This statement triggered new protests dominated by women and girls in Sanaʿa and throughout Yemen.[12]

Southerners put on hold their demand for an independent southern state when Yemenis across the country rose up. Already in late spring 2011, however, joint revolutionary action was tenuous when fighting broke out between factions of northern elites, assisted by tribal armed groups under the control of each faction. As southerners became disillusioned by violence and continued power struggles in Sanaʿa, they reiterated the demand to exit a malfunctioning unified state. A middle-aged female Hirak activist expressed a widespread sentiment when she said during a group dinner at a restaurant, "If the North were a paradise, I would still not want it." Her words echoed how women explain their desire to end a marriage: the South wants a divorce because it no longer wants the North. For most southerners the revolution is against the Yemeni regime in Sanaʿa, not northerners as people.

The revolution forced Saleh to step down from his position in November 2011 in response to insistent calls to leave ("Irhal!"), but a Gulf Cooperation Council (GCC) deal sponsored by Saudi Arabia and its U.S. and European Union allies allowed him to remain in Yemen and continue as party leader.[13] Following Saleh's exit from the presidency, the main opposition parties joined the ruling People's General Congress Party to form a "transitory government." The post of president was handed over to Saleh's deputy and party comrade, ʿAbd Rabbu Mansur Hadi. Violent clashes between elite groups and their allied tribes continued to challenge Hadi's presidency. A foreign-sponsored national dialogue process was launched, with handpicked panelists. It culminated in the National Dialogue Conference (Hiwar) held in the Sanaʿa Mövenpick Hotel between March 2013 and January 2014 and paid for with a US$24 million budget. The dialogue even excluded Tawakkul Karman, a Nobel Prize–winning journalist and Islah Party activist. By the time Saleh signed the GCC transition plan in November 2011, the Southern Movement had reaffirmed a desire to separate the South from the North despite people in northern change squares continuing to express dissatisfaction with how Yemeni elites, Gulf royal families, and their U.S. and European "security" guarantors had co-opted the revolution.[14] Southern youth revolutionaries radicalized in 2011 joined Hirak, while demonstrations and protests continued in northern cities. Following the big rallies in early 2011, revolution efforts in various cities throughout Yemen moved from the streets to government offices to oust corrupt functionaries in local bureaucracies and the army, sometimes successfully. Elite in-fighting culminated in the Houthi movement Ansar Allah marching into Sanaʿa to depose interim president Hadi, who eventually fled to Riyadh. Houthis started their march southward, creating a civil war in spring 2015.[15] Men and women in the heretofore peaceful Southern Revolution took up arms to protect their streets from Houthis allied with the Yemeni Army loyal to former president Saleh.

As in all the Arab uprisings, a crucial dimension in Yemen is competing narratives, one hegemonic and the other trying against all the odds to "imagine new things," to use Gramsci's words. According to the Yemeni regime narrative in Sanaʿa, adopted by international media, the southern question is a regional problem like the Houthi movement. For southerners, however, the unified Yemeni state reached an irresolvable crisis even before the war of 2015. Southerners view their situation not as an internal

Yemeni problem but as a sovereignty question. Southern revolutionaries want to reestablish an independent state, the People's Democratic Republic of Yemen, and allow the people to determine its constitution through democratic means. The southern narrative and political sensibility is nurtured by an alternative public sphere that includes two satellite channels that transmit from outside Yemen, independent newspapers, and Internet-based sites such as *Aden al-Ghad* and *Al-Ayyam*.[16] Southerners follow the print versions of the newspapers, read the news on smartphones, and watch television at home and during afternoon *qat* chews.

Gendered Spatiality in Yemen

I approach public space in the Southern Revolution as a *gendered landscape* of features that mediate intimacy and recognition. Ann Laura Stoler understands intimacy as describing degrees of distance, "involvement, engagement, concern and attention."[17] Lauren Berlant argues that intimacy "creates spaces and usurps places meant for other kinds of relation."[18] The civilpolitics of the Southern Revolution includes projects of recognition that constitute intimacy across difference by attending to proximity, spacing, and timing. Civilpolitics also allows southerners to regroup in a hostile environment and offers a training ground for agitation directed at wider publics,[19] including national and international forces that aim to contain and belittle the revolution.

Public spaces in Yemen are gendered in the sense that they are more or less available to men and women, different behaviors from men and women are expected in them depending on context and time, and gendered and sexual ideologies determine how proximity and intimacy are evaluated. More broadly, mingling across gender and socioeconomic differences in public spaces is considered particularly inappropriate in many areas of the countryside and some towns in the East and North. Such ideologies are not static. The city of Aden became more gender-segregated when the South was unified with the more conservative North Yemen in 1990. In addition to marginalizing them, southerners argue that unity imposed an alien social imaginary with gendered components. Public spaces became male-dominated in Aden as most women left their home only to go to specific destinations, often in a car and hidden behind a face veil. In spring 1994 a war broke out between northern and southern factions of the army, reflecting southern disillusionment with the outcomes of unity.[20] During the war Adeni industries seemed to be special targets of destruction, leading to job losses for thousands of factory women. Fighting ended on 7 July, when the northern army marched into Aden to establish what many southerners continue to call a "northern occupation" (*ihtilal shimali*).[21] After the war southerners were discriminated against in civil service jobs and the army. For young southern men this meant that they were stripped of state employment and a secure income. Employment is attached to full masculinity since a young man without a steady income cannot expect to marry. When southern air force pilots were sacked following the war, they joked they had been sent home to "sit with their wives," something a real man would not do. But their responses were not generally directed at the home front;[22] rather they were expressed in political terms. Despair produced by the 1994 war led some southern women to refuse to leave their home; among these was the famous case of Radhia Shamsir, a long-time women's rights activist who declared a self-imposed curfew in 1994.[23] When I was in Yemen in the 1990s and 2000s, many women complained there were no public activities for them, and thus they restricted their own mobility.

Women's massive engagement in public life since 2011, while radically new, also evokes something old in the South because it reflects deep attachment to collective memories and, for older southern Yemenis, experiences of the PDRY state's commitment to *tahrir al-mar'a*, or women's emancipation and social integration. In mid-twentieth-century British colonial Aden, modernity and women's rights were discussed and promoted by indigenous elites in men's cultural clubs and intellectual circles and two radicalized women's associations, echoing debates in major Arab cities of the time.[24] Soon after independence in 1967 a leftist vanguard party, the National Liberation Front, together with the two women's associations (which united into the General Union of Yemeni Women), established a "women's emancipation" project to bring in women as active partners with men "in all fields of life." Women soon formed one-third of the labor force in Aden. Women graduates of Aden University were hired as supervisors in agriculture and industry. Public administration and schools relied on women cadres, and women occupied a remarkable share of judiciary positions, including as judges. But few women held positions in state and party leadership.[25] Nevertheless, in radical contrast to the colonial era, PDRY leaders discouraged men from using degrading language when referring to women.[26] By the late PDRY period, 1989, highly educated women had

FIGURE 3.1.
A mass funeral was
held in an ad hoc
revolution square
in Maʿalla, the old
port area of Aden,
for three southern
pilots killed by un-
identified gunmen
earlier that week.
This woman was a
volunteer organizer
of the mass funeral
and the long car
procession that
followed it. Photo-
graph by Susanne
Dahlgren.

become critical of state policies that targeted only poor and uneducated
women, believing that the regime had little more to offer for their advancement. I am alert to the limits of gender-based categories in Yemen given
differences in social status, education, ethnic group, ideology, tribal connections, access to state resources, age, and cohort experiences.

With unification in 1990, inclusion was replaced with state-orchestrated
"women's participation" in the Republic of Yemen. A gender-conservative
public sphere emerged that downplayed the policies of the PDRY period.

Women were no longer described as "partners of men in building up society"; now women were expected to focus on nurturing their family, which was described as fulfilling the "requirements of Islamic religion." Southern women lost many rights when the progressive Family Law No. 1 of 1974 was revoked. Women's public presence and participation were bureaucratized with the establishment of the National Committee of Women in 1994.[27] The ruling elite nominated femocrats to key positions in women's "nongovernmental" organizations to address "women's concerns" and represent the state in international fora. Women activists were marginalized or co-opted by the conservative state.[28] Western-funded human rights organizations centered on one figure proliferated, with leaders meeting each other in workshops held in five-star hotels and hosting occasional training sessions for target groups. These organizations largely limited their activities to the framework set by the regime, codified in the Law of Associations and Foundations (Law No. 1 of 2001). A newly adopted covering costume soon meant donning a face veil.[29]

The new freedoms and proximities in public space produced by the Southern Revolution appeal to many young southern men and women, who, although they were educated in the gender-segregated schools that replaced PDRY mixed schools, were accustomed to a gender-mixed global youth culture disseminated by satellite channels and the Internet. For older men the revolution and the social imaginary of a civil state offers the chance to again enjoy the company of nonkin women in public places, something they missed very much. For these men intimacy in public space includes being able to see a woman's face and communicate with her in a context of reciprocity and mutual recognition. Meeting so many men over the years who deeply value seeing a woman's lips, eyes, and expressions during interactions, I often thought of the cruel power over men exercised by women who wear face veils. Younger women who did not know a different life grew to understand a woman's friendly face as a powerful resource in social interactions with men and a concealed face as an asset in the marriage market. They also became talented at using the face veil to carve out a space in male-dominated sites.[30] While there is no public debate on the face veil, the Southern Revolution empowered some men to condemn it. After a middle-aged female colleague wearing a niqab left the room, a high-positioned male civil servant abruptly commented to me, "We hate those!" His bare-faced middle-aged female workmate nodded in agreement. Many young and older women view the face veil as an unnecessary impediment in social interaction, although I found that revolution squares in Aden respected the remarkable diversity in women's sartorial practices.

A common refrain in southern Yemen since PDRY times is that women are "half of society" (*nusf al-mujtama'*), implying that men should not monopolize life outside the home. Southern Revolution activists wanted to reproduce women's active participation alongside men in all fields of life.[31] Rather than understanding *public* as the opposite of *private* or domestic spaces, I contrast *public* to the sense of being hidden, silenced, and marginalized.[32] Women's voices as material and sonic facts, women's bodies, and women's intellectual presence are central to the way inclusive civility (*madaniyya*) is practiced and understood in the Southern Revolution. The Southern Revolution blurs the line between "formal" and "informal" politics and challenges gendered social hierarchies and exclusions in place and space.

As the Southern Revolution mobilized women, it also produced widespread conviction among men and women that the new civil state required reinventing gendered relations in space and actively bringing women back into public life. The Southern Revolution created excitement and engagement, turning previously homosocial male public spaces into carnivals of gender mingling. Two cohorts of women are notable in light of Yemen's gendered spatial history. Older women who held public roles during the PDRY period but withdrew to their home in the prevailing apathy after the 1994 civil war viewed the Southern Revolution as an opportunity for reengagement. For young women whose only adult experience was during the conservative Republic of Yemen, the Southern Revolution allowed them to be mobile and visible in public spaces for the first time. One young activist explained that she could finally emerge from the shadow of unity culture. It is not surprising, then, that gendered symbolism and relations are important qualities in the transformation of public spaces by the Southern Revolution.

Making Intimate Civilpolitics in Revolutionary Aden

As I rode in a friend's car from Aden Airport to the city in April 2013, I could see how the entire cityscape had changed since my visit in 2010, when the physical and symbolic presence of the Southern Movement was not yet visible and municipal workers painted over political slogans at night. In

2013 old PDRY flags rather than Republic of Yemen flags were hoisted on flagpoles. Graffiti covered walls, and martyrs' images replaced advertisements, official announcements, and pictures of the hated ex-president on billboards. Yemenis wore headscarves and shirts that bore political messages. In the lively cloth market in Aden's old town Crater, so named by the British because the district is the site of an ancient volcano, male tailors sewed PDRY flags and revolution symbols onto clothing, as requested by customers. Residents of Aden were preparing for a southern million-person (*milyuniyya*) mobilization. People spontaneously flashed the ubiquitous V for victory sign on seeing me, one of very few foreigners.

During civil disobedience Saturdays and Wednesdays, all shops and schools and most government offices were closed. Streets were blocked with stones to stop traffic and prevent the military from entering residential areas. The scale of resistance and the dynamic civil society reminded me of documentary film clips of the 1960s that showed the lively indigenous politics of Adenis resisting the tanks and military helicopters of British colonialism. The social geography and cityscape had clearly been rewritten and redesigned. In the civilpolitics of the Southern Revolution, activists authored a political culture made visible and audible everywhere.

Once we arrived at the city it became evident that municipal services were failing more dramatically than usual. Access to water and electricity in hot and humid Aden has been irregular for most people since unity. In contrast, when I lived in Aden in 1988–89, city residents always had access to clean running drinking water and uninterrupted electricity service. In 2013 residents of Aden lived with daily power cuts that could last for hours. Those who could afford it had purchased a generator to run a refrigerator, fans, lighting, and television. Since water was now rationed, only people with storage tanks could count on running water, and drinking water was purchased in plastic bottles. Nevertheless, in contrast to 2010, people I encountered were full of hope and optimism about the future. The majority, including intellectuals, high-ranking government officials, court personnel, teachers, and housewives, supported independence, irrespective of class background, education level, and location in the city. This was a dramatic shift from my previous visit, when many were skeptical about southern independence. While full independence was not the only solution that southerners said they would support, it was the most popular in 2013. Even southerners who continued to support unity criticized the bad treatment of the South by Sanaʿa.

The city of Aden dates to antiquity. It was taken over in 1839 by the East India Company and later became a British colony. After independence in 1967, Aden was the capital of the first and only Marxist state in the Arab world, the PDRY. After unity in 1990 the southern political elite moved to the new capital in the North, Sanaʿa, and Aden was largely excluded from state development interventions. All state services in the South collapsed within a short period, including the health care system, public schools, and cultural and sports activities. According to the post-1990 unity narrative, both northern and southern Yemen suffered lack of development and access to resources until unity brought equal measures of progress and advancement to the whole country.[33] After renovations or repairs, the government changed the founding dates of Aden schools to reinforce the unity narrative. After 1990 school books produced and approved in Sanaʿa stated that Aden had been a "village" prior to unity. Challenging such historical distortions with lectures and educational gatherings was an important aspect of the civilpolitics that proliferated throughout Aden in revolution squares. The squares became schools for learning and rewriting history, the present, and the future.

James Clifford contends that space is never ontologically given but is discursively mapped and corporeally practiced. A city square becomes a social space only through people's active occupation of the space.[34] The urban squares (sing. *saha*) I describe, which existed in almost every Aden district in 2013, acquired their meaning as revolutionary spaces in persistent struggles between activists and security forces on the street and in weekly meetings. The revolution squares became "situated knowledges" that carried revolutionary messages across space and time.[35] The sahas were created in familiar squares, bus stations, and often-traveled alleys in the city that were transformed and vitalized into sites of civilpolitics by enactments and community commentary. Sahas challenged the authority and brutality of state military forces by creating peaceful social spaces free of gender and social segregation and offering mutual care practices to the marginalized and subaltern given the collapse of state-supported municipal services.

The vast majority of participants in the revolution squares had never been politically active, since such activism was rare prior to 2007. In sahas, bodies were canvassed with images of revolution. Women sported homemade revolution symbols on their headscarves and ʿabayas, and men wore such patches on their clothing. The southern flag—a blue triangle with an embedded red star aligned on the left margin and three horizontal stripes in red, white, and black—was knitted from thick woolen thread or combined small patches of different-colored cloth. The sahas usually included some women with a niqab covering their face, paradoxically communicating anonymity and public agency given their colorfully patched overcoats and headscarves. People transformed their bodies into bodyscapes that transported the southern cause everywhere, normalizing the revolution and making it part of the everyday scenery.[36]

Men and women did not dramatically differ in their motivations for participating in weekly saha gatherings, and men welcomed women's attendance. Men's respect for women and their voices promoted an intimate atmosphere that made it easy for girls and women of all ages and social backgrounds to attend. Despite the crowdedness of revolution squares, girls and women were not groped, as misbehaving men were wont to do in other times and places. Most female Hirak activists in the squares seemed to be poor, although there were certainly educated women from wealthier families, including Huda al-Attas, perhaps the most respected younger writer in Yemen and a spokesperson for the southern forces unity conference.[37] I first met al-Attas when she was a sociology student at Aden University and developing a reputation as a fine author. In 2012 she helped establish an organization affiliated with Hirak called Intellectuals for a New South in Mukalla, the southern seaport city in Hadhramaut, about eight hundred kilometers east of Aden.[38] In Aden al-Attas actively worked to convince educated people to join activism dominated by the urban poor, including members of the pariah-like social group akhdam (literally, "servants"), who during PDRY rule were given the chance to advance through education, employment, and even high administrative positions.[39]

Activism in revolution squares and elsewhere provided opportunities for educated wealthy elites, poor people living in shanties, internally displaced people originating outside the town, urbanites, and rural people to mix again. Displaced people active in the Southern Revolution in Aden were originally from Abyan province, forty kilometers east of Aden, and largely lived in an abandoned school building with daily power cuts and limited washing and toilet facilities. They were displaced after the Islamist group Ansar al-Shariʿa, accompanied by al-Qaeda fighters, took over a number of towns in the summer of 2011.[40] When members of local popular committees joined the army to fight the militants, their towns were destroyed.[41]

Old town Crater had two revolution sahas. The first was deep within a narrow street on the hillside in al-ʿAidrus area and was established by

FIGURE 3.2. Al-'Aidrus Revolution Square occupies a narrow alley in old town Aden called Crater. Chairs line the alley, and the best seats are reserved for women. Photograph by Susanne Dahlgren.

Islah, the leading Sunni Islamist party in all of Yemen, a socially conservative formation that united northern tribal figures, business people, moderate and conservative clerics, and Muslim Brotherhood supporters. A Hirak youth group dominated by activists from traditional elite families originally from Hadhramaut and 'Ibb took over this revolution square in 2013, after support for Islah declined precipitously because it supported continued unity with the North and in 2012 joined the ruling People's General Congress to form a new government. Islah lost most of its supporters in the South following violent clashes with Hirak in February 2013 that left several people dead and others wounded.[42] This square was frequented by wealthy, educated men and women but also included less affluent people.

The second revolution square in old town Crater is called Martyr Muhammad al-Bukairi Square, which I also call the Midan Revolution Square because it is close to the central point in the old town market. It was established by activists in 2011 in part of a busy bus and taxi station. The Midan Revolution Square cooperatively shared the narrow space with Toyota HiAce vans, Peugeot nine-passenger 406 cars, and drivers. When I first attended a Thursday gathering in Midan Revolution Square, most of the attendees looked to be very poor: boys were not wearing shoes, and men's outfits and women's black 'abaya robes were old and worn. Most of the women I met in the Midan saha came from poor families and had not previously been politically active. But participants also included male intellectuals, literati, and small entrepreneurs. In contrast, NGO events I have attended are typically run by middle-strata people, and audience members rarely include the very poor. A wooden stage was erected at the rear of the area, and a huge southern flag was painted on the wall. The saha was bounded on one side by a wall plastered with a long row of posters depicting images of martyrs killed in the revolution, including a huge poster of fifteen-year-old Nida Shawqi, a girl killed by unidentified gunmen in downtown Aden on 18 March 2012. A banner with a slogan in English, "Down with occupation—Freedom—Independence," hung from the ceiling. In front of the stage old carpets and clothes covered the ground where the audience sat. A plastic table acted as a podium for speakers who addressed the gathering. The only plastic chairs available for audience members were regularly reserved for women. Men customarily prioritized women's access to the chairs over the five weeks I attended the meetings, in recognition strategies that encouraged their participation.

A typical Thursday gathering in Midan Revolution Square started in the early afternoon after lunch, when men arrived to sit, chew qat, and wait for the program to start.[43] Since Thursday is the beginning of the weekend, even men who do not chew qat daily are likely to engage in this Yemeni pastime. Adeni women seldom chew qat and are certainly not supposed to chew it in public or in the company of unrelated men. Women arrived at the square closer to when the program was about to begin, in the early evening, about an hour before sunset. Men made sure that children did not occupy the best places. There was usually a lot of commotion until the organizing committee addressed the audience. Typical of local culture, in other revolution squares speakers were sometimes interrupted with comments, and lively debates would ensue, but every time I visited this saha the audience sat quietly and listened. Most speakers were men, but women from the audience could ask for the microphone during discussion. In Midan Revolution Square the most popular Hirak leader was Ali Salim al-Bidh, the former leader of the PDRY. Following unity he was a member of the presidential council, but he left in 1993 when irresolvable disagreements arose between him and Saleh. Al-Bidh lived in exile in Beirut and was a controversial figure among Yemenis. When I inquired about his popularity, young Hirak men reluctantly conceded that he was a possible leader in an

FIGURE 3.3. Midan Revolution Square in the central market area of Crater in Aden shares a busy bus station with taxis and buses. Photograph by Susanne Dahlgren.

independent southern Yemen. Although young activists preferred none of the old guard as future leaders, al-Bidh was popular among the poor, who remembered with yearning Socialist Party rule, when life was inexpensive and poor people could send their children to school.

The Thursday program in Midan Revolution Square ended when it was time for the *maghrib* (sunset) call to prayer, which was a bit after 6:00 p.m. when I attended. A prayer leader then conducted a joint prayer, with men praying at the front and women behind them, the way it is done in mosques. Afterward the children and men and women organized themselves into rows and marched slowly along the narrow winding roads of the Crater main market shouting slogans. People carried homemade banners and posters printed by the organizing committee. Men and women marched alongside each other without segregation, and those with children were assisted. Women in particular actively encouraged people standing and watching to join the march. In one demonstration I was approached by "Sara," a twenty-one-year-old student from the local neighborhood, who explained that she became politically active only with the establishment of Hirak and that her entire family supports the southern cause. Together we followed the mass of people to the main market through the busy streets, unlit due to power cuts. As the demonstration carved its way, the humid air became ever more pressing, affecting everyone. Some men left to retrieve small bottles or tiny plastic bags of cold water and offered them to female participants, drinking only after the women and children drank. Showing courtesy to female participants is one way revolutionary men communicated that previously homosocial male public spaces that women occasionally transgressed hidden behind cloaks and face veils now welcomed them. Yet women did not wait for or expect such gestures from men but did as they pleased.[44] Men and women also showed care and solidarity because the squares heightened such sentiments. Every time I visited the square, women gathered around me to tell "the world" through me about their personal tragedies or to give me bottled water, snacks, or candies. They always showed concern about my well-being in the hot and humid climate. They often invited me to group photos that included anyone who entered the frame. I had heard similar accounts of care and concern from colleagues in Cairo's Tahrir Square during the first eighteen days of the revolution,[45] although there is no culture of sexual harassment in Aden. Civilpolitics that relies on mutual care created a radically different space in the middle of insecurity.

Men and women revolutionaries frequently used techniques of recognition to highlight women's presence in male-dominant spaces. On 21 May 2013, Yemeni Unity Day, I observed the million-person independence rally for the southern governorates held in the largest revolution square in Khormaksar, the cantonment area built by the British during colonial rule.[46] The square includes a proper stage with benches for a few dignitaries. During the PDRY period the same area was a parade square for official public ceremonies, and between 1990 and 2011 it was the site for state-orchestrated unity events. Unlike the tiny ad hoc sahas in other parts of Aden, this square accommodates hundreds of thousands of people if the nearby road is also occupied, as it was on the day I attended. When I approached the area in the late afternoon on a bus from old town Crater, all streets leading to the square were blocked with parked cars. Activists stopped us five hundred meters from the square, instructing us to enter on foot. People from all socioeconomic sectors were present in the crowded square, including from the remote countryside and the desert. The participants included well-off professional women and men, officials from the judiciary and ministries, and intellectuals who usually hold their own gatherings in clubs and private homes. A woman physician directed the activities of the temporary health unit in a tent. On the podium I saw some women I had met in neighborhood sahas or other sites of activism. I recognized "Sumia,"

FIGURE 3.4. Women's podium in the Southern Revolution million-person rally in Khormaksar Revolution Square on 21 May 2013, the day the regime celebrates unity. Photograph by Susanne Dahlgren.

an energetic Hirak activist who ran a one-woman campaign against drug use among youth; she had brought her posters.

As was the case in Midan Revolutionary Square, all the seats on the stage were reserved for women in Khormaksar. Men onstage to make a speech, read poetry, or conduct the joint prayer had to step down afterward, transforming all the seated women into dignitaries. When I looked down at the rally from the podium, it seemed to reach to eternity, although men far outnumbered women in the crowd. Indeed I observed no women in the carloads of demonstrators coming from governorates outside of Aden. While walking toward the noisy stage, I encountered an elderly woman I knew from Midan Revolution Square walking away. She greeted me amicably and explained that for her "demonstrations are made for the day." She was on her way home to prepare dinner for her family. Newly politically active, she scheduled work for the revolution into her daily routine as a *sayyidat manzil* (housewife). Women who lived even farther than she could not travel to attend a demonstration and return to their home obligations on the same day.

Women were relevant behind the scenes in the civilpolitics of the Southern Revolution even when they were not visible in public spaces, participating through imagination, creativity, and labor in large and distant mobilizations such as the one in Khormaksar. They prepared food for attending family members and sewed and knitted flags and southern symbols onto their own and family members' clothes. In many homes I spent time with women who watched two satellite channels sympathetic to the revolution while comfortably sitting on cushions in their living room: Aden Live TV (then based in Beirut), which has excellent coverage of large mobilizations, and al-Masier TV (based in Cairo).[47] Even when such women were not present in public revolutionary sites, men activists persistently recognized them as full partners in the fight to end the "occupation" of the South.

Nonviolence is a crucial gendered dimension of civilpolitics. "Peaceful revolution" was understood as necessary to counter regime brutality and to include all social sectors. Nonviolence constituted new spatial relations and intimacies across differences that include gender. On the bus returning to Crater from the Khormaksar rally, a middle-aged woman put her head out of the window and instructed a young soldier at a roadblock to "go home." The young conscript from the North seemed confused and surprised by her sense of political agency. The stone-throwing but otherwise unarmed, often very poor boys who challenge troops frequently get a bullet in response. But women who verbally assault troops are seldom attacked, although young girls and women of all ages are among the several hundred Yemenis killed since 2011.[48] A leading Aden Hirak activist, Zahra Abdullah Salih, was sitting in a bus when masked men threw a grenade at her in April 2014.[49] She survived, but her legs were severely injured. During the 1960s guerrilla struggle, women outside Aden participated in armed struggle and women in Aden acted as messengers for fighters. Most women, however, abstained from any involvement and stayed at home.[50] As the Houthi-Saleh military invasion reached Aden in March 2015, the entire society became militarized. Women who had military training prior to unity took up arms alongside men. Engaging in violence violates the civilpolitics imaginary, but Adeni fighters believe they are in a legitimate war to defend their homeland. The results, for gender relations and otherwise, are unclear at this writing.

Conclusion

The Southern Revolution challenges state authority and builds imaginaries of a future civil state through new intimacy norms enacted by activists in the present. Revolutionaries created nonviolent spaces for making civilpolitics, indeed for rewriting militarized and undemocratic spaces into a civil reality. Civilpolitics produces and privileges civility as the locus of ideal political communities. It respects diversity and participation across social status, gender, and family origin. It offers ways to live out and imagine the future in the present. It constitutes new forms of intimacy depending on mutual care and compassion in a variety of spaces. It values desegregated interactions between men and women and downplays status and other social hierarchies, which many in the Southern Revolution consider specifically southern values and sensibilities.[51] The Southern Revolution succeeded in empowering social groups that had remained outside fields considered political. The revolutionary squares communicated compassion, respect, dignity, inclusion, and care. Civilpolitics transformed public spaces into demilitarized and desegregated spaces in the double sense of refusing violence and allowing unrestrained and democratic mingling between people from various backgrounds, challenging the spatial, ideological, and embodied limits and borders associated with unity culture.

NOTES

Epigraph: As reprinted in Adam David Morton, *Unravelling Gramsci: Hegemony and Passive Revolution in the Global Economy* (London: Pluto, 2007), 171. The letter is dated 25 April 1927.

1. Akhil Gupta and James Ferguson, "Spatializing States: Toward an Ethnography of Neoliberal Governmentality," in *Anthropologies of Modernity: Foucault, Governmentality, and Life Politics*, edited by Jonathan Xavier Inda (Malden, MA: Blackwell, 2005), 105.

2. Hirak was established in 2007 by forcibly retired southern members of the army who were joined by civil servants and unemployed youth. At first Southern Movement demands centered on compensation for lost jobs and properties. These expanded into demands for self-rule and national independence. Franck Mermier, "Le mouvement sudiste," in *Yémen, le tournant révolutionnaire*, edited by L. Bonnefoy, F. Mermier, and M. Poirier (Sanaʿa: CEFAS-Éditions Karthala, 2012), 41–65; Susanne Dahlgren, "The Southern Movement in Yemen," *ISIM Review* 22 (Autumn 2008): 50–51.

3. Charles Taylor, *Modern Social Imaginaries* (Durham, NC: Duke University Press, 2003).

4. For the term *geopolitics*, see Gearóid Ó Tuathail, *Critical Geopolitics: The Politics of Writing Global Space* (London: Routledge, 1996). See also Anna J. Secor, "Toward a Feminist Counter-Geopolitics: Gender, Space and Islamist Politics in Istanbul," *Space and Polity* 5, no. 3 (2001): 191–211.

5. There is wide debate about the concept of a civil state in the North as well, as indicated by an article written by a northern intellectual, Anwar Muʿzib, "Al-Dawla

Al-Madaniyya Al-Haditha Fi al-Yaman Bayna al-Mumkin wal-Mustahil" (The Modern Civil State in Yemen, Between the Possible and the Impossible), *Aden Post*, 18 December 2012, http://m.aden-post.com/news/4126/. He argues that a civil state can be defined as "a state of law and order and the rule of equal justice; a state of safety and security and stability; a state of economic development and urban and state tourism and investment; a state of freedoms that are not limitless; and a state of a free press and audio." See also Marie-Christine Heinze, "On 'Gun Culture' and 'Civil Statehood' in Yemen," *Journal of Arabian Studies* 4, no. 1 (2014): 70–95. On debates and approaches to civility and civil society in other Arab countries, see Amer Katbeh, "The Civil State (*dawla madaniyya*): A New Political Term?," *ifair*, 24 February 2014, http://ifair.eu/think/the-civil-state-dawla -madaniya-a-new-political-term/; Rex Brynen, Bahgat Korany, and Paul Noble, *Political Liberalization and Democratization in the Arab World: Theoretical Perspectives*, vol. 1 (Boulder: Lynne Rienner, 1995); Augustus Richard Norton, introduction to *Civil Society in the Middle East*, vol. 1, edited by Augustus Richard Norton (Leiden: Brill, 2005), 1–25.

6. Antonio Gramsci, *Selections from the Prison Notebooks of Antonio Gramsci*, edited and translated by Quintin Hoare and Geoffrey Nowell Smith (London: Lawrence and Wishart, 1971).

7. See, for example, the Aden University history professor Asmahan Aqlan al-Alas lecturing on preserving Aden's historical town scene at "Let's Be Different: Asmahan Al-Alas, TEDxAden," 11 April 2014, YouTube, https://www.youtube.com/watch?v= bCXY1wsROkc.

8. For the background of the two Yemens entering the unity agreement in November 1989, see George Joffé, "Introduction: Yemen and the Contemporary Middle East," in *Yemen Today: Crisis and Solutions. Proceedings of a Two-Day Conference Held at the School of Oriental and African Studies, University of London, November 25th and 26th, 1995*, edited by E. G. H. Joffé, M. J. Hachemi, and E. W. Watkins (London: Caravel, 1997).

9. In late 2011 the northern faction of the Yemeni Socialist Party joined the government in Sana'a as part of post-Saleh arrangements to try to repair Yemen's fiscal and political catastrophe, most urgently daily power cuts and shortages of running water. The southern faction joined Hirak. Some leading old-guard socialist women have not decided which Socialist Party faction to join.

10. See Morooj Alwazir, "Yemeni Women and the Revolution, Televised," *#Support Yemen*, 2014, accessed 5 May 2014, http://supportyemen.org/blog/yemeni-women-and -the-revolutiontelevised/.

11. The translated transcript can be found here: "April 15th Saleh Speech and Supporters," *Yemen Rights Monitor*, 15 April 2011, http://yemenrightsmonitor.blogspot.com/2011 /04/friday-april-15th-saleh-speech.html.

12. For reactions to Saleh's speech and images from women's protests, see "Saleh's Speech on Mixing the Sexes and Its Implications," *Jadaliyya*, 18 April 2011, http://www .jadaliyya.com/pages/index/1283/salehs-speech-on-mixing-the-sexes-and-its-implicat; "Yemeni Women Protest President's Remarks," Reuters Video, 16 April 2011, http://www .reuters.com/video/2011/04/16/yemeni-women-protest-presidents-remarks?videoId =203035802. The speech also provoked critical videos posted on YouTube; see Nabil al-

Sultan, "The Prohibition of Gender Mixing: The Scholar ʿAli Saleh Issues His Legal Opinion" (Arabic), 26 April 2011, https://www.youtube.com/watch?v=MYKQU48j9tU.

13. The GCC plan granted Saleh immunity from all prosecution, and his properties and millions in stolen wealth would be left untouched. The transition plan included the one-candidate presidential "elections" in February 2012 and the entry of opposition parties in the government. Corruption, favoritism, and mismanagement continued, although former opposition parties could now benefit. UN sanctions were imposed on Saleh in November 2014, after his role in supporting the Houthi coup in Sanaʿa became evident. United Nations, "Security Council 2140 Sanctions Committee Designates Three Individuals as Subject to Assets Freeze, Travel Ban," press release, 7 November 2014, http://www.un.org/press/en/2014/sc11636.doc.htm. The entire GCC plan can be accessed here: "Yemen Transition Agreement, 2011," Al Bab, accessed 17 June 2015, http://www.al-bab.com/arab/docs/yemen/yemen_transition_agreement.htm.

14. Sheila Carapico, "Demonstrators, Dialogues, Drones and Dialectics," Middle East Report 269 (2013): 24. When young activists from the northern cities of Sanaʿa and Taʿizz and the southern cities of Aden and Mukalla were interviewed about their grievances, southerners largely differed by explaining their alienation in north/south terms: Saleem Haddad and Joshua Rogers, "Public Protest and Visions for Change: Voices from within Yemen's Peaceful Youth Movement (Al-Haraka Al-Shababiya Al-Silmiya)," paper presented at BRISMES Annual Conference, London, 26–28 March 2012.

15. Ansar Allah took over Sanaʿa on 21 September 2014, after weeks of demonstrations in the capital against the government's revocation of fuel subsidies. Stacey Philbrick Yadav and Sheila Carapico, "The Breakdown of the GCC Initiative," Middle East Report 273 (December 2014): 2–6.

16. Al-Ayyam, the most popular independent newspaper in the South, has been closed by the government since 2009 on the charge of advocating "separatism." See Reporters without Borders, "Major Crackdown on Independent Media," 7 May 2009, http://en.rsf.org/yemen-major-crackdown-on-independent-05-05-2009,32909.

17. Ann Laura Stoler, "Intimidations of Empire: Predicaments of the Tactile and Unseen," in Haunted by Empire: Geographies of Intimacy in North American History, edited by Ann Laura Stoler (Durham, NC: Duke University Press, 2006), 15.

18. Lauren Berlant, "Intimacy: A Special Issue," Critical Inquiry 24, no. 2 (1998): 281, 282. Informed by Foucauldian and Deleuzian understandings, John Allen suggests that subjects are constituted by the spacing and timing of practices as much as by those who seek to shape their conduct. John Allen, Lost Geographies of Power (Oxford: Blackwell, 2003), 9.

19. Nancy Fraser, "Rethinking the Public Sphere: A Contribution to the Critique of Actually Existing Democracy," in Civil Society and Democracy: A Reader, edited by Carolyn M. Elliott (New Delhi: Oxford University Press, 2003), 91, 93.

20. About 150 southern Socialist Party activists had been assassinated in suspicious circumstances; public services and economic development in southern governorates were neglected; and thousands of former factory, agricultural cooperative, and state farm laborers had lost their jobs. For perspectives on the developments that led to the war, see Fred Halliday, "The Third Inter-Yemeni War and Its Consequences," Asian Affairs 26, no. 2 (1995): 131–40; Joffé et al., Yemen Today.

21. Abu Bakr al-Saqqaf, a University of Sana'a professor and friend of Hirak's, calls the northern takeover internal colonialism. Abu Bakr al-Saqqaf, "Equal Citizenship: The Big Absence," in Joffé et al., *Yemen Today*, 127–30. See also Abu Bakr al-Saqqaf, "Three Faces of a State Waging War on Society," *Yemen Times*, 4 February 2008.

22. As in any society, domestic violence exists in Yemen and has been addressed in civil society organizations and state agencies under the slogan "Violence against Women." See Mohamed Ba-Obaid and Catherine Bijleveld, "Violence against Women in Yemen: Official Statistics and an Exploratory Survey," *International Review of Victimology* 9 (2002): 331–47.

23. Susanne Dahlgren, "Segregation, Illegitimate Encounters, and Contextual Moralities: Sexualities in the Changing Public Sphere in Aden," *Hawwa: Journal of Women in the Middle East and the Islamic World* 4, no. 2 (2006): 214–36. Also see the chapter on Radhia Shamsir in Marta Paluch, *Yemeni Voices: Women Tell Their Stories* (Sana'a: British Council, 2001).

24. J. Leigh Douglas, *The Free Yemeni Movement 1935–1962* (Beirut: American University of Beirut, 1987); Asmahan Aqlan al-'Alas, *Awdha' al-mar'a al-yamaniyya fi zul al-idara al-britaniyya li 'adan min 1937–1967* (The Situation of Yemeni Women during the Time of British Administration in Aden 1937–1967) (Aden: Aden University Printing and Publishing House, 2005); Susanne Dahlgren, "Welfare and Modernity: Three Concepts for the 'Advanced Woman,'" in *Interpreting Welfare and Relief in the Middle East*, edited by Nefissa Naguib and Inger Marie Okkenhaug (Leiden: Brill, 2008), 129–48.

25. Tareq Y. Ismael and Jacqueline S. Ismael, *The People's Democratic Republic of Yemen: Politics, Economics and Society* (London: Frances Pinter, 1986), 126.

26. Susanne Dahlgren, *Contesting Realities: The Public Sphere and Morality in Southern Yemen* (New York: Syracuse University Press, 2010), 133–34.

27. The National Women's Committee was established in 1994 by Yemen Cabinet Decree No. 61. The initial mission was to prepare for the UN Fourth Conference on Women: Women National Committee, "Status of Woman in Yemen," 1996, accessed 11 June 2014, http://www.yemen-women.org/.

28. Paluch, *Yemeni Voices*; Susanne Dahlgren, "Readjusting Women's Too Many Rights: The State, the Public Voice, and Women's Rights in South Yemen," in *Feminist Activism, Women's Rights and Legal Reform*, edited by Mulki al-Sharmani (New York: Zed Books, 2014), 48–72.

29. Although the all-covering women's outfit emerged at the same time as unification, the state did not mandate it. Boushra AlMutawakel, a Yemeni photographer, has commented in an illustrative way on the "disappearance" of women wearing clothes that render them invisible. See her "Vanishing Women" in "The Hijab/Veil Series," Muslima, accessed 11 June 2015, http://muslima.imow.org/content/hijab-veil-series.

30. Dahlgren, "Segregation, Illegitimate Encounters, and Contextual Moralities."

31. In Dahlgren, *Contesting Realities*, 131–69.

32. Farha Ghannam, *Remaking the Modern: Space, Relocation, and the Politics of Identity in a Global Cairo* (Berkeley: University of California Press, 2002), 96.

33. This argument is critiqued in H. M. al-'Aqil, *Qadiyya al-janub wa haqa'iq nahb mumtalakat dawla jumhuriyya al-yaman al-dimuqratiyya al-sha'biyya, al-juz'u al-awwal,*

al-tabʿa al-thaniyya (The Southern Cause and Truth about the Plundering of the People's Democratic Republic of Yemen State Property, Part 1, Second Printing) (Cairo: Al-Markaz al-ʿArabi li Khidmat al-Sahafa wal-Nashr "Majid," 2012); Fadhl ʿAbdulla al-Rabiʿi, *Fashl mashruʿ al-wahda bayna jumhuriyya al-yaman al-dimuqratiyya al-shaʿbiyya wal-jumhuriyya al-ʿarabiyya al-yamaniyya: Madkhal li fahm qadiyya al-janub wal haraka al-silmiyya* (Failure of the Unity between the PDRY and the Yemen Arab Republic: An Introduction to Understanding the Southern Cause and the Peaceful Movement) (N.p.: Madar, 2013).

34. James Clifford, "Spatial Practices: Fieldwork, Travel, and the Disciplining of Anthropology," in *Anthropological Locations: Boundaries and Grounds of a Field Science*, edited by Akhil Gupta and James Ferguson (Berkeley: University of California Press, 1997), 185–222.

35. Donna Haraway, "Situated Knowledges: The Science Question in Feminism and the Privilege of Partial Perspective," *Feminist Studies* 14, no. 3 (1988): 575–99.

36. Nicholas Mirzoeff, *Bodyscape: Art, Modernity and the Ideal Figure* (New York: Routledge, 1995), 17.

37. Amira Augustin, "An Interview with Huda al-Attas," Middle East Research and Information Project, 15 May 2014, http://www.merip.org/mero/mero051514?ip_login_no_cache=d6feaafb3f426387baoce4174755cc4d.

38. "'Intellectual[s] for a New South' Political Group Inaugurated," *National Yemen*, 25 June 2012, accessed 5 May 2015, http://nationalyemen.com/2012/06/25/intellectual-for-a-new-south-political-group-inaugurated/. Hadhramaut is the area from which many respected families traditionally originate and from where some leading politicians and intellectuals hail. Residents have historically been at odds with the Sanaʿa regime. Most Yemeni oil reserves are located in this area. In December 2013 a tribal uprising started in Hadhramaut against the regime following the killing of a notable tribal figure. The uprising has since halted oil production and expelled army posts from the area. A Million-Person Rally was held for the first time in April 2014 in Mukalla with Hirak slogans, although many Hadhramis opt for regional independence without the other southern provinces. Susanne Dahlgren, "Southern Yemeni Activists Prepare for Nationwide Rally," *Middle East Research and Information Project*, 24 April 2014, http://www.merip.org/southern-yemeni-activists-prepare-nationwide-rally.

39. Akhdam is a social group whose members specialize in doing work considered unclean, such as barbering, masonry, and sweeping. Recently they have organized into an association that promotes their social and political concerns and have claimed a new identity as *al-muhamishin* (the marginalized). On their involvement in the 2011 uprising in Sanaʿa and Taʿizz, see "Yemen: Akhdam Community Angered by Government Neglect," *IRIN News*, 20 April 2012, http://www.irinnews.org/report/95324/yemen-akhdam. More recently the akhdam community leaders have given contradictory announcements of alliance in the warfare between the Houthis and the regime. See Sadeq Al-Wesabi, "Will the Houthis Help Empower the Muhamasheen?," *Yemen Times*, 12 February 2015, http://www.yementimes.com/en/1858/report/4889/Will-the-Houthis-help-empower-the-muhamasheen.htm.

40. Many Yemenis believe that President Saleh allowed Ansar al-Shariʿa to take over the towns to send a message to the United States and its Gulf partners that if he were forced to resign, Islamists would take over large areas in Yemen. See Yemeni blogger Afra Nasser's post "Who Are Ansar al-Sharia?," *Afra Nasser's Blog*, 17 February 2012, http://www.afrahnasser.blogspot.fi/2012/02/who-are-ansar-al-sharia.html.

41. See Augustin's photo essay on the destroyed Abyan: Amira Augustin, "My Journey to Yemen's Southern Borderline," *Muftah*, accessed 5 May 2014, http://muftah.org/my-journey-to-yemens-southern-frontline/#.U2EE7hCEcXg.

42. "Six Killed in Separatist Unrest in South Yemen—Sources," Reuters, 21 February 2013, http://uk.reuters.com/article/2013/02/21/uk-yemen-violence-idUKBRE91K0 K620130221. Islah claims to represent Islam in politics but remains divided in Parliament on a number of questions, including child marriage. At this writing it is unclear which political party garners the most support because activists avoid working with all of them.

43. Lisa Wedeen, "The Politics of Deliberation: *Qāt* Chews as Public Sphere in Yemen," *Public Culture* 19, no. 1 (2007): 59–84.

44. Leila Ahmed argues that rather than being top-down, the policy of women's emancipation during the PDRY period emerged from a history of women's agency in the Arabian Peninsula, including in the independence struggle in Aden: Leila Ahmed, "Feminism and Feminist Movements in the Middle East, a Preliminary Exploration: Turkey, Egypt, Algeria, People's Democratic Republic of Yemen," in *Arabian and Islamic Studies*, edited by Robin Bidwell and G. Rex Smith (London: Longman, 1983), 155–71.

45. Personal communication with Samuli Schielke.

46. These mobilizations had been regular events since 2008. See Dahlgren, "Southern Yemeni Activists"; Susanne Dahlgren, "Rebels without Shoes: A Visit to Southern Yemeni Revolution Squares," *Muftah*, 22 April 2014, http://muftah.org/rebels-without-shoes-visit-south-yemens-revolution-squares/#.U2eaARCgCE0. This old parade square was recently renamed Sahat al-iʿtisam (Sit-in Square) to mark the standing occupation that started on 14 October 2014 to commemorate the 1963 revolution to speed the declaration of independence from British rule. The revolutionary square terminated after the situation in Sanaʿa deteriorated and President Hadi went into exile.

47. Aden Live is managed by supporters of the former southern leader al-Bidh, and al-Masier is managed by the former southern leaders Ali Nasir Muhammad and Haider Abubakr al-Attas.

48. According to the Southern Observatory for Human Rights, cases of regime violence against citizens exceeded one hundred fatalities during 2013 alone. Southern Observatory for Human Rights, "Southern Observatory for Human Rights Annual Report for 2013," accessed 5 May 2014, https://ia600404.us.archive.org/20/items/deport_23 /Sohr2013English.pdf.

49. This took place on 3 April 2014. See "Naja al-Munadhila al-Janubiyya Zahra Salih min Muhawalat Ightiyal" (The Southern Struggler Zahra Salih Survives an Assassination Attempt), *Aden al-mnarh*, accessed 11 June 2015, http://www.adenalmnarh.com/news /1609166.

50. Maxine Molyneux, "Women and Revolution in the People's Democratic Republic of Yemen," *Feminist Review*, no. 1 (1979): 10–11.

51. See Ali al-Kathiri, "Ila al-Doktor Muhammad al-Haydara: Naʿam . . . al-Mafhum al-Yamani Li-hawiyya al-janub huwa asas al-warita" (For Doctor Muhammad Haydara, Yes, Linking the South with Yemen Is the Basis of the Dilemma), *Aden al-Ghad*, http://adengd .net/news/98569. According to al-Kathiri, it was a mistake to link "South" to "Yemen" when the country adopted the name People's Republic of South Yemen during the three first years after independence because it implied that the South belongs to Yemen.

4 THE SECT-SEX-POLICE NEXUS AND POLITICS
IN BAHRAIN'S PEARL REVOLUTION FRANCES S. HASSO

My interest in gendered embodiments in built environments in the Arab revolutions emerged as I watched videos and photographs of contrasting masculinities in Bahrain in early 2011. Particularly striking were images of unarmed young men in denim jeans, often shirtless, arms raised and hands gesturing in peaceful appeal to police. Occupying the clean avenues of the business district of central Manama, they faced sophisticated military vehicles and an array of fully armed, shielded, and helmeted security men, usually naturalized as citizens and non-Arabic-speaking (figure 4.1). Such scenes coexisted with equally compelling large gender-segregated marches organized by al-Wefaq National Islamic Society. In these contrasting visual tableaux black-robed and veiled girls and women walked on one side of major thoroughfares, separated by sometimes invisible medians from boys and men wearing a variety of clothing styles who walked in parallel. Bahrain's small geographic area, residential partitions on the basis of sect and class, maldistribution of resources, and a post-1979 culture of gender segregation inspired by the Iranian revolution persistently foreground such embodied-spatialized dynamics. I argue that gendered and sect boundaries increasingly "interarticulated,"[1] or worked through each other, as longstanding conflict between the majority of citizens and Al Khalifa rulers intensified into the 14 February Revolution, also called the Pearl Revolution. Rather than further conservatizing the society, such imbrications paradoxically worked to shift gendered norms and embodiments in public space as dramatically as had the 1979 Iranian revolution.

FIGURE 4.1. A Bahraini antigovernment protester gestures in front of riot police on an overpass near the Pearl Roundabout in Manama, Bahrain, 13 March 2011. AP Photo / Hasan Jamali.

I understand sectarianism to be produced like racism, through "racial-izing" projects that transform difference,[2] in this case religious difference, into inequality and violence. The "racial formation" approach, developed by Michael Omi and Howard Winant to understand U.S. racial history and revisited multiple times since initial publication of their book in 1986, chal-lenges categorical understandings of difference (e.g., "the Shiʿa" and "the Sunna") by attending to institutional, especially state-sponsored, proj-ects that "accrete over historical time to shape both the racialized social structure and our psychic structure as racial subjects."[3] Racial formation assumes race to be "neither an essential fact nor an illusion," a judgment that also applies to ethnic, linguistic, and religious difference.[4] Zaheer Ba-ber examines violent religious-based communalism in India through a "racialization" framework, arguing for "structural and ideological similari-ties" between communal and racial conflicts. Too often, he contends, ex-planations for communal violence rely on the "internal logic" of religions, "underplay[ing]" institutional factors, including law. This is a rare scholarly example that applies the racial formation approach to non-U.S. contexts. In Baber's case, and in many examples of sectarianism in the Middle East, identities are racialized "through the construction and deployment of an identifiable discourse of quasi-biological, immutable differences," despite indistinguishability on the basis of phenotype or morphology.[5] In a germane study of violence in mid-nineteenth-century Mount Lebanon, Ussama Makdisi illustrates the modernity of a "culture of sectarianism," challenging linear progress-oriented historiographical explanations that attribute sectarianism to primordialism and tribalism.[6] Examining conflict in Bahrain through a racialization framework, where sectarian formation is understood as resembling racial formation, even when Arabic "race" words such as *jins* and *'irq* are not explicitly used, allows us to see how sect, ethnicity, religion, and citizenship status become resources for categorical boundary-building, facilitating repression, material extraction, and regime maintenance in Bahrain and elsewhere.

Gender and sexuality are crucial symbolic, embodied, and institutional resources for sect-based racialization in the sect-sex-police nexus in Bahrain. As Priya Kandaswamy argues, Omi and Winant's *Racial Formation* neglects gender and naturalizes sexual difference despite the centrality of gender and sexuality to racial formation.[7] Scholarship on sectarianism in the Middle East also avoids the centrality of sex and gender to the reproduction and policing of such boundaries. Sectarianism and racism are similar in their reliance on state and nonstate forms of law to restrict miscegenation and to control gendered and sexual behavior, marriage, and divorce. Informed by the work of Jacques Rancière, I understand *police* to be any system or sensibility of separation, partition, and distribution designed to produce hierarchy and inequality, and *politics* as enacted and shared transgressions of such systems and sensibilities.[8] Police in Bahrain works through sectarian discourse, racialized naturalization policies, security forces dominated by non-Bahrainis, and gendered and sexual forms of violence and control. In contrast the Pearl Revolution offered a politics of multiple emancipatory enactments and transgressions whose results have been new gendered imaginaries, subjectivities, and ways of inhabiting space. Attention to visibility, embodiment, and symbolic enactments in space—sartorial practices, vocal expressions, activist visual and sound productions—illuminates sect-sex-police dynamics and politics in Bahrain.

Doing independent research in a highly repressive state such as Bahrain is difficult, to say the least. The state monitors public and private expression on email, telephone, streets, Twitter, websites, Facebook, YouTube, Internet cafés, and Skype, and even in Shi'a community spaces such as *ma'tams*.[9] Bahraini ministries use human intelligence, filtering technologies, electronic targeting programs, CCTV cameras, surveillance blimps, and face recognition software for these practices.[10] Antiregime expression by identifiable Bahrainis may lead to prison, torture, dismissal from government and private-sector jobs, restrictions on international travel, and loss of citizenship. My tourist visa to enter Bahrain to conduct research was revoked within a week of its approval by the Ministry of Interior on 17 June 2013, four days before I was scheduled to travel, with no reason provided by the Bahraini ambassador to Washington or the Bahrain Ministry of Interior in Manama. This chapter instead relies on open-ended, largely recorded interviews with ten informants in England in July 2013, evenly split between men and women, informal discussion and observation, including at two Bahraini community events in London, and conversations by telephone and email with activists and informants. I do not attribute most quoted material because anxiety was pervasive. I analyze visual and textual material gathered from independent media, regime and opposition websites, Facebook organization pages, satellite channels, YouTube channels, and Twitter feeds.

In this chapter I first use a historical lens to examine regional and local dynamics and the mechanism of rule in relation to inequalities and distinctions in Bahrain based on sect, class, citizenship, and gender. I offer an account of the making of politics in the 14 February Revolution, with particular attention to spatiality and embodiment. I discuss the crucial role of symbolic and discursive action in the Pearl Revolution and examine gendered turning points and anxieties to substantiate my argument of a sect-sex-police nexus in Bahrain.

Lines of Control in the Corporate Family-State

Inequality genealogies are based on citizenship, indigeneity, religious affiliation, ethnicity, gender, and class or wealth in Bahrain. Bahrain is a state in the internally differentiated region of lower Asia Minor, which has long-standing histories of circulation and crossing. Bodies and spaces are nevertheless divided, contained, and distributed through a number of modern mechanisms. Such containments and subjectifications are not only impositions from the top; they work through bodies, minds, feelings, and space on multiple scales.[11] These containments are occasionally ruptured in daily life and at historically significant moments.

A Sunni Arab family-based authoritarian regime, Al Khalifa, rules a country whose majority of 700,000 citizens are Shiʿa Arab.[12] Noncitizens, especially long-term and structurally itinerant migrant workers from South Asia, compose about half of the 1.2 million residents of Bahrain.[13] The regime distributes resources and manipulates citizenship rules to demographically buttress its subordination of Bahrainis of Shiʿa origin, whom it considers disloyal. These processes in turn feed a sensibility of disadvantage and claims making among Bahraini Shiʿa, especially in relation to foreign men and their families.

Sheyma Buali illustrates how the built environment in Bahrain "maps the marginals," or indexes racialized and classed forms of partition and containment through differentially available housing and housing quality based on sect, ethnicity, citizenship status, and class; permanent and mobile checkpoints, patrols, and barricades; and cyber and other surveillance.[14] The ruling family privatizes land and water for its benefit and invests low amounts in health, education, and infrastructure for the majority of Bahrainis.[15] Environments have been transformed in the past fifteen years to include towns and reclaimed islands subcontracted by the state to foreign developers, horizons dotted with icons of financialization, shopping malls, fake harbors, and vast housing developments and gated private communities for the rich—what a non-Bahraini Arab who often visits Bahrain calls "bubbles within bubbles."

"Bahrain Economic Vision 2030" brands Bahrain as "business friendly," a campaign slogan plastered on London cabs in 2010, although Buali tells me the buildings in the "computer-generated landscapes" do not exist.[16] The corporate report, website, and images of this campaign express a capitalist modernity that hides its exclusions and appropriations. Similarly since 2006 "Northern Town" has existed as a plan and series of images to ameliorate a housing crisis for the vast majority of Bahrainis but has yet to materialize.[17] Spaces of luxury living and consumption that actually exist include communities such as the Amwaj island private housing development.[18] Built for expats, residency is limited to wealthy Bahrainis and non-

Bahrainis.[19] In contrast Shiʿa majority towns and villages are "hemmed in and securitized," in the words of a young male Bahraini academic, experiencing enclosure without luxury.

Residential segregation between Shiʿa and Sunni majority villages and towns, as well as urban and rural cultural divisions, often map onto class divisions in Bahrain.[20] The capital city of Manama, explained Abdulhadi Khalaf, has long "been cosmopolitan in the sense that while neighborhoods were generally segregated, there were always a couple of houses that belonged to this or that family from the other side." A young male revolutionary contended that an ideological aspect of this rural-urban divide disappeared after 14 February 2011: "The families that live in Manama are usually citified, well-educated and stayed back from social movements, and in villages the families are usually workers or peasants who were the most politically involved.... In the latest movement this division melted because the state targeted everyone, including the Shiʿa merchants of Manama, who were formerly allies of the ruling family."[21]

State jobs are distributed to reinforce regime wealth and power, "coup-proof" rulers, and reduce opportunities for cross-sect class or ideological solidarities.[22] According to Khalaf, public works jobs are "dominated by Sunni menial laborers," while "sweepers, orderlies, and grounds workers" in the electricity and health departments are largely Shiʿa. In other sectarian formation projects, when the Bahrain Defense Force was established in 1968, all the officers were men from the ruling family, while rank-and-file soldiers represented Bahraini men broadly. Over time, however, service work in the military went to Shiʿa men and soldiering positions to Sunni men. While the Bahrain women's police force established in 1970 includes Shiʿa and Sunni Bahrainis,[23] the much larger male police force excludes Shiʿa Bahrainis and relies on Sunni men of Bahraini and non-Bahraini origin. Policemen are recruited externally, trained, and offered "political naturalization" (citizenship) and housing to assure their loyalty. These practices transform the demographics of Bahrain, harden racialized partitions, and increase the disfranchisement of Baharna indigenous people. They also assure significant divisions between men in the police force, who often do not speak Arabic, and the policed.[24] Institutionalized partitioning, Khalaf contended in an interview, was necessary because the country is "too small to maintain physical segregation."

Unlike in the Kingdom of Saudi Arabia, less than twenty miles away, Bahraini women drive and hold high-level political and professional positions in most economic sectors. Unlike in the Kingdom of Saudi Arabia and the United Arab Emirates, university classrooms are gender-integrated.[25] Like much of the lower Arabian Peninsula, however, Bahrain expresses a habitus of gender segregation and male dominance through built environments, social and political institutions, and everyday practices. On public buses women sit in front seats and men in the back, although the well-off eschew public transportation altogether as low status. Gender segregation is the comfortable and taken-for-granted practice in most settings.

Nevertheless gendered relations and discourse seem less misogynistic and patriarchal than they are in more and less gender-integrated settings I have studied in Egypt, Jordan, the Occupied Palestinian Territories, and the United Arab Emirates. Verbal and physical sexual harassment of girls and women in public spaces is rare in Bahrain.[26] A female Bahraini informant who has been imprisoned observed, "In protests, and especially in difficult circumstances where you are rounded up, it is not a sexualized environment. I don't know what explains it." A religiously conservative Shi'a man in his late thirties agreed that the gender environment in Bahrain differs from that in surrounding Arab countries. Seeming to realize the significance of his words as he responded to my question about gender culture in Bahrain, he elaborated that when he was growing up, the Quran teacher (al-mu'allima) in villages "was usually a woman. Between six and nine years old [in the early 1980s], I learned Quran from a woman." When I asked why that was, he responded, "It might be because she could read and was better-educated than village men, so she taught the boys and girls." Such accounts indicate the importance of a contextualized rather than linear understanding of gender relations in Bahrain.

Hussain al-Shabib, a human rights activist in his twenties, stressed that before 1980 mixed-gender socializing "was normal": "My father tells me that when he visited his friends' homes, their mothers and sisters would sit with them without hijab, wearing mishmars [colorful shawls]. When I was recently comparing family photographs of my grandmothers and my mother, I noticed my grandmother wearing a fancy [nonreligious] headdress as a younger woman, and they are standing in the street by a car." He asked her teasingly, "Grandma, where was this?" She replied, "No, no, no! No one could see us!'" In contrast to a weak culture of gender segregation in the 1970s indicated by his grandmother's clothing, his mother "is wearing a hijab and 'abaya [black robe] in the 1980s."[27] Shi'a Bahrainis, he continues, were definitely impacted by the Iranian revolution. In my religious classes as a child [in the late 1990s], most of the lessons were about what? "Do not talk with women, it is *haram*. There must be segregation. It is banned to sit like we are, with a foreign woman, blah, blah, blah." They made us think that religion completely revolves around these matters. My grandmother is religious, but it is the religiosity of our grandparents, in opposition to my mother, who was raised by movement Islam, which is so different. Even my great aunt is more open [than the younger generation] and named her daughter after [a Lebanese singer]. We were shocked when she told us. We were raised to think that singing is haram. "How could you name your daughter for a singer?"

In Bahrain women's rights are instrumentalized by the government to reinforce sectarian divisions between a masculinist undemocratic regime and the majority Baharna, whose main opposition organization is also masculinist and led by men. The largest political mobilization in Bahrain before February 2011 occurred on 5 November 2005, as 100,000 Baharna marched to protest a campaign to allow parliamentarians and state appointees to codify family law, subsuming Sunni and Shiʿa jurisprudence systems. For pious Shiʿa codification requires a shift from revered sources of religious authority in Lebanon, Iraq, or Iran to laws and policies produced in Manama by a government that does not represent them. King Hamad bin Khalifa has used the threat of codification against the opposition al-Wefaq Society whenever Shiʿa Bahrainis push for increased political rights. Many Sunni and Shiʿa women's rights activists supported codification in 2005, arguing against the unfairness, misogyny, and corruption in marriage, divorce, and child custody matters in shariʿa courts, where male judges use "independent reasoning" based on Islamic jurisprudence. The rights activists had allies among parliamentarians, Sunni and Shiʿa. Most Shiʿa religious scholars in Bahrain, all men, were against codification since it undermines Shiʿa clerical institutions.[28]

In the end marriage law was codified only for Sunni Bahrainis in May 2009. As a secular male Bahraini human rights activist in his late twenties put it during an interview, the regime excels at strategically claiming its gender "modernity," but "when it comes to the hardcore issues related to women, they make it a bargaining chip with the opposition because they know they can press the buttons of the community. . . . If you are an outsider, you might say 'Yes, by God, the government has a right to make this [family] code. Why does al-Wefaq stand against the rights of the people?' But when you take a closer look you see that they used the family law as a political bargaining chip and the opposition was stupid enough to play this game."[29]

Sect differences have seldom led to sustained clashes in Bahrain, and such clashes have rarely been triggered simply by sect affiliation.[30] Like other racializing formations, Sunni-Shiʿa differences are inflamed into sectarianism by institutional practices and systems, particular incidents, and storytelling. Cyber activists in their twenties and thirties reported in interviews that in the decade before 2011, intense sectarian attacks by pro-regime forces largely occurred in digital spheres and state-sponsored media. Visual and textual material triggered "comment wars" that have been "amplified a thousand times" since 2011. Attacks on Shiʿa Bahrainis frequently articulate racism through sexualization. In built environments sectarianism has reached unprecedented levels since 14 February 2011, as shrines, mosques, and cemeteries were destroyed or vandalized by regime or pro-regime forces.[31] "Sunni public figures" for the first time called for economic boycotts of some Shiʿa-owned business.[32]

"In the Gulf There Isn't a Public Square"

For Bahraini activists the conflict with the regime broadly turns on expressing the existence of a disfranchised majority through disruption and transgression of space, place, and dominant discourse. The revolutionary mobilizations in Tunisia and Egypt offered an undeniable opportunity to world-build with others, particularly after 25 January 2011. As a leftist male activist in his twenties stated, "Just the thought that we would be the third group of people to go to the streets—we couldn't wait [*ma sadaqna*]!" Activists picked 14 February as the mobilization date because it marked the tenth anniversary of a referendum that overwhelmingly approved the National Action Charter put forth in late 2000 by the newly installed ruler, Emir Sheikh Hamad bin Isa Al Khalifa, who declared himself king in 2002.[33]

As for location, the Bahraini activist and intellectual Alaʾa al-Shehabi explained:

> Some guy started carrying out a field study, asking, "Where is our Tahrir?" In the Gulf there isn't a public square, a public space that

has history or meaning. He studied various locations and made the case on Bahrain Online [which has fifty thousand members] for the Pearl Roundabout given its numerous exits and the symbolic monument.[34] People started throwing out other ideas and critiquing them and voted on three locations. It was only an idea that, ideally, if we could occupy a place, it would be the Pearl Roundabout given its accessibility to villages. But people differed on strategy: Should we all gather at the Pearl Roundabout, or should we start in our areas and try to get to the Pearl Roundabout? There was no leadership on that.

The choice of the traffic roundabout with the iconic Pearl Monument of six massive white spires (representing sails) carrying a pearl is ironic. It was built by the Khalifa regime in 1982 as an homage to the six kingly governments of the Gulf Cooperation Council in advance of the third GCC meeting in Manama (figure 4.2).

The "14 February Announcement from Bahraini Youth for Freedom" was released on 3 February 2011 at 1:33 a.m. on the Facebook page of Bahrain Online (Multaqa bahrayn).[35] The statement "calls on the people of Bahrain to take to the streets" and to choose "a central and lively location that is easy to reach in the capital." Mobilization rhetoric, communicated through graffiti and Twitter, repeatedly called for unity across sect, ethnic, and class differences. Bahraini activists held a solidarity event with Egyptians outside the Egyptian Embassy in Manama on 4 February and joined Egyptian expats in celebration outside the embassy on 11 February, when President Hosni Mubarak was compelled to step down.[36] On 14 February marches and protests occurred in at least twenty-seven villages. Al-Shehabi explains that residents would hear "a rumor of people going out at eight a.m. from a particular mosque. You never knew who made the call or whether it was genuine, you just showed up. Someone would say, 'Allahu akbar,' and people would start marching, with others coming out to join them from every corner. That's how it happened. I saw people walking, so I started walking with them."

Police shot twenty-one-year-old ʿAli Abdulhadi Mushaima in the back late in the afternoon on 14 February, killing him as he returned to his home in the village of Daih from a protest.[37] Tensions were high as riot police and a few hundred mourners waited outside the morgue in Salmaniyya Medical Complex in Manama on the morning of 15 February to take Mushaima's body for a procession and burial. Police lobbed teargas and shot at mourn-

FIGURE 4.2. Demonstrators gather at Pearl Square in Manama, 25 February 2011. Reuters / Caren Firouz.

ers outside the hospital, killing thirty-one-year-old Fadhel al-Matrook of ʿIsa Town and injuring others.[38] As news spread, thousands joined the funeral procession for Mushaima as it moved to Daih. After his burial mourners were motivated by a "whisper": "Let's go to the roundabout. We have buried him, but we are not done." They marched 1.5 kilometers back to Manama using a road they were surprised was open, arriving in the early afternoon for an unprecedented gathering that became an encampment.[39]

By the evening of 16 February, the 14 February Revolution Youth Coalition was established in the roundabout, according to a male activist who helped found it, "although it did not come out publicly until March."[40] By this account al-Wefaq Society did not request "authorization from the roundabout [*takhwil min al-duwwar*] to speak as our representative. So we tried to establish this logic by forming youth demands that were finalized between 18 and 19 February." The tame demands emerged from negotiation between youth activists and "the majority of opposition groups and figures in Bahrain."[41] A member of the National Democratic Action Society, the largest leftist organization in the country, gathered statements of support for the document from political societies and individuals, "creating a reality." Afterward "the machine began to work and things were running on Bahrain Online, where we didn't have a say." This informant reported that "the opposition in London didn't agree to the statement" because it was too moderate. To roundabout activists' satisfaction, the demands were the basis "of the seven negotiating points announced by the crown prince on 13 March 2011."

Despite generational and ideological differences between al-Wefaq and activists in the 14 February Revolution Youth Coalition, and occasional tension apparent in interviews and published accounts, the distinctions between opposition trends *in* Bahrain can be overdrawn.[42] The main ideological tensions are between some London-based opposition leaders and activists living in Bahrain. As a second male revolutionary noted, "All these things are mixed together in Bahrain. You cannot, for example, clearly categorize the followers of al-Wefaq as separate from the followers of the 14 February Coalition or the followers of other groups. We cannot determine the space each occupies or the membership size of each. In terms of the 14 February Coalition, it is an unknown matter [*shaghla ghamitha*] because nothing [membership and leadership] is clear to anyone."

Police violently cleared the roundabout encampment before dawn on 17 February, killing four people that day and another the following day and injuring hundreds. Police withdrew on 19 February, and protesters tore down the barbed wire and reoccupied the roundabout.[43] After this "hit" activists "cut lines of communication with each other because we did not even know some of the people we were sitting with. We were very worried about who might be a *dabbous* [undercover spy]."

In late afternoon of 22 February tens of thousands of Bahrainis poured into the Pearl Roundabout encampment in a march called by al-Wefaq, demanding the resignation of the longtime prime minister and the end of Khalifa rule.[44]

On 14 March, invited by some of the Khalifa rulers, the GCC sent in a "Peninsula Shield Force" of about one thousand Saudi Arabian national guardsmen and five hundred Emirati police. They entered through the sixteen-mile-long King Fahd Causeway that connects Saudi Arabia and Bahrain and attacked the Pearl Roundabout encampment on 15 March.[45]

On 18 March, in a shocking three-hour operation, state forces demolished the Pearl Monument itself, deeming it too dangerous to exist.[46] Police and military forces barricaded the area, renamed it "Farooq Junction," although it remained closed to human and vehicular traffic, and imposed a security cordon around Manama.

FIGURE 4.3. The logo of the 14 February Revolution Youth Coalition, established March–April 2011. The words "Steadfastness" and "Struggle/Resistance," an image of the Pearl Monument as an ever-present shadow, and the fist of struggle are depicted in the colors of the Bahraini flag.

Resisting, Resignifying, and Cyber-Amplifying

Representations of the destroyed concrete object that was the Pearl Monument, sometimes with splatters of blood and an attached Bahraini flag calling it "Martyr's Square," are ubiquitous in Bahrain and cyberspace. In a brilliant essay Amal Khalaf describes how English-language foreign media eager to have a narrative parallel with Cairo's Tahrir Square called the Pearl Roundabout (Duwwar) the Pearl *Square* instead. Bahraini revolutionaries went from mocking this designation to adopting the word *midan* for signifying a discursive civic square of engagement on multiple scales. Khalaf shows how the destroyed Pearl Monument has "many afterlives" as an "image-memory" that Bahraini activists refuse to allow to disappear (figure 4.3).[47]

A symbolic turning point occurred in 2011 when opposition forces encouraged use of the red and white Bahrain flag—redesigned and decreed by a new king in 2002 as the official state flag—to express the indigenous, nonsectarian, national or *watani* nature of the revolt. Shiʿa Bahrainis are regularly accused by regime and pro-regime partisans of being traitors with strong affinities to Shiʿa in Iran, Lebanon, or Iraq. In turn Arab Shiʿa Bahrainis generally understand the Khalifa as a settler-colonial family from central Arabia who, with British intervention, have consolidated their control on the indigenous population for over two hundred years. A male revolutionary explains why the resignification of the flag is remarkable:

I never recognized the Bahraini flag as the flag of the country because it was imposed by a colonial power. Now it has become our flag by coincidence [ʿalamna bil sudfeh]. The irony is that when the crackdown came, the government relied on Saudi Arabia to help them. During the crackdown, if we were caught at a checkpoint with a Bahraini flag, we would have to be artful [in how to explain it]. Before 14 February protesters regularly carried Hizbollah and other flags. But people were instructed not to carry any flag except the Bahraini flag and not to carry banners and placards with the picture of any one individual.

These previously common male visages at demonstrations included well-known Shiʿa religious and political authority figures from Lebanon, Iraq, and Iran. Nevertheless, he continued, revolutionaries were "hit with the broken record of sectarianism, treason, and national betrayal that the government relies on. They were defeated and could rely on nothing but bullets and lies. The regime was desperate to build the issue of sectarianism [mawthuʿ al-taʾifiyya] in response to this uprising. Our strategy was to minimize opportunities for a sectarian discourse as much as possible," although revolutionaries did not always meet this goal in his opinion.

Resignification of meaning and space on multiple scales remained an explicit aspect of the Pearl Revolution. The 14 February Revolution Youth Coalition #Decisive Moment 3 mobilization campaign on 15 June 2013, which repeats an action from December 2011,[48] blurred divisions between home, neighborhood, and street; incorporated people less likely to travel significant distances from home or neighborhood; and resignified the front stoop as a site of collective politics. Using graffiti, Twitter, and Facebook, the campaign coordinated a "first call" of alert at 3:15 p.m., a "second call" at 3:45, and a "third call" at 5:15.[49] During the second call people were invited "to gradually peacefully gather *in front of their homes* without raising any slogans or banners" and "furnish" and occupy spaces outside the front door.[50] Families and friends sat in front of homes on plastic chairs and mats, drinking tea, eating, and talking. During the third call people participated in marches.[51] When I shared my thesis that decentralized methods facilitate broad inclusion, activists insisted in contrast that they strategize under enclosure conditions. Given residential segregation and the limited number of roads leading to the heart of power in Manama, they see a regime "containment strategy" that "isolates and fragments people in a small country," according to the sociologist Abdulhadi Khalaf. He continued, "If I were the police, I would welcome decentralized protest because protesters . . . spoil their space but not the space that the regime wants to move in." Activists in the 14 February Revolution Youth Coalition prefer to stage events in Manama and Muharraq to assure media visibility and curtail business as usual. Protests in these sites erode containment of Shiʿa villages.

Activists nevertheless magnify dissensus despite geographical containment by using YouTube and other cyber venues to post videos and images of protest. A cyber activist reported that every village in Bahrain has a YouTube channel. Cyberspace is a central site of politics, as illustrated by a video from February 2012 of young activists in the village of Sitra attacking with Molotov cocktails the large and likely unoccupied fortress-like local police station in the night hours. The video illustrates staging attentive to the impressive nighttime effects of light and sound on a cyber audience and scheduling when no police were likely to be hurt. The video had been watched over 230,000 times on YouTube when I viewed it.[52]

Turning Points, Ruptures, and Anxieties in Gendered Body Politics

There is little doubt that the 14 February Revolution opened space for "new actors, new layers, and new groups," maintains Alaʾa al-Shehabi. Activists in the Pearl Roundabout quickly realized that "even the old opposition was part of formal politics," as were organizations such as the Bahrain Center for Human Rights, because these formations

worked within restrictions and boundaries that existed before February 14. With the uprising you had informal task-oriented collectives forming. . . . But they realized they needed new organization. So the heads of the committees in the Pearl Roundabout had nightly meetings. . . . We are talking about a very intensive period that lasted three or four weeks. You could see that a new public sphere was forming, with its own power. . . . There were definitely women at the committee level, at the medical tent, the media tent, they were everywhere. They were very organized. When you start off on the same footing on a blank page there is no space for previous social boundaries to be enforced. So when al-Wefaq tried to come to the Roundabout to say we need gender segregation, there was definitely resistance in the crowd. But it was decided that if there was an area where some women feel more comfortable, that was fine. There was still mixing, and no one was enforcing segregation. As the revolution continued, you got a sense of the tension women's activism produced, with statements from al-Wefaq such as "I urge our good women to please retreat [from] confrontations." You don't go telling [the activist] Zainab al-Khawaja to retreat. She goes looking for a confrontation!

As mentioned, spatial segregation by gender is common in large public gatherings organized by al-Wefaq. Most women wear black ʿabayas and hair covers and group behind or beside men during marches (figure 4.4). These practices visibly communicate conservative notions of respectability and propriety but do not necessarily represent women's and men's gendered or religious motivations and subjectivities. ʿAbayas have become anonymizing uniforms that hide decentralized activities that are less sanctioned by dominant institutions.[53] Sartorial and gender-segregated spatial practices also hide the degree to which spatial gender norms and acceptable forms of embodiment have been seismically shifted by events since February 2011. Al-Shehabi, who covers her hair, noted that when "non-hijabi" women get comments these days, such as "Why the hell are you not properly dressed?," the critics are typically other women, while men may insist, "It's her right. It's her freedom." Even in her conservative village, where she could "not be out without a ʿabaya as a child" in the late 1980s and 1990s, dress standards for girls and women have "loosened enormously" since 2011.

On the island of Sitra, where about half of households have boys or men in jail, according to Amal Khalaf, women's participation is "about bodies, numbers of bodies, and the recognition that bodies have power in space in Bahrain. . . . So it is really important that people make themselves visible." Girls and women are indeed active in barricade building, general strikes, graffiti actions, noise making, and chants. They also make and throw Molotov cocktails, disrupt the contentious Grand Prix Formula 1 race, and engage in pitched battles with riot police.[54] Notwithstanding the use of Molotov cocktails and firebombs by some girls and women, their

FIGURE 4.4. Bahraini antigovernment protesters march toward the Pearl Roundabout on 1 March 2011, men on one side of the road and women on the other, in the capital of Manama. Tens of thousands of Bahrainis, largely Shiites, participated in the march, urging unity among Sunnis and Shiites in demanding political reform. AP Photo / Hasan Jamali.

activism is likely facilitated by the nonmilitarized nature of the Bahrain uprising, which may not remain so.

Hussain al-Shabib noted that women's leadership and participation in the 14 February Revolution at all levels is "pivotal" (*mihwari*) and "impossible to overstate at this point. It would have been impossible to sustain the revolution without women." There are many "distinctive indications" of a gendered cultural turning point linked to 14 February 2011. Among these is that women "who do not wear hijab returned to the front [*raja'at lal-wajih*]" and that "the social restriction against the presence of women who do not wear hijab is gone." This coming out is illustrated most dramatically by covered and uncovered women physicians and nurses of both sects who, with male colleagues, treated the injured across sects, protected them from police and security forces, and have been outspoken against the Khalifa government. Many of these medical personnel were beaten, imprisoned, and tortured and have become national figures in their own right.[55]

A male revolutionary in his midthirties substantiated a shift in gender norms with regard to the inhabitation of space: "The generation of 14 February is more liberal and uses public space with a larger sense of freedom. Ten years ago a young woman could not go to a meeting without having her little brother with her. This is no longer true as girls attend meetings like everyone else and go to places like Costa Coffee, which include men and women. This is true even for the most conservative families. I suspect this scares conservative forces." He cautioned that "matters of religious conservatism" are nevertheless unresolved in Bahrain. He feared "the jihadi, Salafi, or Wahhabi forces, who hate the king. Women's representation is not a major Sunni or Shi'a problem in Bahrain, even among conservative forces. The current female minister is from the Muslim Brotherhood, and al-Wefaq has women at the highest levels now.[56] It is the Salafi-Wahhabi forces who may really be against any opening of public space or expanding women's rights." This activist distinguished women's participation from women's substantive influence in high-level decision making and leadership in al-Wefaq and the government, however. He thought such influence "doubtful" because "the dominant frameworks remain conservative and Islamic, and the masculinist point of view continues to be present and concentrated in Bahraini society."

Widely significant and unprecedented was the bold sonic breach of a mixed-gender space by Ayat al-Qurmezi, a twenty-year-old college student from a modest class background who performed an original poem onstage during the Pearl Roundabout encampment in February 2011. The poem was structured around a fictional encounter between (King) "Hamad" and Satan (Idlis), where Satan is the humane character, and included xenophobic remarks about South Asians awarded citizenship, housing, and other resources by Hamad at the expense of his own people. In the YouTube version the carefully listening men in the audience are heard to say "Clever, clever" and to laugh. They seem startled by Qurmezi's audacity and egg her on during the performance. A young Bahraini intellectual who spoke to me in English called it a "radical performance": "You can hear her voice cracking. She is expressing something that they never had the eloquence or gall to say." He criticized her at the same time for breaking "with the radical message when the poem becomes xenophobic. . . . It is orgiastic xenophobia coupled with a kind of precise critique of power." In addition to the thousands who heard the performance live in the Pearl

Roundabout, videos circulated widely on the Internet and led to Qur-mezi's arrest and torture.[57]

In another kind of gendered-ideological breach, this one increasingly common in corporate space, a widely disseminated video posted to You-Tube on 23 September 2011 by a pro-regime man shows Bahraini girls and women wearing black robes and hair covers, marching and chanting in young feminine voices for the downfall of the regime on the bottom floor of the posh City Centre Mall while apparently Sunni men on the higher atrium floor counterchant, record, and look down on them. In the "about" section on YouTube, the pro-regime uploader explains to his presumed English readers (lightly edited by the author): "Bahraini citizens in City Centre Mall refused this type of action and replied to the protesters against their political chanting and demanded that they get out. City Centre is commercial property that is owned by a business group. Protesting inside private property is against the law and the security forces took action to enforce the law against these illegal actions."[58] In this passage the author constitutes himself and his group as "citizens," in contrast to the protesters; the mall as private property available to him but not the protesting voices; and his alignment with the Law and Police against the women protesters.

Zainab al-Khawaja, born when her parents were in exile in Denmark, is probably the most outspoken and publicly confrontational Bahraini woman activist. She was in prison during most of 2013 and rearrested in December 2014, the latest of many arrests. On 15 December 2011 police attacked a demonstration and sit-in of several hundred people, mostly women. Then twenty-seven years old, al-Khawaja, whose father and hus-band were imprisoned at the time, remained to occupy, in Amal Khalaf's words, "the grassy area of the Bergaland [Burgerland] traffic roundabout, just her one body. She is looking at the police, she is not scared, and they are literally dragging her across the roundabout." The series of European Pressphoto Agency photographs of the incident quickly became powerful iconography (figure 4.5).[59] Like al-Khawaja, many Bahraini women who have been named and targeted by the regime for revolutionary activity are in their twenties or thirties, married, and with young children. Al-Khawaja discussed the difficulty of prioritizing motherhood in an English-language radio interview on February 2012 before one of her arrests.[60]

Confrontational activism by girls and women and the repression of po-lice, intelligence, and security services have produced multiple responses

FIGURE 4.5. The activist Zainab al-Khawaja screaming while being arrested during a protest at the Bergaland traffic roundabout in Abu Seba village, north of Manama, Bahrain, 15 December 2011. European Pressphoto Agency / Mazen Mahdi.

from Baharna men and male-dominated institutions, including admiration, protectiveness, and an impulse to pull them back into comfortable zones of appropriate behavior. Abdulhadi Khalaf maintained that women's disproportionate involvement in the revolution is "more women-led than men-approved." Many men "have a problem seeing this kind of activism." Those interested in "self-preservation" are happy for women's involvement but would rather they not engage in risky activity that forces men to "become macho" and "take more action than we should" given the attached danger. "We have to defend them when the police come," these men say, but they must "learn that women can suffer too." His analysis is consistent with a casual discussion I had with two Bahraini women later that day in July 2013 in a car in London. They agreed that through their actions and words Bahraini women force men to be more militant than may be comfortable or safe. They revealed that many Bahraini women are angered by cautiousness and use language that queers men who do not participate in confrontation.

Calls for girls and women to restrain themselves come from at least two other masculine subject positions, argued Abdulhadi Khalaf. First, there is competitiveness and "envy that women are more daring, really daring.

During the Grand Prix Formula 1 Race in 2012 and 2013, it was women who got into the track" despite security restrictions. Rihanna al-Musawi and Nafissa al-Asfur were indeed arrested in April 2013 for such a breach on the second day of the race and were accused of being part of the leadership of the 14 February Revolution Youth Coalition. Both women reported being tortured, beaten, and abused in detention, including rape, forced disrobing, and other forms of sexualized humiliation and assault.[61] Similarly, Abdulhadi continued, "Zainab al-Khawaja has daring that very few men have. There are many others like her: Fatima Hajji, a medical doctor, the nurse Rula al-Saffar—they do not confront police, but they have not succumbed to pressure from the regime."

The main Shi'a cleric for al-Wefaq, 'Isa Qasem, and the leader of al-Wefaq, Ali Salman, are motivated by a third gender logic when they try to restrain or police women, Khalaf argued: "They have actually voiced objection that women are so active." The warnings are typically in a patronizing language: "For their own good, girls and women should not seek confrontation with the police. They should not go in the forefront because the police are godless, and so on, and will attack anyone." He found "the consequences fascinating because no one listened to them." There is a "self-synergizing process that is moving on its own." Even young Bahraini women students who are so religious they will not shake their male professor's hand are "so immersed in the struggle that I don't think they will ever listen to such a call. This is notable but does not mean they will not fall in line sometime in the future."

The Sect-Sex-Police Nexus

Family and community forms of gender-sexual policing to some degree respond to regime apparatuses in Bahrain that use sexualized measures to control men and women activists through shame.[62] Such methods include rape, sexual assault, forcing detainees to disrobe, removing women's hair covers, monitoring sexual behavior to blackmail activists, and using sexual seduction to bait potential spies. I term this the sect-sex-police nexus. It is widely known among Bahrainis that intelligence forces have blackmailed male activists video-recorded having sex and have used other sexualized methods in attempts to trap them. There are stories of women (*mujannadat*) hired by the National Security Agency to pretend to admire or be in love with men activists on social media, offer Shi'a temporary marriage (*mut'a*), and put men in compromising intimate situations to elicit information on their activities and networks.[63] In another method a man and woman activist will be arrested at the same time, but the woman will be released "in two minutes," putting her under suspicion as a collaborator. The names of released women are sometimes "publicized by opposition forums," leading one woman to attempt suicide. Al-Shehabi criticized "the sexual undertones" of the opposition focus on women collaborators because "everyone became suspicious of any woman who was a successful activist. Is she really an infiltrator or an activist?"

The regime and its supporters have been preoccupied with the sexual activities of activists since the early days of the revolution. Regime and sectarian Sunnis used state-sponsored television and digital venues to spread a sectarian-sexual narrative with multiple layers that accuses activists of gender-mixing and using the roundabout for sex and mut'a. Soon after police and military forces destroyed the Pearl Monument, according to a young male activist, King Hamad's information advisor and president of *Al-Ayyam* newspaper, Nabil al-Hamer, "published a picture of women's underwear on his personal Facebook page with the caption, 'Leftovers of the Roundabout [*Min mukhalafat al-duwwar*].' He deleted it, but people had taken a screenshot." A group called Bahrain Shield, reportedly affiliated with Chief of Police Tareq al-Hassan, on 7 June 2011 posted on YouTube an unintentionally campy video produced in a solemn evidentiary genre that staged women's panties and bras, unused condoms, and condoms with "semen" in them purportedly left behind in razed tents of the encampment.[64]

In another Bahrain Shield video, posted on YouTube on 15 June 2011, male teenagers and young men are accused of luring schoolgirls to the Roundabout for nefarious purposes. After aerial video footage that follows a group of teenage girls walking through the encampment into a tent, sequential title cards of stark white Arabic against a black background declare: "As you saw . . . these young students [fem.] were taken into one of the tents surrounded by adolescents [masc.] and young men." The next title card asks: "And the question here is *why*? And what happened *to them* [*bi-hinna*, feminine plural] inside these tents?" (emphasis added). Rather than voice-overs, the videos intersperse Arabic text with pictures and video, accompanied by ominous instrumental music.[65] The "why" implies that the *real* reason activists occupied the Pearl Roundabout was to sexually exploit girls and women. The phrase *to them* represents men as moti-

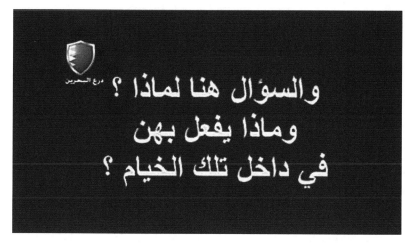

والسؤال هنا لماذا ؟
وماذا يفعل بهن
في داخل تلك الخيام ؟

مع التحرير

FIGURE 4.6. "And the question here is why? And what happened to them inside these tents?" Screenshot from Bahrain Shield, "Witness What Happened to Girl Students in the Roundabout," YouTube, 15 June 2011, 2:22, http://www.youtube.com /watch?v=9dyoIwoHLmQ.

vated by greed and sexual desire rather than political principles and girls and women as objects of exploitation and victims rather than political or sexual subjects (figure 4.6).

Male pundits had free rein on Bahrain state television to accuse women of sexual improprieties. Other material distributed virtually by sectarian forces labels Shiʿa as Zoroastrian and of Iranian origin, with Shiʿa women subject to special vitriol.[66] Sectarian rhetoric from regime and pro-regime forces, contends al-Shabib, aims "to trash" revolutionaries by referring to the roundabout as *duwwar al-mutʿa* (the temporary marriage roundabout). It urges activists to "go back to the [demolished] mutʿa circle" and calls oppositional Shiʿa *wilad al-mutʿa* (children of temporary marriage) and *aʿyal al-mutʿa* (families of temporary marriage). This "basically say[s] we are illegitimate bastards."

Activists are accused of having sex in Tent 6 of the Roundabout, which was near a palm tree the Manama municipality identified by this number, according to al-Shehabi. Interrogations of men and women frequently focus on Tent 6, said al-Shehabi: "'Tell us what you were doing there.' They built this idea that Tent 6 was where people were having mutʿa relations.

They tell people, 'You just wanted to go there for whores.' But you know what? There was no privacy. Everything was open. I spent most of my time there. For the regime, either Iran was behind this or it was about sex." Another woman reported that having sex at the Roundabout "would have been really difficult, [because] there were many families. If you were going to have sex with a boyfriend or girlfriend, maybe you would drive your car far away from kids, and you won't do it anywhere where anyone in your family would ever, ever find out."

A Bahraini woman whose male relative's torture sessions included sexual assault said he was regularly asked, "Tell us who you slept with. You've got to tell us!" A woman arrested in 2012 with a group of journalists and a young man they had paid to drive them during the Formula 1 Race reported, "The first thing I was asked by police was, 'What were you doing in the car with five men anyway?'" She responded, "Can you tell me what law I broke? Are you going to charge me with a violation of honor?" When they asked her about packaged condoms they found in the glove compartment of the vehicle, she responded, "'It's not my car. It's not my responsibility.' They wanted to intimidate me and say 'We have something on you.'" A well-known woman activist who spent many months in prison told Amal Khalaf that a woman police officer taunted her through the cell door, "We found condoms in your car. Are you having sex in the car, you whore?" Such language is ubiquitous online, according to Khalaf, given the desire of pro-government social media "to discredit protesters in any way, shape, or form." The focus on sex, she argued, feeds into a Sunni racist discourse that Shiʿa "are just animals." While most opposition people "didn't care," according to al-Shabib, others "went to the extreme and attacked the other side by calling them 'wilad al-misyar,'" or children of a Sunni form of convenience marriage.[67] These activists also dubbed the al-Fatih Sunni mosque in Manama *tajammuʿ al-misyar*, or the misyar gathering.

Sex and racialization were frequently co-articulated, casting aspersions on the reputations of women activists, making suspicious nonmarital relationships between consenting adults, and increasing family pressure on especially women activists to avoid the appearance of impropriety. As a male Bahraini scholar in his twenties astutely observed, sexual and racial discourse "criminalizes the entire edifice" of the Pearl Roundabout and the opposition. I contend it also *trivializes* the opposition and forces activists to define sex, intimacy, and joy as separate from politics when they are rarely so.

Conclusion

Anxieties about authenticity, rootedness, allegiance, and legitimate belonging remain crucial in Bahrain, animated by a variety of policing practices and discourses. Despite boundary building, Bahraini elites are part of regional and global networks of clerics and religious authorities, rulers, military leaders, weapons merchants, intelligence and security entrepreneurs, capitalists, and culture ministers. Affinities and connections overlap and exceed the bounded and purist assumptions of nationalist, patriarchal, and racializing ideologies in other ways. For example, there are thick lines of family relations between Bahrainis and people in Iran, Hasa in coastal eastern Saudi Arabia,[68] Qatar, Kuwait, the United Arab Emirates, and Iraq.

Global and regional networks also include independent Bahraini intellectuals, feminists, and liberal and radical bloggers, journalists, webmasters, artists, filmmakers, hackers, and other cyber and media activists who have informally worked with each other on a number of scales for many years before 2011. Despite challenges, Bahraini activists have constituted new spaces, embodiments, and imaginaries by enacting freedom and equality in what Gillian Rose has termed "paradoxical space," where it is "impossible to find a position that is outside of hegemonic discourse" and yet people try. It remains important in Bahrain that these emancipatory imaginaries and practices do not depend on what Rose calls "exclusions" or "dualities."[69]

This chapter shows how sex and gender and sectarianism are embodied and work through each other, the built environment, discourse, and digital space in Bahrain. Gender and sexuality are foundational to sectarianism, which I treat as a racializing dynamic that is central to policing. I use verbs rather than nouns—for example, *racializing, gendering, making,* and *sexualizing*—to stress the productions and enactments of police and politics on many scales, in contrast to assumptions of givenness and stability. The 14 February Revolution marks a historical turning point in that it transformed relations between bodies and space, loosened gendered restrictions, and produced new sex-gendered subjectivities, embodiments, and tensions. Among the revolution's notable dimensions is a rise in women-led confrontational street politics not necessarily authorized by Bahraini opposition men, which has produced sublimated tensions not captured by images of orderly gender-segregated marches. For their part Bahraini state officials and their supporters strategically deploy conservative ideologies of sexual respectability and purity to discredit women and men activists and consolidate police.

NOTES

This project was generously supported by research grants from the Duke Islamic Studies Center ("Transcultural Islam" project funded by the Carnegie Corporation) and the Duke Trent Memorial Fund Foundation. I appreciate the assistance provided by Dean Laurie Patton, Gil Merkx, Kelly Jarrett, and Keri Mejikes, especially during the compressed period of visa denial and itinerary changes. I am grateful to the following people for their generosity and openness. They taught me, corrected me, connected me with others, shared published and unpublished sources, and helped me in innumerable other ways: Abdulnabi Alekry, Ali Abdulemam, Ghassan Saʿeed Asbool, Ali al-Mahdi al-Aswad, Sheyma Buali, Salma Dabbagh, Ahmed al-Dailami, Lamees al-Dhayf, Munira Fakhro, Farida Ismael Ghulam, Abdulhadi Khalaf, Amal Khalaf, ʿAdel Marzouk, Nicola Pratt, Alaʾa al-Shehabi, May Seikaly, Hussain Abdullah al-Shabib, Nadia Yaqub, and Banu Gökarıksel. Finally I thank the participants in the Geographies of Gender in the Arab Revolutions Workshop held at Duke University in December 2013 for their generous and extremely helpful feedback.

1. I borrow this term from Judith Butler. Vikki Bell, "On Speech, Race and Melancholia: An Interview with Judith Butler," *Theory, Culture and Society* (April 1999): 168.

2. Michael Omi and Howard Winant, *Racial Formation in the United States: From the 1960s to the 1990s*, 2nd edition (New York: Routledge, 1994).

3. Michael Omi and Howard Winant, "Once More, with Feeling: Reflections on Racial Formation," *PMLA* 123, no. 5 (2008): 1567.

4. Priya Kandaswamy, "Gendering Racial Formation," in *Racial Formation in the Twenty-First Century*, edited by Daniel Martinez HoSang, Oneka LaBennett, and Laura Pulido (Berkeley: University of California Press, 2012), 23.

5. Zaheer Baber, "'Race,' Religion and Riots: The 'Racialization' of Communal Identity and Conflict in India," *Sociology* 38, no. 4 (2004): 702–3, 706, 711. On phenotype and morphology in the racial formations approach, see Nikhil Singh, "Racial Formation in an Age of Permanent War," in HoSang et al., *Racial Formation in the Twenty-First Century*, 277.

6. Ussama Makdisi, *The Culture of Sectarianism: Community, History, and Violence in Nineteenth-Century Ottoman Lebanon* (Berkeley: University of California Press, 2000), 5–7.

7. Kandaswamy, "Gendering Racial Formation," 24, 25, 40.

8. Jacques Rancière, "Ten Theses on Politics," *Theory and Event* 5, no. 3 (2001): 1–4 (Thesis 1), 11–13, http://muse.jhu.edu/journals/theory_and_event/v005/5.3ranciere .html; Jacques Rancière, "The Thinking of Dissensus: Politics and Aesthetics," in *Reading Rancière: Critical Dissensus*, edited by Paul Bowman and Richard Stamp (London: Continuum, 2001), 1–17.

9. Bahrain has separate maʾtams for women and men and more than one of each of these structures in most villages, towns, and cities; sometimes they are attached to

Shiʿa mosques. For more information, see Fuad Khuri, *Tribe and State in Bahrain: The Transformation of Social and Political Authority in an Arab State* (Chicago: University of Chicago Press, 1980), 154; Sophia Pandya, *Muslim Women and Islamic Resurgence: Religion, Education, and Identity Politics in Bahrain* (London: I. B. Tauris, 2012), 83–87; Sophia Pandya, "Women's Shiʿi Maʾatim in Bahrain," *Journal of Middle East Women's Studies* 6, no. 2 (2010): 31–58.

10. Reporters without Borders, "Countries under Surveillance: Bahrain," n.d., http://en.rsf.org/surveillance-bahrain,39748.html; "Bahrain to Set Up New Surveillance System," *TradeArabia Business News Information*, 7 September 2013, http://www.tradearabia .com/news/LAW_242349.html; Privacy International, "Surveillance Briefing: Bahrain. The Role of Surveillance Technology Companies," 2012, accessed 2014, https://www .privacyinternational.org/reports/surveillance-briefing-bahrain/the-role-of-surveillance -technology-companies; English News Today—Russia Today, "Surveillance for Sale: UK Exports Spyware to Bahrain," YouTube, 5 August 2013, accessed 2014, https://www .youtube.com/watch?v=90-hkiT8fHw.

11. For an interview-based discussion with Judith Butler on subjection and subjectification in relation to gender and racialization, see Bell, "On Speech, Race and Melancholia."

12. Citizens include Shiʿa and Sunni of Arab and Persian origin, Jews and Christians of Arab and Persian origin, Muslims of African and South Asian origin, and other ethnicities, identifications, and mixtures. The state gathers no public data that I am aware of on sect proportions among citizens, but it is widely known and accepted that Shiʿa of Arab origin composed about two-thirds of citizens at the beginning of the twenty-first century.

13. Andrew M. Gardner, *City of Strangers: Gulf Migration and the Indian Community in Bahrain* (Ithaca: Cornell University Press, 2010); Bahrain Census 2010 (Arabic), accessed 28 September 2013, http://www.census2010.gov.bh/results.php. The 2010 data indicate a dramatic rise in foreign residents since 2001, but without extensive research I cannot provide a definitive explanation for this.

14. Sheyma Buali, "Mapping the Marginals," unpublished paper, 26 June 2013, kindly provided by the author.

15. See article, diagrams, and especially videos on land appropriation by the ruling regime: Justin Gengler, "How the Failure of Gulf Air Explains the Failure of Bahrain," *Bahrain Politics*, 29 January 2012, http://bahrainipolitics.blogspot.com/2012/01/how -failure-of-gulf-air-explains.html; Joshua Eaton, "What's Really Going On in Bahrain: An Interview with Activist Alaʾa al-Shehabi," *Spare Change News*, 14 June 2013, http:// sparechangenews.net/2013/06/whats-really-going-on-in-bahrain-an-interview-with -activist-alaa-shehabi/.

16. Prime Minister Sheikh Khalifa bin Salman al Khalifa, King Hamad bin Isa al Khalifa, and Crown Prince and Deputy Supreme Commander Sheikh Salman bin Hamad al Khalifa, "Our Vision: From Regional Pioneer to Global Contender. The Economic Vision 2030 for Bahrain," 2008, http://www.mofa.gov.bh/img/partners/Vision2030Englishlow resolution.pdf. Tellingly the Arabic hyperlink in the top right hand of the page resulted in "404 not found" (last checked 23 February 2016): http://www.bahrainedb.com/en /about/Pages/economic%20vision%202030.aspx#.UkLxJW3ODTT. See images: http:// humanette.blogspot.com/2010/06/gulf-ads-on-black-cabs.html.

17. For articles and images on Northern Town in construction and business publications, see Bahrain Projects and Construction Forum, SkyscraperCity, http://www.skyscrapercity.com/showthread.php?t=321441; "Bahrain Will Not Meet Housing Targets—Minister," *Construction Week Online*, 30 March 2013, http://www.construction weekonline.com/article-21633-bahrain-will-not-meet-housing-targets—minister/#.UkML-W3ODTR; "Bahrain Building 30,000 Homes for Citizens," *TradeArabia Business News Information*, 23 January 2013, http://www.tradearabia.com/news/CONS_229451.html.

18. For information on and images of Amwaj Islands, see the corporate website http://www.amwaj.bh/; http://www.amwaj-islands.com/about-amwaj-islands/; "Bahrain Developments," *Click Bahrain*, n.d., http://www.clickbahrain.com/clickbahrain_developments.asp, which includes information on many development projects in Bahrain; and the *Amwaj Families Bahrain* Facebook page, with over eight hundred likes: https://www.facebook.com/AmwajfamiliesBahrain.

19. Currently with about two thousand residents, Amwaj was one of a few places it was safe enough for organizers to physically meet to plan the 14 February 2011 uprising. Those who could afford to moved there in February and March 2011, although public figures such as the physician Nada Dhaif were arrested on the island beginning in late March.

20. Nelida Fuccaro, "Understanding the Urban History of Bahrain," *Critique: Critical Middle Eastern Studies* 9, no. 17 (2000): 49–81. During a July 2013 interview with me in London, the Bahraini sociologist Abdulhadi Khalaf explained that residential segregation based on sect decreased in the 1920s and 1930s with the establishment of common places of interaction such as the British oil company BAPCO and public schooling. By the mid-twentieth century Bahrainis who had "improved their income" had moved to new neighborhoods "open to everyone." In response sects were determined in advance in state public housing projects such as ʿIsa Town, built in the 1960s, although "in the end the township, markets, clinic, and so on were common to both groups, which worked nicely for the integrationists but not the regime."

21. ʿAbbas Mirza al-Marshad and ʿAbdulhadi Al-Khawaja provide a history of Bahrain's political organizations since the early twentieth century in *Political Organizations and Societies in Bahrain: A Descriptive Human Rights Study* (Arabic) (Manama, Bahrain: Faradis, 2008).

22. Khuri, *Tribe and State in Bahrain*, 123–33.

23. Staci Strobl, "The Women's Police Directorate in Bahrain: An Ethnographic Exploration of Gender Segregation and the Likelihood of Future Integration," *International Criminal Justice Review* 18, no. 1 (2008): 39–58.

24. The sociologist Abdulhadi Khalaf describes the Bahraini system as a classic case of "vertical segmentation," whereby people relate to each other and access resources through patrons who are either part of the ruling regime or obsequious to it. The logic of the Bahrain police force strongly resembles that of *fidawi* personal militias of Al Khalifa estate sheikhs in the nineteenth and twentieth century. Composed of nontribal Sunnis, slaves of African origin, and Baluchis, fidawis were "the coercive instrument[s] of the estate" and its Khalifa sovereign until the estates were abolished by the British in the early 1920s (Khuri, *Tribe and State in Bahrain*, 47, 114). For more on policing in Bahrain, see Khuri,

Tribe and State in Bahrain, 89–90, 110, 122, 114–15; Staci Strobl, "From Colonial Policing to Community Policing in Bahrain: The Historical Persistence of Sectarianism," *International Journal of Comparative and Applied Criminal Justice* 35, no. 1 (2011): 19–39; Nelida Fuccaro, *Histories of City and State in the Persian Gulf: Manama since 1800* (Cambridge: Cambridge University Press, 2009), 157–60. Bahraini Shiʿa clerics benefit from a similar system of segmentation based on allegiance of followers that in turn translates into resources for their *mathhab* (school of religious authority). Certain Sunni and Shiʿa clerics benefit from government appointments to oversee *waqf* (religious) properties, which they may lease out for their rent-seeking interests, including to relatives and friends.

25. The first Parliament, of 1973, considered a polarizing proposal by an alliance of Sunni and Shiʿa clerics to gender-segregate medical services and higher education, which "the government considered positively." The matter was superseded by other conflicts, and Parliament was dissolved by the emir in 1975, according to Abdulhadi Khalaf, who was elected to that Parliament.

26. A well-traveled activist in her thirties who is alert to gender inequalities among Bahrainis noted that Bahraini men are "very respectful of women" and that rates of gendered violence are comparatively low. It is difficult to ascertain this matter systematically or to know if it is as proportionally true for low-status migrant workers in their relations with each other or with Bahraini employers who sponsor their residency. See Gardner, *City of Strangers*, for forms of "structural violence" faced by Indian migrant men in Bahrain.

27. For a historical snapshot of daily lives, food, dress styles, built environment, and gendered dress, mobility, and spatial practices in analysis, diagrams, and photographs, see a rare PhD dissertation based on 1960 fieldwork in the Bahrain village of Saar by the Danish anthropologist Henny Harald Hansen, "Investigations in a Shiʿa Village in Bahrain," PhD diss., National Museum of Denmark, 1968.

28. Sandy Russell Jones, "God's Law or State's Law: Authority and Islamic Family Law Reform in Bahrain," PhD diss., University of Pennsylvania, 2010, especially 2–18, 177–78, 210.

29. Shiʿa women in Bahrain may choose to follow the Sunni family law code as an option in family courts.

30. Laurence Louër, *Shiism and Politics in the Middle East*, translated by John King (London: C. Hurst, 2012), 102; Khuri, *Tribe and State in Bahrain*, 194–97; Fuccaro, *Histories of City and State in the Persian Gulf*, 151–60.

31. Between mid-March and mid-May 2011, the Bahrain Ministry of Justice and Islamic Affairs and Waqf demolished over twenty-eight Shiʿa mosques and religious buildings on the stated basis that they were unlicensed, including a mosque in Aali that was over two hundred years old and another in Sitra that was about one hundred years old; a McClatchy story reports the number of demolitions to be "far greater." The regime has made it difficult to rebuild mosques and has demolished licensed building in progress. See "Bahrain Targets Shia Religious Sites," *Al Jazeera*, 14 May 2011, http://www.aljazeera.com /video/middleeast/2011/05/201151311201638948.html; Roy Gutman, "While Bahrain Demolishes Mosques, U.S. Stays Silent," Truthout, 8 May 2011, http://www.truth-out.org /news/item/977:while-bahrain-demolishes-mosques-us-stays-silent; Bahrain Center

for Human Rights, "Mosques under Construction Re-Demolished by Authorities in Bahrain," 9 December 2012, http://www.bahrainrights.org/en/node/5550. YouTube videos sourced to *Al Jazeera*'s website could not be watched in the United States.

32. Louër, *Shiism and Politics in the Middle East*, 102.

33. The full text of the National Action Charter can be found at http://www.bahrain-embassy.or.jp/en/national_action_charter.pdf. In gendered terms this is a conservative document but includes commitments to enfranchise Bahrainis of Shiʿa origin and address economic and social inequalities. The key provisions of this charter have not been implemented.

34. Bahrain Online was established by Bahraini cyber activists in 1999.

35. Bahrain Online's Facebook page is at https://www.facebook.com/note.php?note_id=138126829585520.

36. Wikimedia Commons image of the 4 February 2011 event is at http://en.wikipedia.org/wiki/File:Bahrain_protest_Egypt_embassy.jpg. See "Bahrain Opposition Calls for Rally," *Al Jazeera*, 13 February 2011, http://www.aljazeera.com/news/middleeast/2011/02/2011213185556388117.html.

37. "Death of Ali Abdulhadi Mushaima," Wikipedia, http://en.wikipedia.org/wiki/Death_of_Ali_Abdulhadi_Mushaima.

38. Video outside Salmaniyya Medical Complex is at "Bahrain: The Fall of the Martyr Fadhel Matruk" (Arabic), YouTube, 15 February 2001, http://www.youtube.com/watch?v=o_-UjXiEoBg. "Death of Fadhel Al-Matrook," Wikipedia, http://en.wikipedia.org/wiki/Death_of_Fadhel_Al-Matrook.

39. Images from 13–15 February 2011 (in reverse order): "Bahrain Protest Photos," Cryptome, 17 February 2011, http://cryptome.org/info/bahrain-protest/bahrain-protest.htm. An op-ed by an observer about the early days of the encampment: Ayesha Saldanha, "Three Days at the Pearl Roundabout," *New York Times*, 18 February 2011, http://www.nytimes.com/2011/02/19/opinion/19battuta.html?_r=0%20%28op%20ed%20about%20pearl%20roundabout.

40. Roundabout activists reported pressure from Bahraini opposition leaders in London to name an organization because those outside worried that the moderate al-Wefaq, established in 2001, "would take over."

41. The statement (provided to me by an activist who was part of the encampment) called for a new constitution drawn by a democratic parliament, a parliament-elected prime minister, an independent judiciary, freedom of opinion and expression, a constitutional monarchy based on "separation of three powers," release of all political prisoners, an end to "political naturalization," investigations of corruption and return of looted wealth, and accountability for torture, killing, and other violence.

42. Al-Wefaq, for example, ran parliamentary candidates in the 2000s, all of whom resigned in 2011. The main oppositional trends in Bahrain eschewed such participation given a problematic constitutional framework.

43. A series of images that include 17 and 18 February is available here: Alan Taylor, "Deadly Attacks against Protesters in Bahrain," *Atlantic*, 18 February 2011, http://www.theatlantic.com/infocus/2011/02/deadly-attacks-against-protesters-in-bahrain/100011/; "Bahrain Protests: Your Stories," *BBC News*, 19 February 2011, http://www.bbc.co.uk/news

/world-middle-east-12516237. The following joint statement was released following the 17 February statement: "Statement of Civil Society Organizations in Bahrain Regarding the Brutal Attack on Protesters in the Pearl Roundabout," *Jadaliyya*, 29 February 2011, http://www.jadaliyya.com/pages/index/688/statement-of-civil-society-organizations-in-bahrain-regarding-the-brutal-attack-on-protesters-in-the-pearl-roundabout.

44. "Thousands Protest Government in Bahrain," Reuters, 22 February 2011, http://www.reuters.com/article/video/idUSTRE71IoX320110222?videoId=189186386; "As Protest March Unfolds, Bahrain Urges 'National Dialogue,'" CNN, 22 February 2011, http://www.cnn.com/2011/WORLD/meast/02/22/bahrain.protests/.

45. YouTube postdating is based on time in California. See hyya999, "Video of Repression of the Pearl Roundabout for Today 16/3/2011" (Arabic), YouTube, 15 March 2011, http://www.youtube.com/watch?v=ebTu9Z6qRiQ#t=60; Xgotfiveonitx, "Bahrain: Hundreds of Bahraini Police Launch Assault on Pro-Democracy Protesters in Capital Manama," YouTube, 16 March 2011, http://www.youtube.com/watch?v=PrBLzjJQqks.

46. Martin Chulov, "Bahrain Destroys Pearl Roundabout: Focal Point of Pro-Democracy Protests Demolished as Authorities Try to Rid Capital, Manama, of Demonstrators," *Guardian*, 18 March 2011, http://www.guardian.co.uk/world/2011/mar/18/bahrain-destroys-pearl-roundabout. Also see videos of the 17 February attack on protesters in the Pearl Roundabout on "Pearl No More: Demolishing the Infrastructure of Revolution," *Jadaliyya*, 18 March 2011, http://www.jadaliyya.com/pages/index/956/pearl-no-more_demolishing-the-infrastructure-of-re.

47. Amal Khalaf, "The Many Afterlives of Lulu: The Story of Bahrain's Pearl Roundabout," *Ibraaz*, 28 February 2013, http://www.ibraaz.org/essays/56. A slightly revised version of this essay was later published as Amal Khalaf, "Squaring the Circle: Bahrain's Pearl Roundabout," "The Arab Uprisings of 2011," special issue, *Middle East Critique* 22, no. 3 (2013): 265–80.

48. See Facebook page of The Decisive Moment (Arabic), https://www.facebook.com/pages/%D8%A7%D9%84%D9%84%D8%AD%D8%B8%D8%A9-%D8%A7%D9%84%D8%AD%D8%A7%D8%B3%D9%85%D8%A9-The-Decisive-Moment/195331817226817; Abu Haider, "#Bahrain: #Sitra-Avnu 6 Clashes on 31-12-2011. #The Decisive Moment," YouTube, 31 December 2011, http://www.youtube.com/watch?v=M5YykRCmdIw.

49. The Coalition of 14 February Youth Facebook page, 15 June 2013, https://www.facebook.com/photo.php?fbid=572121369505565&set=a.178717292179310.64487.178269738890732&type=1&theater.

50. The Coalition of 14 February Youth Facebook page, 15 June 2013, https://www.facebook.com/photo.php?fbid=572127979504904&set=a.178717292179310.64487.178269738890732&type=1&theater.

51. The Coalition of 14 February Youth Facebook page, 15 June 2013, https://www.facebook.com/photo.php?fbid=572151832835852&set=a.178717292179310.64487.178269738890732&type=1&theater.

52. Al-Shahid Muhammad (Arabic), "Bahrain: Burning a Police State after Killing a Protester," YouTube, 8 February 2012, accessed 3 July 2014, https://www.youtube.com/watch?v=NniIgQNsphk.

53. "Voices of the Network: Bahraini Women Are the Frontline of Protests" (Arabic), *France 24 Arabic*, YouTube, 19 January 2012, https://www.youtube.com/watch?feature =player_embedded&v=Lr-pqYQ-CKY. The segment is based on an interview with a twenty-something Bahraini woman (face is blurred) describing women's activism.

54. The active involvement of women and men in Formula 1 protests is illustrated in "Bahrain Grand Prix Formula 1 Highlights Tensions between Government and Protesters," *World Post*, 20 April 2013, http://www.huffingtonpost.com/2013/04/20/bahrain -grand-prix-formula-1_n_3123285.html. A rare film of revolutionary action and interviews made undercover by the French filmmaker Stéphanie LaMorré is "Documentaire: Bahrein, plongé dans un pays interdit," 17 August 2012 (Arabic and French, with occasional English), https://www.youtube.com/watch?feature=player_embedded&v=ToD_FjjK _bc (URL terminated).

55. A moving representation of the release of women medical personnel is Biladi4feb, "Greeting the Freed Heroine Rula Al-Saffar 2011-8-21" (Arabic), YouTube, 21 August 2011, https://www.youtube.com/watch?feature=player_embedded&v=Q3_32Xsu4N4. A story about the physician Nihad al-Shirawi is in *Al-Wasat*, 12 November 2011, http://www .alwasatnews.com/3353/news/read/607954/1.html. A video of a nurse, Rula al-Saffar, giving a talk at an al-Wefaq event with her hair uncovered is Bahraini Bahrani, "Daih Video" (Arabic), YouTube, 12 May 2012, https://www.youtube.com/watch?feature=player _embedded&v=SqRsqoggACU.

56. Thirty percent of al-Wefaq board members are women; the Shura Council includes elected women; and women are three of ten members of the General Secretariat, according to al-Wefaq leaders I conversed with in London.

57. A video recording of al-Qurmezi's performance is at Shayala13alam, "Ayat Al-Qormezi—A Poem Worth a Year of Brutal Torture and Imprisonment [Eng Subs]," YouTube, 15 June 2011, http://www.youtube.com/watch?v=mcCEk9s82ac. The xenophobic remarks appear at 6:09. Richard Spencer, "Bahraini Woman Poet Tells of Torture While in Custody," *Telegraph*, 14 July 2011, http://www.telegraph.co.uk/news/worldnews /middleeast/bahrain/8638396/Bahraini-woman-poet-tells-of-torture-while-in-custody .html. The video "Verses of Bahrain and the Revolutionary Poet" (Arabic), uploaded to YouTube by AhrarQatif on 6 May 2011, discusses her imprisonment and torture and includes an interview with her mother: http://www.youtube.com/watch?feature=player _embedded&v=PhdBVszx5Io#at=51.

58. Hsamar, "City Center Protest #Bahrain," YouTube, 23 September 2011, https://www .youtube.com/watch?feature=player_embedded&v=JJdaqApuA2EIn.

59. Eeyore, "Caught on Camera: Female Human Rights Activist Handcuffed and Dragged along Ground for Sitting on a Roundabout (and Now SHE's Been Charged with Assault)," *Vlad Tepes*, 17 December 2011, http://vladtepesblog.com/2011/12/17/caught -on-camera-female-human-rights-activist-handcuffed-and-dragged-along-ground-for -sitting-on-a-roundabout-and-now-shes-been-charged-with-assault/.

60. Melissa Bell, "'Angry Arabiya,' Bahraini Activist and Danish Citizen, Released from Jail," *Washington Post*, 21 December 2011, http://www.washingtonpost.com/blogs /blogpost/post/angry-arabiya-bahraini-activist-and-dutch-citizen-released-from-jail /2011/12/21/gIQAmooD9O_blog.html. This account is notable for al-Khawaja's tweets

upon release from prison; she comments on a woman political prisoner left behind as well as "hugging and cuddling" her daughter Jude. Preethi Nallu, "The Khawajas on Valentine's: Heartbeats of Activism," *Al-Akhbar English*, 14 February 2012, http://english.al-akhbar.com/node/4157/. Her remarks on motherhood appear at 16:10.

61. Sadeq Shehab, "Rihanna Al-Musawi Astonishing Court Hearing Strikes Bahrain with Anger," Corbis Images, 12 July 2013, http://www.corbisimages.com/stock-photo/rights-managed/42-49764509/rihanna-almusawi-astonishing-court-hearing-strikes-bahrain; Yumna Marwan, "Bahraini Women Activists Detained, Beaten," *Al-Akhbar English*, 2 May 2013, http://english.al-akhbar.com/node/15687; "Naked Regime: This Is Why Rihana Al-Musawi Was Targeted," *Bahrain Mirror*, 17 July 2013, http://bhmirror.no-ip.biz/news/10266.html.

62. Abdulhadi Khalaf, "Double Efforts to Contain Women's Mobility in Bahrain" (Arabic), *Al-Safir Al-Arabi*, 10 October 2012, http://arabi.assafir.com/article.asp?aid=344&refsite=arabi&reftype=home&refzone=slider.

63. "Recruited Activists in the Dirtiest Game . . . the Latest Trap by the Authorities" (Arabic), *Mirat al-Bahrayn*, 16 July 2012, http://bh-mirror.no-ip.org/news/5069.html.

64. Khalaf, "The Many Afterlives of Lulu," 17.

65. Bahrain Shield, "Pictures of the Scandals of the Mut'a Roundabout Published for the First Time" (Arabic), YouTube, 7 June 2011, http://www.youtube.com/watch?v=A1h5LZzcd9I&list=PLTOgz3bT-TwV7tgKYDDJFYFR1DkDmIer&index=14&feature=plpp_video; Bahrain Shield, "Witness What Happened to Girl Students in the Roundabout" (Arabic), YouTube, 15 June 2011, http://www.youtube.com/watch?v=9dyoIwoHLmQ.

66. Lualua, "Stations with Lamees al-Dhayf: The Exploitation of Women's Sexuality" (*Jinsaniyyat al-mar'a*), YouTube, 1 June 2013, https://www.youtube.com/watch?v=epecpU4NWWw. This is a weekly segment on the satellite television station Lualua. Bahrain material begins about four minutes into the video, and remarks described in the text are at 4:37 and 5:10.

67. Frances S. Hasso, *Consuming Desires: Family Crisis and the State in the Middle East* (Stanford, CA: Stanford University Press, 2011), 124–25.

68. Hasa is the area between Qatif and Salwa, a Shi'a-dominant oasis region that was part of historic Bahrain.

69. Gillian Rose, *Feminism and Geography: The Limits of Geographical Knowledge* (Minneapolis: University of Minnesota Press, 1993), 137, 138.

5 **"THE WOMEN ARE COMING"** Gender, Space, and
the Politics of Inauguration ZAKIA SALIME

The rise of the 20 February Movement in Morocco (Feb20) took many by
surprise. The movement's call for protests on 20 February 2011 raised questions about its ability to destabilize the state and bridge divisions among
an elite invested in the rule of King Mohamed VI. Many have since argued
that the movement's inability to change the regime indicates multiple class,
ethnic, and gender divisions among political elites and the youth movement. Political elites and established feminist groups support the king as
the symbol of stability, the guarantor of urbanite-neoliberal mobility, and
the enforcer of a state-feminist gender policy. As the North African revolts
took sexist, sectarian, and militarized turns, anxiety regarding instability
deepened the disengagement of these elites from the 20 February Movement. These anxieties reinforced elite rhetoric of Morocco's "exceptionalism" and contentions that Feb20 would have a limited impact on the political field.[1]

I argue, in contrast, that Feb20 inaugurated a process that multiplied
feminist and political spaces of expression, including by "ordinary" people,
or those individuals whose subjectivities, senses of self, and conceptions
of rights and desires cannot be contained within the discursive regimes
of gender equality, rights, or legal rationality.[2] The Feb20 Movement interrupted politics conceived around *already given* identities, spaces, and
strategies of mobilization by forging new categories of nationhood and belonging that opened multiple possibilities for the discursive, performative,
and aesthetic co-imbrication of sex, gender, culture, and politics. Feb20

incorporated gender struggle into a social justice and equality framework while initiating new modalities around which political, gendered, and sexual identities could be formed, narrated, and performed. I am particularly interested in the feminist enunciations the movement generated, as well as the gap between an imagined egalitarian gender order and disappointing everyday encounters with male activists. Rather than limiting feminist spaces, these gaps multiplied the possibilities of feminist activism within and beyond the movement.

Political theorists argue that space inaugurates politics and vice versa.[3] Hannah Arendt contends that politics can emerge only in "a space of appearance," where people appear to one another in public space.[4] As bodies create their own space of appearance, they interrupt the stabilization of "politics" as "discourses, practices and institutions" and open possibilities for the emergence of "politics" in Jacques Rancière's terms, as dissensus.[5] Rancière argues, "The essence of politics is the reconfiguration of its own space. It is to make the world of its subjects and its operations seen. The essence of politics is the manifestation of dissensus, as the presence of two worlds in one."[6] Consistent with Arendt's understanding of politics as a "space-making plurality" that inaugurates "a new beginning" and sets "something into motion,"[7] Feb20 activists understand themselves as a "dynamic," *harakiyya* or *dinamiyya*, rather than a "social movement," *haraka ijtima'iyya*. Whereas "a movement can rise and fall, a dynamic, once inaugurated, is here to stay," an activist explains. Harakiyya opens new spaces, generates possibilities, and creates tensions and contradictions that enable multiplicity and dissensus.

In this chapter I map the Feb20 Movement and explore the fissures, tensions, and connections it generated. I analyze the movement's politics of inauguration in two video mobilization calls that challenged the partition of time, space, and voice among men and women as socially situated bodies. I examine gendered dynamics within the many spaces of encounter between men and women and explore the multiplicative effect of Feb20 on feminist modes of protests. I show how these protests took a *sexual turn* that brought women's bodies and body parts to the core of public debate, cyber activism, artistic production, and performance. I have observed Feb20 events and interacted with activists through social media and other virtual sites and in face-to-face meetings over the past few years. I completed in-depth interviews with thirty members of the movement, fifteen men and fifteen women, between May 2011 and January 2014. I attended a

November 2013 meeting in Rabat where more than sixty activists from all over Morocco gathered to assess their movement's successes and failures. I interviewed four members of the National Council of Support for Feb20 and made several visits to al-Wassit, a nongovernmental organization in Rabat that includes many Feb20 activists. I examined virtual sources, including Facebook, blogs, online feminist magazines, and YouTube clips. Though Feb20 members do not work in secrecy, I protect the identities of participants at various points in the chapter given the continuous state policing of protests and intimidation of male activists. Several Feb20 male activists are under arrest; others were killed in early demonstrations and during periodic government crackdowns on protesters. Recurrent state targeting of Feb20 male activists speaks to the gender-specific criminalization and "hypervisibility" of male bodies, which also works to make women invisible as agents of political dissent.[8]

Lines of Division

In euphoric responses to the uprisings in North Africa, virtual groups, notably the Network of Solidarity with the Peoples (Shabakat al-tadamun maʿ al-shuʿub), organized street protests in front of the Tunisian, Egyptian, and Libyan Embassies in Rabat. Debates about Morocco's political system preexist the uprisings in 2011, including several social media networks and groups that formed, merged, or dissolved.[9] The ousting of presidents Zine al Abidine Ben Ali and Hosni Mubarak encouraged activists to articulate proper demands for Morocco: "We thought it was possible, after we had seen how quickly Ben Ali just vanished." The Facebook group Freedom and Democracy Now inaugurated the Moroccan revolutionary scene in early February by calling for street rallies on 20 February and establishing the Twitter hashtag #Feb20, which produced the 20 February Movement for Change.[10]

Two video calls released in mid-February 2011 and a press conference held on 17 February publicly announced the Feb20 Movement's demands. Soon after the group's establishment, members of small leftist political parties (including al-Taliʿa, the Unified Socialist Party, and Annahj al-dimuqrati) and most labor unions and human rights organizations formed the National Council of Support (NCS) of Feb20, a coalition of 130 organizations. The main political parties, including Istiqlal, Union Socialiste des

Forces Populaires, and the Parti du Progrès et du Socialisme, did not want to join the coalition. The NCS adopted a gender quota requiring that at least one of the three representatives of each member organization had to be a woman. The Moroccan Human Rights Association played an instrumental role by hosting the press conference and offering logistical support for production of the video calls.

During the press conference publicly announcing the Feb20 demands, nineteen-year-old Tahani Madmad read a memorandum that highlighted the many organizational committees and the peaceful character of the planned protests.[11] She defined the movement as a "youth dynamic" that was "secular, modernist [*hadathi*], democratic, and independent of all foreign agendas or political affiliations." The movement's goal was to see the "flag of freedom, equality and social justice reign over Morocco through peaceful means." She warned that "no sectarian, political, or religious slogans that would point to a particular affiliation are authorized" during the protests.

By stressing the civil, nonsectarian, and secular sensibilities of the movement, Feb20 activists positioned themselves against the main sources of legitimation of political power in Morocco. The Moroccan Constitution stipulates the shari'a as one of the sources of legislation, Islam as the official religion of the nation, and Arabic as the national language. It proclaims the king "Commander of the Faithful." Founding members of Feb20 claimed, in contrast, that the Moroccan Constitution separates "state and religion," that "human rights are universal," and that faith has a "personal character." These secular sensibilities manifested in a ban on all religious slogans during protests.

The movement located its demands at the nexus of an "interlocking system" of political, economic, and cultural oppressions:[12] dissolution of Parliament and the government, a new constitution, decent housing and free education, access to jobs and better wages, and recognition of Tamazight as a national language. Activists called for representative institutions, a *civil* state, and a modern political system in which the king "reigns but does not rule," which they initially called "a constitutional monarchy." The calls for social justice did not emerge in a vacuum since most of the founding members had been active in the Moroccan Association of Human Rights, as well as radical leftist political parties and labor unions, most notably the Tali'a and Annahj al-dimuqrati parties. The demands reinforced what

FIGURE 5.1. Tahani Madmad introducing the 20 February Movement at a press conference, 17 February 2011. Screenshot from "Conférence de Presse du Mouvement 20 Fevrier," YouTube, 17 February 2011, http://www.youtube.com/watch?v=-i9mEB _sWnw.

activists called *tarbiyya huquqiyya*, ideological rearing in labor struggles, socialist groups, and Moroccan human rights organizations that produce a human rights sensibility or culture.

In a highly significant early moment of the protests, Feb20 pointed to the fusion of economic, religious, and symbolic power in the hands of the king and the privileges enjoyed by his entourage, and called for an end to the corruption and social injustices related to these privileges.[13] At the onset of Feb20 mobilizations, two French journalists published *Le Roi Predateur*, which fueled the debate about social justice in an already inflamed street.[14] In response to the mobilization calls, hundreds of thousands of Moroccans rallied in more than fifty cities and towns on 20 February under the unifying slogans "Dignity, Liberty, Social Justice" and "End Corruption."

Because Feb20's founding members wanted to communicate the civil and secular sensibilities of the new movement, they did not allow the banned Islamist Justice and Spirituality Movement to be part of the first waves of protests. Justice and Spirituality is without a doubt the largest political opposition to the monarchy and, according to many studies, the largest Islamist force in the country.[15] Its decision to participate in Feb20 protests offered thousands of bodies easily mobilized, since members are regulated by a pyramidal structure of authority based on obedience to the late Sheikh Abdessalam Yassine, follow a Sufi tradition of self-discipline, have long experience with civil disobedience, and mobilize a Gramscian understanding of change as produced by intervention in civil society. Hence accepting this mobilizing and mobilized force in the 20 February Movement was not only a strategic decision but also reflected Feb20's commitment to political pluralism. However, this inclusion required Justice and Spirituality to adhere to the general goals of the Feb20 Movement, including the ban on all religious expression during protests, which explains why it was integrated only after the first rallies on 20 February 2011. The second Islamist force in Morocco is the Justice and Development Party, which initially announced its support of peaceful protests and then withdrew support, allowing its youth, organized under the label Baraka, to take to the street if they wished. Justice and Development won the elections after the uprising. The leading feminist organizations—the Democratic Association for Women's Rights, the Democratic League for Women's Rights, and the Union of Women's Action—were absent from the NCS despite being instrumental in the institutionalization of "gender equality" in the family code, previously known as the *mudawwana*.[16] Leaders of these feminist organizations shared with me their concerns that in the early period, Feb20 marginalized gender equality under the general goal of political change. They feared that women's issues were again subsumed under broad categories of social justice and worried that weakening the authority of the king could mean the loss of painfully gained rights in case Islamists won elections.

These divisions reflected ideological and strategic differences among political elites in relation to the protest scene and the state, viewed mainly through a cost-benefit logic, as well as generational and class divides.

After the initial large rallies, Feb20 organized weekly protests across the country as determined by each locality's needs. A monthly national rally provided opportunities to unite local independent coordinating committees (*tansiqiyyat*) under similar slogans. As in most Arab uprisings, Feb20 does not have a center or a leader,[17] although the coordinating committee in Rabat is an important engine.

Recognizing an emerging crisis of legitimacy, on 9 March 2011 King Mohamed VI addressed the nation on television, responding to some of Feb20's demands without explicitly acknowledging the movement. He called for a referendum on a new constitution on 16 May and early legislative elections in November. He stipulated equal citizenship rights for women, or "gender parity," and recognized Tamazight as a national language along with Arabic. But Feb20 rejected such "a gifted constitution" and called for a boycott of the referendum.[18] Most political parties and mainstream media nevertheless rallied behind the king's reforms. Established feminist organizations rushed to prepare proposals for gender equality and parity for the newly appointed Royal Committee of Constitutional Reform, an opportunistic approach that widened the breach between them and Feb20 activists. During the November legislative elections the Islamist Justice and Development Party won the majority of seats and formed the first Islamist-led government in Morocco's history.

Languages of Performative Pluralism

The 20 February Movement circulated calls for protest in two video clips released in mid-February on YouTube.[19] The "I Am Moroccan" and "Who Are We?" videos stage ethnic, class, and gender sensibilities through the distribution of bodies, faces, languages, and clothing. Men and women alternated in claims making that announced the "end of fear." They were carefully selected to voice different Moroccan accents, dialects, and languages. The translations of the mobilization videos into English and French facilitated transnational circulation, as Feb20 members formed sections on European and North American university campuses.

The video calls disrupted conventional understandings of spatiality and politics by challenging normative divisions between private/public, male/female, and politics/culture. The redistribution of bodies in these visual and virtual enactments showed that bodies are not merely surfaces for inscription of certain political and gendered regimes but material spaces for interruption of normative orders. The video clips also demonstrated the space-body nexus as the site for new political possibilities and openings. This orchestration of gendered bodies in virtual spaces illustrates politics as "dissensus," a "reconfiguration of the distribution of the sensible," as is clear in the repartitioning of languages, voices, and faces in the videos.[20]

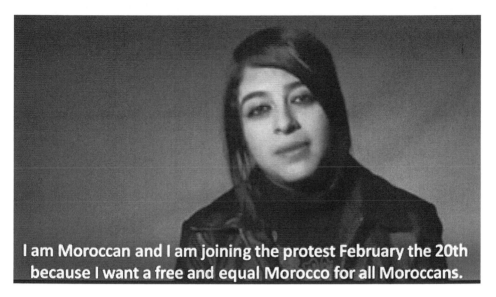

I am Moroccan and I am joining the protest February the 20th because I want a free and equal Morocco for all Moroccans.

FIGURE 5.2. Amina Boughalbi, a founder of the 20 February Movement, in the "I Am Moroccan" video clip. Mariamelmas9, "Morocco Campaign #Feb20 #Morocco," YouTube, 16 February 2011, http://www.youtube.com/watch?v=S0f6FSB7gxQ.

In the "I Am Moroccan" clip Feb20 activists weave the goals of the movement in a clear redistribution of time, space, signs, voices, and images. The clip is only two minutes long and includes fourteen people, five of them women. The speakers alternate to make their demands in Arabic, Darija, and Tamazight beginning with the first-person statement "I am Moroccan and I am joining the protest on 20 February because I want . . ." The statements move to the collective "all Moroccans" in the same sentence: "I am Moroccan. I am joing the protest on 20 February because I want free education for all." The statements were filmed against a plain backdrop, and the YouTube video is captioned in English. With the exception of an older woman, the speakers are in their teens and twenties.

Gender is central to the performative pluralism of the "I Am Moroccan" video clip, which opens with the face and voice of a young woman, Amina Boughalbi, wearing a black, leather-like jacket and closes with the strong words and expressive face of an older woman whose prominent screen presence betrays signs of age, class membership, and religious modesty. The first and last women in the video differ in their positionalities, attire,

I am joining the protest on February the 20th, I will protest and more than that! Because food prices are too high and I am suffering from that.

FIGURE 5.3. The older woman in the "I Am Moroccan" video clip. Mariamelmas9, "Morocco Campaign #Feb20 #Morocco," YouTube, 16 February 2011, http://www .youtube.com/watch?v=Sof6FSB7gxQ.

bodily posturing, and language, while sharing the same "space of appearance," this one digital.[21]

Boughalbi, a twenty-three-year-old journalism student at the time, is a founding member of Feb20. In her performance she combines the individual "I" and the collective "all" in the same sentence: "I am Moroccan, and I will go out to the streets on 20 February because I want freedom and equality for all Moroccans." She does not explicitly name gender equality in the video clip because, she said later, at "this first stage gender equality was considered as part of the general call for equality for all Moroccans." Another Feb20 activist, Hanane, argued that by their very "bodily presence, commitment to the movement, and strong voice, many women believed that the movement's call for freedom and equality for all Moroccans was a recognition of gender equality." The male and female activists I interviewed understand *gender equality* as equality before the law, including in inheritance, access to resources, opportunities, and political representation.

The older woman who closes the "I Am Moroccan" video, who speaks to an imagined audience for fifty seconds, almost half the length of the video, foregrounds issues of social justice. The camera pans her expressive face closely, as if to show the lines of time and economic stress. She speaks of high food prices and describes her struggles with economic marginality and police oppression. She emphasizes, "I am going out on 20 February and I will protest *and protest* because high food prices are killing me." The clip ends with a complaint of injustice and a rhetorical question: "When I go out to peacefully protest the high cost of living, I am faced with police brutality. . . . I am in my country and I am oppressed. How can I be oppressed in my own country?"[22]

The face and voice of the older woman normalize ordinary women's subjectivity and political agency, typically silenced in revolutionary struggles. Her emphatic "I will protest *and protest*" reflects an understanding that political change is produced by active occupation of the space of protest by poor women.

The "Who Are We?" clip, released a few days later, explains the movement to an audience that had grown suspicious in response to defamation by a group called the Royalist Youth. It was designed in a question-and-answer format to explain the reasons behind the Feb20 mobilization. This video was filmed against a black and white banner that repeats *20 February Movement* in Arabic, Tamazight, French, Spanish, and English. The images include each question printed in Tamazight, Arabic, and French. The seven speakers, three of them women, alternate between Darija and Tamazight to answer each question. The speakers use the first-person plural, *we*, to make demands, illustrating Sari Hanafi's argument that the individual actor who emerged during the Arab uprisings is different from the neoliberal subject in that she became "a source of unification for all the civilians in opposition to the regime" and embodied the nation.[23] The video call illustrates this new political subjectivity by capturing linguistic and ethnic pluralism. Darija, colloquial Arabic, and three versions of Tamazight (from the Rif, the Atlas, and the South) alternate and coexist.

The display of written Darija and Tamazight—both mainly used orally— and the marginalization of classical Arabic reflected Feb20 members' desire to speak to Moroccans in their mother tongues and destabilize the centrality of Modern Standard Arabic as the national language of the constitution, instruction, and religion.[24] The nationalist urban elites had situated Morocco within an "imagined geography" of the Arab world,[25] disconnecting it from multiple roots and geographies, through the institutionalization of Arabic as the national language, first to fight French colonialism and

FIGURE 5.4.
A banner proclaiming "20 February Movement" in several languages, including Tamazight (Berber).

second as a source of national unity after the independence of Morocco. The inclusion of everyday language practices and embodiments in the videos addressed culturally situated viewers in Morocco's various geographic regions and subverted the supremacy of Arabic by upholding the everyday languages of ordinary people, notably Darija. Moroccan spoken Arabic is a hybrid language attached to the home, feminine sensibilities, and elderly wisdom. It evokes popular memory, "cultural authenticity,"[26] music, and masculinist (dis)order in the street since it is often used by men in ways that intimidate or shame women. It is also associated with illiteracy, humor, and political satire. Tamazight words and structures, as well as French and Spanish Arabized terms, are interwoven in the everyday conversations of ordinary Moroccans.

People contested the Arabization of Moroccan historical memory and the denigration of spoken languages in rap music, social media chats, and everyday conversations well before the North African uprisings. Among younger people Darija is the dominant language of chats, text messages, YouTube, and Facebook.[27] Rap music informed the revolutionary imagination of Feb20 members, who consider themselves part of "the hip hop generation," in the words of an activist. These resistance sensibilities are part of a genealogy of youth "cultural politics" that I call "aesthetic citizenship."[28] They began with the revolutionary songs of the group Nass El Ghiwane in the 1970s and have continued in rap music since the mid-1990s. Nass El Ghiwane's dialect and lyrics use coded language to denounce political and economic oppression and are grounded in the socioeconomic realities and cultural sensibilities of new migrants to metropolitan Casablanca, especially in the shantytown of Hey Mohammadi. The valorization of Darija and its aestheticization in music enabled the creation of a "third space" onto which hybrid language practices are mapped and *aesthetic citizenship* forged. For Homi Bhabha a third space "initiates new signs of identity, and innovative sites of collaboration and contestation."[29] The speech acts and language performances in the video clips express the contingencies of national identity and the importance of grounding the transnational "revolutionary imagination" of the Arab revolts in multiple localities.[30] The videos carried messages that resonated with every Arab revolutionary struggle but were specific to Morocco given its diversity, postcolonial form of Arab nationalism, and geographical situatedness as a borderland.

Stating, "I am Moroccan and I want . . ." in various dialects and languages and from plural embodied positionalities appropriated national belonging through a "differentiated citizenship" that requires that difference be recognized and valued, to use David Harvey's terms.[31] Such an inclusive revolutionary imagination recognized subalternity, indigeneity, socioeconomic inequalities, and generational interdependence. It acknowledged national identity as contingent, plurally lived, and open to transnational forms of recognition and action. The men and women in the two videos articulated desires for differentiated belonging based on gender, geography, class, and language.

Feminism and Its Discontents

Women were prominent in the Feb20 Movement. At the outset the Rabat and Casablanca coordinating committees were headed by women. Women led street campaigns and general assemblies and spoke on behalf of the movement in national and international forums, such as Boughalbi's Paris intervention at the Centre Mosellan des Droits de l'Homme in June 2011.[32] Women constitute over a third of the speakers in the "I Am Moroccan" video clip and almost half of the speakers in the "Who Are We?" clip. Nevertheless no feminist group joined the Feb20 Movement due to ideological tensions.

Moroccan feminism stands out in Arab and Middle Eastern contexts. In 2004 the feminist movement won the most progressive codification of women's rights in the region with a Family Code that stipulates gender equality, revokes marital guardianship and obedience laws, provides women with the right to initiate divorce and gain custody of children, abolishes repudiation, and restricts polygamy. In 2007 Moroccan women were able to pass their nationality on to their children, and in 2008 the state lifted its reservations on the UN Convention to Eliminate All Forms of Discrimination against Women.

The latest youth dynamic in Morocco must be situated within a genealogy of spaces and debates already opened by feminist activism and negotiations with the state since the 1980s. Many Moroccan feminists wondered whether the Family Code victory would in fact diminish the appeal of feminism to a generation unfamiliar with the struggle. There are no systematic studies on the impact of a feminist epistemology of rights on youth identifications in Morocco. A UNICEF-FNUAP study is suggestive in showing that only 7 percent of young people surveyed were connected to a feminist organization, despite growing involvement by Moroccan youth in the third sector of nongovernmental organizations.[33] Nevertheless this percentage from ten years ago is likely higher than reported feminist affiliation rates in the United States. Rather than indicating a postfeminist era,[34] as most studies claim, the low rate of involvement points to the irrelevance of feminism to youth subjectivities and political identifications. The few late twentieth-century studies available on Moroccan youth emphasize the influence of family, difficult economic conditions, and political Islam.[35] The centrality of gender and women in the Feb20 Movement testifies, however, to the importance of feminism as discourse and practice in the mobilization of youth.

Feb20 was clearly secular in its demand for the separation of state and religion in the Moroccan Constitution, testifying to what Asef Bayat calls "post-Islamism," Islam as a sphere of personal rather than political identification.[36] Many activists believed that the pluralistic and secular foundations of Feb20 offered an opportunity for established liberal feminist organizations to "renew their base" and expand it to include the impoverished groups targeted for mobilization by Feb20 youth. For Feb20 activists such as Nabil, one "cannot speak of women's rights in the context of a constitution that puts religion and the king's authority above international law." To these activists Moroccan liberal feminists' emphasis on the "specificity of women's issues" "isolated their movement" and facilitated "the intervention of state bureaucrats, foreign funds, and global players in women's lives."

Feb20 activists believed that gender equality could be accomplished only if "men and women are together in the struggle" and "represented by institutions accountable to them." These activists understood the king's March 2011 address as a turning point in this regard, as established feminist organizations withdrew their already hesitant support by openly dismissing the Feb20 Movement, allowing the government to use a more muscular approach against their protests.

Liberal feminist groups have a complicated relationship with the state, however. They have built activism around a legalistic framework that necessitates the involvement of state agents and the king as a constitutional arbitrator. The reform of family law, for example, owes a great deal to the complicated negotiations among political parties, feminist groups, Islamist players, and King Mohamed VI. Since the 1990s feminist groups have positioned themselves as allies rather than opponents of the Moroccan state. These established feminists believe that if they had endorsed the goals of Feb20, they would upset these alliances and empower Islamist players. Despite tensions between feminist organizations and Feb20, I argue that feminism as a discourse of equality not only informed the younger generation's activism but also penetrated their sensibilities and the material and virtual spaces they carved out for resistance and mobilization. Ironically, even as it heightened tensions between old and new feminist sensibilities, the king's March 2011 address foregrounded feminist sensibilities and tensions *within* Feb20.

Negotiating Gender

Equality and parity were constituted, displayed, and tested in the neighborhood committees and general assemblies of the Feb20 Movement. Its mobilization strategies were decentralized and relationship-based, which was extremely conducive for the involvement of women. Committees that included men and women instituted gender parity, which facilitated door-to-door contact with local residents. The neighborhood committees also enabled the organization of rallies "close to where people live." The involvement of Feb20 women in neighborhood committees and mobilizing based on proximity made it easier for marginalized communities to make their own claims and for building determined activism from the grassroots.

During protests Feb20 pedagogy consisted of one person using a megaphone to outline each goal of the movement and the marchers repeating each goal to magnify, teach, and reinforce it. Chants enunciated feminist politics as they called for the "voice of the sons of the people" and "the voice of the daughters of the people" to be heard:[37]

Smaʿa saout al-shaʿab.
Listen to the voice of the people.
Smaʿa ouled al-shaʿab.
Listen to the sons of the people.
Smaʿa bnat al-shaʿab.
Listen to the daughters of the people.
We want
Isqat al-hukuma
the fall of the government
Isqat al-barlaman
the fall of the Parliament
Isqat al-fasad
the end of corruption.

Debates about women's rights and equal representation within the movement were part of the initial conversations that established Feb20. These conversations frequently became "agonistic" because the publics involved in Feb20 included leftists, secularists, liberals, Islamists, and Salafis.[38] While Salafis energetically challenged gender equality, Feb20 activists did not necessarily consider Islamist participation in negative terms. Founding Feb20 women who interacted with Islamist men in neighborhood committees and street protests in Rabat and Casablanca argued that their participation "enriched the movement by providing opportunities for discussions and networking among seculars, leftists, and Islamists." Islamist participation also instigated debates about gender equality, which is often taken for granted among leftists and secularists rather than discussed or foregrounded.

A Feb20 leftist and feminist activist in charge of a coordinating committee in Casablanca of twenty-six members, half of them women, argued that she had witnessed "positive changes" in the "attitudes" of Islamist men on her committee, who largely interacted with non-Islamist women activists. These changes included more openness to working with "secular and leftist women" and "changing perceptions on both sides" created by teamwork. In Rabat and Casablanca women reported that Islamist men from Justice and Spirituality physically sheltered them from police violence. "Unlike our friends, the Islamists do not run away when the police crack down. They stay with us and try to protect us," two activists claimed. According to these activists, the Islamists did not distinguish between women based on ideology. Rather they engaged in what Engin Isin calls "solidaristic modes" of resistance.[39] According to one Islamist activist, "Feelings of solidarity emerged as women's and men's bodies are in proximity and congregate around a common cause." He added that caring for one's neighbor is "a religious duty, especially when that neighbor is a woman." Despite the patriarchal foundations of these statements, the women I spoke with appreciated knowing they were not alone. The presence of Islamist men on the battlefield created emotional bridges that converted regimes of distrust and fear into support and care. But the inclusion of Islamists also produced tensions, as reflected in semiotics and the distribution of bodies in space. Symbolically debates raged over protest slogans, signs, and colors used by Feb20. At the outset secularists and Islamists agreed to avoid colors and slogans that pointed to particular religious, ideological, or sexual claims or affiliations. They adopted white and black for all the signs and banners during street protests. When Justice and Spirituality decided to withdraw from Feb20 after the electoral victory of the Justice and Development Party in November 2011, the physiognomy of protests drastically changed as the number of bodies taking to the streets dropped. While some activists lamented the end of "practical solidarity" with Islamists,[40] others perceived of it as "a liberation from a binary of black and white," arguing, "[This] binary does not reflect the diversity of the movement and the wide scope of rights, including religious and sexual, that Feb20 fights for."

Feb20 general assemblies were also platforms of gendered struggles. Decision making was formally consensual, in dramatic contrast to "dictatorship of the majority" logic. This gave all voices the same weight in the decision-making process while assuring that several hours of discussion were necessary to reach a consensus. However, political alliances that formed at the margins of open meetings practically limited this formal equality of voice, including for women activists. The spatial metaphors *kawlassa* and *tkoulis* (derived from the French term *coulisse*, "backstage") illustrate this dynamic. During assemblies backstage negotiations facilitated the emergence of certain blocks and disproportionately empowered the legitimacy of certain claims in open meetings, including on gender issues. To female activists such backstage politics marginalized gender equality matters. Male activists often argued that raising the issue would further divide the movement and divert attention from general struggle for political change. The marginalization of women's issues follows a historically consistent pattern whereby women's concerns are often pushed aside for the sake of the overall goal of revolution, as Nadje al-Ali argues.[41]

Nevertheless women described the general assembly as a political space where they learned how to address a crowd, make arguments, and acquire a voice. They instituted "equal time slots to express their opinion" and made sure they were not interrupted when speaking. Even if this sounds basic, women believed these meetings became a feminist pedagogy at work, for male friends learned how to listen to women, take their opinion into account, and alternate with them in heading assemblies and moderating debates. Many activists claimed that Feb20 inaugurated new political subjectivities among men and women as political actors and "equal partners."

The rally in Rabat on 24 April 2011 shook the fragile foundations of this pedagogy, because for the first time Feb20 women faced spatial segregation and the dominance of religious slogans at a protest. As Salafis and Islamists began dividing protesters into separate men's and women's columns, women screamed slogans about gender equality, which were "met with disdain." As the women chanted in Darija, "Men and women have equal rights" (*a-rijal wa-nisa' fil-huquq fhal fhal*), the Islamists responded, "Men and women are equal in struggle" (*a-rijal wa-nisa' fil-kifah fhal fhal*). A female activist riding on a man's shoulders and shouting slogans through a megaphone was shocked to find herself thrown to the ground by a man who appeared to be Salafi.

Disputes over spatial organization, symbolism, and chants extended to contentions over the master frame of the three-month-old movement. The subversion of "equality in rights" into "equality in struggle" by Islamists and Salafis compelled many Feb20 activists to adopt a bolder understanding of equality that included "inheritance rights," according to an NCS member. In places with a longer history of feminist activism, such as Rabat and Casablanca, young men were more receptive to the "social imaginary" of an egalitarian gender order.[42] Women activists in other regions of the country, however, complained of "entrenched sexism." In an audio testimony published in the online feminist magazine *Qandisha*, two women Feb20 activists from the southern region of Agadir describe how people watching a rally responded to the slogan "Dignity to women" with sarcastic slogans of "Dignity to men" and "Dignity to children." One of the two women interviewed describes her arrest and the gender-specific techniques of intimidation used by the police against her, including asking her, "Are you a virgin?" and "How do you think your family is going to receive the news about your arrest?" This experience made her doubt the efficacy of full inclusion of women's issues when movements have generic justice demands: "Women need their specific organizations, to take care of our specific needs. . . . There is no equality, it is a mirage. I am a Feb20 member, but this does not mean that we should not have our own voice as women with specific issues. . . . At the same time we cannot isolate women's issues from the broader cause of gender and social justice. . . . But I am not gaining anything from chanting slogans about justice if I am not treated with dignity."[43]

When evaluating the feminist impact of the Feb20 Movement it is important to assess the kind of subjectivities it generated and shaped. The movement multiplied the spaces in which gender, body, sexuality, and politics are interwoven. These new feminist spaces are different from those opened in the 1980s by liberal feminist groups. The latter became the place for the governmentality of women's rights within the platform of economic restructuring and development, as Inderpal Grewal argues.[44] The "new feminism," in contrast, interrogates the existing institutionalized sites of feminist mobilization.[45] It is embodied instead in artistic expression, street performances, and cyber activism. The multiplication of these spaces illustrates emergent ontologies and epistemologies of the body, sexuality, class, and ethnicity, as is clear in the shift from issues of social justice broadly defined to specific questions of gender justice.

The Sexual Turn

Feb20 inaugurated a plurality of new feminist spaces in which groups and individuals address bodies, sexuality, and gender oppression in languages and platforms shaped by emerging and renewed understandings of class, subalternity, and gender justice.

Ishriniyyat Febrayer started as an online network of women who identify with Feb20 across Morocco. Unlike the gender-neutral and singular Arabic term for *twenty* in 20 February, the term *ishriniyyat* feminizes and pluralizes the number and makes it a noun in relation to *February*. The group launched a Facebook page to discuss gender issues, create events, provide news about Feb20, and mobilize for feminist- and gender-focused meetings, sit-ins, and artistic events supported by a variety of groups.

Al ʿyalat jayyat (The Women Are Coming) is another independent group that emerged after 2011. Its Facebook banner page contains the line "No dignity, no freedom, no social justice without women's access to full rights."[46] The online magazine of the group, *Nisf al-sama ʾe* (Half of the Sky), quotes Lenin, draws on Maoist Cultural Revolution language, and uses anticapitalist rhetoric that relates women's oppression to private property. The magazine defines women as a proletariat,[47] explicitly stresses gender justice, and challenges middle-class positionalities that contain women's rights within the liberal framework of gender equality. Rabia Bouslama, a cofounder of the group, explained that they chose the name to document an event that took place during a street protest in which an antiriot agent pushed an old woman. Upset by his action, the woman shouted a reprimand to the officer that included the promise "Wait, the women are coming."[48] This threat by an ordinary woman underscores the vocalization of feminist sensibilities and "end of fear" beyond class boundaries. The video clip of a woman fighting police while carrying her child on her back—a sign of low status in urban Morocco—turned viral during the first weeks of protests to become the symbol of the Feb20 movement.[49] The movement's decision to move protests to impoverished neighborhoods facilitated "this articulation of social justice claims by subaltern women as revolutionaries," argued Khadija, a feminist and human rights activist. Mobilizing poor neighborhoods also created possibilities for the emergence of a new generation of women leaders from these neighborhoods. Demands for social justice chanted in these neighborhoods have now become part of widely shared sensibilities that extend well beyond urban and middle-class professionals, as indicated by the uproar that occurred after Amina Filali's suicide.

Filali was a sixteen-year-old girl who ingested rat poison in March 2012 to end a marriage to her alleged rapist. The multisited mobilization that resulted illustrates the feminist body politics that flourished as a result of Feb20 dynamics and the unprecedented mediations between established and emergent feminist sites. The new group Woman-Choufouch was the prime champion of Filali after her death. The group's name is a play on words that appropriates an expression of sexual harassment commonly heard in the streets of Morocco: "Why don't we see [you]?" It began as an anti–sexual harassment group in March 2011 when its first members, three women and two men students in their early twenties, called for the organization of SlutWalk Morocco on 13 August 2011. The SlutWalk became an annual event in many locations in the world after the first took place in Canada in 2011.[50] Though the planned SlutWalk never took place in Morocco, the group retained the SlutWalk designation as part of their name on their Facebook page. Woman-Choufouch grew out of the sexualized and embodied dynamics in the North African uprisings that included sexual harassment, rape, and sexualized violence by state and nonstate actors.[51] These dynamics produced what I call the "sexual turn" in these revolutions.

Woman-Choufouch increased public awareness about Filali's suicide and, by mobilizing against "legalized rape," helped change the law in Morocco. The group coordinated sit-ins before the parliament building in Rabat, online petition campaigns, and calls for protests.[52] The Facebook pages *We Are All Amina Filali* and *#RIPAmina* had several thousand supporters in a few days.[53] The group located its intervention at the intersection of cyberfeminism, human rights discourse, and gender justice claims, bringing together old and new feminist activists and initiating new sites of sexuality talk. The well-established feminist group Union de l'Action Feminine and the Moroccan Association for Human Rights helped with logistics, opened their offices for meetings, and undertook legal investigations of the case.

The actions taken on behalf of Filali reflect the hybrid nature of this new feminism, which includes actions online and offline, directed toward the government and toward mobilizing the street and led collectively and individually by "cultural entrepreneurs."[54] Artists are particularly important in mobilizations that illustrate the sexual turn in documentaries, satire, plays, and other productions. Nadir Bouhmouch's film *475: When Marriage Becomes Punishment* (2012) and Hind Bensari's film *Trêve de Silence* (Break the Silence, 2013) are individual interventions by young artist activists who inserted the voices of rape victims into the debates about social justice.[55]

The online publication *Qandisha Collaborative Feminine Magazine* facilitated wide-ranging personal engagement with the Filali case under the heading "I Was Raped." The title attracted a stream of testimonies and responses by women victims of rape. The physicist and founder of the magazine, Fedwa Misk, explained the call for narrating rape stories: "The aim was to demonstrate that no woman who underwent this physical and psychological injury could find comfort in the legal union to the abuser."[56]

The Aquarium Theater is another site of artistic rearticulation of sex talk.[57] Its president and producer, Naima Zitane, reacted to the violence in the stories of rape and sexual violence and to taboos associated with women's sexuality with a seven-month investigation into women's sexuality that included workshops and focus groups involving 150 women from all social backgrounds. The interviews were shaped into a play titled *Dialy* (Mine), a Darija reference to the vagina.[58] Referring to a vagina and explicitly naming it in a public forum created by women disrupted a logic of respectability and shame attached to "that thing" that no respectable person should mention in public. The result was a major uproar. Performed for the first time in December 2012, the play was part of an array of vibrant new sites where the sexualization of women's bodies and denigration of body parts is challenged by their naming and reappropriation by women. Thanks to multisited knowledge and creative production, dispersed yet connected audiences, crowdfunding, and open discussion, sexual freedoms and rights are now part of a vibrant urban artistic space. The display of women's bodies in street performances and the embodied forms of protest invented by activists transformed public space into a "space of engagement" and co-imbricated politics and aesthetics.[59]

The Aesthetics of Protest

Street-cleaning campaigns, distribution of flowers, graffiti, and songs staged scenes of dissensus.[60] The 2011 Arab revolutions also foregrounded a protest aesthetic of *still* and naked micro-rebellious bodies, such as those of the Egyptian Aliaa Elmahdy and the Tunisian Amina Tyler. In the Moroccan streets men and women enacted a collective aesthetics of dissensus in the Freeze campaigns, which were confounding spectacles for police.

The Freeze for Freedom took place in front of the Moroccan Parliament on 6 March 2012.[61] In this collective performance several men and women froze in positions that showed police brutality or disabled such brutality by freezing the violent act.[62] Unemployed university graduates and other Moroccans have for decades staged demonstrations, camped, engaged in hunger strikes, and attempted to immolate themselves in front of Parliament. The architecture of the place underwent a transformation a decade

FIGURE 5.5. Freeze for Freedom in front of Parliament, Rabat, 6 March 2011.

ago when urban planning divided the central part of Avenue Mohamed V into small lawns separated by stones, ostensibly to create leisure spaces for city dwellers. Decoupage and greening were technologies of pacification that attempted to depoliticize this Parliament space, reduce the number of bodies that can gather or camp there, and impede the mobility of protesters in major events. Hence decolonizing public spaces through embodied dissent and bodily performance became one of the major struggles of the Arab Spring, as Nadia Shabout claims.[63] The Freeze for Freedom enactment is a compelling and dramatically visible reclamation and decolonization of space through embodied action in the Arab revolutions.[64] Freeze events had previously taken place in Fez and Meknes in the Northwest in October 2010.[65] An organizer explained in an interview that these events tested youth's ability to "mobilize online for the event and draw hundreds to the street to participate or watch and document online." Their success illustrated to activists the possibility of mobilizing isolated individuals and scattered groups. Most important, public display of the women's bodies in Freeze events challenged hegemonic notions of public morality and a shared understanding of the street as a place women pass through but rarely inhabit, especially in conservative cities. Although the physical distance between men and women is carefully orchestrated and staged, women enacted new reclamations of the street in these mixed-gender performances.

After the Rabat Freeze, art and resistance came together in a more for-mal and collective way in the Festival of Resistance and Alternatives, which was held in February 2012 (Rabat), 2013 (Rabat), and 2014 (Casablanca).[66] In these festivals activists creatively reclaimed streets that had become sat-urated with police violence. They also offered a radical alternative to the annual Festival Mawazine, established by the king in 2001, which activists, including Islamists, have for years criticized for drawing on public funds to pay high-profile international artists and singers in foreign currency and use them to portray the monarchy as culturally and politically open.

In contrast the Festival of Resistance and Alternatives, conceived and organized by Feb20, produces countercultural spaces of dissensus for youth. A wide variety of artistic productions and youth performances line the schedules, including documentaries produced by Feb20 members, en-gaged art and rap, exhibitions, poems, and workshops focused on many topics, including violence against women. During the second edition of the Festival, in 2013, these creative entrepreneurs organized flash mobs to engage the street, making sounds to attract people's attention, chanting a few slogans against the Makhzen, and then enacting a performance by clowns that lasted two minutes, ending before the arrival of police. Many Feb20 activists are now part of this vibrant scene, contributing to the pro-liferation of artistic and performative politics in Rabat and elsewhere. The long-term impact of such politics is too early to assess, but its creative energy is palpable and diffuse.

Conclusion

The 20 February Movement no longer has the intensity and urgency that was apparent in 2011, but it inaugurated dynamics that informed several protest movements across the country. The movement's slogan, "Dignity, Freedom, Social Justice," continues to resonate in protests organized by professional groups, the unemployed, and labor activists and in scattered agitations in various cities and remote regions. Feb20 multiplied spaces for the embodiment of gender sensibilities and citizenship desires and dis-rupted ethnicized, classed, and sexualized hierarchies and differences. The movement generated a multiplicative and open-ended process, enabled the proliferation of virtual and material spaces to negotiate feminist sensi-bilities, and produced a sexual turn that takes seriously gendered and sexu-alized bodies and desires and sexualized violence.

Though the Moroccan state did not systematically deploy sexual violence against women, Feb20 opened new ways to address the everyday sexualization of public space and the gendered violence of many laws. Feb20 enabled women to vocalize these concerns on artistic platforms, at symbolic sites, and within political groups. These new modes of feminist engagement addressed the material conditions and discursive fields of gendered and sexual sensibilities and practices. They enacted politics through new language, speech acts, bodily dispositions, and artistic performances. One of the most enduring impacts of Feb20 was the rise of these plural modes of politics in multiple spaces.

NOTES

I am grateful to Khadija Merwazi, president of the Mediator for Democracy and Human Rights, for supporting this research, including by establishing contact with activists and opening her NGO's office in Rabat for my meeting with them. Financial support for this research came through Rutgers University's School of Arts and Sciences research fund.

1. On the notion of exceptionalism in relation to Feb20, see Driss Maghraoui, "Constitutional Reforms in Morocco: Between Consensus and Subaltern Politics," *Journal of North African Studies* 16, no. 4 (2011): 679–99.

2. Zakia Salime, "Arab Revolutions: Legible, Illegible Bodies," *Comparative Studies of South Asia, Africa and the Middle East* 35, no. 3 (2015): 525–38; see also Asef Bayat, *Life as Politics: How Ordinary People Change the Middle East* (Stanford, CA: Stanford University Press, 2006).

3. On the notions of inauguration, space, and politics, see Mustafa Dikeç, "Space as a Mode of Political Thinking," *Geoforum* 43, no. 4 (2012): 669–76; Lorraine Dowler and Joanne Sharp, "A Feminist Geopolitics?," *Space and Polity* 5, no. 3 (2001): 165–76; Judith Butler, "Bodies in Alliance and the Politics of the Street," European Institute for Progressive Cultural Policies, last modified September 2011, http://www.eipcp.net/transversal /1011/butler/en.

4. Hannah Arendt, *The Human Condition*, 2nd edition (Chicago: University of Chicago Press, 1998), 198.

5. Chantal Mouffe, *On the Political* (London: Routledge, 2005), 260–63; also Dikeç, "Space as a Mode of Political Thinking," 670. Jacques Rancière, *The Politics of Aesthetics: The Distribution of the Sensible*, translated by Gabriel Rockhill (New York: Continuum, 2004), 128.

6. Jacques Rancière, *Dissensus: On Politics and Aesthetics*, translated by Steven Corcoran (London: Continuum, 2010), 37, 38, 39.

7. On Hannah Arendt, see Dikeç, "Space as a Mode of Political Thinking," 671–73.

8. On the notion of hypervisibility, see Paul Amar, "Turning the Gendered Politics of the Security State Inside Out?," *International Journal of Politics* 13, no. 3 (2011): 308–9.

9. Media networks include the Facebook groups Moroccans Who Speak to the King, People Want Change, and Freedom and Democracy Now.

10. Freedom and Democracy Now, accessed September 2012, https://www.facebook .com/events/186929851346887/?ref=52&source=1.

11. The press conference can be viewed at Yousfi adil, "Conférence de Presse du Mouvement 20 Fevrier," 17 February 2011, YouTube, http://www.youtube.com/watch?v=-i9mEB _sWnw.

12. Patricia Hill Collins, *Black Feminist Thought: Knowledge, Consciousness, and the Politics of Empowerment* (Boston: Unwin Hyman, 1990), 221.

13. This was not the first time the king's wealth and his entourage's gifted economic privileges were subjected to domestic scrutiny. "Le salaire annuel du Roi Mohamed VI, 6 millions de dirhams," Biladi, 21 November 2012, http://www.bladi.net/salaire-annuel -roi-mohammed-6.html.

14. Catherine Graciet and Eric Laurent, in *Le Roi predateur: Main basse sur le Maroc* (Paris: Seuil, 2012), offer incredible details about the tactics allegedly utilized by the king, who used his entourage and privatized companies to monopolize every sector of the Moroccan economy. Banned in print format, the book was already circulating online thanks to the diasporic extensions of Feb20 in Europe and North America. In a bolder act of dissent, cyber activists created a Facebook page from which the book could be downloaded, comments generated, and more knowledge disseminated: https://www.facebook.com /RoiPredateurVosReactions.

15. See Mohamed Tozi, *Al-Malakiyya wal-Islam al-Siyasi* (The Kingdom and Political Islam) (Casablanca: Le Fennec, 1999).

16. On the reform of family law, see Zakia Salime, *Between Feminism and Islam: Human Rights and Sharia Law in Morocco* (Minneapolis: University of Minnesota Press, 2011); Houria Alami Mchich, *Genre et politique au Maroc: Les enjeux de l'egalité hommes-femmes entre islamisme et modernisme* (Gender and Politics in Morocco: The Stakes of Male-Female Equality between Islamism and Modernism) (Paris: L'Harmattan, 2002).

17. On the leaderless character of the Arab Uprisings, see Mohamed Bamyeh, "Arab Revolutions and the Making of New Patriotism," *Orient German Journal for Politics, Economics and Culture of the Middle East* 52, no. 3 (2011): 6–7.

18. On the debate about the reform of the constitution and Feb20 boycott of the elections, see Maghraoui, "Constitutional Reforms in Morocco," 681–83.

19. The videos were released on 16 and 18 February, respectively. The first call, "I Am Moroccan," with English captions, is at Mariamelmas9, "Morocco Campaign #Feb20 #Morocco," YouTube, 16 February 2011, http://www.youtube.com/watch?v=S0f6FSB 7gxQ. The second, "Who Are We," with Arabic, Tamazight, and French captions, is at Badu004, "Jeunes 20 février: Vidéo explicative," YouTube, 18 February 2011, http://www .youtube.com/watch?v=XqfcopNyV3Q/.

20. Rancière, *Dissensus*, 37, 38, 39–40; Rancière, *The Politics of Aesthetics*, 128; Mariamelmas9, "Morocco Campaign #Feb20 #Morocco."

21. Arendt, *The Human Condition*, 198.

22. She begins speaking at 1:19. Mariamelmas9, "Morocco Campaign #Feb20 #Morocco."

23. Sari Hanafi, "The Arab Revolutions: The Emergence of a New Political Subjectivity," *Contemporary Arab Affairs* 5, no. 2 (2012): 203.

24. Amazigh intellectuals have been invested in this sociolinguistic engineering of a counterdiscourse that highlights the North African and Amazigh sources of the historical memory of Moroccans, notably after the creation of the Royal Institute for Amazigh Culture in 2001.

25. Dowler and Sharp, "A Feminist Geopolitics?," 166.

26. Moha Ennaji, "Multiculturalism, Gender and Political Participation in Morocco," *Diogenes* 57, no. 1 (2010): 49.

27. Alexander Elinso, "Darija and Changing Writing Practices in Morocco," *International Journal of Middle East Studies* 45, no. 4 (2013): 715–30. Because of Morocco's integration into the French zone of influence, most people use the Latin alphabet to communicate in Darija on keyboards, resorting to the numbers 3, 7, and 9 for missing Arabic sounds.

28. Amy Mills, "Critical Place Studies and Middle East Histories: Power, Politics, and Social Change," *History Compass* 10, no. 10 (2012): 780; Zakia Salime, "I Vote, I Sing: The Rise of Aesthetic Citizenship in Morocco," *International Journal of Middle East Studies* 47, no. 1 (2015): 136–39.

29. Homi Bhabha, *The Location of Culture* (London: Routledge, 1994), 1.

30. Marie Josefina Saldana-Portillo, *The Revolutionary Imagination in the Americas and the Age of Development* (Durham, NC: Duke University Press, 2006).

31. Iris Marion Young, "Polity and Group Difference: A Critique of the Ideal of Universal Citizenship," *Ethics* 99, no. 2 (1989): 251; David Harvey, "Class Relations, Social Justice and the Politics of Difference," in *Place and the Politics of Identity*, edited by M. Keith and S. Pile (London: Routledge, 1993), 41.

32. See Amina Boughalbi's talk at the Centre Mosellan des Droits de l'Homme (CMDH), Paris, 19 June 2011, at Saïd Laayari, "COLLOQUE CMDH intervention d'Amina BOUGHALBI.wmv," YouTube, 29 June 2011, http://youtu.be/bwowqZCxilA.

33. Driss Bennani, "Dans la tête des jeunes marocains," *Yabiladi*, accessed 18 March 2016, http://www.yabiladi.com/article-societe-2226.html. FNUAP is the French acronym for the United Nations Population Fund.

34. On the notion of postfeminism, see Stéphanie Genz, "Third Way/ve: The Politics of Postfeminism," *Feminist Theory* 7, no. 3 (2006): 333–53.

35. See Soumia Bennani-Chraïbi, *Soumis et rebelles, les jeunes au Maroc* (Paris: CNRS, Éditions Méditerranée, 1994); Rahma Bourqia, Mohammed El Ayadi, Mokhtar El Harrass, and Hassan Rachik, *Les jeunes et les valeurs religieuses* (Casablanca: Eddif, CODESRIA, 2000).

36. Asef Bayat, "A New Arab Street in Post-Islamist Times," *Foreign Policy*, 26 January 2011.

37. Nadir Bouhmouch's film *My Makhzen and Me* (http://vimeo.com/36997532) documents this pedagogy.

38. Chantal Mouffe, "Deliberative Democracy or Agonistic Pluralism," Institute for Advanced Studies, Vienna, December 2002, http://www.ihs.ac.at/publications/pol/pw_72.pdf.

39. Engin Isin, "Engaging, Being, Political," *Political Geography* 44, no. 3 (2005): 381.

40. Bamyeh, "Arab Revolutions and the Making of New Patriotism," 6.

41. Nadje al-Ali, "Gendering the Arab Spring," *Middle East Journal of Culture and Communication* 5, no. 1 (2012): 26–31.

42. Charles Taylor, "Modern Social Imaginaries," *Public Culture* 14, no. 1 (2002): 91–124.

43. "M20F: Où sont les revendications féministes?," *Al-badil al-tawri*, 5 May 2013, http://badiltawri.wordpress.com/2012/03/05/m20f-ou-sont-les-revendications -feministes-extrait-du-site-www-qandisha-ma/.

44. Inderpal Grewal, *Transnational America: Feminisms, Diasporas, Neoliberalisms* (Durham, NC: Duke University Press, 2005), esp. chapter 3.

45. Zakia Salime, "New Feminism as Personal Revolutions: Micro-Rebellious Bodies," *Signs: Journal of Women in Society and Culture* 40, no. 1 (2014): 18.

46. Al ʿyalat jayyat, Facebook, https://www.facebook.com/events/511352895573931.

47. Their magazine, *Nisf al-sama ʾe*, can be viewed at http://moitieduciel.wordpress .com/2012/02/12/%D8%AD%D8%B1%D9%83%D8%A9-%D8%A7%D9%84%D8%B9% D9%8A%D8%A7%D9%84%D8%A7%D8%AA-%D8%AC%D8%A7%D9%8A%D8%A7 %D8%AA%D8%8C-%D8%B4%D8%B1%D9%88%D8%B7-%D8%A7%D9%84%D8% A7%D9%86%D8%AB%D8%A7%D9%82-%D9%88/. For some of their actions, see the Facebook page of the Fes section: https://www.facebook.com/groups /327830280582108/.

48. See the interview with Rabia Bouslama: http://www.aufaitmaroc.com/actualites /maroc/2011/12/5/un-nouveau-mouvement-different-du-m20#.UavrT-uA7-Q (accessed 15 September 2013).

49. Samia Errazouki, "Working-Class Women Revolt: Gendered Political Economy in Morocco," *Journal of North African Studies* 19, no. 2 (2014): 259.

50. The first SlutWalk was held in Ontario in early April 2011 after women students and staff at Osgoode Hall Law School complained about a statement from a Toronto officer at a campus safety event in late January that women should avoid dressing like sluts in order not to be victimized. See more on the SlutWalk on the website http://www .slutwalktoronto.com.

51. See Amar, "Turning the Gendered Politics of the Security State Inside Out?"; Mona Eltahawi, "Why Do They Hate Us? The Real War on Women Is in the Middle East," *Foreign Policy*, 23 April 2012; Sara Mourad, "The Naked Body of Alia," *Jadaliyya*, 1 January 2013, http://www.jadaliyya.com/pages/index/9291/the-naked-bodies-of-alia; Sherene Seikaly and Maya Mikhdashi, "Let's Talk about Sex," *Jadaliyya*, 25 April 2012, http://www .jadaliyya.com/pages/index/5233/lets-talk-about-sex.

52. *The Uprising of Women in the Arab World*, https://www.facebook.com/intifadat .almar2a?hc_location=stream.

53. *We Are All Amina Filali*, Facebook, https://www.facebook.com/pages/We-Are-All -Amina-Filali/392757007401977; #RIPAmina, Facebook, https://www.facebook.com /RIPAminaNonAuViolAvecLaCompliciteDeLEtat.

54. Loubna Hanna Skalli, "Youth Media and the Politics of Change in North Africa: Negotiating Identities, Spaces and Power," *Middle East Journal of Culture and Communication* 6, no. 1 (2013): 6.

55. *475: When Marriage Becomes Punishment* can be viewed at http://vimeo.com /60159667. *Trêve de Silence* can be viewed at http://vimeo.com/63390276.

56. The English version of "I Was Raped" is at http://www.qandisha.ma/2012/03/26 /i-was-raped/, posted 26 March 2012.

57. Théâtre Aquarium Facebook page: https://www.facebook.com/TheatreAquarium.

58. Lorraine Pincemail, "Dialy: La pièce de théâtre qui brise les tabous au Maroc," *Le Petit Journal*, 19 June 2013, http://www.lepetitjournal.com/casablanca/societe/156682 -dialy-la-piece-de-theatre-qui-brise-les-tabous-au-maroc.

59. Nada Shabout, "Whose Space Is It?," *International Journal of Middle East Studies* 46, no. 1 (2014): 163. On the relationship of politics and aesthetics, see Rancière, *The Politics of Aesthetics*, 13.

60. See Rancière, *Dissensus*, 140.

61. Portail E-joussour, "Freeze mob' Rabat 6 mars 2011," YouTube, 6 March 2011, https://www.youtube.com/watch?v=qmWTm5edE4A.

62. The call for a SlutWalk spread to more than two hundred countries, including Morocco.

63. See Shabout, "Whose Space Is It?," 163.

64. Kaveh Ehsani, "Radical Democratic Politics and Public Space," *International Journal of Middle East Studies* 46, no. 1 (2014): 161.

65. Souhail snakez, "Freeze Flashmob party a Fez—Maroc," YouTube, 6 October 2010, https://www.youtube.com/watch?v=Y4DCt8OF6ck. Freeze in Meknes: Othmane Ben-hamid, "Freeze à Meknes le 23/10/2010," YouTube, 25 October 2010, http://www.youtube .com/watch?v=T8MMcxiSm3A.

66. The website of Festival de résistances et d'alternatives is http://framaroc.wordpress .com/the-first-edition/.

6   CAUTIOUS ENACTMENTS   Interstitial Spaces of
Gender Politics in Saudi Arabia   SUSANA GALÁN

> Thursday night after a social obligation, she tucked her kids into bed and waited
> until they fell asleep. At about 1:30 am she put on one of her husband's shmaghs
> (Saudi head-dresses), opened the garage door and drove out! And this is not
> some reckless teenager; she's a working mother in her thirties. She told me that
> it was the most liberating feeling she had ever experienced.
> —Eman al-Nafjan, 31 October 2009

On 17 June 2011 a group of activists organized the Women2Drive campaign
to demand the lifting of the ban on women driving in the Kingdom of
Saudi Arabia (KSA). Inspired by the affective wave that shook the region
with promises of social change in the winter and spring of 2011, organizers aimed to capitalize on the revolutionary momentum to push for a very
concrete gain for Saudi women: the right to drive. This initiative built upon
a legacy of driving activism that went back to the 1990s as well as upon individual, often spontaneous transgressions of the ban that had been documented for years in Saudi women's blogs and on YouTube. Acknowledging this past, activists opted for staging a decentralized protest in order to
avoid the legal and social reprisals that had historically followed any attempt to challenge the prohibition to drive; unlike in Tunisia, Egypt, Yemen, Bahrain, or Morocco, there was no occupation of squares, no waving
of banners, no chanting of slogans, no meeting point or time. Each participant decided on her own when and where to drive, videotaped it, and
shared it on Facebook, Twitter, YouTube, or her personal blog.

In this offline-online configuration the action was conceived to operate on multiple scales: At the individual level participants could take over the driving and lay claim to the streets and roads, while the dispersed character of the protest allowed them to maintain a low profile to avoid detention. At the collective level women across the country, from the capital, Riyadh, to Jeddah in the west and Khobar in the east, could bridge the distance that separated them through a coordinated use of social media. While the physical acts of dissent remained practically invisible to Saudi publics and authorities, in cyberspace the multiplication of YouTube videos showing Saudi women driving produced a visually suggestive performance that articulated a demand for the lifting of the ban directed to a wide audience in the KSA and beyond.

The Women2Drive campaign is an example of cautious enactments staged by Saudi women activists to defy state and clerical control over women's mobility while minimizing the risk of repression and social condemnation. Similar tactics are implemented by women and girls in the KSA for a variety of actions, from flirting with strangers within the strictures of gender segregation to contravening the prescribed dress code and norms of appearance. Through the informal adoption of micropractices such as *targim* (described later) and nail polishing, Saudi women and girls erode conservative and religious systems of control aimed at disciplining their bodies and regulating their inhabitation of space. These careful explorations of the limits of dissent do not take place in the open space of the public square, nor do they remain confined to the private space of the home, but they are often enacted in the interstitial spaces that emerge between the public and the private.

The architect Aldo van Eyck conceptualized the *interstice* in 1961 as "a place of two spatial programmes, often indicating a meeting of private and public spaces."[1] Similar to other spaces and places, interstices are not preexistent but are brought into being, often as a result of an always temporary arrangement of "interactions and affections" between individuals.[2] In the KSA, where many fundamental freedoms are limited by a sexist gender regime, interstices offer a "possibility for action," where Saudi women and girls can enact "potentially new and atypical performances."[3] The interstitial space of the private car, the shopping mall, and online platforms like personal blogs and YouTube have become places where activist and nonactivist women and girls in the KSA have individually and collectively contested a range of prohibitions, transforming these regulated and surveilled mediums of mobility, consumption, and expression into sites of cautious resistance. Rather than simply reflecting existing sensibilities, these ongoing and multiple enactments produce emergent embodiments, subjectivities, and communities. While prudent and often paradoxical, the outcomes of these transgressions are not controllable or predictable. Indeed by performing such cautious acts women and girls in Saudi Arabia open up new spaces where they can jointly imagine radical futures and, in the process, stage less restrictive presents.

Controlling Bodies and Space

The KSA was founded in 1932 by Abdulaziz bin Saud (popularly known as Ibn Saud) from an amalgamation of tribes in the Arabian Peninsula. The state was established as an absolute monarchy in alliance with Wahhabi religious authorities, who applied a restrictive interpretation of Islam. According to Wahhabi ideology, women are "icons for the authenticity of the nation and its compliance with God's law," a conception that fit well with the patriarchal traditions of tribal cultures.[4] With the discovery of oil in the 1930s, existing structures of social control were replaced by a centralized bureaucratic apparatus that institutionalized state scrutiny of women's movement and appearance.[5] The development of the oil industry required massive inflows of foreign expertise and guest labor, particularly men, a demand that became acute during *tafra*, the period of high oil production between the mid-1970s and the mid-1980s.[6]

The control of Saudi women's mobility and visibility intensified as national religious discourse concentrated on "protecting" women from the gaze of foreigners. As Madawi al-Rasheed notes, the ultimate aim was to "guard" the honor of men and limit "the possibility of 'shame' being inflicted on [them] as a result of female behaviour or the violation of females by outsiders."[7] To that end the Saudi government devoted part of its oil profits to enforce and promote a costly system of gender segregation and regulation that included duplicated schools, workplaces, and health care systems.[8] As Amélie Le Renard remarks, these regulations were not traditional or conservative remnants of tribal systems but the materialization of a Saudi version of state-led urbanization and modernity.[9]

Instead of confining women to the domestic sphere, Le Renard argues, the oil revenue was used to create a parallel "'female sphere' consisting of a mosaic of new female spaces where entry is forbidden to men."[10] Yet in this gendered partitioning of space and bodies, men are usually allotted the best areas or most convenient hours.[11] In addition women's employment opportunities are severely constrained by this logic: until 2011 they were restricted to working in education and health care; it was not until 2011 and 2012, respectively, that they were allowed to work in lingerie shops and retail stores, such as supermarkets.[12]

The dominant ideology in the KSA considers men and women to be complementary or "equivalent" to each other rather than equal.[13] Although Saudi Arabia ratified the UN Convention on the Elimination of All Forms of Discrimination against Women on 7 September 2000, the government reserved the right to negate any article that contradicts "the norms of Islamic law."[14] Inside the country the institution of male guardianship reduces women to the status of minors subordinated to the authority of a father, husband, son, or other male relative in questions affecting their own and their children's lives. This institution particularly impacts women's mobility and their ability to marry, divorce, or seek employment.[15] Husbands are the legally designated heads of household and control key decisions, such as choosing the family residence and applying for official documents. Saudi women cannot confer citizenship on their children, obtain a national identity card, or travel outside the country without the permission of their legal guardians.[16]

In Saudi Arabia women's bodies are considered "a source of *fitna* (chaos)" that must be concealed.[17] For that reason, women's appearance and their visibility in public are regulated by an official dress code that requires them to wear a full black cloak (*'abaya*) and a face veil (*niqab*). To ensure compliance, streets and other mixed-gender spaces are policed by the infamous Committee for the Promotion of Virtue and the Prevention of Vice, also known as the religious police (*mutawwi'in*), who control "public moral behavior, including proper dress and the interaction between men and women."[18] As a general rule, according to Eleanor Doumato, it is considered "shameful" and "dangerous for women" to be in public, even when veiled.[19] The blogger Saudi Stepford Wife confirms this point: "There's no public transportation and a lone woman takes a chance with her safety and moral standing any time she takes a taxi alone."[20]

As part of these gendered restrictions on mobility, Saudi Arabia is the only country in the world where women are not allowed to drive. Although there is no written law stating the prohibition, government clerics have issued fatwa rulings that ban such driving, the Department of Traffic refuses to grant driving licenses to women, and police officers and religious police-men customarily arrest women caught driving. The driving ban is not en-forced everywhere, however; women drive in the ARAMCO complex, the Saudi national oil and natural gas company in Dhahran, as well as on the campus of the coed King Abdullah University for Science and Technology, founded in 2009.[21] Moreover Bedouin women are known to drive trucks and other farm equipment in the desert and countryside, as the blogger Sabria Jawhar documents: "I remember as a child my uncle in one of the Yanbu villages going to work at 4 each morning, leaving the management of the house, the family and the harvesting of their crops to my aunt. She drove all over the region to make sure not only her kids but the extended family were cared for."[22]

The right to drive is a very practical concern for women in the KSA. A report published by Human Rights Watch in 2011 found that public trans-portation is insufficient in the country and that women's everyday depen-dence on cab rides, costly full-time drivers, or male family members seri-ously hinders their "ability to study, work, and participate in public life."[23] Far from popular representations in the KSA and abroad of Saudi women as pampered queens chauffeured around by their South Asian drivers, personal bloggers attest to the economic and practical difficulties they en-counter to secure their daily transportation needs.[24] As the activist Manal al-Sharif stresses in a YouTube video, some women devote "90% of their salary" to pay for a driver. She recounts the experience of a friend: "She wakes up at 5am, though her work starts at 7am. When the driver picks her up, he has to go and pick up other women. She gets home at 5pm though her house is only 10 minutes from her work. If she is five minutes late [the driver] will leave her."[25]

While lifting the ban on women driving would immediately solve many of these problems and radically improve Saudi women's lives, conserva-tive sectors strongly oppose this step, arguing that freedom of movement would lead to the disintegration of the system of gender segregation and, ultimately, to immorality.[26] Blogger Rasha explains this reasoning: "If a woman drives she will be free to go where ever and see who ever she please[s], and that scares them."[27] The blogger Eman al-Nafjan explains that the fear that women driving could be used as "a tool of rebellion against husbands and families" may explain why any attempt to defy this prohibition has received exemplary punishments.[28] In particular, driving activism in the KSA is haunted by memories of the harsh repercussions that followed the first Saudi women's driving protest, on 6 November 1990. On that day a group of women met in the parking lot of a supermarket in Riyadh, distributed themselves into fourteen cars, and drove around the city for half an hour until the religious police stopped them. In response to their act of defiance, forty-seven women—among them university professors and public school teachers—were arrested, publicly vilified, and suspended from their jobs.[29]

This disproportionate response occurred in an important political context. Several months before the driving action, in August 1990, King Fahd requested the deployment of U.S. forces on Saudi soil to protect the territory and oil fields after Saddam Hussein's troops invaded Kuwait. U.S. women military personnel became, Doumato remarks, a "highly visible—though controversial—presence" as they openly drove military vehicles in the kingdom.[30] Possibly feeling the pressure, the Saudi government issued an edict promoting the enrollment of women volunteers in social and medical positions in government agencies.[31] Saudi women's rights activists interpreted these shifts as signs that the Saudi monarch was open to reform. Yet, the activists did not anticipate that the regime, criticized for its alliance with the United States, would find in the punishment of women drivers an opportunity to divert attention from the regional conflict while pleasing religious and conservative voices critical of Saudi Arabia's rapprochement with the West.[32]

The severe repression of the participants in the 1990 driving action shaped subsequent actions—and inactions—related to women's driving rights and inflected blog discussions on this issue. In the years that followed, activists continued to ask for an end to the ban by petitioning the king, a tactic that presented less risk.[33] Reflecting these sentiments, the blogger Hala al-Dosari objected to the strategy used by the Saudi activist Wajeha al-Huwaider, who posted a video of herself driving in March 2008.[34] Al-Dosari criticized al-Huwaider's "individual" solution: "It's not only me who would be harshly punished if I challenge the authority, it's my old father as well, this is what happened with the women who demonstrated for the right to drive before." She proposed instead "other meaningful, and less confrontational methods to reach the decision makers, without inciting negativity."[35] At the same time, and despite the risk of reprisals, Saudi bloggers continued to use blogs and other online platforms to discuss and explore ways of pushing for what they considered to be a reasonable demand and to experiment with actions that maintained a delicate balance between legality and trespass.

Moving Alone and Together

On 17 June 2011 around fifty women took part in the Women2Drive campaign by driving in the KSA, many of them in the company of women friends and relatives, fathers, husbands, brothers, and sons.[36] The drivers were aware of the dangers associated with their action: less than a month before, the police had detained al-Sharif, one of the leaders and the face of the campaign, for posting a video of herself driving.[37] The blogger al-Nafjan did not yield to intimidation and participated in the protest as a passenger. Shortly afterward she shared her impressions on her blog, highlighting the affective connections established between the participants through social media: "I was fortunate enough to be able to be a part of it, even though I've never learned to drive. I got into a car with another Saudi woman, Azza Al Shmasi. As I videotaped, she drove for 15 minutes close to a main street in Riyadh. When I got home I excitedly shared the video with my followers on Twitter, as did all the women who drove that day."[38]

While the action explicitly defied the driving prohibition, it was staged in a way to avoid confrontation and assure the anonymity of the participants. To stress its legitimacy, organizers limited participation to women who already had an international driving license and urged drivers to buckle up, obey traffic laws, respect the dress code, and "not challenge the authorities."[39] Ironically the strict adherence to religious rules on women's dress allowed those preferring to remain anonymous to participate without being recognized, tactically using the ʿabaya and the niqab as protection against identification. Despite precautions two drivers were stopped by the police and released after signing a pledge that they would not reoffend. Those who published their names on YouTube, Twitter, Facebook, or a blog were contacted by the Ministry of Interior and their male guardians were summoned to sign the pledge.[40]

The mild reaction of the authorities to the rather faceless protest starkly contrasts with the repression of the drivers in 1990 and al-Sharif's detention on 22 May 2011. Al-Rasheed reads this "indifference" toward the driving action as a sign of the state's effort to maintain the "loyalty of women" in the turbulent context of the 2011 Arab revolutions, a strategy that aims

FIGURE 6.1. Azza Al Shmasi drives during the Women2Drive action, recorded by the blogger Eman al-Nafjan. ScarceMedia, "Driving in Saudi with @saudiwoman," YouTube, 17 June 2011, https://www.youtube.com/watch?v=1rb77qKZseI.

to "feminize the masculine state" in a controlled manner to limit internal dissent and international embarrassment.[41] Following this line of action, the Saudi press ignored the campaign or denied it had occurred, quoting traffic police officers saying that "no women driving incidents have been reported at all." This statement was readily challenged by one of the drivers, who posted on her Twitter account a picture of a ticket she had been issued for driving without a Saudi license, thereby proving that the protest had actually taken place.[42]

The dispersed acts of defiance would have gone largely unnoticed were it not for their virtual presence and magnification online. The participants uploaded the videos of their drives on the YouTube channel "SaudiWomen2Drive" and commented on them on Facebook and Twitter using the hashtag #Women2Drive. In many aspects the action resembled "smart" or "flash mobs" in how it mobilized strangers through social media to perform in concert in the physical space.[43] However, unlike these online-offline interventions, in this case the online presence was not a mediated echo of the action but the political act itself, as it was only in virtual space where the singular transgressions—some of them carried out and video-recorded in the middle of the night to avoid detection—became visible and legible as protest. Taken individually these videos seemed to be rebellious anecdotes, but together they brought "into being" a space of politics that was promptly filled with images of Saudi women behind the wheel.[44]

The introduction of the Internet in 1994 and its spread in 1999 opened new avenues of dissent and multiplied the spaces from which Saudi women could negotiate their "loyalty" to the state.[45] Moreover since the mid-2000s, when Web 2.0 and social media platforms became available in the kingdom, women and girls in the KSA have increasingly used the blogosphere, YouTube, and other digital forums to communicate, share grievances, express dissent, and constitute new forms of consciousness and community within and beyond the country's boundaries.[46] According to unofficial statistics, women represented two-thirds of Internet users in Saudi Arabia in the early 2000s.[47] More recent figures indicate widespread Internet use among both men (56.6 percent) and women (45.6 percent).[48] The estimated number of Internet users in the KSA in December 2011 was 13 million, or 49.0 percent of the population, an increase partly fostered by the multiplication of smartphones and other individual and private access points favored by Saudi women over cyber cafés.[49]

On the other hand, cyberspace is heavily surveilled in Saudi Arabia in ways that evoke Foucault's panopticon, the "all-seeing place" used to discipline individuals by manipulating their presumption that they are under observation.[50] The department responsible for providing Internet services in the country, the Internet Services Unit, states on its website that it filters the web and blocks "pages of an offensive or harmful nature to society, and which violate the tenants of Islamic religion or societal norms."[51] According to the OpenNet Initiative, the KSA also targets web pages that discuss reformist or oppositional issues, human rights, women's rights, LGBTQ rights, family planning, Christianity, or Shiʿa Islam. Over the years Saudi Arabia has detained a number of bloggers and cyber activists for their online activities and regularly appears on the list of the "most net-repressive countries."[52] Despite such close monitoring, online platforms offer a space for mobilization around common causes.[53] Unlike texting, a medium used for political activism in Gulf countries in the late 1990s and early 2000s,[54] the Internet enables complete strangers to take part in concerted actions without communicating with each other. By mobilizing a "negative collectivity" of people who are not members of an established group and do not know each other, social media allows participants to remain anonymous even to the organizers, reducing the risk of identification or co-optation.[55]

The participatory nature of Web 2.0 also encourages computer-literate users to create content online by publishing texts or uploading their own images and videos.[56] In addition, through these platforms Saudi netizens can gain access to information that may not be available in the kingdom and interact with strangers across gender lines, circumventing family and governmental control.[57] As Loubna Skalli has noted for women in the Arab region, bloggers and users of Facebook, Twitter, and YouTube also use these sites to create "alternative discursive spaces" that contest or qualify dominant political and religious views.[58]

Yet these portals not only reflect and communicate but also dialectically constitute new embodied counterhegemonic subjectivities, as exemplified by the suggestive video performance "Flowing through Saudi Arabia— A Hoop Dance," by the Saudi visual artist Balqis AlRashed.[59] The fifteen-second YouTube clip shows AlRashed in her ʿabaya and niqab, swinging a hula hoop, her body swirling freely "through Saudi Arabia" in what appears to be the intimate space of her home. Like the moving images, the accompanying English-language text, titled "A State of Play," explicitly challenges a range of hegemonic embodied restrictions, using evocative spatial language to constitute her identity on her own terms:

I am not gender.
I am not religion.
I am not expectations.
. . .
I am movement and growth,
A series of expansions and contractions.
I am opposition and sameness.
. . .
But, I am not what you think of me,
I am what I think of myself.
I am not what you made of me,
I am what I make of myself.
. . .

Interventions like AlRashed's coexist and often converge with other "microrebellions proliferating in the fluidity and interwoven pathways of cyberspace," as Zakia Salime has described these individual acts of defiance online.[60] Another example is the video posted by the twenty-four-year-old student Loujain Al Hathloul on 24 January 2013 on the social

FIGURE 6.2. Still of Balqis AlRashed's "Flowing through Saudi Arabia—A Hoop Dance," *Balqis AlRashed,* 4 October 2014, http://www.balqis-alrashed.com/2014/10 /hooping-in-saudi-arabia-flow-dance.html.

network Keek. The otherwise inoffensive clip, which shows Al Hathloul mocking Saudi ultraconservatives with her face and hair uncovered, caused "a commotion" when it went viral, as al-Nafjan recalls on her blog.[61] Several months after her "unveiling" Al Hathloul became the face of a second driving action, organized on 26 October 2013, and participated in the protest by driving in the company of her father and posting the video of her drive online.[62] The confluence of Al Hathloul's "personal revolution" and the activism of the Women2Drive campaign illustrates one of the many ways in which these singular gestures that are proliferating in Saudi cyberspace reproduce and propagate themselves, interact with each other, and coalesce around common causes.[63]

Blogs as Sites of Cautious
Interstitial Politics and Radical Imaginings

Blogs are personal online spaces whose particular architecture facilitates and even promotes the interaction between author and readers through the comments section. While open to judgment and critique, these sections are often perceived as safe spaces for debate, as bloggers can moderate comments and retain control over published content. Scholarship on women's blogging in Egypt and Iran indicates that blogs facilitate a largely "unregulated narrative, which counters hegemonic norms without directly confronting the state."[64] In the KSA, blogs such as al-Nafjan's *Saudiwoman's Weblog*, Jawhar's Sabria's *Out of the Box*, al-Dosari's *Hala in Wonderland*, *Saudi Stepford Wife*, and *Omaima Al Najjar* have been some of the sites used by Saudi netizens since the mid-2000s to discuss the driving ban, "get [their] viewpoint out," and "express [their] opinion" on many social and religious questions.[65]

Constituted as hybrids between personal diaries and online forums, blogs encourage informal expression in ways that, for Saudi Stepford Wife, resemble "any typical bitching session I have with my friends when we get together."[66] In addition the possibility of writing anonymously allows bloggers to communicate more freely and create spaces for controversial discussion. While al-Nafjan, Jawhar, al-Dosari, and Al Najjar write under their real names, others are well aware of the risks associated with expressing certain opinions online in Saudi Arabia and prefer to use a pseudonym. This is the case with Saudi Stepford Wife, who states in her first post, from 2007, "I will try to remain as anonymous as possible so in case I get too vocal on touchy subjects, it won't impact my life negatively (I can only speculate as to how)."[67]

At the personal level blogs represent for many of these authors one of the few available outlets to release steam and voice their frustrated responses to various restrictions on their lives and mobility. At the social level the comments section provides an "opportunity for dialogue between the genders" that is otherwise infeasible in gender-segregated physical spaces and facilitates the creation of cross-gender alliances.[68] For example, in response to one of al-Nafjan's posts, several Saudi men expressed their solidarity with the driving cause, disrupting the hegemonic masculinist discourse articulated by state and religious authorities and conservative publics:

HAITHAM: I await the day when women in Saudi Arabia will be ... issue[d] driving licences and drive freely. As for my part, I will personally teach my mother and sister how to drive and help them [get] driving licences.

ABDULLAH: Same here.

SAUDIMAJIX: My friends and I were talking about this, and one of my friends said, if each one of us is whiling [*sic*] to let his wife, sister or mother drive and sit by her said [*sic*] no one could say anything about it.⁶⁹

In the KSA, as in most parts of the world, bloggers are educated and relatively privileged people. As we learn from their posts, al-Nafjan is a lecturer at King Saud University, where she teaches English as a foreign language, and lived in the United States when she was a child. Jawhar is an assistant professor at King Saud bin Abdulaziz University and got her PhD and driving license in Newcastle, in the United Kingdom.⁷⁰ Al-Dosari studied in the United States, where she learned how to drive.⁷¹ According to her blog profile, Al Najjar is a "nurse becoming a doctor" who "appreciate[s] good classical & Baroque music, good Italian food and comedy movies/ shows."⁷² Saudi Stepford Wife is an "American/Saudi" graduate student who writes in English to establish a "dialogue with the world" that can be read "in the furthest reaches of the planet."⁷³

By addressing an international audience, these bloggers weave transnational networks of solidarity that support their cause and put further pressure on the Saudi regime to improve women's situation in the KSA. Jawhar notes, "If Saudi Arabia wants to be a player in the international business community, it's going to have to make some dramatic changes. . . . Westerners observe, and, yes, judge our society . . . by how we treat our own citizens, the expatriates that work here, and whom Saudi society thinks [of] as our national treasure—women."⁷⁴ These English-language blogs also serve as a megaphone with which these authors challenge Orientalist stereotypes that portray them as passive victims. As al-Nafjan notes in her post "Why do we stay the way we are?," "Outsiders looking in think to themselves why do Saudi women put up with all this oppression. The guardianship system, the ban on driving and all our other societal peculiarities draw looks of pity, shock and for some a fixation. Why don't we all just go out into the streets without *abaya*s? Why don't we just get behind a wheel and drive? Why don't we run away? The short answer is we don't want to." She concludes, "Before you judge us, relate to us. This is what we are born into and we would feel lost without our community's approval and backing. And just like every individual in this world, Saudi women are just trying to find their way."[75]

These contextualizing remarks, however, should not be confused with compliance. As a matter of fact, bloggers are very critical of Saudi society and discriminatory norms. With regard to the prohibition to drive, their posts often take the form of bitter complaints about the necessity of hiring a driver, its cost, the negative impact of the ban on working women, and the driver's bad driving. By narrating specific problems and grievances, authors "relate to one another and generalize experiences."[76] Not unlike feminist consciousness-raising practices, Saudi bloggers in conversation with each other develop a critical perspective that links individual lived experiences to a larger social and political context. By expressing "individual sentiment" in blogs, bloggers make their sensibilities communal and open the way for "collective action."[77] For example, in response to a post by al-Nafjan on 28 October 2010 expressing frustration about the ban, Al Najjar wrote, "2 months ago I was driving the car on the beach and there was this voice inside of me [that] whispers . . drive in the main street Omaima. . Man . . . couldn't helpt [sic] it. . I turned right on to the main street—and it was day time, windows open . . . I drove 80km\h and I felt so good. Perhabs [sic] you should do the same." To that confession a second commenter replied, "Omaima, what do you mean you drove on the main street? What city? What happened? No one said anything? Maybe that's what has to happen. A collective 'intifada' where all women that CAN drive, agree on the day and just DO it!! Can you imagine!!!!!!!" A third commenter added, "If you could gather 3,000 women to protest . . . really what will the Saudi men do? I think what needs to happen is a good old fashioned large number protest. There is strength in numbers and the small handfuls of 100 here 20 there isn't enough to overwhelm. Are there enough Saudi women willing to be brave and organize for something this big?"[78]

The Women2Drive campaign of June 2011 was the materialization of online reflections of this kind. As a commenter to one of al-Nafjan's posts noted, discussions such as these are "like the single drops accumulating" and, over time, creating a "ripple effect" that can produce change.[79] Indeed the protest succeeded in raising international awareness of the driving ban and set a precedent that served as a reference for subsequent actions, organized on 26 October 2013 and 2014. While the Saudi state has continued to monitor and silence this activism by blocking the website of the campaign and the mirror websites created to circumvent censorship,[80] women's blogs discussing this question have not been subjected to comparable tactics of state intervention, possibly because they are understood as personal spaces where women share concerns not considered political. The framing of the driving issue in terms of lived experience and the fact that bloggers use the familiar and informal language of social life camouflage the degree to which blog conversations radically challenge fundamental contradictions of the Saudi state.

"One day it will rain cars and I'll drive my own," wrote al-Nafjan in a post of 5 September 2012 titled "Optimism."[81] By envisioning and sharing an alternative reality, and by enacting it in the present time through clandestine interventions like the Women2Drive protest, activists create a sort of virtual heterotopia, Foucault's "other space" that is "in relation with all the other sites, but in such a way as to suspect, neutralize, or invert the set of relations that [it] happen[s] to designate, mirror, or reflect."[82] In this real place, located at the interstice between private and public space, where the personal and the political meet and the individual becomes collective, Saudi women drive, interact with like-minded strangers from around the world, engage in conversations with unrelated others, and, by imagining radical futures, pave the way for the desired present.

Paradoxes of Interstitial Spaces and Enactments

> For your information the video is on its way to Twitter and Facebook!
> —Saudi Nail Polish Girl, 23 May 2012

In *Feminism and Geography* Gillian Rose discusses the subversive potential of occupying a "paradoxical space," a location imagined by the subject of feminism to contest dominant masculinist spatial thinking and articulate a more productive relation between dichotomous notions of self and other, inside and outside, or power and resistance. As she provocatively suggests, paradoxical sites can emerge in any context through "partial and strategic" yet potentially radical emancipatory action.[83] In "An Ontology of Everyday Distraction: The Freeway, the Mall, the Television" Margaret Morse contends that highly regulated and predictable places can offer conjunctural spaces where "kinks in the road" unexpectedly appear.[84]

In Saudi Arabia, shopping malls promote private consumption while safeguarding "public decency" by means of a double security presence: private security personnel protect businesses from theft while religious police patrol the walkways, shops, and entrances to ensure that men attend the mosque and vendors close shops for prayer times. The CCTV surveillance system is used to monitor women's dress practices as well as interactions between unrelated men and women.[85] In addition many malls enforce family-only policies that ban (at all times or on particular days and hours) single men from entering shopping centers by themselves.

Yet the shopping mall also generates productive possibilities in the KSA. Despite surveillance and control, malls in Saudi Arabia have become one of the few spaces where unrelated men and women have opportunities to mingle.[86] Saudis use different strategies to communicate with each other in malls, including targim, whereby one person discreetly drops a note containing their mobile number in front of another person, and more recently by using Bluetooth.[87] In the absence of bars, movie theaters, and other entertainment facilities, Saudi single men resort to different tactics to gain access to these spaces of consumption and leisure, including disguising themselves as women, bribing security personnel, and persuading female customers to enter with them.[88] Saudi women and girls visiting these spaces frequently transgress dress practices—for example, by letting their headscarves fall on their shoulders or showing their makeup, thereby pushing social boundaries and redefining "gendered norms of conduct in public."[89]

On 23 May 2012 a self-recorded video by a young Saudi woman confronting the religious police in a shopping mall went viral after she posted it on YouTube.[90] For approximately four minutes she argues with the officers who ask her to leave the premises because she is wearing nail polish and showing her hair. While this episode has been downplayed by al-Rasheed as a "futile disconnected" incident "grounded in sensationalism and imagined heroism,"[91] it should not be dismissed out of hand. Indeed the online reproduction of this act of defiance speaks to other personal transgressions, like those performed by AlRashed and Al Hathloul. Moreover its occurrence in a shopping mall and the Nail Polish Girl's audacious remark "I am free to walk around this mall as I like!" reveal the paradoxical perception of this privatized space as a place where women, as consumers, are entitled to freedom of movement, a right that is denied to them in public space.

Like in many other cities and countries, political activities are prohibited in Saudi shopping malls. Yet in the absence of suitable alternative venues, organizers of petitions for the right to drive have gathered signatures on their premises, and malls have occasionally become sites of protest, especially after the 2011 Arab revolutions.[92] Far from being *nonplaces* that create "neither singular identity nor relations; only solitude, and similitude,"[93] malls are places of intense sociability in the kingdom. By disrupting their "predictable and schematized" character,[94] Saudis of all genders produce malls as interstitial spaces for unauthorized interaction and expression, albeit with some limitations. Commercial hubs are often located in suburban areas with limited connections to public transportation, and therefore shopping malls are not accessible to Saudis across the economic spectrum, particularly women who cannot afford a full-time driver or cab fare.

Like shopping malls, automobiles are linked to notions of freedom. Ironically, cars require the fossil fuels that allowed the ruling Saud family to consolidate its political control in alliance with Western corporations and imperial interests. Moreover, the oil-based rentier economy funds the current system of gender segregation in KSA. Nevertheless, having a car and being able to navigate Saudi roads fulfill "symbolic and affective functions" and can elicit feelings of autonomy, safety, and sociability as well as anxiety.[95] Within the mosaic of "aesthetic, emotional and sensory responses" associated with the automobile,[96] driving their own cars is imbued with special significance for many Saudi women. While sitting in the backseat reproduces relations of domesticity and dependence, taking the wheel represents "the materialization of fantasies and desires for independence," while providing a certain sense of safety.[97] As al-Sharif affirms in a video recorded by the activist al-Huwaider while she drove in the city of Khobar, "No one dares to humiliate me or bother me [in my own car]."[98]

Saudi women bloggers frequently write about driving and their desire for increased mobility. Walking involves several dangers; in Saudi Stepford Wife's words, among these is the risk of becoming a "moving target for this country's unskilled drivers" because there are no sidewalks. In addition women who venture alone on the streets "may be apprehended by the religious police on accusations of soliciting sex," as Doumato remarks, or subjected to violence.[99] In fact an incident of this kind catalyzed al-Sharif's driving activism: "I almost got kidnapped trying to find a taxi in the street. .... In Saudi Arabia, it's not normal for a woman to walk in the street alone, and I don't cover my face, so I am an open target. I was walking at 9 p.m. trying to find a taxi for a ride home, and someone followed me and I had to throw a stone at this guy to protect myself."[100]

At another level those bloggers who have an international driving license, like Stepford Saudi Wife, find a sense of autonomy and competence in the driver's seat: "I make it a point to renew my driver[']s licence every time I go to the States, even if it hasn't expired yet. I use it in Bahrain and the Emirates when we go. My hubby know[s] as soon as we cross the border I'll tell him to scoot over." Conversely, her inability to drive in the KSA is a "core issue which sinks its razor-sharp, rank teeth into almost every aspect of [her] family life," as she depends on her husband to run daily errands.[101]

For Saudi women who rely on hired drivers, the safety usually identified with the "secluded, highly structured space" of the car is relative.[102] Jawhar remarks, "I depend on a stranger driving his own less-than-safe vehicle to get me around [on] time. I am at the mercy of his whims and moods."[103] The lack of privacy in the interior of the car and the permanent physical proximity of the driver add a "suffocating" layer to women's lack of autonomous mobility, as illustrated by al-Nafjan: "When my husband cannot reach me on my cell phone, he contacts the driver because wherever I am, the driver will of course be there too."[104] In other cases bloggers see in their chauffeurs a potential threat to themselves or their children.[105]

Although the state justifies the driving ban on the grounds of preventing gender mixing between unrelated men and women, the inability to drive forces many women in the KSA to spend significant amounts of time with an unrelated male. Al-Nafjan attributes this paradox to the ways class, race, and citizenship interarticulate with gender and sexuality in Saudi Arabia. Most hired drivers are of South Asian origin, and their work and living conditions resemble those of other low-status migrant workers in the Gulf. For these "guest" workers, "being considered a human being" is not self-evident, as Rhacel Parreñas has amply documented.[106] Al-Nafjan candidly explains this matter in a post titled "Saudi Women's Man-O-Meter": "To completely understand how this came about you have to go back in history to when slavery was the norm. Back then, women did not stringently cover from their male slaves and in some families they did not cover at all. The neutering of some male slaves was socially acceptable. This attitude somehow transferred to the modern day drivers. Women who are religious strictly cover from their drivers but the majority treat drivers like a little less than a man."[107]

Yet despite the socially constituted boundaries that designate South Asian men as not quite human, "just another auto part," the relatively intimate interior of the car allows for "multiple socialities."[108] In particular it is conducive to the development of relations that violate such boundaries, as driver and passenger share an important part of their everyday lives alone together in that "quiet spot, removed from the world outside."[109] Stories of romance and marriage between Saudi women and their drivers are common and feed anxieties regarding miscegenation between Saudi citizens and these "perpetual outsiders."[110]

Adding to these social concerns, reports of women driving have multiplied in Saudi blogs, as have authors confessing their transgression of the driving ban. These disclosures sometimes appear as fleeting references in a comments section, as when Saudi Stepford Wife replied to a reader, "Personally, I've driven veiled in the east and in the west (I've even driven in SAUDIA - Shhhh!)."[111] Sometimes women offer detailed descriptions of their clandestine rides. For example, in response to al-Nafjan's blog post "Saudi Shewolf," where she shared the story of a friend's driving escapade in the middle of the night, several readers disclosed similar experiences produced by a variety of circumstances, ranging from family emergencies to adventurous outings.[112] Describing these episodes as "hilarious," "great fun," or "very liberating," bloggers set a joyful and playful tone that contrasts with the stern admonitions of state and religious authorities regarding women's driving. By sharing these experiences and bringing together complaints and confidences with humor and irony, Saudi bloggers recognize commonalities in the spaces they inhabit and build the necessary trust to establish common ground for engagement and community. It is in the paradoxical space that emerges that they can collectively ponder existing closures and potential openings within the limits of the strict system of gender segregation.

Conclusion

The Arab uprisings that swept the region in 2011 left toppled governments and disrupted regimes. As the contributors to this volume demonstrate, these ruptures went beyond the realm of formal politics, affecting gender and sexual orders in fundamental, though not always emancipatory ways. In the KSA, King Abdullah's royal decree to grant Saudi women the right to suffrage in 2015, announced on 25 September 2011, was read as a symbolic gesture of the monarch in response to "Saudis' restlessness to pick up the pace of reform" in the context of the so-called Arab Spring.[113] While women's rights activists have welcomed this step, the contradictions of this legal advance have not escaped them, as al-Nafjan pointedly observed in a post of September 2011: "In 18 months' time a Saudi woman can be a member of parliament providing that her male guardian allows her to and she finds a man to drive her there."[114]

Yet beyond this formal—and highly publicized—development that offers limited potential for the advancement of women's rights in the less-than-democratic KSA,[115] activist and nonactivist Saudi women and girls continue to push in informal and less visible ways to enact change in quotidian life. The interstitial spaces of automobiles, shopping malls, and cyber sites such as personal blogs and YouTube have become particularly productive for this modality of cautious politics that unfolds where public and private, and by extension personal and political, become "intermeshed."[116] As individual expressions of resistance against state- and religiously dictated restrictions on movement, appearance, and interaction or as a collective articulation of a demand for the right to drive, these interventions should be understood to be in dialogue with each other. Indeed if we consider them separately, we risk seeing these ruptures as a mere compilation of anecdotes. Collectively they constitute a repository of cumulative resistance. The sum of these single contributions in conversation with each other creates what Ananda Mitra calls a "hypervoice" that emerges from the "numerous voices all connected together." Jointly they articulate the narrative of a diverse and complex collectivity, calling "in unison . . . for recognition within the public sphere of cyberspace" and beyond.[117] The combination of these voices and actions in online and offline spaces helps generate new forms of consciousness, community, and politics.

The outcomes of these performances, moreover, are not easy to control or delimit. The mediated resistance that came into being during the 2011 driving campaign did not vanish once the action concluded. It has been sustained by regular feeds in the blogosphere, on Facebook, and on Twitter using the hashtag #Women2Drive. Blogs and social media persistently address and challenge the driving ban, follow the detention of women caught driving, and express solidarity with initiatives fostering this cause.[118] In 2013 and 2014 these platforms were reactivated for similar driving actions, and they will continue to function in future driving campaigns. The next protest is scheduled for the nonexistent date of 31 November, a move that actualizes an indefinite demand and encourages Saudi women to take the wheel any day and every day, tactically producing the *paradoxical time* of an imminent future for Saudi women.[119]

NOTES

This chapter greatly benefited from comments from a variety of generous colleagues. First and foremost I am indebted to the editors, Frances Hasso and Zakia Salime, whose constructive criticism and insight prompted me to push my analysis further. I am grateful to the participants in the 2013 Geographies of Gender workshop at Duke University for their provocative and thoughtful remarks. I thank the anonymous reviewers for their valuable suggestions, which greatly contributed to improving the final version. This chapter also profited from discussions at earlier presentations of this research: the 2012 Gender and Women's Studies in the Arab Region Conference (American University of Sharjah, UAE), the 2012 Hemi G SI Convergence: The Geo/Body Politics of Emancipation (Duke University), Theorizing the Web (Brooklyn, 2014), and Féminismes du XXIe Siècle (Université de Cergy-Pontoise and Université Paris Diderot, 2014). Finally, I would like to thank Ian Alan Paul for his constant support and stimulating advice throughout the writing of this chapter.

Epigraph: Eman al-Nafjan, "Saudi Shewolf," *Saudiwoman's Weblog*, 31 October 2009, http://www.saudiwoman.me/2009/10/31/saudi-shewolf.

1. Mattias Kärrholm, "Interstitial Space and the Transformation of Retail Building Types," in *Urban Interstices: The Aesthetics and the Politics of the In-Between*, edited by Andrea Mubi Brighenti (Farnham, UK: Ashgate, 2013), 136.

2. Henri Lefebvre, *The Production of Space* (1974; Oxford: Blackwell, 1991); Andrea Mubi Brighenti, introduction to Brighenti, *Urban Interstices*, xviii; Andreas Philippopoulos-Mihalopoulos, "Spatial Justice in the Lawscape," in Brighenti, *Urban Interstices*, 89.

3. Luc Lévesque, "Trajectories of Interstitial Landscapeness: A Conceptual Framework for Territorial Imagination and Action," in Brighenti, *Urban Interstices*, 23; Kärrholm, "Interstitial Space and the Transformation of Retail Building Types," 137.

4. Madawi al-Rasheed, *A Most Masculine State: Gender, Politics, and Religion in Saudi Arabia* (New York: Cambridge University Press, 2013), 17.

5. S. F. al-Ghamidi, *Structure of the Tribe and Urbanization in Saudi Arabia* (Jeddah: Al-Shrooq Press, 1981), 32–35.

6. Hélène Thiollet, "The Ambivalence of Immigration Policy in Saudi Arabia: Public and Private Actors in Migration Management," in *Migrant Labor in the Gulf: Working Group Summary Report,* edited by Center for International and Regional Studies (Doha: Georgetown University, School of Foreign Service in Qatar, 2011), 23, https://repository .library.georgetown.edu/bitstream/handle/10822/558543/CIRSSummaryReport2 MigrantLaborintheGulf2011.pdf?sequence=5.

7. Madawi al-Rasheed, *Contesting the Saudi State: Islamic Voices from a New Generation* (New York: Cambridge University Press, 2006), 164.

8. Al-Rasheed, *Masculine State,* 24; Roel Meijer, "Reform in Saudi Arabia: The Gender-Segregation Debate," *Middle East Policy* 17, no. 4 (2010): 81.

9. Amélie Le Renard, "'Only for Women': Women, the State, and Reform in Saudi Arabia," *Middle East Journal* 6, no. 4 (2008): 610.

10. Le Renard, "'Only for Women,'" 610.

11. Eleanor A. Doumato, "Saudi Arabia," in *Women's Rights in the Middle East and North Africa: Progress amid Resistance,* edited by Sanja Kelly and Julia Breslin (New York: Freedom House, Rowman and Littlefield, 2010), 432.

12. Doumato, "Saudi Arabia," 426; Human Rights Watch, "World Report 2013: Saudi Arabia," accessed 24 June 2015, http://www.hrw.org/world-report/2013/country-chapters /saudi-arabia; Katherine Zoepf, "Shopgirls," *New Yorker,* 23 December 2013, http://www .newyorker.com/reporting/2013/12/23/131223fa_fact_zoepf.

13. Sanja Kelly, "Hard-Won Progress and a Long Road Ahead: Women's Rights in the Middle East and North Africa," in Kelly and Breslin, *Women's Rights in the Middle East and North Africa,* 19.

14. UN Women, "Declarations, Reservations, and Objections to CEDAW," Convention on the Elimination of All Forms of Discrimination against Women, accessed June 22, 2015, http://www.un.org/womenwatch/daw/cedaw/reservations-country.htm.

15. Doumato, "Saudi Arabia," 427.

16. World Bank, *Women, Business and the Law 2014* (Washington, DC: World Bank, Bloomsbury, 2013).

17. Al-Rasheed, *Masculine State,* 116.

18. Doumato, "Saudi Arabia," 427.

19. Eleanor Abdella Doumato, "Women in Civic and Political Life: Reform under Authoritarian Regimes," in *Political Change in the Arab Gulf States: Stuck in Transition,* edited by Mary Ann Tetreault, Gwenn Okruhlik, and Andrzej Kapiszewski (Boulder: Lynne Rienner, 2011), 202.

20. Saudi Stepford Wife, "Sorry, Can't Help Ya," *Saudi Stepford Wife,* 2 October 2007, http://www.saudistepfordwife.blogspot.com/2007/10/sorry-cant-help-ya.html.

21. Doumato, "Women in Civic and Political Life," 194.

22. Sean Foley, "All I Want Is Equality with Girls: Gender and Social Change in the Twenty-First Century Gulf," *Middle East Review of International Affairs* 14, no. 1 (2010): 25. See also "Rising Number of Bedouin Women Enter Work Force," *Al Arabiya,* 1 July 2012, http://english.alarabiya.net/articles/2012/07/01/223783.html; Sabria Jawhar, "Let Rural Women Drive, as They Always Have in Past," *Saudi Gazette,* 14 October 2009,

http://web.archive.org/web/20150328144324/http://www.saudigazette.com.sa/index.cfm
?method=home.regcon&contentID=2009101451500; "To Drive or Not to Drive . . . the
Gender Debate Continues in Saudi Arabia," *Asharq Al-Awsat*, 20 June 2005, http://www
.aawsat.net/2005/06/article55271101; Sabria Jawhar, "Saudi Rural Women's Freedom to
Drive Cars and Trucks under Renewed Threat," *Sabria's Out of the Box*, 13 October 2009,
http://www.saudiwriter.blogspot.com/2009/10/saudi-rural-womens-freedom-to-drive
.html.

23. Human Rights Watch, "Saudi Arabia: Free Woman Who Dared to Drive," 23 May
2011, http://www.hrw.org/news/2011/05/23/saudi-arabia-free-woman-who-dared
-drive.

24. Ordinary Girl, "It Is Going to Be O.K.!!," *A Girl Who Is Trying*, 21 August 2008,
http://ordinarygirl9.blogspot.com.es; Omaima Al Najjar, "What Is It Like to Be a Saudi
Woman?," *Omaima Al Najjar*, 27 April 2010, https://omaimanajjar.wordpress.com/2010
/04/27/whats-like-to-be-a-saudi-woman-2; Sabria Jawhar, "Let Women Drive!," *Sabria's
Out of the Box*, 25 September 2007, http://saudiwriter.blogspot.com.es/2007/09/let
-women-drive.html.

25. See Manal al-Sharif's video in "Saudi Woman Driver Faces Jail Again—'This Is
against Religion and Logic'—Video," *Guardian*, 26 May 2011, http://www.theguardian
.com/world/video/2011/may/26/saudi-arabia-woman-driver-video.

26. Eman Al Nafjan, "The Saudi 'Study' That Finds All Women Drivers on the Road to
Immorality," *Guardian*, 6 December 2011, http://www.theguardian.com/commentisfree
/2011/dec/06/saudi-study-women-drivers.

27. Rasha, "Saudi Girls Involved with Their Drivers," *Mideast Youth*, 4 May 2007, http://
www.mideastyouth.com/2007/05/04/saudi-girls-involved-with-their-drivers.

28. Eman al-Nafjan, "The Reasoning behind the Ban on Women Driving," *Saudiwoman's Weblog*, 27 June 2008, http://www.saudiwoman.me/2008/06/27/the-reasoning
-behind-the-ban-on-women-driving.

29. Doumato, "Women in Civic and Political Life"; Foley, "All I Want Is Equality with
Girls."

30. Eleanor A. Doumato, "Gender, Monarchy, and National Identity in Saudi Arabia,"
British Journal of Middle Eastern Studies 19, no. 1 (1992): 31.

31. Foley, "All I Want Is Equality with Girls," 26.

32. Doumato, "Gender, Monarchy," 44.

33. On 23 September 2007 the Society for Protecting and Defending Women's Rights,
founded by Wajeha al-Huwaider and Fawzia al-Ayouni, launched a petition addressed
to the king to lift the driving ban. For more information, see Ebtihal Mubarak, "Saudi
Women Petitioning Govt for Driving Rights," *Arab News*, 16 September 2007, http://
www.arabnews.com/node/303391. To read the full text in Arabic, see www.web.archive
.org/web/20071219024436/http://www.womengateway.com/arwg/News/2007/Sep
/saudinews.htm.

34. See Yes2WomenDriving, "Wajeha Al-Huwaider for Women's Day 2008" (Arabic),
YouTube, 7 March 2008, www.youtube.com/watch?v=54pRJkJ6B6E. See also Amira Al
Hussaini, "Arabeyes: Rebelling the Saudi Way," *Global Voices*, 18 March 2008, http://www
.globalvoicesonline.org/2008/03/18/arabeyes-rebelling-the-saudi-way.

35. Hala al-Dosari, "Claiming Women's Rights [I Don't Need Support]," *Hala in Wonderland*, 29 June 2009, http://www.hala1.wordpress.com/2009/06/29/claiming-women%E2%80%99s-rights-i-don%E2%80%99t-need-support.

36. Ahmed Al Omran, "'A Historical Moment': The Saudi Women Challenging a Government by Driving," NPR, 19 June 2011, http://www.npr.org/blogs/thetwo-way/2011/06/19/137271964/a-historical-moment-the-saudi-women-challenging-a-government-by-driving.

37. Manal Al-Sharif, a computer security consultant at ARAMCO, posted a YouTube video publicizing the protest on 18 May 2011: "Questions and Answers about June" (Arabic), http://www.youtube.com/watch?v=zLOjlG59GYU. Four days later she was arrested for driving and uploading the video of her drive online (see "Saudi Woman Driver Faces Jail Again").

38. Eman al-Nafjan, "English Version of Piece Published in Stern," *Saudiwoman's Weblog*, 6 October 2011, http://www.saudiwoman.me/2011/10/06/english-version-of-piece-published-in-stern.

39. Al-Sharif listed the instructions in "Questions and Answers about June."

40. Al-Nafjan, "English Version of Piece Published in Stern."

41. Al-Rasheed, *Masculine State*, 292–93.

42. Al Omran, "'A Historical Moment.'"

43. Howard Rheingold, *Smart Mobs: The Next Social Revolution* (Cambridge, MA: Perseus, 2002), xii; Almira Ousmanova, "Flashmob: The Divide between Art and Politics in Belarus," *Art Margins Online*, 15 July 2010, http://www.artmargins.com/index.php/2-articles/588-flashmob-divide-between-art-politics-belarus.

44. Judith Butler, "Bodies in Alliance and the Politics of the Street," European Institute for Progressive Cultural Policies, last modified September 2011, http://www.eipcp.net/transversal/1011/butler/en.

45. Communication and Information Technology Commission, "Internet in Saudi Arabia," accessed 22 June 2015, http://www.internet.sa/en/?s=internet+in+saudi+arabia&x=0&y=0.

46. Web 2.0 and social media platforms are "web-based platforms that predominantly support online networking, online community-building, and maintenance, collaborative information production and sharing, and user-generated content production, diffusion, and consumption." Christian Fuchs et al., *Internet and Surveillance: The Challenges of Web 2.0 and Social Media* (New York: Routledge, 2012), 3. This includes, among others, Facebook, Twitter, YouTube, Blogger, Wordpress, and Wikipedia.

47. Joshua Teitelbaum, "Dueling for Daʿwa: State vs. Society on the Saudi Internet," *Middle East Journal* 56, no. 2 (2002): 234.

48. Asbar Center for Studies, Research and Communications, "Uses of the Internet in the Saudi Society," accessed 22 June 2015, http://web.archive.org/web/20150626192904/http://www.asbar.com/en/studies-researches/social-research-studies/350.article.htm.

49. Internet World Stats, accessed 23 June 2015, http://www.internetworldstats.com/middle.htm#sa; Sunila Lobo and Silvia Elaluf-Calderwood, "The BlackBerry Veil: Mobile Use and Privacy Practices by Young Female Saudis," *Journal of Islamic Marketing* 3, no. 2 (2012): 193. At the same time, however, women in impoverished and rural areas with

poor telecommunications infrastructure are "at a higher risk of being marginalized" due to a traditionally male-dominated ICT sector, unequal access to training, and scarcity of Internet content in Arabic. Ayman Elnaggar, "Towards Gender Equal Access to ICT," *Information Technology for Development* 14, no. 4 (2008): 280. According to the Asbar Center for Studies, Research and Communications, 91.1 percent of women (82.0 percent of men) prefer to use the Internet at home, and only 10.4 percent of women (53.3 percent of men) access the web from an Internet café ("Uses of the Internet in the Saudi Society").

50. Rheingold, *Smart Mobs*, 189; Michel Foucault, *Discipline and Punish* (New York: Random House, 1977).

51. Internet Services Unit, "Introduction to Content Filtering," http://web.archive.org /web/20150813041026/http://www.isu.net.sa/saudi-internet/contenet-filtring/filtring .htm.

52. OpenNet Initiative, "Internet Filtering in Saudi Arabia," last modified 2009, http:// www.opennet.net/sites/opennet.net/files/ONI_SaudiArabia_2009.pdf. See also Reporters without Borders, "Attacks on Journalists and Media in Iraq and Yemen, Two Bloggers Freed in Saudi Arabia," 1 June 2011, http://en.rsf.org/saudi-arabia-attacks-on-journalists -and-media-01-06-2011,40389.html; Reporters without Borders, "Beset by Online Surveillance and Content Filtering, Netizens Fight On," 29 March 2012, http://en.rsf.org/beset -by-online-surveillance-and-13-03-2012,42061.html. The Committee to Protect Journalists ranked the KSA eighth on the list of the ten most censored countries in 2012: "10 Most Censored Countries," 2 May 2012, http://www.cpj.org/reports/2012/05/10-most -censored-countries.php.

53. Serpil Yuce, Nitin Agarwal, and Rolf T. Wigand, "Mapping Cyber-Collective Action among Female Muslim Bloggers for the Women to Drive Movement," *Lecture Notes in Computer Science* 7812 (2013): 331.

54. Steve Coll, "In the Gulf, Dissidence Goes Digital," *Washington Post*, 29 March 2005, http://www.washingtonpost.com/wp-dyn/articles/A8175-2005Mar28.html.

55. Ousmanova, "Flashmob."

56. Rheingold, *Smart Mobs*, 197.

57. Deborah L. Wheeler, "Blessings and Curses: Women and the Internet Revolution in the Arab World," in *Women and Media in the Middle East: Power through Self-Expression*, edited by Naomi Sakr (London: I. B. Tauris, 2004), 156.

58. Loubna H. Skalli, "Communicating Gender in the Public Sphere: Women and Information Technologies in the MENA," *Journal of Middle East Women's Studies* 2, no. 2 (2006): 39.

59. Balqis AlRashed, "Flowing through Saudi Arabia—A Hoop Dance," *Order Out of Chaos*, blogger.com, 4 October 2014, http://www.balqis-alrashed.com/2014/10/hooping -in-saudi-arabia-flow-dance.html.

60. Zakia Salime, "New Feminism as Personal Revolutions: Microrebellious Bodies," *Signs: Journal of Women in Culture and Society* 40, no. 1 (2014): 16.

61. Eman Al Nafjan, "Loujain Al Hathloul," *Saudiwoman's Weblog*, 9 November 2013, http://www.saudiwoman.me/2013/11/09/loujain-al-hathloul.

62. See Loujain Al Hathloul's video announcing the 26 October driving campaign: Keek, 19 September 2013, http://www.keek.com/keek/4uRkdab. See the video of

Al Hathloul's drive during the protest, recorded by her father: Keek, 23 October 2013, http://www.keek.com/keek/Og6udab.

63. Salime, "New Feminism as Personal Revolutions," 16.

64. Yasmine Rifaat, "Blogging the Body: The Case of Egypt," *Surfacing* 1, no. 1 (2008): 51. See also Sharon Otterman, "Publicizing the Private: Egyptian Women Bloggers Speak Out," *Arab Media and Society* 1 (February 2007): 2; Masserat Amir-Ebrahimi, "Transgression in Narration: The Lives of Iranian Women in Cyberspace," *Journal of Middle East Women's Studies* 4, no. 3 (2008): 101.

65. Eman al-Nafjan, *Saudiwoman's Weblog*, http://www.saudiwoman.me; Sabria S. Jawhar, *Sabria's Out of the Box*, http://www.saudiwriter.blogspot.com; Hala al-Dosari, *Hala in Wonderland*, http://www.hala1.wordpress.com; *Saudi Stepford Wife*, http://www .saudistepfordwife.blogspot.com; Eman al-Nafjan, "Hello World!," *Saudiwoman's Weblog*, 1 February 2008, http://www.saudiwoman.me/2008/02/01/hello-world; Omaima Al Najjar, "About Me," *Omaima Al Najjar*, http://www.omaimanajjar.wordpress.com /about.

66. Saudi Stepford Wife, "Stay Tuned," *Saudi Stepford Wife*, 27 February 2007, http:// www.saudistepfordwife.blogspot.com/2007/02/stay-tuned.html.

67. Saudi Stepford Wife, "Stay Tuned."

68. Yeslam Al Saggaf, "The Effect of Online Community on Offline Community in Saudi Arabia," *Electronic Journal on Information Systems in Developing Countries* 16, no. 2 (2004): 9. A study conducted by Al Saggaf in Saudi Arabia in 2001–2 showed that participants in an online community (seven men and eight women) gained self-confidence and became more open-minded, more aware of the characteristics of individuals in their society, and less inhibited about and more appreciative of the opposite gender as a result of these interactions (13).

69. Eman al-Nafjan, "Women Driving Cars . . . How Do We Start Its Implementation," *Saudiwoman's Weblog*, 18 April 2010, http://www.saudiwoman.me/2010/04/18/women -driving-cars%E2%80%A6how-do-we-start-its-implementation/#comments.

70. Sabria Jawhar, "Jeddah's 'Lord of the Flies' Driving Habits," *Sabria's Out of the Box*, 23 September 2012, http://www.saudiwriter.blogspot.com/2012/09/jeddahs-lord -of-flies-driving-habits.html.

71. Hala al-Dosari, "I Can Drive!!!," *Hala in Wonderland*, 16 February 2008, http://www .hala1.wordpress.com/2008/02/16/i-can-drive.

72. Al Najjar, "About Me."

73. See Saudi Stepford Wife Daisy, "About Me," Blogger, http://www.blogger.com /profile/09934386285333242262; Saudi Stepford Wife, "Stay Tuned."

74. Jawhar, "Let Women Drive!"

75. Eman al-Nafjan, "Why Do We Stay the Way We Are?," *Saudiwoman's Weblog*, 3 April 2010, http://www.saudiwoman.me/2010/04/03/why-do-we-stay-the-way-we-are.

76. Stacey K. Sowards and Valerie R. Renegar, "The Rhetorical Functions of Consciousness-Raising in Third Wave Feminism," *Communication Studies* 55, no. 4 (2004): 535.

77. Yuce et al., "Mapping Cyber-Collective Action among Female Muslim Bloggers for the Women to Drive Movement," 332.

78. Eman al-Nafjan, "My Favorite Daydream," *Saudiwoman's Weblog*, 28 October 2010, http://www.saudiwoman.me/2010/10/28/my-favorite-daydream/#comments.

79. Al-Nafjan, "My Favorite Daydream."

80. Osama Khalid, "Saudi Authorities Block Women Driving Websites," *Global Voices*, 8 October 2013, http://www.globalvoicesonline.org/2013/10/08/saudi-authorities-block-women-driving-websites.

81. Eman al-Nafjan, "Optimism," *Saudiwoman's Weblog*, 5 September 2012, http://www.saudiwoman.me/2012/09/05/optimism.

82. Michel Foucault and Jay Moskowitz, "Of Other Spaces," *Diacritics* 16, no. 1 (1986): 24.

83. Gillian Rose, *Feminism and Geography: The Limits of Geographical Knowledge* (Cambridge: Polity, 1993), 159.

84. Margaret Morse, *Virtualities: Television, Media Art, and Cyberculture* (Bloomington: Indiana University Press, 1998), 121.

85. Ibrahim Alhadar and Michael McCahill, "The Use of Surveillance Cameras in a Riyadh Shopping Mall: Protecting Profits or Protecting Morality?," *Theoretical Criminology* 15, no. 3 (2011): 315.

86. The only exception is the shopping mall of the Kingdom Centre in Riyadh, which features a women-only floor. For a discussion of this "space liberated from the constraints of social control—and consecrated to consumption," see Amélie Le Renard, "The Ladies Kingdom and Its Many Uses: A Shopping Mall in Riyadh for Women Only," *Metropolitics*, 30 March 2011, http://www.metropolitiques.eu/The-Ladies-Kingdom-and-Its-Many.html.

87. Alhadar and McCahill, "The Use of Surveillance Cameras in a Riyadh Shopping Mall," 324. For more information, see Kevin Sullivan, "Saudi Youth Use Cellphone Savvy to Outwit the Sentries of Romance," *Washington Post*, 6 August 2006, http://www.washingtonpost.com/wp-dyn/content/article/2006/08/05/AR2006080500930.html; Associated Press, "In Saudi Arabia, a High-Tech Way to Flirt," NBC News, 8 November 2005, http://www.nbcnews.com/id/8916890/ns/world_news-mideast_n_africa/t/saudi-arabia-high-tech-way-flirt/#.UhoVqhtSiAg; Rajaa Alsanea, "My Saudi Valentine," *New York Times*, 13 February 2008, http://www.nytimes.com/2008/02/13/opinion/13alsanea.html?_r=0.

88. For more information, see Nadia al-Fawaz, "Young Saudis Invent Ploys to Enter Family-Only Malls," *Arab News*, 29 December 2011, http://www.arabnews.com/node/402436. The family-only regulations were lifted in the emirate of Riyadh in 2012. See "Riyadh Eases Ban on Single Men in Shopping Malls," *Gulf News*, 23 March 2012, http://gulfnews.com/news/gulf/saudi-arabia/riyadh-eases-ban-on-single-men-in-shopping-malls-1.998695.

89. Amélie Le Renard, "Young Urban Saudi Women's Transgressions of Official Rules and the Production of a New Social Group," *Journal of Middle East Women's Studies* 9, no. 3 (2013): 113.

90. YouTube video of the Nail Polish Girl incident: MEMRITVVideos, "Saudi Woman Defies Religious Police: It Is None of Your Business If I Wear Nail Polish," YouTube, 24 May 2012, https://www.youtube.com/watch?v=OpUUOYRLW3k.

91. Madawi al-Rasheed, "Imagined Heroism of the Saudi 'Nail Polish Girl,'" *Al-Monitor*, 30 May 2012, http://www.al-monitor.com/pulse/originals/2012/al-monitor/imagined -heroism-of-the-saudi-na.html.

92. For more information, see Faiza Saleh Ambah, "Saudi Women Petition for Right to Drive," *Washington Post*, 24 September 2007, http://www.washingtonpost.com/wp-dyn /content/article/2007/09/23/AR2007092300862.html; Saudi Jeans, "Protest to Release Detainees in Riyadh Mall," *Saudi Jeans*, 6 June 2012, http://saudijeans.org/2012/06/06 /protest-in-riyadh-mall.

93. Marc Augé, *Non-places: Introduction to an Anthropology of Supermodernity* (London: Verso, 1995), 103.

94. Kärrholm, "Interstitial Space and the Transformation of Retail Building Types," 140.

95. Linda Steg, "Car Use: Lust and Must. Instrumental, Symbolic and Affective Motives for Car Use," *Transportation Research Part A* 39, nos. 2–3 (2005): 147. See also Mimi Sheller, "Automotive Emotions: Feeling the Car," *Theory, Culture and Society* 21, nos. 4–5 (2004): 221–42; John Urry, "Inhabiting the Car," *Sociological Review* 54, no. S1 (2006): 17– 31; Kai Eckoldt et al., "Alternatives: Exploring the Car's Design Space from an Experience-Oriented Perspective," proceedings of the 6th International Conference on Designing Pleasurable Products and Interfaces, Newcastle upon Tyne, 2013, 156–64.

96. Sheller, "Automotive Emotions," 222.

97. Urry, "Inhabiting the Car," 23; Eckoldt et al., "Alternatives," 156.

98. See al-Sharif's video at "Saudi Woman Driver Faces Jail Again."

99. Saudi Stepford Wife, "The Flirty-Go-Round," *Saudi Stepford Wife*, 3 May 2007, http://saudistepfordwife.blogspot.com.es/2007/05/flirty-go-round.html; Doumato, "Saudi Arabia," 432.

100. Cited in "Manal al-Sharif May Be Saudi Arabia's Most Awesome Woman," *Saudi Women Driving*, 15 March 2014, http://www.saudiwomendriving.blogspot.com/2014/03 /manal-al-sharif-may-be-saudi-arabias.html.

101. Saudi Stepford Wife, "Sorry, Can't Help Ya."

102. Eckoldt et al., "Alternatives," 156.

103. Jawhar, "Let Women Drive!"

104. Eman al-Nafjan, "Saudi Women and Their Drivers," *Saudiwoman's Weblog*, 12 September 2008, http://www.saudiwoman.me/2008/09/12/saudi-women-and-their -drivers.

105. Manal al-Sharif discusses how she used to be harassed by her driver ("Saudi Woman Driver Faces Jail Again"). See also Saudi Stepford Wife, "Sorry, Can't Help Ya."

106. Rhacel Salazar Parreñas, *Servants of Globalization: Women, Migration, and Domestic Work* (Stanford, CA: Stanford University Press, 2001), 180.

107. Eman al-Nafjan, "Saudi Women's Man-O-Meter," *Saudiwoman's Weblog*, 27 September 2008, https://saudiwoman.me/2008/09/27/saudi-women%E2%80%99s-man-o -meter.

108. Al-Nafjan, "Saudi Women and Their Drivers"; Urry, "Inhabiting the Car," 19.

109. Eckoldt et al., "Alternatives," 160.

110. Rasha, "Saudi Girls Involved with Their Drivers"; Wafa Sultan, "The World of Fatwa in 2009," *My World and More*, 20 December 2009, http://www.wafagal.com/2009/12/world-of-fatwa-in-2009.html; Karen Leonard, "South Asian Workers in the Gulf: Jockeying for Places," in *Globalization under Construction: Governmentality, Law, and Identity*, edited by Richard Warren Perry and Bill Maurer (Minneapolis: University of Minnesota Press, 2003), 131.

111. Saudi Stepford Wife, "Women Can't Drive If She Wears a Veil . . . Bull!," *Saudi Stepford Wife*, 2 April 2007, http://www.saudistepfordwife.blogspot.com/2007/04/women-cant-drive-if-she-wears-veilbull.html.

112. "30 Responses to 'Saudi Shewolf,'" *Saudiwoman's Weblog*, http://www.saudiwoman.me/2009/10/31/saudi-shewolf/#comments.

113. Sabria Jawhar, "Gaddafi's Death May Bring Tribal Warfare before Democracy," *Sabria's Out of the Box*, 27 October 2011, http://saudiwriter.blogspot.com/2011/10/gaddafis-death-may-bring-tribal-warfare.html.

114. Eman al-Nafjan, "Life for Saudi Women Is a Constant State of Contradiction," *Saudiwoman's Weblog*, 29 September 2011, http://saudiwoman.me/2011/09/29/in-the-guardian-life-for-saudi-women-is-a-constant-state-of-contradiction.

115. King Abdullah's 2011 royal decree allowed Saudi women to become members of the consultative Shura Council and to participate in elections for municipal councils. In January 2013, thirty women were appointed to the Shura Council. See Sara Hamdan, "Women Appointed to Saudi Council for First Time," *New York Times*, 16 January 2013, http://www.nytimes.com/2013/01/17/world/middleeast/women-appointed-to-saudi-council-for-first-time.html. On 12 December 2015 Saudi women participated in the municipal elections for the first time. According to official sources, 130,000 women and 1.36 million men cast their ballots. Women candidates won 21 of the 2,100 seats. Although municipal councils have limited power and one-third of their members are appointed, historian Hatoon al-Fassi regards Saudi women's performance of their "right of being a citizen" as a defining moment for women's rights in the kingdom. See Ian Black, "Saudi Arabia Elects up to 17 Female Councillors in Historic Election," *Guardian*, 13 December 2015, http://www.theguardian.com/world/2015/dec/13/saudi-arabia-elects-up-to-17-female-councillors-in-historic-election.

116. Mimi Sheller and John Urry, "Mobile Transformations of 'Public' and 'Private' Life," *Theory, Culture, and Society* 20, no. 3 (2003): 116.

117. Ananda Mitra, "Voices of the Marginalized on the Internet: Examples from a Website for Women of South Asia," *Journal of Communication* 54, no. 3 (2004): 503.

118. See, for example, Mona Kareem, "Saudi Arabia: Outrage over 10 Lashes for Female Driver," *Global Voices*, 15 November 2011, http://www.globalvoicesonline.org/2011/11/15/saudi-arabia-outrage-over-10-lashes-for-female-driver; Eman al-Nafjan, "Cornering Saudi Women," *Saudiwoman's Weblog*, 8 June 2012, http://www.saudiwoman.me/2012/06/08/cornering-saudi-women; Eman al-Nafjan, "My Attempt to Break the Driving Ban in Saudi Arabia," *Saudiwoman's Weblog*, 28 February 2013, http://www.saudiwoman.me/2013/02/28/1793. Al-Nafjan was detained on 10 October 2013 while she filmed another activist driving in preparation for the 26 October action; see Human Rights Watch, "Saudi Arabia:

End Driving Ban for Women," 24 October 2013, http://www.hrw.org/news/2013/10/24/saudi-arabia-end-driving-ban-women.

119. Other hashtags used in relation to women's driving activism in Saudi Arabia are #SaudiWomenRevolution, created on 7 February 2011 as a reaction to the successful uprisings in Tunisia and Egypt, and #Oct26Driving, created on 25 September 2013 to coordinate the 26 October action. The website of the 26 October 2013 campaign is no longer available but can be found at https://web.archive.org/web/20130923225331/http://www.oct26driving.com. See also "Saudi Women Drivers: Leading Female Campaigner Stopped," *Saudi Women Driving*, 29 November 2013, http://www.saudiwomendriving.blogspot.com/2013/11/saudi-women-drivers-leading-female.html.

7 REVOLUTION UNDRESSED The Politics of Rage and
Aesthetics in Aliaa Elmahdy's Body Activism KARINA EILERAAS

My message is gender equality and my body is no sin.
—Aliaa Magda Elmahdy, Femen protest, Stockholm, 1 July 2013

If we don't invent a language, if we don't find our body's language, it will have too few gestures to accompany our story.
—Luce Irigaray, *This Sex Which Is Not One*

On 17 November 2011 a group of Egyptian Islamic law graduates filed suit against the Egyptian blogger Aliaa Magda Elmahdy and her boyfriend Kareem Amer for "violating morals, inciting indecency and insulting Islam."[1] A few weeks earlier, on 23 October, the nineteen-year-old middle-class Elmahdy had posted nude selfies and images of naked men to her blog, *A Rebel's Diary*.[2] This was a radical act that resulted in calls to punish and kill her.

Elmahdy's activism emerged at a historical moment of despair regarding the direction of the Egyptian revolution, as the military had consolidated power in the previous months despite mass mobilizations that forced President Hosni Mubarak to step down in February. In a November 2011 interview Elmahdy explained her act as part of an ongoing struggle for sex equality in the new Egypt: "The (sexism) against women in Egypt is unreal, but I am not going anywhere and will battle it until the end."[3] Immediately preceding Elmahdy's nude protest, Egyptian parliamentary campaign posters for the Salafist al-Nour Party advertised its belief that women should stay out of the public eye; even campaign material for women candidates used images of flowers or a photo of their husband instead of their own face. For this the party earned widespread ridicule in Egypt.[4] Elmahdy's nude protest also followed revelations by Samira Ibrahim that the military had conducted "virginity" tests on her and other unmarried Egyptian women activists whom police had violently cleared out of Tahrir Square on 9 March 2011. As the military state bolstered itself against deeper transformations, harassment and violence against fully dressed girls and women in public spaces had intensified rather than improved, especially in Cairo. In sum, the context in which Elmahdy took her radical action was particularly hostile to women's presence in public spaces and their political activism. Elmahdy's activism restages political dissent and the "tensions around national identity that animate the contemporary Arab public sphere."[5]

This chapter offers a theoretically informed analysis of Elmahdy's blog prose, image posts, street actions, and wider responses in three phases of corporeal protest. Her initial launch of self-taken images in October 2011 in a post titled "Fan 'ari" (Nude Art) criticized "sexual hang-ups," "chauvinism," and restrictions on freedom of expression and artistic representation in contemporary Egypt. In December 2012 Elmahdy founded a branch of the Ukrainian feminist organization Femen in Egypt, and in early 2013 she fled to Sweden, where she was granted political asylum. She continued her body activism in what I term a second phase, this time in street theater in Sweden and postings on her blog. Elmahdy was unable to control the narrative in the street phase as she became a public spectacle and was required to comply with the Femen message and parameters of nude protest.[6] She initiated the third phase in October 2013 and continues her body activism through visual and narrative blog posts that often focus on resisting sexual violence and control.

I argue that Elmahdy is a revolutionary subject who provocatively fuses aesthetics and disidentification politics in a self-branding, digital age. Elmahdy sexes (and sexts) revolution by calling attention to its embodied sexual-gendered elisions and exclusions. She challenges revolutionary and iconographic registers that subordinate matters related to gender, the feminine, sex, and the body. Her digital activism foregrounded sex and the female body in a way that underscored their political primacy. In effect she used fantasy to stage a revolt against the sexual status quo. Elmahdy's activism illustrates the "paradoxical" nature of all spaces, which offer opportunities for counterhegemonic rupture even when they are sexist, racist, or homophobic.[7] When she performatively inserted her body where it was least expected, she reshaped the landscape of feminist protest and female nudity in aesthetics despite the perils of cyberspace, the complicated charge attached to female nudes, and the ideological disagreements that immediately emerged among feminists in Egypt and the Arab world about Elmahdy's strategy.

Elmahdy's controversial nude activism uses digital circuits to express and incite rage against the gendered and sexual status quo in Egypt. She is part of a transnational genealogy of radical artists who use their bodies to disrupt the normative social order by challenging exploitation. Such performances nonviolently force audiences to consider the sexual, gendered, and vulnerable body. Whatever her intentions, Elmahdy, like the young activist Amina Tyler of Tunisia, could not control responses to her nude activism in a hyperdigital age that remains structured by imperialism, racism, and sexism.

Bodies Out of Place

Donna Haraway dreamed of the fractured identities and epistemological ruptures that might become possible in the figure of the cyborg, an integrated circuit of the human body and digital technology that is necessarily disloyal to the myth of a singular origin.[8] This hybrid infidelity speaks powerfully to a contemporary moment in which personal identity is negotiated alongside and through digital circuits and online communities. Elmahdy's body activism contributes to a networked feminist public square invigorated by an open-ended, heterodox, nonhierarchical, kaleidoscopic swirl of voices and visions.[9] We have entered the era of the rhizome or *heteroglossia* as blueprint for the public square: a dynamic space of exchange in which multiple tongues, epistemological sources and registers, and sexualities collide to forge perennially evolving stories and pathways of personal and political becoming.[10]

Yet human bodies still exert unique force, even in the digital age. Bodies represent humanity in its most primal form. Our bodies are fragile, prone to bruises, breaks, cuts, wrinkles, fractures, and scars.[11] Bodies offer a means of expression and are the last line of defense. The potency of embodied expression, certainly if it is unarmed, is very much lodged in vulnerability to physical, emotional, and social injury, exclusion, and death. Bodily forms of protest, Marwan Kraidy writes, communicate "a radically superior commitment to one's cause, because putting one's body in harm's way reflects far higher stakes."[12] When protesters obstruct the paths of tanks and soldiers, light themselves on fire, or go on a hunger strike, they pose a metaphysical question: "What is my body—my life—worth to you?" Bodily protest asks how different lives are valued and whose experiences are officially named, muted, or sacrificed in collective memory.

Protest that includes the "deliberate stripping of clothing," Hamid Dabashi writes, "is an act of staged formal destruction that disrupts the banality of socializing norms for a deliberate pause. It is the staging of the body for a momentary reflection."[13] Women's bodies offer particularly fraught symbolic terrain, especially when they are naked and out of place, because they disrupt sacrosanct gendered dichotomies of public/private. Women's oppositional nakedness demands a pause not only because it is improper, as it might be for men under similar circumstances. The legal theorist Amy Adler maintains that the live nude woman in the U.S. context is especially jarring because of profound cultural anxiety regarding agentic female sexuality that manifests in the collective unconscious in the figure of the Medusa.[14] Elmahdy deliberately occupied digital and material public squares "improperly" on a number of scales. By so doing she "re-membered"—in Homi Bhabha's sense of working through traumatic memory—and battled with masculinist, colonialist, and imperialist repressions and appropriations.[15]

The gender-sexual agency expressed by nudity depends on context and intent. The body in varied states of dress has a long history as an agent of global protest. African women have staged naked protests in Kenya, Uganda, Liberia, and Nigeria. The most prominent of these was the 1929 Igbo Women's War in Eastern Nigeria, when thousands of indigenous women challenged colonial rule and Western colonial hypersexualization of their bodies by encouraging unmarried women to appear naked in public.[16] The elders challenged the British colonial rule that women must be clothed to be proper. Oppositional nakedness was also part of the 1980–81 Armagh Prison Dirty Protest held by Irish Republican women political prisoners in Northern Ireland. The women disrobed, refused to bathe, and smeared the walls with their feces and menstrual blood in an environment that intended to silence, if not erase, them as female political subjects.[17] In the twenty-first century women Greenpeace activists use nudity to protest animal cruelty and environmental abuse.[18] In 2015 the African American artist Nona Faustine posed nude in front of historical slave-trading sites in New York, including Wall Street. In so doing she raised powerful questions regarding the devaluation of black female bodies and their historical status as commodities within systems of global finance and commerce.[19]

Feminist Rage as Incitement

State-sanctioned violence against women in Egypt did not begin with the 2011 uprising centered in Tahrir Square, nor is Elmahdy the first Egyptian feminist actor to rise up in protest. She is part of a legacy of advocacy for social, political, and economic justice. Elmahdy's protest, however, thoroughly violated respectability norms. By launching her nude body into cyberspace to viral effect,[20] Elmahdy criticized not only Islamist regulation of women's visibility but also state policing of women's bodies and masculinist ambivalence about the presence of women in public space. Like most urban centers, Cairo is a space of paradoxes with respect to women's bodies. A high percentage of women cover their hair even as the "public display of the sexualized female body" is ubiquitous in "film posters, ads, and publicity campaigns."[21] Not surprisingly, given cultural and religious taboos against public female nudity, most Egyptians consider Elmahdy's activism outrageous. Her October 2011 posting quickly went viral, with over 1.5 million blog hits in the first week. Elmahdy incited rage, condemnation, threats of rape and death, and solidarity. If, as Roland Barthes contends in *Camera Lucida*, every image is open to infinite readings, Elmahdy's embodied activism is no exception.[22] In the wake of her online protest she was cast as a heroine, feminist icon, prostitute, madwoman, traitor, and heretic. Egyptian feminists have understood her as alternately obscene, courageous, disloyal, groundbreaking, and naïve. These readings are not reducible to being "for" or "against" her actions;[23] instead they are symptomatic of class, ideological, and even generational divides within the women's movement.

Egyptian feminism has been shaped by the intersecting forces of colonialism, capitalism, nationalism, militarism, and Islamism. The feminist field in Egypt today includes leftists, Islamically oriented activists, nationalists, liberal-modernists, human rights advocates, and sexual rights activists. It also includes research centers, Facebook and Twitter campaigns, and ad hoc coalitions. Regardless of this diversity, feminists are frequently charged with being agents of Western colonialism or imperialism, as reactions to Elmahdy's activism show. Elmahdy deploys an individualistic, rights-based narrative of sexual agency and free expression that she regards as no less authentically Egyptian. She regularly speaks out against sexual violence and sexual control of women in Egypt. Like most Egyptian feminists, she is aware that since at least 2005 successive governments have been complicit in campaigns of sexual violence against women protesters.[24] These penetrations by the state, as the scholar Maya Mikdashi argues, serve "to terrorize, and the aim of terrorism is always to instill fear and hope that fear will incite self-policing in a civilian population. Sex as terror has been used in Abu-Ghraib, at Guantanamo Bay, in Iraq, Libya, the Democratic Republic of Congo, Argentina, and in US-occupied Afghanistan. Physical violation is commonplace and always public, because the point is to demonstrate the impunity with which these citizens' bodies can be violated by foreign and local powers."[25]

Reactions to Elmahdy's activism blur the division between secularists and Islamists. As Sara Mourad contends, "Demands for sexual freedom are not part of mainstream secular discourse in Egypt." Indeed secular Egyptians "were the first to denounce Aliaa's photograph as evidence of her immaturity; her disrespect for social, cultural, and religious norms; and her mimicry of the West."[26] Many leftist feminists condemned her endorsement of Western nudity as liberation. Naheed Mustafa, for example, contests "the persistent idea that by turning our bodies into objects, even if by choice, women will somehow break through age-old cultural taboos, customs and laws that keep us socially and legally constricted."[27] Sex-positive feminist critics, while agreeing that sexual freedom and bodily integrity are imperative, did not necessarily view Elmahdy's act of self-exposure as a meaningful act of liberation.[28] Liberals worried about conservative social backlash against the Egyptian revolution and feared that Elmahdy's focus on sexual freedom would give the revolution "a bad name."[29]

Conversely Elmahdy's supporters appreciated the audacity of the embodied sex-gender critique she launched against masculinist and repressive dynamics in the first months of the Egyptian revolution. Her activism resonated with feminist campaigns that exploded throughout the region in 2011, including a billboard campaign and web-based group called The Uprising of Women in the Arab World, which has become a key visual site of feminist revolutionary protest.[30] This campaign began with the phrase

"I am with the Arab women's uprising because . . ." and asks supporters to finish the sentence. Elmahdy completes the sentence with "because they harassed me and threatened to rape me, jail me, and kill me when I posted an artistic naked picture of myself and blogged about women's rights and had a relationship with my love and left my 'father's house.'"[31] In the virtual sphere these activists "forge an 'other space'—akin to Foucault's 'heterotopias'—where they can engage in discussions about sexuality and the female body, jointly redefine notions of honor and shame, and collectively imagine Egypt free of gender inequality and sexual violence."[32]

Many Arab men and women activists, including in Egypt and the Egyptian diaspora, rallied to support Elmahdy, either publicly or privately. The Egyptian American actress Amanda Banoub defended Elmahdy's nudity as an expression of humanity and commended her for "displaying genuine purity and modesty without a single layer of clothing."[33] The Lebanese journalist Joy Majdalani Habib writes, "Somehow, something about el Mahdy's exposed body has been interpreted as a tremendous threat to patriarchal society. Not only did Aliaa el Mahdy break the taboo of nudity, she also countered the tyranny of the male gaze that constantly strives to enclose the female body in one of two categories: either a desirable object to lust upon or a shameful object to hide under heavy sheets. This change of perspective is, in my opinion, what was the most scandalous in Aliaa el Mahdy's act."[34] Mikdashi further notes that Elmahdy "is not 'waiting' for the 'right moment' to bring up bodily rights and sexual rights in post-Mubarak Egypt. She is not waiting her turn, and she is not trying to turn us on. Her nudity aims to reinvigorate a conversation about the politics of sex and the uneven ways it is articulated across the fields of gender, capital, and control. She is staring back at us, daring us to look at her and to not turn away. Daring us to have this debate."[35] The Egyptian American journalist Mona Eltahawy, herself beaten and sexually assaulted in Cairo, argues that Elmahdy "is the Molotov cocktail thrown at the Mubaraks in our heads—the dictators of our mind." This "Molotov," she continues, "insists that revolutions cannot succeed without a tidal wave of cultural changes that upend misogyny and sexual hypocrisy."[36] Mourad suggests that Elmahdy's nude protest be read "against its socially conservative and repressive Arab context" and contends that her "choice to strip in the name of politics retains a transgressive edge."[37]

By forcing attention to the naked female body, Elmahdy questions persistent paradigms that frame women's nudity, sexuality, political activism, and presence in public spaces as either irrelevant distractions or sources of shame. In addition to opening a different kind of conversation about the relationship between women's bodies, sexuality, and revolution, El-mahdy directs attention to a shifting landscape in feminist and queer praxis wherein a feminist guard meets a vibrant new generation of performers and artist-activists and conventional street organizing collides with new forms of protest in social media and cyberspace.

Proponents of liberation technology believe that the digital revolution expands freedom by facilitating decentralized mobilization efforts, including smart and flash mobs and digital shaming.[38] Yet digital expression of "imagined violence" in a "place of rage" has in many ways superseded physical "critical mass" mobilization in the cyber era.[39] For Jack Halber-stam, imagined violence is the artistic staging of rage by the marginal-ized. In this reading rage is a revolutionary "ground for resistance" or "a political space opened up by representation in art, in poetry, in narrative, in popular film, of unsanctioned violences committed by subordinated groups upon powerful white men." The boundary between imagined and real violence is fragile, "unstable, contested and radically unpredictable," partly because "representation and fantasy" have the power to "make the system nervous."[40] By trespassing in the public square, Elmahdy inserts her naked body into the chasms and fissures of a national political imaginary that routinely erases the female body, gender-based violence, and sexual-ity. Her political striptease plays on the limits of a binary between the real and imagined to ignite fear in the collective unconscious. Her tactics open up the "tightly patrolled and highly ambiguous" space of fantasy wherein expression threatens to become action.[41]

Activist netizens in the iPhone, YouTube, and Facebook digital era con-tribute to an attention economy that thrives on the global exchange of in-formation, images, memes, and ideas. This economy sustains subcultures of rage and resistance and shapes new visions of identity, belonging, and civic responsibility. Elmahdy's digital embodied activism, I contend, chal-lenges the structural inequalities of public spheres and spaces. It revolts against the "symbolic violence" of a status quo that naturalizes domination, "pound[ing]" it "into the deepest layers of the body" and encouraging the marginalized to participate in their own subjugation.[42] Elmahdy underlines the body's capacity to be an agent of change, not only a passive surface for subordinating inscription. Through the force of fantasy she invites the marginalized to enact alternative political communities that decenter sexist visions of belonging and offer sex(t)ed registers of revolution.

Elmahdy's activism occurs within feminist traditions that insist on the centrality of women, gender relations, and sexuality to national politics, revolution, and decolonization. By performing oppositional nakedness against inequality online and on the streets, she "dispossesses" herself of a legacy of sex inequality.[43] Her performance of sexy citizenship opens up productive *lieux de mémoire*, or places and objects that embody national memory, and opportunities for disidentification with sexual mandates.[44] Elmahdy activates imaginaries of body futures that work past gender inequality, heteronormativity, racism, and empire and insist on the political register of the visual act, or that which resides in our inner cinema.

Elmahdy's corporeal protests may be read as acts of "diva citizenship" that confront the body politic as a sexualized battleground.[45] Her actions demonstrate that "the gendered human body is at once a medium of expression and a discursive battlefield."[46] She challenges a figurative landscape where women's bodies too often serve as symbolic war zones between Western and Eastern actors and ideologues. On one side are those who invoke women's status and bodies as in need of liberation or modernization. And on the other are those who constitute them as repositories of national, cultural, or religious tradition. Elmahdy refuses such binary frames when she rages against sexual inequality, gendered double standards, and political marginalization that reduce women to silent victims or erotic spectacles. If, as Ernest Renan suggests, nationalism depends on forgetting, Elmahdy uses embodied digital and street protest to remember sexuality- and gender-based violence as sources of trauma historically integral to projects of revolution and state formation.[47] She expands the theaters and sites of politics.

Aesthetic Body Politics

As a feminist scholar of performance and body art, I am especially struck by how Elmahdy rewrites the female nude from an object of heteronormative fantasy and the male gaze to an autonomous feminist subject. In the Orientalist painterly tradition of the odalisque, naked women wait passively for men to enter, narrate, and direct the scene. John Berger argues that the surveyed female nude is dominated by the male spectator.[48] Laura

Mulvey theorizes a similarly dominating and normalizing "male gaze" in narrative Hollywood cinema.[49] Elmahdy reworks the overlap between fantasy, violence, and the symbolic. She provocatively restages the classical aesthetic genre of the gazed-upon female nude through self-authored, sex-positive nakedness. She deploys her body as "erotic capital" whereby the desired return is not the voyeuristic male gaze but increased social and political capital for women.[50] In the process she challenges the conventional staging of heteronormative, sexual, and nationalist fantasies.

Art history sheds invaluable light on bodies as canvases of dissent. Performance art is especially potent for addressing relations between bodies and violence. In the 1960s and 1970s conceptual and performance artists, including Joseph Beuys, Chris Burden, Yoko Ono, and Ana Mendieta, staged their bodies as vulnerable—inviting their violation and reminding audiences of human fragility and mortality. In her performative work *Cut Piece*, for example, Ono sat next to a pair of scissors and invited audiences to cut off her clothing at will.[51] Burden pushed this interventionist approach one step further with his danger piece, *My God, Are They Going to Leave Me Here to Die?* Burden inhabited the threshold between life and death by lying next to a bucket of water on a museum floor and strapping his body to electrodes, inviting audiences to electrocute him.[52] Especially in her *Silueta Series* the Cuban artist Ana Mendieta posed nude in endangered environments throughout the United States and Mexico to protest human exploitation of Mother Nature by drilling, mining, logging, and other invasive activities.[53] More recently the band Pussy Riot staged naked protests in Russia to disrupt public and sacred spaces, and contemporary feminists in China have engaged in body and performance art as a means of political activism to challenge the sexual status quo.[54]

Elmahdy's oppositional nakedness is difficult to reduce to narcissistic expression or personal catharsis because she uses her blog to state that women have been effaced as subjects in history, politics, and art. As Cynthia Enloe notes, the refrain "Not now, later" often greets feminist demands within revolutionary movements.[55] Like other feminist activists, Elmahdy refused to postpone addressing gender and sexuality within revolutionary Egypt's milieu of sexual harassment, sexual assault, gang rape, and public shaming of women activists. She was distinct, however, for absolutely rejecting norms of propriety and respectability while so doing, exposing herself to significant condemnation and danger. Outraged by exclusionary and hypocritical forms of citizenship and revolution, Elmahdy stages activism that demands a response from those who encounter it. It enacts productive sites of disturbance to promote alternative registers of revolution from a space that often resists telling within patriarchal nationalist and revolutionary realms.

When Elmahdy initially uploaded her photos to Facebook, the administrators deleted them within a few hours to comply with a corporate policy that prohibits nudity. In response she uploaded the photos to her blog.[56] In the cyber traffic jam that followed her 23 October 2011 posting, the most viewed image was a full-body self-portrait taken at home with "a delayed-action shutter release of her digital camera."[57] In it Elmahdy wears only patterned stockings that end at her thighs and red flats with a red flower arranged playfully in her hair (figure 7.1). In the caption that appears below the portrait, Elmahdy defends women's bodily pride and freedom of expression: "Put on trial the artists' models who posed nude for [Egyptian] art schools until the early 70s, hide the art books and destroy the nude statues of antiquity, then undress and stand before a mirror and burn your bodies that you despise to forever rid yourselves of your sexual hangups before you direct your humiliation and chauvinism and dare to try to deny me my freedom of expression."[58]

On her blog postings and Twitter profile Elmahdy identifies as an atheist and a "secular, liberal, feminist vegetarian" influenced by the work of the Egyptian feminist and scholar Nawal El Saadawi.[59] In excerpts published in November 2011 Elmahdy states that she "was never into politics. I first joined the protests on 27 May because I felt the need to participate and decided I might be able to change the future of Egypt and refused to remain silent."[60] Despite her self-reported disinterest in politics, Elmahdy's intimate relationship with a dissident political activist and early interest in El Saadawi and the Egyptian feminist movement betray disillusionment with established forms of political activism and the status quo. She does politics in Jacques Rancière's sense of "making visible what had no business being seen."[61] Her unruly body signifies a will to reconfigure the body politic and reimagine the spaces of revolution. She describes her nude photos in explicitly political terms, as "screams against a society of violence, racism, sexism, sexual harassment and hypocrisy."[62]

Elmahdy takes issue with media portrayals that misrepresent her intent.[63] She explains on her blog, "I like being different. I love life, art, photography and expressing my thoughts through writing. That is why I studied media and hope to take it further to expose the truth behind the lies we

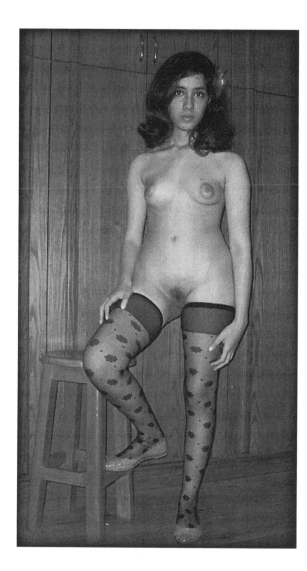

FIGURE 7.1. Aliaa
Magda Elmahdy,
"Nude Art."
Courtesy of the
photographer.

endure everyday."[64] Prior to posting her photos online, she had moved out
of her parents' strict home to live with her boyfriend Kareem Amer, a well-
known Alexandrian blogger and critic of the Mubarak government, liberals, and Islamists.[65] Amer, who is about seven years older than Elmahdy,
was imprisoned for four years by Mubarak, the first Egyptian blogger to be
imprisoned for cyber activism.[66]

   Elmahdy insists that her protests challenge sexist views held by most
Egyptians, including her parents.[67] She elaborates in a print interview pub-

lished by CNN: "I am not shy of being a woman in a society where women are nothing but sex objects harassed on a daily basis by men who know nothing about sex or the importance of a woman. The photo is an expression of my being and I see the human body as the best artistic representation of that. I took the photo myself using a timer on my personal camera. The powerful colors black and red inspire me."[68]

Before posting the photo, Elmahdy writes, she considered writing on it, "My body is not property or a sex tool."[69] She is especially critical of a double standard within Islamist thought that simultaneously shames female nudity, suppresses female sexuality, prescribes female modesty, and excuses sexual violence on the premise that male sexuality is insatiable. This logic of containment and regulation, argues the Moroccan feminist Fatima Mernissi, assumes female sexuality to be an active force of potential disorder (*fitna*).[70] Taking up a feminist and visual vocabulary that is distinctly sexual and revolutionary in scope, Elmahdy publicly declares she is not a virgin, challenges the virgin/whore dichotomy, and decries the practice of virginity testing in Tahrir Square.[71] She invites followers to post nude artwork and other feminist praxis to her blog. In this way she gestures toward promising forms of transnational feminist solidarity *à venir* (still to come). She writes, "Education teaches us that female sexual desire is to be silenced, that women exist to be used by men. Men claim that they have uncontrollable lust which makes them prey on us if we don't disappear (cover, stay at home, be quiet, hide from shame). Claiming that male sexual deprivation is the cause of sexual harassment implies that men have sexual libido, but women don't, and that women are a sexual supply for men. I get horny, but I don't get an urge to harass people. Sexual harassment is a hate crime, a tool society uses to oppress women."[72]

How might we read Elmahdy's efforts to rewrite the female nude? Does the turn to nudity reinforce the patriarchal Western philosophical views of Rousseau and Kant regarding the value of the feminine as purely sexual and ornamental?[73] Does it speciously equate nudity with liberation? Can it be viewed as a feminist effort to reclaim the body and the space of female sexuality as part of emancipatory politics rather than voyeuristic titillation? These complex questions animate the ideological divide among Arab feminists with respect to Elmahdy's activism. I argue that Elmahdy's activism opens up all these possibilities at once. Her nudity and words both incite and destabilize.

Elmahdy's self-portrait stands in stark contrast to Orientalist odalisques reclining nude in the imagined domestic space of the harem. The odalisque stares into the distance while presumably waiting for a masculine subject to enter. Most striking is her languor and passivity, which does not allow the viewer to imagine her as an active participant or a subject of history. Conversely Elmahdy stands erect in her self-portrait, with an energy that radiates. She faces the camera head-on with one leg elevated on a stool, directly confronting her own camera lens with her gaze. Her bold stare communicates proud ownership of her naked body and sexuality; it is defiant and provocative, a look that bell hooks might describe as "oppositional."[74] This gaze is the *punctum* of her portrait—the "lightning bolt, sting, pin prick"—or element that most offends those who read her image as vulgar, scandalous, and sacrilegious.[75]

Similar to French feminists' emphasis on *l'ecriture feminine*, which celebrates women's bodies as outside the control imposed by masculine culture, Elmahdy insists that women's bodies are central to revolutionizing space, art, politics, and history.[76] She retools the female nude, investing it with explicitly confrontational sexual and political agency, as feminist postcolonial producers of writing and film have done in the Maghreb.[77] When she opens her legs and exposes her genitals in her original portrait, Elmahdy defies conventional expectations of female modesty and decorum. In its content and composition her nude self-portrait conveys an innocent and insouciant sexiness that has been described as seductive, alluring, sultry, erotic, and unintentional. It is certainly insolent.[78] Her portrait is arresting in its simplicity and iconic in its determination to put sexuality into conversation with revolution. With her clothing choices she fuses the intimate, hidden chamber of the boudoir with a conversation about power in public space, cyberspace, and representational space more broadly. Rather than occupying the least amount of space, as girls and women are often conditioned to do,[79] Elmahdy dominates the space in her self-presentation. She transforms the photographic field into a space of possibility by writing herself into history as a political and sexual agent. By recomposing her body as a photographic subject and object, she also captures the elegiac quality of photography as testimony to "time's relentless melt."[80] She queers the public square—as well as the female nude—by challenging the primacy of the male gaze and a hetero-uterine framing of female sexuality.[81] She confronts men who "cannot see beyond tits and ass" with a gaze of rage and resistance.[82]

Troubling Transnational Feminist Solidarity

Some of the worldwide solidarity with Elmahdy's activism was problematic. Western white activists, feminist and nonfeminist, some racist and Islamophobic, were particularly supportive of her. As previously mentioned, Elmahdy established a Femen branch in Cairo and then worked with the organization in Sweden until late 2013. Femen is a Ukraine-based global feminist organization that uses nude theatrics and antireligious rhetoric to advance Western humanist ideals of liberation and freedom. Although Femen claims to disavow all organized religion, its actions disproportionately target sites of Islamic and Catholic worship.

On 20 December 2012 Elmahdy demonstrated naked with Femen outside the Egyptian Embassy in Stockholm, raising the Egyptian flag behind her head to protest Egypt's draft constitution (figure 7.2). On her body was written in English, "Shariʿa is not a constitution!" Elmahdy was the only Femen protester that day who did not cover her vagina. While some critics view her uniquely naked genitals as a symptom of racialized exploitation,[83] I read this as a deliberate decision that mirrors the self-exposure she chooses on her blog. Her naked body was a potent reminder of how fraught is any effort to negotiate polyvalent sites of "freedom," empowerment, agency, and resistance within transnational feminist praxis.

Femen sparked worldwide controversy by staging International Topless Jihad Day on 4 April 2013 in front of mosques and Tunisian embassies across Europe to oppose Islamism and shariʿa law in solidarity with Amina Tyler, the founder of a Femen chapter in Tunisia. In March Tyler had posted topless photos of herself on Femen Tunisia's Facebook page with the Arabic phrases "Fuck your morals" and "My body belongs to me and is not the source of anyone's honor" scrawled across her chest.[84] Almi Adel, a Salafi cleric and leader of Tunisia's Commission for the Promotion of Virtue and Prevention of Vice, called for her to be stoned to death. Her family kidnapped and beat her and held her in captivity for three weeks, subjecting her to a virginity test. Femen representatives in France immediately issued a statement in support of Tyler: "We show our support through topless photos and we deliver a clear message to the Islamists: We will not let them oppress women's bodies by hiding [them] and locking them [up]!"[85]

In response to International Topless Jihad Day, a group of Muslim women organized Muslimah Pride Day "to show the world that we oppose Femen and their use of Muslim women to reinforce Western imperi-

FIGURE 7.2. Femen protest in Stockholm, 29 June 2013. Everydayrebellion.net.

alism." Using Twitter and Facebook thousands of women posted portraits of themselves holding signs directed at Femen such as "Nudity does not liberate me—and I do not need 'saving.' You do not represent me!"[86] For many Muslim women and feminists, Femen resurrects the specter of colonial, racist, and Islamophobic feminism. Many critics note that Femen members overwhelmingly resemble thin, white, young, blonde models. Femen's founder, Inna Shevchenko, rebuts that claim by pointing out that Femen enjoys a diverse membership base, yet the press chooses to zoom in on young, white, blonde members in its coverage of live protests.[87] In any case, Tyler renounced the organization's staging of International Topless Jihad Day on her behalf: "They burned the Islamic flag in front of a mosque in Paris. I am against it." While not disavowing her connection to Femen, she feared, "Everyone is now going to think that I encouraged them. It's unacceptable."[88] Tyler continues to speak out with Elmahdy in public forums regarding their political mission to reclaim the female nude body from the realm of passive object of titillation for the theater of militant action.[89]

Elmahdy's activism with Femen in Sweden can be read on a continuum with her efforts to queer the meanings of the female nude and revolution. Street protest activates a vulnerable body-that-feels yet also leaves visual archives in photographic and video footage, especially when it involves naked women. Elmahdy tells *Al Arabiya English*, "[We want to] affirm that we own our bodies, they are not public property. If we want to make change, we have to do it unlike the way it is already done." Many liberal critics, including a spokesperson for Egypt's 6 April Movement, Mahmoud Afifi, characterized Elmahdy's nude protests with Femen as obscene.[90]

Elmahdy's bodily alliance with Femen in Sweden thrust her into a transnational feminist public square that simultaneously amplified her presence while erasing her political personhood. The collaboration reinforced stultifying binaries, including not recognizing the possibility of religious subjectivity coexisting with feminist critique. Femen advances at worst racist and at best ethnocentric understandings when it equates nudity with liberation and renounces veiling as a monolithic sign of subordination. The Lebanese feminist Joumana Haddad, writing critically of Elmahdy's nudity in Femen protests, contends that genital and breast exposure by women draws attention to them within a patriarchal setting, whereas the "more powerful weapon" is for women to use their "voice."[91] While it is true that Elmahdy's naked body is read within sexist and racist representational fields and histories, these fields and histories do not necessarily take women's voices seriously either.

In October 2013, after participating in five actions with Femen, Elmahdy left the group because she believed she had compromised her autonomous authorship: "I don't accept Femen leaders to decide about my actions before I do them."[92] In her most recent body activism she continues to speak out against sexual oppression and violence on her own terms, via social media and her blog.[93] Elmahdy provoked scandal again in December 2013 when she posted a feminist version of the Muslim call to prayer and a Quranic verse on her Facebook page, inserting the phrase "Woman is great" in place of "God is the greatest."[94] In March 2014 she joined Fitnah: Movement for Women's Liberation, which "demands freedom, equality, and secularism and calls for an end to misogynist religious and moral laws and customs, compulsory veiling, sex apartheid, sex trafficking, and violence against women."[95] Fitnah argues for positive chaos inspired by female sexual and political agency.

Conclusion

Aliaa Elmahdy's staged revolt against the status quo underscores the primacy of gender, sexuality, and embodiment to revolutionary squares. By projecting her body in places where it is least expected, Elmahdy remakes those sites and reminds everyone that the public square belongs to women like her as well. In ancient Greece, by contrast, an elite body of white male elders (the *theoria*) was the only group granted the political legitimacy to tell the "truth." Through their privileged positionality they monopolized the production of knowledge and the narration of history. In her revolutionary undressing Elmahdy questions ideological and ontological borders that police and delimit thinking, expression, and embodiment in a variety of spaces. She troubles the borders of conventional organizing as well as the presumed divide between the political and the aesthetic by locating the physical body as a creative agent within the "body politic." Her embodied performances yield a rich symbolic vocabulary of resistance and disidentification.

We live in the screen age, a period in which material bodies seem increasingly irrelevant to daily transactions. Commerce, creative exchange, scholarly research, and even interpersonal relationships are now often conducted entirely online with cyber bodies. The Internet, especially YouTube, has democratized access to knowledge in the public sphere such that virtually anyone with a cell phone and Internet access may narrate unfolding political events and record history. The Internet allowed Elmahdy to rupture the status quo with self-authored images and analysis. While physically safer than a city block, virtual sites are more socially dangerous than a gallery, museum building, or art seminar. Digitally and physically, Elmahdy's activism demonstrates that bodies continue to matter.

Whatever our intent, our bodies are to a large degree read in ways we cannot control. Judith Butler emphasizes how we are in this sense simultaneously invested and disinvested of our bodies: "Constituted as a social phenomenon in the public sphere, my body is and is not mine."[96] Similarly, the Elmahdy and Tyler cases reinforce that no author of an image that may circulate controls how it is read. However innocently one might approach the task of celebrating and empowering the naked body, the female nude arrives on scene invested with an erotic charge. Retraining the public eye and cultural assumptions is no small task. Nude women's protest attracts more visibility in the global media than any other feminist effort, yet how effective is the message if it unfolds in a theater in which women's naked bodies are instantly sexualized? If, as Foucault contends, "visibility is a trap," this is especially true for women.[97]

Elmahdy's campaign of oppositional nakedness encourages the mapping of alternative spaces of feminist and queer solidarity even as it illustrates limits, divides, and fractures within the transnational digital public square. Her alliance with Femen compels feminists to confront anew how and what the body, nudity, and visual culture signify in transnational solidarity and resistance. Elmahdy's body activism dares us to imagine what may happen when people disidentify with rules of belonging, community, and resistance. She wrote on her blog in January 2014 that "when we fight for our right to become ourselves, we are called crazy" within national and cultural frameworks that value conformity and compliance above all.[98] Charges of insanity are not new for unruly subjects who live in spaces of double consciousness, cyborg infidelity, and heteroglossia. Elmahdy's naked activism points to a paradoxical feminist body politic fractured by its differences and limits and yet actively undoing boundaries between self and other for times and spaces still to come. Whether we choose to view Elmahdy as a feminist performance artist, naïve idealist, or irrepressible fighter, her oppositionally naked body inserts a sexually charged pause for reflection that invites us to consider anew the possibilities of genuinely inclusive revolutionary symbolic spaces, digital republics, and squares.

NOTES

1. Gianluca Mezzofiore, "Aliaa Magda Elmahdy, the Egyptian Nude Blogger, Sued for 'Insulting Islam,'" *International Business Times*, 18 November 2011, http://www.ibtimes.co.uk/aliaa-magda-elmahdy-egyptian-nude-blogger-sued-252058.

2. Aliaa Elmahdy, "Nude Art," *A Rebel's Diary*, 23 October 2011, http://arebelsdiary.blogspot.com/2011_10_01_archive.html.

3. Mohamed Fadel Fahmy, "Egyptian Blogger Aliaa Elmahdy: 'Why I Posed Naked,'" CNN, 19 November 2011, http://www.cnn.com/2011/11/19/world/meast/nude-blogger-aliaa-magda-elmahdy/.

4. See, for example, Mohammed Abdel Rahman, "Effacing Women in Salafi Campaign Bid," *Al-Akhbar*, 15 November 2011, http://english.al-akhbar.com/node/1505; "Female Salafist Candidate Is Using Her Husband's Photo on Campaign Posters," *Al Arabiya*, 10 November 2011, http://www.alarabiya.net/articles/2011/11/10/176372.html.

5. Sara Mourad, "The Naked Body of Alia: Gender, Citizenship, and the Egyptian Body Politic," *Journal of Communication Inquiry* 38, no. 1 (2014): 62.

6. Aliaa Elmahdy, "Scattered Thoughts," *A Rebel's Diary*, 10 May 2014, http://arebelsdiary.blogspot.com/2014/05/scattered-thoughts.html.

7. Gillian Rose, *Feminism and Geography: The Limits of Geographical Knowledge* (Cambridge: Polity, 1993), 20.

8. Donna Haraway, *Simians, Cyborgs, and Women: The Reinvention of Nature* (New York: Routledge, 1991), esp. chapter 8.

9. Gilles Deleuze and Félix Guattari, *A Thousand Plateaus: Capitalism and Schizophrenia*, translated by Brian Massumi (Minneapolis: University of Minnesota Press, 1987), 3–25.

10. Mikhail Bakhtin, *The Dialogic Imagination*, translated by Michael Holquist (Austin: University of Texas Press, 1981), 270–78.

11. This discussion is drawn from my earlier analysis of Elmahdy, which views her body as a litmus test for transnational feminist solidarity. Karina Eileraas, "Sex(t)ing Revolution, Femen-izing the Public Square: Aliaa Magda Elmahdy, Nude Protest, and Transnational Feminist Body Politics," *Signs: Journal of Women in Culture and Society* 40, no. 1 (2014): 40–52. This essay in contrast emphasizes Aliaa's nakedness as an act of rage and aesthetic re-visioning.

12. Marwan M. Kraidy, "The Revolutionary Body Politic: Preliminary Thoughts on a Neglected Medium in the Arab Uprisings," *Middle East Journal of Culture and Communication* 5, no. 1 (2012): 73.

13. Hamid Dabashi, "La Vita Nuda: Baring Bodies, Bearing Witness," *Al Jazeera*, 23 January 2012, http://www.aljazeera.com/indepth/opinion/2012/01/20121211238688792 .html.

14. Amy Adler, "Performance Anxiety: Medusa, Sex, and the First Amendment," *Yale Journal of the Law and Humanities* 21, no. 2 (2009): 224–50.

15. Homi Bhabha, "Remembering Fanon: What Does the Black Man Want?," *New Formations* 1 (Spring 1987): 118–24.

16. Samantha Mallory Kies, "Matriarchy, the Colonial Situation, and the Women's War of 1929 in Southeastern Nigeria," MA thesis, Eastern Michigan University, 2013, http://commons.emich.edu/cgi/viewcontent.cgi?article=1910&context=theses. See also Maryam Kazeem, "Bodies That Matter: The African History of Naked Protest, FEMEN Aside," *Okay Africa*, 28 March 2013, http://www.okayafrica.com/news/naked-prostest -bodies-that-matter-femen-african-history/.

17. Leila Neti, "Blood and Dirt: Politics of Women's Protest in Armagh Prison, Northern Ireland," in *Violence and the Body: Race, Gender and the State*, edited by Arturo Aldama (Bloomington: Indiana University Press, 2003), 77–93.

18. See, for example, Greenpeace International, "600 Strip Naked on Glacier in Global Warming Protest," 18 August 2007, http://www.greenpeace.org/international/en/news /features/naked-glacier-tunick-08182007/.

19. For more on this, see Black Girl with Long Hair, "Black Woman Artist Poses Nude at Former New York City Slave Trading Sites, Including Wall Street," 4 July 2015, http:// blackgirllonghair.com/2015/07/black-woman-artist-poses-nude-at-former-new-york -slave-trade-sites-including-wall-street-and-city-hall/.

20. Maggie Michael, "Activist Posts Herself Nude, Sparks Outrage," *Daily News Egypt*, 17 November 2011, http://www.dailynewsegypt.com/2011/11/17/activist-posts-herself

-nude-sparks-outrage/. See also Kyle Kim, "Aliaa Magda Elmahdy Nude Photos Spark Controversy," *Global Post*, 17 November 2011, http://www.globalpost.com/dispatch/news/regions/middle-east/egypt/111117/egyptian-activist-posts-nude-photos-herself-sparking-.

21. Maya Mikdashi, "Waiting for Aliaa," *Jadaliyya*, 20 November 2011, http://www.jadaliyya.com/pages/index/3208/waiting-for-alia.

22. Roland Barthes, *Camera Lucida*, translated by Richard Howard (New York: Hill and Wang, 1981).

23. Mourad, "The Naked Body of Alia," 62.

24. Mikdashi, "Waiting for Aliaa."

25. Mikdashi, "Waiting for Aliaa."

26. Mourad, "The Naked Body of Alia," 64.

27. Naheed Mustafa, "Put Your Shirts Back On, Ladies," *Foreign Policy*, 8 April 2013, http://foreignpolicy.com/2013/04/08/put-your-shirts-back-on-ladies/.

28. See, for example, Joumana Haddad, "Look Me in the Eyes . . . I Said the Eyes," *Now Media*, 28 December 2012, https://now.mmedia.me/lb/en/jspot/look_me_in_the_eyes_i_said_the_eyes.

29. Michael, "Activist Posts Herself Nude, Sparks Outrage"; Sami, "Different Faces of Extremism?"

30. The Uprising of Women in the Arab World, http://uprisingofwomeninthearabworld.org/?lang=en.

31. Aliaa Elmahdy, "Femen Egypt," *A Rebel's Diary*, 30 December 2012, http://arebelsdiary.blogspot.com/search?updated-min=2012-01-01T00:00:00%2B02:00&updated-max=2013-01-01T00:00:00%2B02:00&max-results=22.

32. Susana Galán, "'Today I Have Seen Angels in Shape of Humans': An Emotional History of the Egyptian Revolution through the Narratives of Female Personal Bloggers," *Journal of International Women's Studies* 13, no. 5 (2012): 19.

33. Gianluca Mezzofiore, "Aliaa Magda Elmahdy, Nude Blogger, Gains Support from Egyptian Diaspora," *International Business Times*, 18 November 2011. http://www.ibtimes.co.uk/aliaa-magda-elmahdy-nude-blogger-gains-support-252301.

34. Joy Majdalani Habib, "Who's Afraid of Alia el Mahdy?," *Middle Eastern Women's Rights Knowledge Base: Red Lips High Heels*, 11 March 2013, http://www.redlipshighheels.com/whos-afraid-of-aliaa-el-mahdy/.

35. Mikdashi, "Waiting for Alia."

36. Mona Eltahawy, "Egypt's Naked Blogger Is a Bomb Aimed at the Patriarchs in Our Minds," *Guardian*, 18 November 2011, http://www.guardian.co.uk/commentisfree/2011/nov/18/egypt-naked-blogger-aliaa-mahdy.

37. Mourad, "The Naked Body of Aliaa," 64.

38. Larry Diamond, "Liberation Technology," *Journal of Democracy* 21, no. 3 (2010): 69–83. See also Ulises A. Mejias, "Liberation Technology and the Arab Spring: From Utopia to Atopia and Beyond," *Fibreculture Journal* 20 (June 2012), http://twenty.fibreculturejournal.org/2012/06/20/fcj-147-liberation-technology-and-the-arab-spring-from-utopia-to-atopia-and-beyond/.

39. Judith Halberstam, "Imagined Violence, Queer Violence: Representation, Rage and Resistance," *Social Text* 37 (Winter 1993): 187. See also Pratibha Parmar, *A Place of Rage*, documentary (London: Women Make Movies, 1991).

40. Halberstam, "Imagined Violence," 187, 188, 190. See also Michael Taussig, *The Nervous System* (New York: Routledge, 1992), 2.

41. Halberstam, "Imagined Violence," 191–92.

42. Pierre Bourdieu, *La Domination Masculine* (Paris: Editions du Seuil, 1998), 44, my translation.

43. Judith Butler and Athena Athanasiou, *Dispossession: The Performative in the Political* (Cambridge: Polity, 2013), xi.

44. Pierre Nora, "Between Memory and History: *Les Lieux de mémoire*," *Representations* 26 (Spring 1989): 7–24.

45. Lauren Berlant, *The Queen of America Goes to Washington City* (Durham, NC: Duke University Press, 1997), 223.

46. Kraidy, "The Revolutionary Body Politic," 73.

47. Ernest Renan, "What Is a Nation?," paper delivered at the Sorbonne, 11 March 1882, in *Qu'est-ce qu'une nation?* (Paris: Presses-Pocket, 1992).

48. John Berger, *Ways of Seeing* (New York: Penguin, 1972).

49. Laura Mulvey, "Visual Pleasure and Narrative Cinema," *Screen* 16, no. 3 (1975): 6–18.

50. Catherine Hakim, "Erotic Capital," *European Sociological Review* 26, no. 5 (2010): 499–518.

51. Sha-Lene Pung, "Yoko Ono 'Cut Piece' Performance Art," YouTube, 26 March 2010, http://www.youtube.com/watch?v=Zfe2qhI5Ix4.

52. Roger Ebert, review of Chris Burden, *My God, Are They Going to Leave Me Here to Die?*, 25 May 1975, http://www.rogerebert.com/interviews/chris-burden-my-god-are -they-going-to-leave-me-here-to-die; Matt Potter, "From Sewage to Art and Back Again," *San Diego Reader*, 2 December 1999, http://www.sandiegoreader.com/news/1999/dec/02 /sewage-art-and-back-again/.

53. Ana Mendieta, *Silueta Series*, various sites throughout the US & Mexico, 1973–1980. See Erin Dziedzic, "Ana Mendieta: Earth Body, Sculpture and Performance 1972–85: *One Universal Energy Runs through Everything*," *Drain*, November 2015, http://www.drainmag .com/contentNOVEMBER/REVIEWS_INTERVIEWS/Ana_Mendieta_Review.htm.

54. Pussy Riot, "A Punk Prayer," Cathedral of Christ the Savior, Moscow, 21 February 2012. For video footage see Rpmackey, "Russian Riot Grrrl Protest," YouTube, 6 March 2012, https://www.youtube.com/watch?v=yZKaBh9pX64. For more on Pussy Riot, see the HBO documentary *Pussy Riot: A Punk Prayer* (2013), http://www.hbo.com /documentaries/pussy-riot-a-punk-prayer#/. Pussy Riot, *Pussy Riot! A Punk Prayer for Freedom* (New York: Feminist Press, 2012), is available on Kindle: http://www.amazon .com/Pussy-Riot-Punk-Prayer-Freedom-ebook/dp/B009DQG2R2. I am indebted to Yuxin Pei, 2014–15 Fulbright Scholar at USC, for sharing her research related to performance art–based feminism in modern China.

55. Cynthia Enloe, *Bananas, Beaches and Bases: Making Feminist Sense of International Politics* (Berkeley: University of California Press, 1990), 62.

56. Sami, "Different Faces of Extremism?"

57. Takis Würger, "From Icon to Exile: The Price of a Nude Photo in Egypt," *Spiegel Online*, 17 December 2013, http://www.spiegel.de/international/world/the-price-egyptian-aliaa-elmahdy-paid-for-posting-nude-photo-online-a-939541.html.

58. Elmahdy, "Nude Art."

59. From Elmahdy's Twitter profile at https://twitter.com/aliaaelmahdy. See also Mohammed Shoair, "Elmahdy: Egypt's Nude Rebel," *Al Akhbar*, 15 November 2011, http://english.al-akhbar.com/node/1512.

60. Sami, "Different Faces of Extremism?"

61. Jacques Rancière, *The Nights of Labor: The Workers' Dream in Nineteenth Century France*, translated by Rana Dasgupta (Philadelphia: Temple University Press, 1989), 674.

62. See Sami, "Different Faces of Extremism?"

63. For example, Elmahdy rejects Takis Würger's portrayal of her actions in "From Icon to Exile" as motivated primarily by personal protest against her parents' strictness, sexual repression, and physical abuse. Elmahdy, "Scattered Thoughts."

64. Fahmy, "Egyptian Blogger Aliaa Elmahdy."

65. Shoair, "Elmahdy: Egypt's Nude Rebel."

66. "Egypt Blogger Jailed for Insult," *BBC News*, 22 February 2007, http://news.bbc.co.uk/2/hi/middle_east/6385849.stm; Curt Hopkins, "Egyptian Blogger Kareem Amer Finishes Prison Sentence—Remains in Jail (Updated)," *ReadWrite*, 5 November 2010, http://readwrite.com/2010/11/05/egyptian_blogger_kareem_amer_finishes_prison_sente.

67. Elmahdy, "Scattered Thoughts."

68. Fahmy, "Egyptian Blogger Aliaa Elmahdy."

69. As relayed via status updates on Facebook and on her blog at Elmahdy, "Scattered Thoughts."

70. Fatima Mernissi, *Beyond the Veil: Male-Female Dynamics in Modern Muslim Society* (Bloomington: Indiana University Press, 1987), 31–45.

71. Fahmy, "Egyptian Blogger Aliaa Elmahdy."

72. Aliaa Elmahdy, "Ex-Muslim Women Protest Topless at Misogynistic Islamic Conference," *A Rebel's Diary*, 13 September 2015, http://arebelsdiary.blogspot.com/search?zx=874b5ac44f7ddf2e.

73. Jean Jacques Rousseau, *Emile, or On Education* (New York: E. P. Dutton, 1921). See also Immanuel Kant, *Observations on the Feeling of the Beautiful and the Sublime*, translated by John J. Goldthwait, 2nd edition (Berkeley: University of California Press, 2004).

74. bell hooks, *Black Looks: Race and Representation* (Boston: South End, 1992), 116.

75. Barthes, *Camera Lucida*, 27.

76. See Helene Cixous, "Laughter of the Medusa," translated by Keith Cohen and Paula Cohen, *Signs: Journal of Women in Culture and Society* 1, no. 4 (1976): 875–93.

77. See, for example, Leila Sebbar, *Sherazade: Missing, Aged 17, Dark Curly Hair, Green Eyes*, translated by Dorothy S. Blair (London: Quartet Books, 1991); Assia Djebar, *Fantasia: An Algerian Cavalcade*, translated by Dorothy S. Blair (Portsmouth, NH: Heinemann, 1993); Anne Donadey, *Recasting Postcolonialism: Women Writing between Worlds* (Portsmouth, NH: Heinemann, 2001); Winifred Woodhull, *Transfigurations of the Maghreb: Feminism, Decolonization, and Literatures* (Minneapolis: University of Minnesota Press,

1993); Suzanne Gauch, *Liberating Shahrazad: Feminism, Postcolonialism, and Islam* (Minneapolis: University of Minnesota Press, 2007); Jarrod Hayes, *Queer Nations: Marginal Sexualities in the Maghreb* (Chicago: University of Chicago Press, 2000); Barbara Harlow, *Resistance Literature* (New York: Routledge, 1987).

78. Compiled from comments on Elmahdy's actions expressed in articles in *Global Post, Al Ahram Online*, and *Al Akhbar*. Also see Shoair, "Elmahdy: Egypt's Nude Rebel."

79. Jean Kilbourne, "'The More You Subtract, the More You Add': Cutting Girls Down to Size," in *Gender, Race and Class in Media*, 2nd edition, edited by Gail Dines and Jean Humez (Thousand Oaks, CA: Sage, 2003). See also Sandra Lee Bartky, "Foucault, Femininity and the Modernization of Patriarchal Power," in *Writing on the Body: Female Embodiment and Feminist Theory*, edited by Katie Conboy, Nadia Medina, and Sarah Stanbury (New York: Columbia University Press, 1997), 129–54. For a powerful visual evocation of how this translates to extreme eating disorders, see *Thin*, directed by Lauren Greenfield (Santa Monica, CA: HBO, 2006).

80. Susan Sontag, *On Photography* (New York: Farrar, Straus and Giroux, 1977), 15.

81. Gayatri Spivak, "French Feminism in an International Frame," *Yale French Studies*, no. 62 (1981): 183.

82. Maryam Namazie, "I Will Be Nude, I'll Protest and I'll Challenge You!," *Unveiled: A Publication of Fitnah—Movement for Women's Liberation* 2, no. 3 (2014): 16, http://fitnah .org/fitnah_articles_english/M-Namazie_Nude_I_will_be_Nude.html.

83. "As Women Bare All in Feminist Protest, Germaine Greer Asks: Is This Feminism?," News.com.au, 17 March 2013, http://www.news.com.au/lifestyle/as-women-bare-all-in -feminist-protest-germaine-greer-asks-is-this-feminism/story-fneszs56-1226598414628.

84. Ben Bouazza, "Amina Tyler, Topless Tunisian Protester, Fears for Her Life," *Huffington Post*, 7 April 2013, http://www.huffingtonpost.com/2013/04/07/amina-tyler-topless -tunisian-protester-fears-for-life_n_3033352.html#.

85. "Topless Tunisian Protester at the Centre of Controversy," *Al Jazeera*, 25 March 2013, http://stream.aljazeera.com/story/201303252145-0022635.

86. See "Muslim Women Decry Topless Gender Protests," *Al Jazeera*, 5 April 2013, http://www.aljazeera.com/news/europe/2013/04/2013451183827070101.html.

87. Inna Shevchenko, "Femen Let Victor Syvatski Take Over Because We Didn't Know How to Fight It," *Guardian*, 5 September 2013, http://www.theguardian.com/comment isfree/2013/sep/05/victory-svyatski-femen-man.

88. "Amina Tyler, Tunisia's 'Topless Jihad' Activist, Caught and Under Arrest," *Al Arabiya English*, 21 May 2013, http://english.alarabiya.net/en/News/middle-east/2013 /05/21/Amina-Tyler-Tunisia-s-topless-jihad-activist-under-arrest.html; Naili Hajer, "Femen's Islam-Bashing Disregards Muslim Feminism," *Women's Enews*, 10 April 2013, http://womensenews.org/story/religion/130409/femens-islam-bashing-disregards -muslim-feminism.

89. See, for example, Bread and Roses Nude Protest: Nano GoleSorkh, "It Is My Body, 30 April 2014," YouTube, 1 May 2014, https://www.youtube.com/watch?v=Pqwxd4JC88c.

90. Mustapha Ajbaili, "Egypt Activist Who Protested Nude Says She Wants to Make Change, Differently," *Al Arabiya English*, 21 December 2012, http://english.alarabiya.net /articles/2012/12/21/256345.html.

91. Haddad, "Look Me in the Eyes."

92. Aliaa Elmahdy, "Free the Nipple Photo Shoot," *A Rebel's Diary*, 10 May 2014, http://arebelsdiary.blogspot.com/2014/05/scattered-thoughts.html#links.

93. As evident in 2014 posts containing video and imagery related to sexual assault in Tahrir Square and the "Islamic state." See Elmahdy, "Ex-Muslim Women Protest Topless at Misogynistic Islamic Conference," accessed 5 March 2016, http://arebelsdiary.blogspot.com/2015/09/ex-muslim-women-protest-topless-at.html#links. See also "Photo-Action against ISIS," accessed 5 March 2016, http://arebelsdiary.blogspot.com/2014/09/photo-action-against-isis.html#links.

94. See, for example, Lizzie Crocker, "Egypt's Pioneering Nude Protester," *Daily Beast*, 4 December 2013, http://www.thedailybeast.com/witw/articles/2013/12/04/aliaa-elmahdy-egypt-s-pioneering-nude-protester.html.

95. See Fitnah's website, http://fitnah.org. For more on sexual violence in Egypt, see Mariam Kirollos, "Sexual Violence in Egypt: Myths and Realities," *Jadaliyya*, 16 July 2013, http://www.jadaliyya.com/pages/index/13007/sexual-violence-in-egypt_myths-and-realities-. See also "Egyptian National Council for Women Proposes New Sexual Harassment Law," *Ahram Online*, 5 April 2013, http://english.ahram.org.eg/NewsContent/1/0/68515/Egypt/0/Egyptian-National-Council-for-Women-proposes-new-s.aspx.

96. Judith Butler, *Precarious Life: The Powers of Mourning and Violence* (New York: Verso, 2004), 26.

97. Michel Foucault, *Discipline and Punish: The Birth of the Modern Prison*, translated by Alan Sheridan (New York: Vintage Books, 1977), 200.

98. Aliaa Elmahdy, "My Speech at the Heathen Society's Annual Meeting," *A Rebel's Diary*, 25 January 2014, http://arebelsdiary.blogspot.com/2014/01/my-speech-at-heathen-societys-annual.html.

8 INTIMATE POLITICS OF PROTEST Gendering Embodiments and Redefining Spaces in Istanbul's Taksim Gezi Park and the Arab Revolutions BANU GÖKARIKSEL

A riot policeman in a gas mask and body armor showering a young woman in a red dress with pepper spray became the "iconic leitmotif" of the Gezi Park protests in Taksim Square during the summer of 2013 in Turkey (figure 8.1). Partly in response to the violent police crackdown, the Gezi protests quickly evolved into a popular uprising against the government of the Islamically oriented Adalet ve Kalkınma Partisi (AKP), or Justice and Development Party. The original grievances against neoliberal transformations of the city and their environmental and sociocultural impacts expanded to include concerns about police violence, "creeping authoritarianism," and increasing restrictions on freedom of speech, expression, and assembly.[1]

Unlike most of the cases discussed in this book, the Gezi protests emerged in a democratic context—a fact asserted repeatedly by government leaders and pro-government media in Turkey. Denying any similarity between the Arab revolutions and the Gezi protests, AKP representatives and pro-AKP media argued that what was happening in Turkey was an antidemocratic movement of "marginal" youth against a democratically elected, legitimate government.[2] The carefully grounded chapters in this book show that political resistance in each setting was indeed unique, but there were also many important similarities and connections between revolutionary dynamics across the region, including Turkey.[3] Turkey remains geographically, politically, and culturally tied to its neighbors by multiple historical and contemporary threads. When the Taksim Gezi uprising

FIGURE 8.1. A Turkish riot policeman uses pepper spray against a woman in a red dress on 28 May 2013 in Gezi Park, Istanbul. Osman Orsal / Reuters.

started in 2013, terms such as "Turkish Spring" and "Gezi Spirit" aimed to capture the similarities between the wave of revolutions across the Arab world and resistance in Turkey.[4] The Arab revolutions were inspiring for those in Turkey who were discontented with the government's increasing repression of rights and freedoms, unbridled neoliberalization, and social conservatism. Many were also frustrated with an electoral system they believed did not sufficiently represent their voices.

In all the uprisings in the region urban space was key to the efforts of a diverse set of ordinary citizens to assert a right to the city and to seek justice, dignity, and freedom.[5] Protesters utilized the virtual spaces of chat rooms, blogs, Twitter, and Facebook, and the material spaces of their neighborhoods and cities, occupying streets, squares, and parks. They largely expressed democratic ideals and commitment to pluralism, transforming the spaces they occupied to reflect and foster these ideals. Women's presence was notably at the forefront of all these upheavals and protests.[6] Gendered spatial politics were as crucial in Turkey as they were in Arab settings examined in this book. Using the analytics of feminist political geography and "critical visual methodology," I highlight the dynamics of gender and space across the cases analyzed in this book to develop an embodied and spatial understanding of the uprising in Turkey and to identify shared tactics and discourses of protest and revolution in the region and beyond.[7]

My argument about the intimate politics of the Turkish uprisings connects with the main analytical contributions of this book. I use the term *intimate politics* to underline the significance of the body, the "geography closest in," and its representations.[8] All the chapters illustrate the centrality of the gendered and sexualized body as a political site of revolutions and uprisings, as well as repression. Further, they indicate that protest strategies often domesticated public spaces and blurred spatial binaries (public/private, material/virtual, formal/intimate) and their gendered and sexual registers. The revolutions and uprisings disrupted hegemonic definitions of politics, spaces, and bodies and enabled the imagining of alternative forms of life and society. Thus the book indicates the spatial and embodied significance of gender and sexuality well beyond an empirical tallying of the visible presence or absence of women and girls. Approaching the Arab and Gezi uprisings from a feminist spatial perspective that attends to multiple scales and spaces offers new insights into their social and political dynamics.

The image widely dubbed "the woman in red" (*kırmızı elbiseli kadın*) that became an icon of the Gezi resistance in Turkey is akin to the "woman in the blue bra" image and to the activist Aliaa Elmahdy's nude self-portrait in Egypt in 2011, discussed by Karina Eileraas in this volume. These images draw on, reproduce, or subvert gendered, sexual, and ideological assumptions about how power is distributed across bodies and in space. Taken together the photographs reveal the intimate politics of revolution and how gendered and sexualized bodies are the main sites of political struggle. As important, such bodily representations are crucial to how struggle was made legible to wider publics.

After examining the intimate politics of the revolutions, I outline the historical and political context of the Gezi uprisings and the significance of Taksim as a public space; analyze embodiments of gender and sexuality in iconic images and stories of the Gezi uprising; show how spatial divisions were destabilized by a politics of intimacy in public space in the Arab and Turkish cases; and illustrate the domesticating of public spaces as central to many of the strategies and methods used in the Arab and Turkish revolutions and uprisings.

Intimate Politics

When the mass upheavals erupted in the Middle East and North Africa in 2011, they were instantly hailed as Facebook or Twitter revolutions.[9] This initial hype of new technologies and social media seemingly rendered material space irrelevant to popular uprisings of the twenty-first century. Yet as the images of city squares and main streets where thousands gathered filled the pages and screens of mainstream news sources, it became impossible not to recognize the continuing significance of public space for political movements, leading to a corrective reorientation that focused on the importance of the material architecture of mass protest.[10] This attention to public space was crucial and welcome but problematic when it primarily treated space as a setting or stage for political events. At times it perpetuated the myth of the public/private divide, the notion that public spaces are the only spaces of politics, and an understanding of politics that is limited to elections and constitutions, evacuating many other registers and scales, including embodied relations and intimate life. Feminist scholarship has long challenged such masculinist and ahistorical assumptions and their effects. Dovetailing with research in other disciplines, feminist geographers destabilized the public/private binary by showing that the personal is often political and the home is a key space for political mobilization.[11] Such scholarship provides embodied accounts of political practice attuned to difference and multiple scales, connecting bodies to nation-states and global politics.[12]

Doreen Massey and Cindi Katz have called for feminist geographical analysis that does not treat places as isolated, exclusive, and discreet units but rather examines connections between them across space and time.[13] The contributors to this volume, with their meticulous attention to connections between "revolution squares" and bedrooms, homes, neighborhoods, online chat rooms, blogs, and cars in different revolutionary settings, demonstrate this sensitivity to spatial connectivity with particular attention to embodiment. Each author destabilizes binary understandings of virtual/material and public/private and highlights the centrality of embodiment, subjectivity, and ideology in the character of such divisions and destabilizations. Sonali Pahwa, Susana Galán, and Eileraas illustrate that women activists operated across virtual and material space, complicating neat divisions between them. Frances Hasso, Susanne Dahlgren, Pahwa, and Galán show that protesters also crisscrossed the boundary between private and public space, politicizing domestic spaces and domesticating public spaces. And Zakia Salime, Lamia Benyoussef, Dahlgren, and Hasso demonstrate that revolutionaries and protesters challenged gender and sexual ideologies and formed new political subjectivities as they occupied city squares and parks.

Bodily and virtual encounters across age, gender, ethnicity, and sexual identity, as well as ideological orientations, led to disagreements and exclusions, most clearly indicated in the chapters by Salime and Benyoussef. Indeed disidentification was an important dimension of these revolutions and uprisings, as discussed by Pahwa, Eileraas, and Dahlgren. But these encounters also produced shared understandings, alliances, and coalitions, as indicated in the chapters by Dahlgren and Salime. Authors in this book remind us that whether metaphoric or physical, center, margin, and border are contingent and ideologically, socially, and discursively constructed.

Feminist scholarship has taken issue with disembodied accounts of politics that exclusively focus on state institutions and electoral politics. Feminist geopolitics has instead peopled the "world without people" that is constructed by conventional geopolitics.[14] Similarly wary of NGOs and their gender-mainstreaming agendas, feminist approaches within geopolitics have turned to the everyday and corporeal as critical categories. Politics is studied as it is enacted, materialized, and transformed by embodied and grounded relations and practices in the private *and* public spaces of everyday life. The emphasis on the body and embodiment in feminist geopolitics crystallizes in Jennifer Fluri's understanding of "the gendered corporeal as a geographic space that is a symbolic, material and at times violent agent of geopolitics."[15] Sara Smith has put forth the concept of *intimate* geopolitics to show the entanglement of territorializing practices with sites of "love and babies" where "geopolitical strategy is animated."[16]

My approach takes the body as a central site of politics, not merely as the surface upon which discourses are inscribed.[17] It is the material space for the making of political subjects, social reproduction, and social change. The body is the site of the symbolic *and* the material, the source of visual and textual representations, the target of ideologies, *and* the fleshy, messy, and leaky physical substance of who we are.[18] The concept of intimate politics helps foreground the corporeal and capture its complexity while enabling us to trace emotions and affect, including relations of power and resistance across space.

A focus on intimate body politics, I suggest, is crucial because revolutions and uprisings are deeply bodily and affective affairs. For example, the memorable and widely discussed Clock Tower scene in Tunis examined by Benyoussef was produced by daring young men who climbed the tower. At discursive levels, she argues, music, art, and activism create competing "mythspaces" that stretch from prerevolutionary to revolutionary Tunisia and from local to transnational actors, practices, and spaces. Revolutions are thoroughly intimate in their strategies and effects, inaugurating new political subjectivities, spaces, feminisms, and modes of citizenship. Pahwa's analysis of Egyptian women bloggers shows how the bloggers' intimate, gendered performances and voices were crucial to the formation of their political subjectivities and direct engagement with the revolution and its aftermath. She argues that blogs were where the women formed a political repertoire, rehearsed new roles and relationships, and transformed personal emotions and sentiments into politically charged public affects. Salime argues that the 20 February Movement in Morocco proliferated material and discursive spaces of activism, producing many kinds of "aesthetic citizenship." Although much organizing nowadays occurs through spatially dispersed social networks and social media, these activities are no less embodied in their stakes, but in different ways, as indicated by Galán's discussion of illicit protest driving by Saudi women, Eileraas's examination of Elmahdy's nude protests, and Pahwa's study of Egyptian women's blogging activism. When Saudi women collectively post on YouTube videos of themselves driving or Egyptian women bloggers create "intimate publics" and find a political voice, their practices are both embodied and produce bodily affects on their blog and YouTube communities.

A demonstration or confrontation ultimately requires the material, bodily presence of protesters in the same place and time. Material bodies occupied space in the Pearl Roundabout in Manama, Freedom Squares in Aden, Bardo Square in Tunis, the streets of Rabat, and Gezi Park in Istanbul, transforming the people involved and the course of each revolution and uprising. Protesters walked, ran, carried banners, and gathered together. They stood side by side and held hands. They used their voices in ways that changed each other and listeners as they recited poetry, chanted, and sang. Some camped out for days. Others came with their family and friends for a few hours. Some hurled themselves in front of earthmovers or water cannons. Others built barricades or threw stones at or gave flowers to armored riot police. The eyes and throats of protesters burned from tear gas and pepper spray; their skin was sprayed with high-pressure water laced with chemicals; and their bones were crushed by the police. They were injured, lost eyes, and died from bullets, bombs, and beatings. In the cases of Mohamed Bouazizi in Tunisia and Fadwa Laroui in Morocco, the destruction of one's body became a form of "microrebellion" that helped to shape revolutionary imaginaries.[19]

Zeynep Gambetti eloquently argues for Gezi, "If history is being rewritten, then its subject is the body."[20] Sherine Hafez similarly underlines the significance of the corporeal, "not simply as a repository of disciplinary power ... [but] as a fluid and culturally mediated form with the potential to be disruptive, destabilizing, and transformative."[21] Not all bodies are present at protests, as Benyoussef, Dahlgren, Galán, Hasso, and Salime point out. Sometimes they are excluded, and sometimes they participate but are not necessarily in iconic scenes. They may be in the living room, watching the protests on television in solidarity as they care for children and cook meals, as Dahlgren shows us. This reminds us that gender, sexuality, and class systems help to constitute bodies, their presence or absence in various spaces, and even how we respond to them. In many of the protests across the Middle East and North Africa, women were present alongside men, including in Gezi Park, the Pearl Roundabout, Bardo Square, and Freedom Squares. Gender differences were seemingly suspended as both women and men shouted slogans, chanted, and made peace signs. However, gender differences were accentuated when women were subjected to virginity tests, accused of promiscuity by the government and the police, or objectified in iconic images.[22] As Hasso argues, gendering, sexualization, and racialization worked together in a sex-sect-police nexus to intensify sectarianism in Bahrain. Women's bodies in all settings became the artistic, representational, discursive, and material substance for competing claims about the nation, morality, justice, freedom, and dignity.

The Politics of Space and Bodies in Taksim Gezi

A series of political and social developments, many related to gender relations, expression, and embodiments in public space, generated popular discontent before the Taksim Gezi protests, contributing to their rapid escalation. The AKP emerged in 2001 out of a long history of political contention between Islamist political parties and the secular establishment (including the military and judiciary) in the second half of the twentieth century. Although continuously professing Islamic values and exhibiting Islamic lifestyles, members of the AKP disavowed the party's roots in Islamist politics when established in 2001 and presented themselves as reformist, liberal "Muslim democrats." The AKP gained successive victories in national legislative elections between 2002 and 2011, and its leaders, Abdullah Gül and Recep Tayyip Erdoğan, respectively, became president in 2007 and 2014.

Initially AKP policies liberalized the political system in Turkey and aggressively neoliberalized the economy; the economy grew rapidly and the government began negotiations for EU candidacy.[23] Senior politicians curtailed the role of the military and broached many sensitive issues concerning religious and ethnic minorities. At the same time, AKP leadership made frequent references to Islam and encouraged previously suppressed, outlawed, or unacceptable displays of religiosity to become more public. This combination of Islamic identity politics and economic and political liberalism led to talk of the "Turkish model" as a possible ideal for the region. Some pundits even argued it would be the model for the democratic transformation of Arab Muslim polities shaken up by popular unrest in 2011.

In Turkey, however, political developments especially since 2007 demonstrated the limits of democracy under AKP rule. The AKP government and the prime minister (later president) consolidated power.[24] According to a nationwide study, many felt pressure to appear as devout Sunni Muslims for economic success and social mobility.[25] The "alcohol law" of May 2013 restricting the sale, marketing, and advertising of alcoholic drinks was perceived as another indication of increasing disciplinary power over nonconformist lifestyles.[26]

Two organizations that focused on protecting Taksim, Taksim Gezi Parkı Koruma ve Güzelleştirme Derneği (Association for the Protection and Beautification of Taksim Gezi Park) and Taksim Dayanışması (Solidarity for Taksim Square),[27] organized the first sit-in on 27 May 2013 to protest plans to demolish Gezi Park to make way for the construction of a neo-Ottoman–style building. This was part of larger plans to completely redesign the Taksim area, including the square and adjacent Gezi Park. The new structure to be built at Gezi Park would replicate the late Ottoman military barracks torn down in the mid-twentieth century.[28] Redesign of the public green space included controversial upscale, semiprivate spaces such as a shopping mall, art galleries, and a mosque. Many believed the plans were similar to other "top-down" AKP government projects that privatized public spaces and transformed the city according to the lifestyles of the newly ascendant conservative Muslim political and economic elite.[29]

Taksim Square has long been a key contested public space in Turkey.[30] Set in the midst of Istanbul's indisputable cultural center and in close proximity to universities and financial and commercial districts, it was the site of some of the most famous political demonstrations in Turkish history. Despite increased police presence and security measures to prevent protests in the previous two decades, the square remained the main destination for mass public demonstrations.[31] The increasing polarization between Islamists and secularist Kemalists, named after Mustafa Kemal Atatürk, manifested in recurring struggles concerning the image and material composition of the area.[32] Islamists argued that this symbolically significant city center is filled with the iconography of the secularist state, including a statue of Atatürk that symbolized his centrality to the republic and the Atatürk Cultural Center. The square also includes non-Muslim sites, such as Greek and Armenian churches, foreign embassies, restaurants, and upscale hotels. Nothing signified Muslimness in Taksim, according to Islamist politicians.[33] Over the previous decade the municipal government restricted alcohol sales in the outdoor sections of restaurants around the square.[34] Tensions also escalated between visitors and users of the district, as mostly conservative residents contested the use of public space in Taksim. The planned building project would have finally realized the goal of projecting a neo-Ottoman and Muslim image on the square, ensuring that tourists and citizens understood that Turkey was indeed a Muslim country.

Women's organizations gained important victories in the first few years of AKP rule, such as progressive revisions of Turkey's Penal Code in 2004.[35] Nevertheless encroaching social conservatism increasingly intervened in the most private aspects of women's lives, fueling concerns over growing conservatism and limits on rights and liberties. For example, beginning in 2008 Erdoğan repeatedly called for all women to have at least three children; strongly criticized abortion, births by caesarean section, and birth control; and supported public disciplining against displays of affection in state-owned spaces, including after an incident on an Ankara subway in May 2013, when a conductor reprimanded a young couple for kissing.[36] State representatives and religious leaders also targeted pregnant women and their public visibility on city streets.[37]

The historical significance of Taksim for resistance was not lost on protesters. The main protest slogan, "Everywhere is Gezi, everywhere is resistance," poignantly pointed to the spatiality of resistance, underlining the political potential of place-based resistance that is distinct from and yet connected to other places and times. The emphasis on "everywhere" defied the sociopolitical division of space by a disciplinary state. It linked resistance across Turkey and opened up possibilities for global solidarity, making connections to concurrent demonstrations in Brazil, as well as earlier uprisings and occupations in Egypt's Tahrir Square, Bahrain's Pearl Roundabout, New York City, and elsewhere.

Despite an Istanbul court decision to halt the renovation of Taksim, Erdoğan stood behind the Gezi renovation building project.[38] By using terms such as *serseri* (bum or rogue) and *çapulcu* (vandal, looter, or marauder) he dismissed the protesters as marginal youth gendered masculine.[39] His defiant remarks about the protests and open support for the police, who used excessive force, contributed to the intensification and spread of the protests. Erdoğan and other political leaders tried to present the conflict in Gezi as between secularists and Islamists. This is a simplistic framing, similar to Benyoussef's argument for Tunisia. Like the other uprisings across the Middle East and North Africa, the protesters at Taksim Gezi Park in 2013 were remarkably diverse, a dimension that was much romanticized. A previously unimaginable mix of people, protesters included union organizers, neo-Marxist Islamist activists who called themselves "revolutionary Muslims" and "anticapitalist Muslims," shopkeepers, young professionals who had never participated in a demonstration, LGBTQ activists, and soccer fans, among them the now famous Çarşı fan club of Beşiktaş. Thousands gathered daily at the park, which remained occupied until mid-June 2013, when riot police cleared the encampment. At the same time, the AKP organized Respect for National Will (Milli İradeye Saygı) rallies that aimed to counter the Gezi protests by reiterating that the government was democratically elected and represented the "majority" of the population.[40]

Even as the protesters in Taksim Gezi Park were forcefully dispersed, sporadic protests continued through the summer and grassroots organizing culminated in a series of "direct democracy" public forums in neighborhood parks across Istanbul and other cities.[41] In December 2013 scandals related to corruption by top-level government officials led to more demonstrations.[42] In March 2014 protests flared again to mourn the death of a fifteen-year-old boy who had been in a coma since being hit in the head by a tear gas canister on his way to the grocery during the Gezi protests.[43] As of this writing, Gezi Park and its decades-old trees are still standing. However, in July 2015, the 6th Office of the Council of State overturned the decision it made a year earlier to cancel the controversial Taksim Gezi Park project.[44] At the same time, concerns about women's rights, civil liberties, and media freedom have only deepened with Erdoğan's continuing attempts to amass power since 2013.[45]

Embodied Femininities and Masculinities in Taksim and Beyond

The taking or "shooting" of a photograph is typically situated within power relations and contexts, as are acts of seeing and interpreting images. Gillian Rose uses a "critical visual methodology" to systematically analyze photography and other images.[46] This approach assumes that an image does not merely depict an event or setting but also actively constructs social reality through its multiple effects. Images actively work on the social contexts in which they are circulated and interpreted. As Gordon Fyfe and John Law put it, "To understand a visualization is to enquire into its provenance and into the social work it does. It is to note its principles of inclusion and exclusion, to detect the roles that it makes available, to understand the way in which they are distributed, and to decode the hierarchies and differences it naturalizes."[47]

Susan Sontag explains that photography does not work solely as evidence of the real: "In teaching us a visual code, photographs alter and enlarge our notions of what is worth looking at and what we have a right to observe. They are a grammar and, even more importantly, an ethics of seeing. Finally, the most grandiose result of the photographic enterprise is to give us the sense that we can hold the whole world in our heads—as an anthology of images."[48]

The anthology of the world of the Gezi Park protests includes many images that feature feminine and masculine bodies. Broadly speaking, the images and accounts sympathetic to the protests mobilized hegemonic tropes of femininity, such as the vulnerability, innocence, and nonviolence of women, to belie Erdoğan's and the pro-government and dominant media discourse that the protests were dangerous, chaotic, and spurred by radical outliers and others on the fringes of Turkish society. Representa-

tions of revolutionaries, ideological disagreement, and resistance as chaotic, radical, or fringe indicate how crucial spatial thinking, discourse, and
symbolism are to understanding resistance, control, and ideological per-
suasion. The photos of protesting women in headscarves signified that not
all visibly religious people supported the AKP government.[49] A group of
young women and several men doing yoga in perfect harmony implicitly
contrasted with the supposed disorder and violence of the protesters at
the park.[50] The image of a pregnant woman with "#Direngeziparkı geliyo-
rum" (#ResistGeziPark I'm coming) written on her exposed belly above
the sketch of a computer progress bar that was "95%" complete challenged
Erdoğan's presumption that every child born would support his political
ideology.[51] Images of multiple family generations together at protests similarly highlighted the diversity of participants and their nonthreatening
nature.[52]

In the remainder of this section I focus on specific representations
and narratives to more deeply examine the gendered spatial and intimate
politics of the uprisings in Gezi and elsewhere in Turkey. I consider how
gender differences and other asymmetrical power relations are visualized,
imagined, and understood and their wider implications. I am particularly
interested in embodied relations in space and place in such visualizations
and imaginings: how bodies are depicted, where an image is set, and what
kinds of spatial relations are suggested.[53]

THE WOMAN IN RED

The image of "the woman in red" was taken by the Reuters photographer
Osman Orsal on 28 May, the second day of the mass protests in Taksim.
Wearing a casual summer dress and holding onto a white canvas bag, the
woman appears to be a nonviolent, ordinary citizen—not a radical, marginal, or çapulcu, the words Erdoğan used to characterize the Gezi protesters. Her civilian appearance contrasts with that of an armored masked
policeman, crouched and muscles flexed as he sprays her from a short distance.[54] Reuters released more frames from this set of images in response
to the original photo's popularity.[55] Yet it is the image in figure 8.1, typically
cropped so that only the woman and the policeman are in the scene, that
circulated far and wide through social media and cyberspace in Turkey
and abroad.[56] Among the thousands of professional and amateur photographs, it became the "global symbol of anti-government resistance."[57] It

was reproduced in artwork and graffiti and printed in books and on banners and T-shirts. Its many incarnations included hand-drawn versions that removed it from its geographic origin, so that the frame was even more focused on the two bodies.[58]

The image was reprised again and again as thousands joined the protests and similar demonstrations sprung up across the city and country.[59] For many the woman in red encapsulated the escalating violence against protesters who were merely exercising their rights as concerned citizens, initially gathering to prevent the demolition of Gezi, a central city park that bordered the politically and symbolically significant Taksim Square. At a time when mainstream newspapers and news channels in Turkey did not or could not cover the Taksim protests,[60] photographs shared on Twitter, Facebook, YouTube, and Instagram and posted and archived on blogs and websites bypassed such restrictions.

The woman in the image, reluctant to become the representative of the protests, emphasized that she was only one of many to be violently attacked by the police.[61] Despite her reluctance, the image quickly became iconic, probably facilitated by the fact that she was not wearing a headscarf.[62] Indeed the quality, content, composition, framing, colors, and gendered registers all contributed to the reading of this image. First, the compositional elements capture movement despite stillness. A line of riot police is standing behind the officer spraying tear gas, apparently oblivious to the framed interaction. The woman's red summer dress and white tote bag vividly reflect the colors of the Turkish flag, and the folds of her dress reinforce its flag-like quality. The red color also invokes "the sensual realm of pleasure and spontaneity," juxtaposed to the "instrumental rationality, hierarchy, and order" signified by the policeman.[63] She is unarmed, wearing feminine clothing, and not striking an aggressive pose. Although her face is invisible behind her hair, she appears to be young, embodying a vision of a secular, middle-class, urbanized country.

Commentators on the image viewed its wide circulation as playing into gendered binaries and as a distraction from the complexity of the protests.[64] Irrespective of the desires of the protesters and the woman, the image worked as its own riposte in the battle of gendered-sexual discourse. Viewers saw the assumed innocence, vulnerability, and nonviolence of a woman's body that had entered an apparently risky public space. As the journalist Max Fisher noted, she is "a threat to no one."[65] While she invoked

FIGURE 8.2. The "woman in red" on the cover of the satirical magazine *Penguen*: "Protesters are attacking the police!" and "Everyone is selling [themselves]. We also sold the magazine ;)))."

the nation as young, urban, and attractive, the young policeman embodied the active, strong, and combative masculinity that represents the police and the state. The vulnerable woman's victimization by the police officer becomes a visual synecdoche for the brutality of the regime. Indeed *Penguen*, a popular magazine of political satire, played on the image by producing a cartoon in which the woman in red attacks a tote-carrying policeman with pepper spray, poking fun at government and media claims that the protesters were violent (figure 8.2). But the original image also communicates the fortitude of the woman in red, as she stands upright, only her face and upper body turned away from the spray.

The "woman in red" image does not depict the bloody faces and bruised bodies that can be seen in thousands of images archived in blogs and spread through social media—for example, on #Occupygezi. It also differs from photos of triumphant male protesters in forceful confrontations with police. Instead this image is akin to other images that have come to represent unarmed struggle against authoritarian regimes across the region, such as "the woman in the blue bra," a physician who was beaten and partially disrobed by Egyptian police in Cairo on 17 December 2011, an event captured in iconic video and still images.[66] The female body under attack seems a convenient and globally evocative archetype of unarmed, innocent, non-violent resistance against violence, especially violence initiated by males.

Yet "the woman in red" offers a striking contrast to the nude self-portrait of the Egyptian activist Aliaa Elmahdy, discussed by Eileraas.[67] While "the woman in red" relies on idealized notions of women's bodies and political subjectivities, Elmahdy's self-portrait provocatively calls these very assumptions into question by explicitly claiming sexual and bodily agency. The unarmed female body targeted by police violence is the very site of Elmahdy's sexual and political agency. Elmahdy undressed herself, gazed directly at the camera, and took the photograph using her camera's timing mechanism. Both "the woman in red" and Elmahdy's self-portrait point to the significance of gendered and sexualized bodies and embodied practices in these revolutions and uprisings and their representations, which circulate much more widely and intensively than images ever have. As feminist geopolitical scholars assert, however, there is a much longer history of bodies as "public sites of violence on which constructions of the nation and its boundaries take place."[68]

The social life of "the woman in red" image is telling. Its wide circulation on social media and in national and international newspapers fueled popular outrage globally against the severe police crackdown. It was reproduced in cartoons, graffiti, and books, on T-shirts, billboards, and posters, and on numerous paraphernalia, such as mugs, buttons, and pins.[69] The woman in red turned into Little Red Riding Hood and an Ottoman-style miniature illustration.[70] The tear gas was transformed into flowers or a stylized cloud-like fog. The woman herself was sometimes depicted as a tree and, inevitably, as the Turkish flag. The aesthetic play of this artwork drew on the well-known repertoire of symbols of the nation, femininity, masculinity, the environment, and history that was recognizably national but also easily appealed to an international audience given her youthful feminine appearance and her posture.

THE HEADSCARF-WEARING MOTHER WITH BABY

While "the woman in red" mobilized supporters through a gendered and sexualized visual grammar that depicted the violence of the police against peaceful protesters, another story, this one textual, galvanized those opposed to the Gezi protesters. In this account the victimized woman was a headscarf-wearing mother with her infant baby who was simply crossing the street at a busy area of bus stops in Kabataş, near Taksim, and the perpetrators of violence were thirty to forty male protesters who attacked her for being a presumed government supporter.[71] The story began its media circulation in June 2013 and became a linchpin of Erdoğan's speeches at AKP rallies organized to counter the Gezi protests. The ruthless protesters verbally abused the woman, who was minding her own business, and added insult to injury by urinating on her and her baby, according to the story; no visual evidence was offered to substantiate this, despite the many CCTV cameras at the location of the alleged incident. In February 2014, when Kanal D, a major television channel, broadcast a visual recording of the woman waiting in the bus station at the time of the alleged incident, the story was revealed as a fabrication.[72]

Much like the "woman in red" image and its deployments, this story used ideologies of gendered and sexual embodiments. Unlike the "woman in red" example, however, the account did not even require visual evidence to circulate. The story offered political leaders and their supporters an innocent, conservative, veiled mother with her baby attacked and humiliated by protesters. Despite ideological differences in relation to the government, in both accounts merciless men were understood to victimize innocent, even apolitical women. But the story of the woman and her baby resonated with the AKP's persistent rhetoric about the history of the oppression of Islam and devout Muslims by a staunchly secular Turkish state. Erdoğan repeated the story to represent Gezi protesters as wanting to return to the oppressive secularism of the past rather than seeking a pluralistic democratic society. In contrast to the bare-headed woman in red, the mother wearing a headscarf embodied a newfound freedom of religious expression against zealous secularist thugs.

Anecdotal stories of headscarf-wearing women being abused in Istanbul during the Gezi protests only strengthened the depiction of the protests as manifestations of the same old secularist ideology. But the presence of visibly pious Muslim protesters at Gezi complicated such representations. And on 7 June 2013 fifty headscarf-wearing women participated in a protest march that started in Kabataş and ended in Taksim Gezi Park. The women were protesting the harassment of headscarf-wearing women in different parts of the city and violence that targeted any woman, although they also highlighted the lack of such harassment at Gezi and insisted that they would continue to participate in the Gezi protests. Their banners read,

"Taksim is ours, Çarşı is ours, the street is ours," asserting ownership of urban space, enacting a politics of disidentification that refused the alignment of the headscarf with support for the AKP government, and calling for a broad feminist alliance to fight violence against all women.[73]

THE SLINGSHOT AUNTIE

The image of "sapanlı teyze" (the slingshot auntie), first printed in a newspaper on 12 June 2013, provides clues for the visual and social construction of an alternative femininity, albeit short-lived, in the uprisings in Turkey (figure 8.3).[74] The photo by Bülent Kılıç was taken the previous day and captures escalating violence by police and resistance by protesters. The setting is a construction site on the main street leading to Taksim Square, bordering Gezi Park. In the image banners hang on the office buildings lining the street. In the out-of-focus background are four or five men wearing surgical masks, and one wears a white construction hardhat. The image looks like a scene of urban guerrilla warfare, with debris everywhere and graffiti on the barricades spelling PKK, a reference to the armed Kurdish nationalist organization, and "Fight Cops" in English.

The focus of the image is an older woman using a slingshot to attack the police from behind a barricade. The police are out of frame for the viewer. The woman has gray hair tied into an untidy bun and wears dark loose athletic pants, a flowery print blouse, and a bulky brown fanny pack around her waist. A white surgical mask covers her mouth and nose. She is in a combat position, with one leg in front and her arms stretching the slingshot, which has a stone lodged in it ready to fly. Her blood type is written on her arm, signaling her expectation of and preparation for bodily harm. Except for the incongruous slingshot and mask, her clothing and body identify her as an average urban older middle-class woman in Istanbul, an "auntie." It is this "auntie-ness" that surprised many. This disidentification with the customary auntie subject position was noted in the news coverage and discussions of the photograph.

The older, everyday femininity of the slingshot auntie contrasts with the youthfulness, innocence, and apparent nonviolence of the woman in red. The maternalness of the slingshot auntie contrasts with the allegedly attacked headscarf-wearing mother. Rather than using her body to shield a baby, the auntie is attacking armed police. The photo is clearly composed to present her as the hero. According to some news sources, the image was taken up by resistance movements and spray-painted in places as far

FIGURE 8.3. Emine Cansever, nicknamed "the slingshot auntie," aims at riot police on Taksim Square on 11 June 2013. Bülent Kılıç / AFP / Getty Images.

away as Colombia.[75] This image was embraced by many in Turkey who admired the woman's courage as she fought alongside young people. Pro-government pundits discredited the woman, Emine Cansever, when it was revealed she was a member of a labor organization allegedly linked to a left-ist terrorist group.[76] Thus she was no longer an older, nonideological, ma-ternal woman caught in the maelstrom of protest and innocent of political intent. Right-wing and pro-government media sources described her as marginal and even a terrorist. Anonymous online commentators lodged gendered and sexualized insults against her, including that she was sexu-ally frustrated and needed to be "fucked."[77] She was arrested in September 2013 and jailed for three months because of her involvement in other pro-tests in the neighborhood of Gülsuyu, Istanbul.[78] Thus the celebration of the combatant maternal femininity she symbolized was short-lived and quickly attacked by a flood of insults.

IDEOLOGIES OF MOTHERHOOD AND FATHERHOOD

At the peak of the protests, on 13 June 2013, the prime minister issued a threatening demand to the families of the Gezi Park occupiers: "I say to the mothers and fathers, please take your children in hand and bring them out."[79] This call denied the political agency of young people in the protests, constructing them as unruly children in need of protection and guidance from responsible parents. The governor of Istanbul Province made the same call to mothers, adding that their children were not safe at Gezi anymore. In response hundreds of mothers went to Gezi Park the next day.[80] But instead of taking their children home, they lined up holding hands, forming a barricade between the police and the protesters. They figuratively constituted a public maternal protective boundary around the protesters that refused attempts to depoliticize motherhood.[81] Some chanted for mothers of the police to take *their* children home. By joining en masse as mothers, the women asserted that they and their children were not "extremists" or "marginal" and that the protesters were justified.[82] The images of mothers at the Gezi protests legitimized the protesters in the eyes of some precisely because of gendered assumptions about mothers. Good mothers could not be vandals or bums or support the delinquency of children.

Some feminists were skeptical of the gendered ideologies at play in protest strategies that reinforced normative femininities and masculinities — for example, the chain of mothers. Especially given Erdoğan's strong rhetoric about motherhood as the primary role of women, there are limits to the transformative possibilities of activism on the basis of maternity. One activist, a mother, emphasized that she was at Gezi as a woman, pointing to the difficulty of feminist challenges to unequal gender relations through the framework of motherhood.[83] Regardless of their intentions, women are conventionally read as embodying peacefulness and requiring protection. Thus their political potency too often paradoxically depends on the perceived rupture between the gendered stereotype of women's physical vulnerability and the strength of the women depicted.

THE GAS-MASKED, PINK-SKIRTED WHIRLING DERVISH

Images and accounts of men protesters and their embodiment operated through a gender-oppositional set of meanings. In Gezi images men mostly appear either as active combatants (whether police or protesters) or as unquestionable victims of the police, with bloody faces, black eyes, and broken bones. In an iconic instance of combative masculinity, a group of men on 2 June commandeered an excavator machine in Beşiktaş and drove it all the way to the Dolmabahçe Palace, the historic Ottoman palace that Erdoğan used as his office when he was in Istanbul during his term as prime minister.[84] The photos and accounts of rival soccer fans, dressed in the uniforms of their respective teams and marching in Taksim, hint at the potential violence lurking beneath the common cause made in opposition to government infringement on civil liberties.[85]

Images of the "whirling dervish" wearing a gas mask and the "standing man" represent alternative masculine embodiments that contrast with hegemonic masculine images and accounts during the Taksim Park protests. The photograph of the whirling dervish captures its subject in the midst of his turn, his pink skirt flowing elegantly through the air.[86] At the edges of the photo are people lined up to watch and photograph him. He is whirling in front of a sign for the State Opera and Ballet and the State Theater declaring "We are Everywhere" (Her Yerdeyiz) atop a graffiti-covered wall.

The whirling dervish image acquired visual potency and global aesthetic appeal by contrasting a welcoming, accommodating Islam of aestheticized embodied performance with the aggressive, combative masculinities of police, some protesters, and Erdoğan himself.[87] But this dervish was unlike other male adherents to mystical forms of Islam. Many commentators remarked on the vulnerability of this "shirtless" dervish, whose bare chest dramatically contrasts with traditional fully clothed dervishes.[88] Moreover the bright pink skirt and red belt of Gezi's dervish are far more vibrant, feminine, and sexual than the solemn, gender-neutral white skirt and black belt of conventional dervishes. The man was revealed to be Ziya Azazi, a performance artist who uses the whirling dervish as a theme in his provocative dance performances and choreography.[89]

By referencing the Sufi teachings of Jalal al Din Rumi, much celebrated for his acceptance and accommodation of difference, antimaterialistic ambitions, and complete devotion to Allah, such performances appeal to a version of Islam perceived as radically different from the conservative Sunni Islam that had come to dominate the public sphere in Turkey in the previous decade. The Gezi "whirling dervish" image was quickly made into widely used stencils, some adding Rumi's famous poetic invitation to Sufism, "Come whoever you are" (Sen de gel).[90] Taking up this message, the LGBTQ activist organization Kaos painted images of the gas-masked dervish in rainbow colors, superimposing an explicit LGBTQ sensibility.[91] Thus this performance and its representations and iterations brought together seemingly contradictory signifiers that opened up dominant masculinity to criticism, questioned normative heterosexuality, and asserted an intimate politics that incorporated such questioning into the history of Gezi.

Another embodied performance of masculine disidentification from the Gezi protests was illustrated by *duran adam*, the "standing man," who emerged on June 17, 2014, after the government forcefully cleared the Gezi Park occupation and "cleaned" and reopened the square.[92] Erdem Gündüz, a performance artist, stood still for eight hours gazing at the Atatürk Kültür Merkezi (Atatürk Cultural Center) in Taksim Square.[93] Wearing a white shirt and jeans, his hands in his pockets, he is the central subject in images of the protest, while a curious crowd stands behind him. His long hair is pulled into a disheveled ponytail and his backpack lies at his feet in front of him. The police were "startled by this act of passive resistance" and searched his backpack multiple times, looking for explosives.[94] Others joined his vigil, so that the number of standing men and women reached three hundred at Taksim Square that day.[95] Rather than protesting with movement, violence, or sound, "standing man" asserted the material stillness and silence of his body in place, a "dignified defiance" that challenged combative masculinities.[96] Thus the standing man "manifests a brilliant act of subversion, whereby a male figure occupies public space creating a spectacular instance of passivity."[97]

In an interview with Hürriyet TV following his protest, Gündüz explained his choice of location.[98] He used Taksim Square to get the attention of journalists and the public and to protest the government leaving the Atatürk Kültür Merkezi arts and performance center in disrepair during the preceding four years. The building became the operation headquarters for riot police during the protests. The act of standing silently condemned police violence but also, Gündüz painstakingly emphasized, the violence of cleaning up the memories and traces of protest that had occurred at the site. Similar standing men and women appeared in the Istanbul neighborhoods of Beşiktaş and Kadıköy and in other city squares across Turkey.[99] A number of standing men and women were arrested in the early hours of the following day.[100]

CODA

The gendered bodies of women and men offered the basic substance for ideological struggles over power and truth in the Gezi protests. Protesters occupied space to assert belonging, claim rights and liberties, disidentify, and redefine, reinforce, or produce new textures, meanings, and boundaries. But embodied actions and their representations and circulations also tapped into, mobilized, or challenged dominant conceptions of femininity and masculinity. At Gezi the legitimacy of protesters claiming a right to the city depended on gendered and sexualized grammars that showed the disproportionate force used by the police against peaceful protesters and countered the government's depiction of protesters as violent, reckless, marginal, and antidemocratic. Widely circulated images and stories of the Gezi protests did much of this ideological work. These accounts relied on, reproduced, or offered possibilities for subverting traditional conceptions of femininity and masculinity, gender-sexual orders, and female and male embodiments.

Bodies reproduce or are used to reproduce dominant ideologies. Bodies also manifest as the most intimate, gendered, and sexualized sites of political resistance and repression. Because bodies regularly cross borders between presumed public and private, they expose the charge attached to disrupting existing spatial orders.

Crossing Borders, Redefining Spaces

Feminist scholars have long questioned the public/private divide and criticized its gendered underpinnings and role in reproducing gender inequalities.[101] Key to gendered orderings of space is the characterization of private space as domestic, feminine, irrational, and apolitical, whereas public space is presented as male and rational, the site of politics and civic engagement.[102] The public/private divide was persistently subverted by activists in the revolutions and uprisings discussed in this book.[103] Repeatedly crossing the line between public and private enabled activists not only to claim city spaces but also to actively reconfigure their material architecture and affective and symbolic elements.[104] The boundaries between public and private were blurred in the uprisings and protests from Yemen to Egypt to Turkey, and activists established linkages between cyberspace and material space and their domestication of public space—for example, through public enactments of intimacy and care.

Social media circuits offer spaces for social interaction and mobilization that challenge the divide between the virtual and the embodied, although Galán, Pahwa, Hasso, and Eileraas show that such circuits and transversals are not without limits and dangers. Though not equally conspicuous, activist bedrooms, blogs, and city squares were fundamentally tied to each other in these revolutions and uprisings. In Galán's analysis Saudi women coordinated driving protests in cars, ambiguous spaces that are public or private, depending on the situation. When the women shared videos online of illicit driving, their violations, often completed individually at night on abandoned streets, the women wearing anonymizing Saudi dress, produced a cyber-collective and cyber-public protest after the fact. Their protests did not require a synchronic collective enactment in a physical setting. Blogging with anonymizing handles similarly complicates delineations between public and private.

Activists in these revolutions and uprisings contested the public/private divide in other ways. Once protesters were in the streets, parks, or squares, the "throwntogetherness" of multiple bodies for a common cause established new intimacies and redefined protest sites as intimate spaces.[105] Practices usually considered intimate, even feminine, were inserted into city squares, reconfiguring them and creating intimate politics. Multiple examples from the revolutions and uprisings indicate the importance of the home, the front yard, and sexual and embodied life as sites of politics, defiance, and repression, as discussed by Benyoussef, Dahlgren, Salime, Hasso, and Eileraas.[106] As Judith Butler notes, such intimacies are politically potent.[107]

Public spaces were often redefined and domesticated through embodied practices. Benyoussef, for example, describes activists sweeping city streets throughout Tunisia, and Salime discusses the Freeze for Freedom spectacle in front of the Parliament building, which reclaimed a pacified protest scene through embodied art performance. In taking on a practice usually seen as the low-status paid work of men or the unpaid home work of girls and women, male revolutionary activists openly transgressed gender and class norms and challenged the gendered public/private divide. The act of sweeping streets asserts common ownership of and shared responsibility for public space. It sent the message that people claim their rights to cities and towns without asking for permission, to use Benyoussef's term.[108] As in Tunisia, protesters at Gezi collectively swept the park, collected garbage, and planted flowers, enlisting children and dogs in such projects.[109] These acts domesticated Gezi and rearticulated it as the responsibility of residents, not only municipal workers and politicians. These enactments were also ideologically performative in that they served to counter pro-government accounts that presented protesters as vagrants and *çapulcu*s who destroyed city buses and peed and defecated in the park.

Revolutions and uprisings often involve spatial politics that expose the power relations embedded in the geographical divisions of everyday life by challenging them. In the Arab and Turkish cases activists attempted to remake places and imaginaries to usher in the desired societal transformation, as indicated by intense struggles over the Pearl Roundabout and the flag in Bahrain and the illuminated Independence Clock Tower on Habib Bourguiba Street in Tunis. This is a plainly powerful strategy. Even when protest is decentralized and shifting in response to changing political situations, streets, neighborhoods, and squares are redefined, certainly in how they are remembered by activists, residents, and bystanders. These dynamics are more pronounced when protest sites are occupied for an extended time, as in the cases of Tahrir Square, the Pearl Roundabout, Bardo Square in Tunis, the many *saha*s in Aden, and Gezi Park.

While encampment and occupation have been central to these revolutions and uprisings, the terms do not do justice to the strategic remaking of spaces by such practices and the ways these practices in turn remake subjectivities and imaginations in interaction with virtual activism. Open-ended unauthorized collective *dwelling* is a radical form of politics that challenges accepted definitions of space, social relations, and sources of power. Moreover the gendered divisions between the political and the everyday, the masculine and the feminine, are challenged as tents are pitched, rugs rolled out, medical tents and libraries established, stages constructed, poetry and dance performed, and meals shared. For example, in Dahlgren's discussion of the Southern Revolution in Yemen, the home spilled out into the sahas, which turned into mixed-gender and mixed-generation living and dining rooms, challenging the gender ideology of the government in Sana'a, as women and men sat together and marched to make "civilpolitics." More than challenging segregation, gender mixing in sahas produced new intimacies between men and women and offered another vision of gendered spatial relations in Yemeni society.

At Gezi protesters similarly transformed the park into a home-like space of encampment as they placed tents, carpets, and pillows in sleeping quarters. Some built makeshift beds out of scrap material, producing a distinct architecture; flags, banners, and signs became curtains in these new dwellings; trees were elaborately decorated.[110] At the same time, these places of living and dwelling were thoroughly communal. As in Tahrir Square, protesters built a library and a pharmacy.[111] Many who could not camp out at Gezi donated books, medicine, water, and food; others do-

nated their time and expertise, including doctors treating wounded protesters free of charge.[112] Protesters shared meals.[113] Some protesters drank,
some sang, and some prayed together. Many slept next to one another.
Such intimate sharing of space cultivated solidarity across difference and
transformed the setting itself, allowing the reimagining of sites as distinct
liberated territories, as captured by the Egyptian revolutionary term "the
Republic of Tahrir."[114]

Some of the most poignant symbols of the revolutions and uprisings
were images of public spaces remade by activists. Sleeping in public, a politically potent act of embodied dwelling, occurred in a number of the upheavals, including Cairo, Manama, Tunis, and Istanbul. Homeless people
sleeping in public spaces upset public/private sensibilities, but they are
commonly dismissed and denigrated. In contrast, activists and revolutionaries who collectively sleep outside can radically destabilize social norms
and the meanings of particular sites, particularly if they mix across socioeconomic differences. Sleeping in public can be a form of dissensus that
calls into question the given distribution of bodies, practices, and objects
across space.[115] That may explain the hundreds of photos of protesters
sleeping at Gezi Park and other locations during extended encampments
in Turkey; most were on blankets, their bodies completely exposed, displaying themselves collectively at their most vulnerable.[116] This intimate
politics required being all there, with no protection and minimal privacy,
removed from the usual material and social environment. A man lying on
his side, an arm tucked under his head, shoes carefully placed at one end of
his blanket; a group of men and women lying next to one another, making
a human jigsaw puzzle—both images depict politically charged forms of
vulnerability and social relationality built by struggle.[117]

In a striking and easily marketable Getty image that was widely circulated, a beautiful young couple dressed in the casual clothing of global
youth lies on a red blanket overlaid with newspapers (figure 8.4). The
woman is on her side, her blonde hair flowing onto the blanket, and the
man's arm is over his face.[118] The impact and cultural message of such an
image differed depending on the ideological frame of the viewer. As illustrated in Hasso's chapter on the Pearl Roundabout and Eileraas's chapter
on Elmahdy, pro-government rhetoric and social and religious conservatives used such images and accounts to tell tales of immorality for the pur-
pose of discrediting protesters. Similarly in Turkey displays of affection
and intimacy at protests, especially between presumably unmarried indi-

FIGURE 8.4. Protesters lie together in Gezi Park on 7 June 2013. Uriel Sinai / Getty Images.

viduals, were inserted into a government discourse that represented the government as primarily concerned with protecting public morality and the protesters as culturally marginal. Yet the significance of the politics of intimacy was not lost on protesters. Precisely because public morality had become a crucial discursive technique of governmentality in Turkey, they continued to organize tango sessions and "kiss-ins" at Gezi, and a sign with hand-drawn symbols of gay, trans-, bi-, and other nonnormative sexual identities astutely asked, "Genel ahlak kimin ahlakı?" (Whose morality is public morality?).[119] This question pointed out the exclusions embedded in hegemonic notions of public morality and drew attention to how power systems define the material and cultural boundaries of the public and its inhabitation.

Conclusion

Activists disrupted the spatial orders of things, materialized political claims, formed alliances, and re-created spaces in the popular revolutions and uprisings across the Middle East. The deliberate blurring of the presumed boundaries between the public and the private during the revolutions and uprisings reworked the spatial allocation of intimacies. In her discussion of the 2011 revolutions Butler writes, "Political claims are made by bodies as they appear and act, as they refuse and as they persist under conditions in which that fact alone is taken to be an act of delegitimation of the state."[120] Indeed the appearance of bodies in digital and material spaces was central to these upheavals. Bodies were persistently present even when subjected to police violence, and governments consistently launched discursive attacks to delegitimize them. In every case this presence was a powerful enactment of politics that called into question the state's legitimacy and revealed the limitations of an existing order, as Rancière describes the police. As "modalities of power," bodies were the main substance of the intimate politics of revolution.[121]

Revolutions and uprisings are intimately political not only because they work through bodies but also because they produce and reconfigure intimacies across space and between people. This intimate politics is a crucial dimension of their power, underlying demands for rights to the city and inclusion of the dismissed and excluded. The embodied practices of protesters domesticated and transformed public sites into home spaces of collective dwelling, even if temporarily. Activists and revolutions forged connections across cyber and material spaces as well as living rooms, kitchens, bedrooms, front stoops, city squares, streets, and parks. These enactments made apparent the essential role of affect—love, anger, care, solidarity, shared vulnerability, and sectarianism—in politics and policing. Despite the fact that many of the encampments and hot and visible confrontations have ended or deteriorated into war in a number of cases, contestations of totalizing and repressive definitions of the public continue in multiple ways in every setting. As Salime argues, the revolutions and uprisings produced many sites for making claims for citizenship rights, community membership, and belonging. Each chapter in this book illustrates their ongoing nature.

This book shows that training the lens on the most intimate of sites, the body, reveals the centrality of gender and sexuality in the revolutions and uprisings. Politics has never been the exclusive business of public spheres and formal party politics. It is part of everyday life and everyday spaces. The uprisings and revolutions confirm the necessity of taking into account this multiscalarity, plurality, and open-endedness. Paying attention to bodies reveals the precariousness of binaries such as public/private and virtual/material space. Bodies are crucial to discursive, symbolic, and ideological struggles over legitimacy and space. Many images in these uprisings and revolutions relied on and perpetuated hegemonic gender norms, roles, and values—including beauty, innocence, nonviolence, and motherhood—even when rulers are being contested, indicating the limits of uniscalar definitions of revolution.[122] A number of chapters in this book show how the revolutions and uprisings created openings that questioned heteronormativity, gendered respectability norms, and dominant masculinities and femininities, which often underpin repressive governments. The revolutions and uprisings enacted alternative embodiments and imaginaries of life itself. Even as structures of power consolidate and rearticulate themselves in a number of settings, the effects continue.

NOTES

1. Aslı Iğsız, "Brand Turkey and the Gezi Protests: Authoritarianism, Law, and Neoliberalism (Part One)," *Jadaliyya*, 12 July 2013, http://www.jadaliyya.com/pages/index/12907 /brand-turkey-and-the-gezi-protests_authoritarianis; Aslı Iğsız, "Brand Turkey and the Gezi Protests: Authoritarianism, Law, and Neoliberalism (Part Two)," *Jadaliyya*, 13 July 2013, http://www.jadaliyya.com/pages/index/12939/brand-turkey-and-the-gezi-protests _authoritarianis; Cihan Tuğal, "Occupy Gezi: The Limits of Turkey's Neoliberal Success" *Jadaliyya*, 4 June 2013, http://www.jadaliyya.com/pages/index/12009/occupy-gezi_the -limits-of-turkey%E2%80%99s-neoliberal-succ. On the environmental and sociocultural impacts, see Ömür Harmanşah, "Urban Utopias and How They Fell Apart: The Political Ecology of *Gezi Parkı*," in *The Making of a Protest Movement in Turkey: #occupygezi* ed. Umut Özkırımlı (Basingstoke, UK: Palgrave Macmillan, 2014), 121–33. The phrase "creeping authoritarianism" is from Ziya Öniş, "Sharing Power: Turkey's Democratization Challenge in the Age of the AKP Hegemony," *Insight Turkey* 15 (2013): 103–22. See also Seyla Benhabib, "Turkey's Authoritarian Turn," *New York Times*, 3 June 2013, http://www .nytimes.com/2013/06/04/opinion/turkeys-authoritarian-turn.html.

2. Emrullah İşler, "Arap Baharindan Gezi Parkini Okumak" (Reading Gezi Park through the Arab Spring), *Yeni Şafak*, 19 June 2013, http://www.yenisafak.com/hayat/arap -baharindan-gezi-parkini-okumak-533684.

3. For a comparison of the Gezi protests and the Arab Spring, see Danya Al-Saleh and Mohammed Rafi Arefin, "Taksim Is/Is Not Tahrir: Comparative Frameworks in Managing Protest," *Jadaliyya*, 27 July 2013, http://www.jadaliyya.com/pages/index/13217/taksim -is-is-not-tahrir_comparative-frameworks-in-.

4. Richard Seymour, "Istanbul Park Protests Sow the Seeds of a Turkish Spring," *Guardian*, 31 May 2013, http://www.theguardian.com/commentisfree/2013/may/31 /istanbul-park-protests-turkish-spring; Onur Bakiner, "Can the 'Spirit of Gezi' Transform Progressive Politics in Turkey?," *Jadaliyya*, 3 July 2013, http://www.jadaliyya.com /pages/index/12616/can-the-spirit-of-gezi-transform-progressive-polit. Protesters' soli-

darity networks stretched across and beyond the region to the Occupy movement in the United States and street demonstrations in Brazil.

5. Berna Turam, *Gaining Freedoms: Claiming Space in Istanbul and Berlin* (Stanford, CA: Stanford University Press, 2015), 3.

6. Nadje al-Ali, "Gendering the Arab Spring," *Middle East Journal of Culture and Communication* 5, no. 1 (2012): 26–31. According to two separate studies of protesters at Taksim Gezi, over 50 percent were women. See Emre Kongar and Aykut Küçükkaya, *Gezi Direnişi* (Gezi Resistance) (Istanbul: Cumhuriyet, 2013), and Konda, "Gezi Report: Public Perception of the 'Gezi Protests' and Who Were the People at Gezi Park," 5 June 2014, 6, http://konda.com.tr/en/raporlar/KONDA_Gezi_Report.pdf.

7. Gillian Rose, *Visual Methodologies: An Introduction to Researching with Visual Materials*, 3rd edition (London: Sage, 2012), 16–17.

8. Robyn Longhurst, "The Geography Closest In—The Body . . . the Politics of Pregnability," *Australian Geographical Studies* 32, no. 2 (1994): 214–23.

9. Catharine Smith, "Egypt's Facebook Revolution: Wael Ghonim Thanks the Social Network," *Huffington Post*, 25 May 2011, http://www.huffingtonpost.com/2011/02/11/egypt-facebook-revolution-wael-ghonim_n_822078.html; Carol Huang, "Facebook and Twitter Key to Arab Spring Uprisings: Report," *National* (UAE), 6 June 2011, http://www.thenational.ae/news/uae-news/facebook-and-twitter-key-to-arab-spring-uprisings-report; Saleem Kassim, "Twitter Revolution: How the Arab Spring Was Helped by Social Media," *Mic*, 3 July 2012, http://mic.com/articles/10642/twitter-revolution-how-the-arab-spring-was-helped-by-social-media; Wael Ghonim, *Revolution 2.0: How the Power of the People Is Greater Than the People in Power. A Memoir* (New York: Mariner Books, 2013).

10. Nezar AlSayyad, "The Virtual Square: Urban Space, Media, and the Egyptian Uprising," *Harvard International Review* (Summer 2012): 58–63. See also Josh Sanburn, "Square Roots: How Public Spaces Helped Mold the Arab Spring," *Time*, 17 May 2011, http://content.time.com/time/world/article/0,8599,2071404,00.html.

11. Eleonore Kofman and Linda Peak, "Into the 1990s: A Gendered Agenda for Political Geography," *Political Geography Quarterly* 9, no. 4 (1990): 313–36; Lynn Staeheli and Eleonore Kofman, "Mapping Gender, Making Politics: Towards Feminist Political Geographies," in *Mapping Women, Making Politics: Feminist Perspectives on Political Geography*, edited by Eleonore Kofman and Lynn Staeheli (New York: Routledge, 2004), 1–13; Lynn Staeheli and Don Mitchell, "Spaces of Public and Private: Locating Politics," in *Spaces of Democracy: Geographical Perspectives on Citizenship, Participation, and Representation*, edited by Clive Barnett and Murray Low (London: Sage, 2004), 147–60.

12. Sallie Marston, "The Social Construction of Scale," *Progress in Human Geography* 24, no. 2 (2000): 219–42.

13. Doreen Massey, *For Space* (London: Sage, 2005); Cindi Katz, "On the Grounds of Globalization: A Topography for Feminist Political Engagement," *Signs: Journal of Women in Culture and Society* 26, no. 4 (2001): 1213–34.

14. Staeheli and Kofman, "Mapping Gender, Making Politics," 5; see also Deborah Dixon and Sallie Marston, "Introduction: Feminist Engagements with Geopolitics," *Gen-*

der, Place and Culture 18, no. 4 (2011): 445–53; Jennifer Hyndman, "Mind the Gap: Bridging Feminist and Political Geography through Geopolitics," *Political Geography* 23, no. 3 (2004): 307–22; Sara Smith, "She Says to Herself, 'I Have No Future': Love, Fate, and Territory in Leh District, India," *Gender, Place and Culture* 18, no. 4 (2011): 455–76.

15. Jennifer Fluri, "Armored Peacocks and Proxy Bodies: Gender Geopolitics in Aid/Development Spaces of Afghanistan," *Gender, Place and Culture* 18, no. 4 (2011): 531.

16. Sara Smith, "Intimate Geopolitics: Religion, Marriage, and Reproductive Bodies in Leh, Ladakh," *Annals of the Association of American Geographers* 102, no. 6 (2012): 1512.

17. This emphasis on the body is not to reproduce the presumption that white men are able to transcend their embodiment while women, blacks, children, and people with disabilities are forever trapped in their bodies. See Robyn Longhurst, *Bodies: Exploring Fluid Boundaries* (London: Routledge, 2000), 13. Nor is it to accept the mind/body dualism. The feminist literature that I draw upon makes the body and embodiment central precisely to destabilize a series of dualisms (mind/body, public/private) and to question the masculinist perspectives inherent in even the most fundamental geographic concepts, such as scale: Gillian Rose, *Feminism and Geography: The Limits of Geographical Knowledge* (Cambridge: Polity, 1993); Marston, "The Social Construction of Scale."

18. Longhurst, *Bodies*; Heidi Nast and Steve Pile, eds., *Places through the Body* (London: Routledge, 1998).

19. Zakia Salime, "New Feminism as Personal Revolutions: Microrebellious Bodies," *Signs: Journal of Women in Culture and Society* 40, no. 1 (2014): 16.

20. Zeynep Gambetti, "Occupy Gezi as Politics of the Body," *Jadaliyya*, 9 July 2013, http://www.jadaliyya.com/pages/index/12806/occupy-gezi-as-politics-of-the-body.

21. Sherine Hafez, "Bodies That Protest: The Girl in the Blue Bra, Sexuality, and State Violence in Revolutionary Egypt," *Signs: Journal of Women in Culture and Society* 40, no. 1 (2014): 22.

22. Salime, "New Feminism as Personal Revolutions," 18; Hafez, "Bodies That Protest."

23. Ziya Öniş, "The Triumph of Conservative Globalism: The Political Economy of the AKP Era," *Turkish Studies* 13, no. 2 (2012): 135–52; Cihan Tuğal, *Passive Revolution: Absorbing the Islamic Challenge to Capitalism* (Stanford, CA: Stanford University Press, 2009).

24. Öniş, "Sharing Power."

25. Binnaz Toprak, Iran Bozam, Tan Murgul, and Nedim Sener, *Being Different in Turkey: Religion, Conservatism and Otherization* (Istanbul: Bogazici University, Open Society Foundation, 2009).

26. Ergun Özbudun, "AKP at the Crossroads: Erdoğan's Majoritarian Drift," *South European Society and Politics* 19, no. 2 (2014): 155–67.

27. Beyza Kural, "Gezi Parkı İçin Nöbetteyiz" (We Are Keeping Guard for Gezi Park), Bianet, 28 May 2013, http://www.bianet.org/bianet/kent/146965-gezi-parki-icin-nobetteyiz.

28. As critics pointed out, the barracks were significant historically as the place of origin for a right-wing, Islamically oriented uprising against the modernization efforts of the late Ottoman state in 1909. See "Topçu Kışlası'nın Tarihî Anlamı" (The Historical Meaning of Topçu Barracks), DW, 13 June 2013, http://www.dw.de/top%C3%A7u-k%C4%B1%C5%9Flas%C4%B1n%C4%B1n-tarih%C3%AE-anlam%C4%B1/a-16879025; Okunma

Sayısı, "Gezi Parkı ve Topçu Kışlası Ardındaki Tarihi Gerçekler" (The Historical Truths behind the Gezi Park and Topçu Barracks), *Milliyet*, 6 June 2013, http://blog.milliyet.com .tr/gezi-parki-ve-topcu-kislasi-ardindaki-tarihi-gercekler/Blog/?BlogNo=417986.

29. Ozan Karaman, "Urban Neoliberalism with Islamic Characteristics," *Urban Studies* 50, no. 16 (2013): 3412–27.

30. Harmanşah, "Urban Utopias and How They Fell Apart," 126; Ayfer Bartu, "Who Owns the Old Quarters? Rewriting Histories in a Global Era," in *Istanbul: Between the Global and the Local*, edited by Çağlar Keyder (Lanham, MD: Rowman and Littlefield, 1997), 31–46; Ayfer Bartu, "Rethinking Heritage Politics in a Global Context: A View from Istanbul," in *Hybrid Urbanism: On the Identity Discourse and the Built Environment*, edited by Nezar AlSayyad (Westport, CT: Praeger, 2001), 131–55.

31. On 1 May 1977, in what has been called the Taksim Square Massacre, government forces opened fire at demonstrators, resulting in thirty-four deaths (Harmanşah, "Urban Utopias and How They Fell Apart," 127). Every year on 1 May, Workers Day, a demonstration takes place at Taksim Square. In 2015, despite the governor's ban on a demonstration and police barricades, a small group carrying Turkish Communist Party flags still gathered at the square. "Valilikten 1 Mayıs Açıklaması: Taksim Yasak" (Governor's Announcement about 1 May: Taksim Is Forbidden), *Hürriyet*, 30 April 2015, http://www.hurriyet .com.tr/gundem/28872549.asp; "1 Mayıs: İstanbul'da Olağanüstü Güvenlik Önlemleri" (1 May: Unusual Security Measures in Istanbul), BBC, 1 May 2015.

32. Harmanşah, "Urban Utopias and How They Fell Apart," 127.

33. Bartu, "Who Owns the Old Quarters?"; Bartu, "Rethinking Heritage Politics in a Global Context."

34. Turam, *Gaining Freedoms*, 32.

35. Feride Acar, "Türkiye'de Kadınların İnsan Hakları: Uluslararası Standartlar, Hukuk ve Sivil Toplum" (Human Rights of Women in Turkey: International Standards, Law and Civil Society), in *Kadın Hakları Uluslararası Hukuk ve Uygulama* (International Law of Women's Rights and Its Implementation), edited by Gökçiçek Ayata, Sevinç Eryılmaz Dilek, and Bertil Emrah Oder (Istanbul: Istanbul Bilgi Üniversitesi, 2010), 17–19; Fatma Umut Beşpınar, "Women and Gender," in *Turkey and the Politics of National Identity: Social Economic and Cultural Transformation*, edited by Shane Brennan and Marc Herzog (London: I. B. Tauris, 2014), 128.

36. "Erdoğan: En Az Üç Çocuk Doğurun" (Erdoğan: Give Birth to at Least Three Children), *Hürriyet*, 7 March 2008, accessed 29 July 2014, http://www.hurriyet.com .tr/gundem/8401981.asp; "Erdoğan: İş İşten Geçmeden En Az 3 Çocuk" (Erdoğan: Before It's Too Late, 3 Kids), NTV, 10 October 2009, http://www.ntv.com.tr/arsiv/id /25008774; "Erdoğan Neden 3 Çocuk İstediğini Açıkladı" (Erdoğan Explained Why He Wants 3 Kids), *Milliyet*, 2 January 2013, http://www.milliyet.com.tr/erdogan-neden -3-cocuk-istedigini-acikladi-/siyaset/siyasetdetay/02.01.2013/1650260/default.htm. Erdoğan described abortion as murder and argued that "each abortion is Uludere," referring to the incident of 28 December 2011 in which a military airstrike killed over thirty civilians. "Erdoğan: Kürtaj Cinayettir" (Erdoğan: Abortion Is Murder), NTV, 25 May 2015, www.ntv.com.tr/arsiv/id/25352507/; "Her Kürtaj bir Uludere'dir" (Each Abortion Is an Uludere), NTV, 26 May 2012, www.ntv.com.tr/arsiv/id/25352590/. On the subway inci-

dent, see "Erdoğan: Twitter Denen Bela Terrorize ediyor" (Erdoğan: The Trouble Called Twitter Is Terrorizing), *Türkiye Gazetesi*, 3 June 2013, http://www.turkiyegazetesi.com.tr /politika/42720.aspx.

37. One critic of pregnant women "flaunting their bellies" was the Sufi thinker Ömer Tuğrul Inançer, who said during an interview for a Ramadan special on state television (TRT1) in July 2013 that women who are visibly pregnant should not be out in public; if they needed air, their husband could take them for a ride in his car. Dugunum, "TRT 1'de iftar sohbeti: Hamile kadın sokakta gezmesin, Ped reklamları Yasaklansin" (Iftar Conversation on TRT 1: Pregnant Women Should Not Be on the Streets, Sanitary Pad Advertisements Should Be Banned), YouTube, 24 July 2013, https://www.youtube.com/watch?v= pVPd_jS5-oM.

38. "Gezi Parkı ile ilgili Mahkemeden Karar" (Court Decision about Gezi Park), Haber7, 31 May 2013, http://www.haber7.com/guncel/haber/1033404-gezi-parki-ile -ilgili-mahkemeden-karar. For an analysis of Erdoğan's masculinity, see Zeynep Kurtulus Korkman and Salih Can Aciksoz, "Erdogan's Masculinity and the Language of Gezi Resistance," *Jadaliyya*, 22 June 2013, http://www.jadaliyya.com/pages/index/12367/erdogan %E2%80%99s-masculinity-and-the-language-of-the-gezi.

39. Protesters creatively appropriated *çapulcu* and started self-identifying as such. See Christiane Gruber, "The Visual Emergence of the Occupy Gezi Movement, Part Two: Everyday I'm Capulling," *Jadaliyya*, 7 July 2013, accessed June 22, 2015, http://www .jadaliyya.com/pages/index/12715/the-visual-emergence-of-the-occupy-gezi -movement-p.

40. "Erdoğan Ak Parti'nin Ankara Mitinginde Konuştu, Gezi'ye 'Müdahale Ederiz' Mesaj Yolladı" (Erdoğan Spoke at AKP's Ankara Rally, Sent the Message "We will Intervene" in Gezi), *Milliyet*, 15 June 2013, http://www.milliyet.com.tr/erdogan-ak-parti-nin -ankara/siyaset/detay/1723383/default.htm; "Erdoğan Kazlıçeşme Mitinginde Konuştu!" (Erdoğan Spoke at Kazlıçeşme Rally), *Milliyet*, 16 June 2013, http://www.milliyet.com.tr /ak-partililer-kazlicesme-ye-akin/siyaset/detay/1723747/default.htm.

41. "Mahalle Forumları, Mahalle Meclisleri—Ural Köroğlu" (Neighborhood Forums, Neighborhood Assemblies—Ural Köroğlu), Sendika, 25 June 2013, http://www.sendika .org/2013/06/mahalle-forumlari-mahalle-meclisleri-ural-koroglu/.

42. "Meydanlarda Yolsuzluk Protestosu" (Protests at Squares against Corruption), DW, 26 December 2013, http://www.dw.de/meydanlarda-yolsuzluk-protestosu/a-17325042.

43. "Berkin Elvan İçin Çeşitli İllerde Gösteriler Düzenlendi" (Protests Organized in Cities for Berkin Elvan), *Haberler*, 12 March 2014, http://www.haberler.com/berkin-elvan -in-olumu-5779957-haberi/.

44. "Danıştay Gezi Parkı Kışlasının Önünü Açtı" (The Council of State Allows the Gezi Park Barracks), *Hürriyet*, 15 July 2015, http://www.hurriyet.com.tr/danistay-gezi-parkinda -topcu-kislasi-nin-onunu-acti-29556112.

45. Tim Arango, "Turkish Leader, Using Conflicts, Cements Power," *New York Times*, 31 October 2014, http://www.nytimes.com/2014/11/01/world/europe/erdogan-uses -conflict-to-consolidate-power.html.

46. In *Visual Methodologies* Gillian Rose develops a framework consisting of two axes for critically analyzing images. The first axis contains three *sites*: the site(s) of the produc-

tion of the image, the site of the image itself, and the site(s) where it is seen by various audiences (19). Three *material* modalities make up the second axis: the visual technology of the image; the compositional or material qualities of the image; and "the range of economic, social, and political relations, institutions, and practices that surround an image" (20).

47. Cited in Rose, *Visual Methodologies*, 12.

48. Susan Sontag, *On Photography* (New York: Picador, 2001), 3.

49. "Başörtülü Taksim Gezi Parkı Mizanseni" (Scene with Headscarf at Taksim Gezi Park), *Haksöz*, 10 June 2013, http://www.haksozhaber.net/basortulu-taksim-gezi-parki-mizanseni-38138h.htm.

50. The images are available at http://www.thetower.org/wp-content/uploads/2013/06/taksim-yoga.jpg. See Jimillenium, "Yoga against Violence and Hate in Gezi Parkı," YouTube, 6 June 2013, https://www.youtube.com/watch?v=h8_kzg6gpO8.

51. Jim Kuras, "#DIRENHAMILE: Pregnancy, Morality, and Resisting Discourses of Seclusion at the Gezi Park Protests," MA thesis, University of North Carolina at Chapel Hill, 2015. The image is available at https://s-media-cache-ako.pinimg.com/474x/38/18/ea/3818ea2cda65840c73375b7fdba3b27c.jpg.

52. "Direnişin Bebekleri Taksim'de" (The Babies of Resistance Are at Taksim), *Halkın Habercisi*, 8 June 2013, http://www.halkinhabercisi.com/direnisin-bebekleri-taksimde.

53. Rose, *Visual Methodologies*, 28.

54. On 10 June 2015 the police officer was sentenced to twenty months in prison and ordered to plant six hundred trees. See "Kırmızılı Kadın Dava Sonucu: Polise 20 Ay Hapis Cezası" (The Result of the Woman in Red Court Case: 20 Months' Prison Sentence for the Police), Direnisteyiz, 10 June 2015, http://direnisteyiz.net/haber/kirmizi-kadin-dava-sonucu-polise-20-ay-hapis-cezasi/.

55. Lewis Williamson, "'Woman in Red' Sprayed with Teargas Becomes Symbol of Turkey Protests," *Guardian*, 5 June 2013, http://www.theguardian.com/world/2013/jun/05/woman-in-red-turkey-protests; *Daily Mail* reporter and Becky Evans, "Horrifying Image of 'Woman in Red' Being Doused with Pepper Spray Becomes Symbol of Turkish Protests," *Daily Mail*, 5 June 2013, http://www.dailymail.co.uk/news/article-2335924/Turkey-Protests-Horrifying-image-woman-red-doused-pepper-spray-symbol-Turkish-protests.html.

56. "Turkey's Riot Icon: Woman in Red Dress" (video), CNN, 4 June 2013, http://www.cnn.com/videos/world/2013/06/04/lead-votell-paton-walsh-turkey-red-dress.cnn.

57. Luke Harding, "Turkey's Resistance Image Forged as Pepper Spray Burns Woman in Red Dress," *Guardian*, 5 June 2013, http://www.theguardian.com/world/2013/jun/05/turkey-lady-red-dress-ceyda-sungur.

58. Jessica Testa, "How the 'Lady in Red' Became Turkey's Most Inspiring Meme," BuzzFeed, 4 June 2013, http://www.buzzfeed.com/jtes/how-the-lady-in-red-became-turkeys-most-inspiring-meme#.shRLLrW60.

59. Estimates of the total number of participants range from 2.5 million to 3.6 million in protests in seventy-nine to eighty cities across Turkey. See "2.5 milyon İnsan 79 İlde Sokağa İndi" (2.5 Million People in 79 Cities Took to the Streets), *Milliyet*, 23 June 2013, http://www.milliyet.com.tr/2-5-milyon-insan-79-ilde-sokaga/gundem/detay/1726600

/default.htm; "Gezi'ye Kaç Kişi Katıldı?" (How Many People Joined Gezi?), CNN, 25 November 2013, http://www.cnnturk.com/2013/guncel/11/25/geziye-kac-kisi-katildi /732168.0/index.html.

60. CNN Turk notoriously showed a documentary about penguins instead of covering the protests and the police crackdown on them; "Taksim Olaylarını Es Geçip 'Penguen' Belgeseli Yayınlayan Kanala Halk Tepki Gösteriyor . . ." (The Public Is Reacting against the Channel That Broadcast a Documentary about Penguins Instead of Covering Taksim Incidents), *Milliyet* blog, 3 June 2013, http://blog.milliyet.com.tr/taksim-olaylarini-es -gecip—penguen—belgeseli-yayinlayan-kanala-halk-tepki-gosteriyor/Blog/?BlogNo =417594. Protesters subsequently appropriated the image of penguins and used it to criticize the mainstream media.

61. Harding, "Turkey's Resistance Image Forged as Pepper Spray Burns Woman in Red Dress." The woman was revealed to be Ceyda Sungur, an academic at nearby Istanbul Technical University.

62. Max Fisher, "The Photo That Encapsulates Turkey's Protests and the Severe Police Crackdown," *Washington Post*, 3 June 2013, http://www.washingtonpost.com/blogs /worldviews/wp/2013/06/03/the-photo-that-encapsulates-turkeys-protests-and-the -severe-police-crackdown/.

63. Gülsüm Baydar, "Embodied Spaces of Resistance," *Women's Studies International Forum* 50 (May–June 2015): 15.

64. Harriet Fitch Little, "The Women of Gezi Park Are Protesters, Not Pin-Up Girls," *New Statesman*, 19 June 2013, http://www.newstatesman.com/world-affairs/2013/06 /women-gezi-park-are-protesters-not-pin-girls.

65. Fisher, "The Photo That Encapsulates Turkey's Protests and the Severe Police Crackdown."

66. Michael Higgins, "Police Beating of 'Girl in the Blue Bra' Becomes a New Rallying Call for Egyptians," *National Post* (Canada), 20 December 2011, http://news.nationalpost .com/2011/12/20/beating-of-blue-bra-woman-reignites-egyptian-protests/; Kainaz Amaria, "The 'Girl in the Blue Bra,'" NPR, 22 December 2011, http://www.npr.org/blogs /pictureshow/2011/12/21/144098384/the-girl-in-the-blue-bra.

67. See also Karina Eileraas, "Sex(t)ing Revolution, Femen-izing the Public Square: Aliaa Magda Elmahdy, Nude Protest, and Transnational Feminist Body Politics," *Signs: Journal of Women in Culture and Society* 40, no. 1 (2014): 40–52.

68. Hyndman, "Mind the Gap," 318.

69. "Taksim Gezi Parkı Direnişinden Güldüren Resimler," MedyaCafe, accessed 18 March 2016, http://www.medyacafe.net/taksim-gezi-parki-direnisinden-gulduren -resimler.html. The mug is for sale at Red Bazaar, http://redbazaar.net/kp14gp02.

70. Yaşarken Yazılan Tarih (The History Written as It Is Lived), http://yasarkenyazilan tarih.com/yasarkenyazilantarih/.

71. "Saldırıya Uğrayan Başörtülü Kadın Konuştu!" (The Headscarf-Wearing Woman Who Was Attacked Spoke), *Dünya Bülteni*, 13 June 2013, http://www.dunyabulteni.net /haber/263540/saldiriya-ugrayan-basortulu-kadin-konustu.

72. "Kabataş'ta Saldırıya Uğradığı Iddia Edilen Başörtülü Kadının Görüntüleri Yayınlandı" (The Images of the Headscarf-Wearing Woman Who Was Allegedly Attacked

in Kabataş Was Broadcasted), T24, 13 February 2014, http://t24.com.tr/haber/kanal-d
-kabatasta-saldiriya-ugradigi-iddia-edilen-basortulu-kadinin-goruntulerini-yayinladi
,251028.

73. "Başörtülü Kadınlara Taciz Tepkisi" (Reaction to the Harassment of Headscarf-
Wearing Women), Haber7, 8 June 2013, http://www.haber7.com/guncel/haber/
1036289-basortulu-kadinlara-taciz-tepkisi.

74. "Taş Atan Teyze . . ." (The Auntie Throwing a Rock . . .), T24, 12 June 2013, http://
t24.com.tr/haber/tas-atan-teyze,231809.

75. Itır Selin Kalyoncu, "Gezi Direnişi'nin 2. Yıldönümünde Direnişçilerin Ağzından 4
Ünlü Fotoğrafın Hikâyesi" (On the Second Anniversay of Gezi Resistance Protesters Tell
the Story of Four Famous Photographs), Onedio, 30 May 2015, http://onedio.com/haber
/gezi-direnisi-nin-2-yildonumunde-direniscilerin-agzindan-5-unlu-direnis-fotografinin
-hikayesi-517511.

76. "Sapanlı Teyze Bakın Kim Çıktı!" (Look Who Turned Out to Be the Slingshot
Auntie!), Internet Haber, 27 October 2015, http://www.internethaber.com/sapanli-teyze
-bakin-kim-cikti-547336h.htm.

77. In the online open source dictionary, Uludağ Sözlük, in the entry on The Slingshot
Auntie, several have posted comments such as "biri siksin la şunu lafına cuk oturan teyze-
dir" (she is the aunt that fits perfectly the term "someone fuck her") and "sikerler öyle
teyzeyi" (we will fuck such an auntie). See http://www.uludagsozluk.com/k/eyleme
-kat%C4%B1lan-sapanl%C4%B1-teyze/.

78. Fırat Alkaç, "Yine Giderim" (I Will Go Again), Hürriyet, 2 January 2014, http://
www.hurriyet.com.tr/gundem/25484142.asp.

79. Reuters, "Turkish PM Erdogan Says Patience Run Out with Park Protesters,"
13 June 2013, http://www.reuters.com/article/2013/06/13/us-turkey-protests-erdogan
-idUSBRE95C0BF20130613.

80. "Gezi'de Anne Zinciri" (Chain of Mothers at Gezi), NTV, 13 June 2013, http://www
.ntv.com.tr/arsiv/id/25448958/.

81. Baydar, "Embodied Spaces of Resistance," 13.

82. Little, "The Women of Gezi Park Are Protesters, Not Pin-Up Girls."

83. Little, "The Women of Gezi Park Are Protesters, Not Pin-Up Girls."

84. Getty Images, "Istanbul Protests Continue," http://www.gettyimages.com/detail
/news-photo/bulldozer-digger-breaks-through-police-lines-as-turkish-news-photo
/169835314.

85. "Gezi'de Renklerin Kardeşliği" (The Sisterhood of Colors at Gezi), Hürriyet, 1 June
2013, http://www.hurriyet.com.tr/spor/futbol/23415269.asp.

86. For the photograph, see Zeynep Tüfekçi's blog post "'Come, Come, Whoever
You Are.' As a Pluralist Movement Emerges from Gezi Park in Turkey," Technosociology,
30 June 2013, http://technosociology.org/?p=1421.

87. Tuğba Taş and Oğuzhan Taş, "Resistance on the Walls, Reclaiming Public Space:
Street Art in Times of Political Turmoil in Turkey," Interactions: Studies in Communication
and Culture 5, no. 3 (2014): 340. One artistic representation of the dervish is at http://
technosociology.org/wp-content/uploads/2013/06/sen-de-gel-ayol.png. See also
Korkman and Aciksoz, "Erdoğan's Masculinity and the Language of Gezi Resistance."

88. An example is this tweet: "(When I saw the gas-mask dervish yesterday, he was shirtless!)," https://twitter.com/BananaKarenina/status/341883653913198592/photo/1.

89. Azazi's website is http://ziyaazazi.com/. For other images of this artist, see http://reframe.sussex.ac.uk/activistmedia/files/2013/08/5.jpg.

90. Stencil images are at http://www.jadaliyya.com/content_images/fck_images/Gruber_figure18.jpg; http://www.exhibitioncritique.com/2014/10/28/occupygezi-art-of-the-gezi-protests/. Rumi's poem is inscribed on his shrine in Konya, Turkey. Here is a translation by Coleman Barks (posted on Tüfekçi, "'Come, Come Whoever You Are'"): "Come, come, whoever you are, / Wanderer, worshiper, lover of leaving. / It doesn't matter. / Ours is not a caravan of despair. / Come, even if you have broken your vows a thousand times. / Come, yet again, come, come."

91. Taş and Taş, "Resistance on the Walls, Reclaiming Public Space," 340.

92. The image is available at http://444.hu/assets/sites/2/2013-06-18T075235Z_896697958_GM1E96I17Y801_RTRMADP_3_TURKEY-PROTESTS-STANDING MAN.jpg.

93. Gündüz's website is http://www.erdemgunduz.org/.

94. Taş and Taş, "Resistance on the Walls, Reclaiming Public Space," 341.

95. Karim Talbi, "Turkey's 'Standing Man' Protest by Erdem Gunduz Spreads across Country," World Post, 18 June 2013, http://www.huffingtonpost.com/2013/06/18/turkey-standing-man-protest-erdem-gunduz_n_3458390.html.

96. Richard Seymour, "Turkey's 'Standing Man' Shows How Passive Resistance Can Shake a State," Guardian, 18 June 2013, http://www.theguardian.com/commentisfree/2013/jun/18/turkey-standing-man; Christopher Burgess, "Duran Adam: Standing Man," World Post, 21 June 2013, http://www.huffingtonpost.com/christopher-burgess/duran-adam-standing-man_b_3475014.html.

97. Baydar, "Embodied Spaces of Resistance," 16.

98. See the interview posted by Murat Reis, "Duran Adam Konuştu" (Standing Man Spoke), YouTube, 19 June 2013, https://www.youtube.com/watch?v=FB84rFANAgM .

99. Hasan Yıldırım and Ozan Ural, "'Duran Adam' Salgını" (The Epidemic of Standing Man), Hürriyet, 18 June 2013, http://www.hurriyet.com.tr/gundem/23530185.asp.

100. "Duran Adam'lara Gözaltı" (Jail for Standing Men) (video), Radikal, 18 June 2013, http://webtv.radikal.com.tr/turkiye/3954/duran-adamlara-gozalti.aspx.

101. See Gillian Rose's discussion of the work of Kate Millett dating back to 1969 (Feminism and Geography, 17–18).

102. See, for example, Linda McDowell, Gender, Identity, and Place: Understanding Feminist Geographies (Minneapolis: University of Minnesota Press, 1999), 12.

103. Judith Butler, "Bodies in Alliance and Politics of the Street," European Institute for Progressive Cultural Policies, last modified 2011, http://www.eipcp.net/transversal/1011/butler/en.

104. Butler, "Bodies in Alliance and Politics of the Street."

105. Massey, For Space, 140–41.

106. Baydar, "Embodied Spaces of Resistance," 14, points to two distinct practices that also transformed the home into protest spaces. The first is residents flickering lights and

banging on pots and pans at exactly 9 p.m. every night in support of the Gezi protests. The second is residents of Taksim hosting the protesters who were running away from the police and tear gas.

107. Judith Butler, *Precarious Life: The Powers of Mourning and Violence* (New York: Verso, 2006).

108. Henri Lefebvre, *Writings on Cities*, translated by Eleonore Koffman and Elizabeth Lebas (Oxford: Blackwell, 1996); David Harvey, *Rebel Cities: From the Right to the City to the Urban Revolution* (London: Verso, 2013); Don Mitchell, *The Right to the City: Social Justice and the Fight for Public Space* (New York: Guilford, 2003).

109. "Titiz Direniş" (Tidy Resistance), *Milliyet*, 3 June 2013, http://www.milliyet.com .tr/titiz-direnis/gundem/detay/1717832/default.htm; "Gezi Parkı'nda Bahar Temizliği" (Spring Cleaning at Gezi Park), *Radikal*, 2 June 2013, http://www.radikal.com.tr/turkiye /gezi_parkinda_bahar_temizligi-1135976; "Day 7," *Show Discontent*, 2 June 2013, http:// showdiscontent.com/archive/gezi-parki/2013-06-02/; for a photo of a little girl helping with cleaning, see http://www.ataturk.org/wp-content/uploads/2013/06/gezi-temizlik2 .jpg; Çiçek Tahaoğlu, "Park Yeniden Çiçeklendi" (Planting Flowers in Park Again), Bianet, 2 June 2013, http://www.bianet.org/bianet/toplum/147146-park-yeniden-ciceklendi.

110. Images are available at Tafline Laylin, "#Occupygezi in Situ Architecture Made with Scrap Materials (Photos)," *Green Prophet*, 28 June 2013, http://www.greenprophet.com /2013/06/occupygezi-in-situ-architecture-made-with-scrap-materials-photos/; http:// everywheretaksim.net/wp-content/uploads/2013/09/taksim_gezi_cadir.jpg; http:// egoistokur.com/wp-content/uploads/2013/06/occupygezi-egoistokur-3.jpg.

111. A photo of the library is at http://egoistokur.com/wp-content/uploads/2013/06 /kutuphane-occupygezi-egoistokur.jpg.

112. "Bianet: Ne İşimiz Var Orada?" (Bianet: What Business Do We Have There?), *Everywhere Taksim*, 29 May 2014, http://everywheretaksim.net/tr/tag/gezi-doktorlari/. A photo of some donations is at http://media-cdn.t24.com.tr/media/stories/2013/06 /page_gezi-parkinda-yiyecek-duvari_109539833.jpg.

113. Eating together became a significant act of protest that continued with simple and intimate *iftar* dinners called "yeryüzü sofraları" (literally, "tables on earth") during Ramadan and after the forced dispersal and demolishment of the Gezi camp.

114. Nathan Swanson, "Embodying Tahrir: Bodies and Geopolitics in the 2011 Egyptian Uprising," *Area*, 16 December 2014, doi: 10.1111/area.12163.

115. Jacques Rancière, *Dissensus: On Politics and Aesthetics*, translated by Steve Corcoran (London: Continuum, 2010); Mustafa Dikeç, "Space as a Mode of Political Thinking," *Geoforum* 43, no. 4 (2012): 669–76.

116. "Turkey Deputy PM Apologises to Gezi Park Protesters," BBC, 4 June 2013, http:// www.bbc.com/news/world-europe-22767622; "Gezi Parkı 13'üncü Gün Temizlik ve Kahvaltıyla Başladı," T24, 9 June 2013, http://t24.com.tr/haber/gezi-parki-13uncu-gun -temizlik-ve-kahvaltiyla-basladi,231596; "Turkey Protesters Vow to Stay in Gezi Park," *Al Arabiya*, 15 June 2013, http://english.alarabiya.net/en/News/world/2013/06/15/ Turkey-protesters-vow-to-stay-in-Gezi-park.html; "Turkey: PM Erdogan to Meet Protesters' Representatives," TVC News, http://www.tvcnews.tv/?q=article/turkey-pm -erdogan-meet-protesters-representatives; Elena Becatoros and Jamey Keaten, "Turkish

Riot Police Disperse Protesters in Istanbul Park," *Concord (NH) Monitor*, 16 June 2013, http://www.concordmonitor.com/news/nation/world/7016362-95/turkish-riot-police -disperse-protesters-in-istanbul-park.

117. The images are at http://www.s-peterson.com/index.php#mi=2&pt=1&pi=10000 &s=1&p=2&a=0&at=0; http://i2.cdn.turner.com/cnn/dam/assets/130613072733-01 -turkey-protests-0613-horizontal-gallery.jpg.

118. "Revealed: First Picture of 'the Woman in Red' Who Became the Unwitting Symbol of Turkey Protests after She Was Tear-Gassed by Police," *Daily Mail*, 8 June 2013, http://www.dailymail.co.uk/news/article-2337788/Turkey-Protests-First-picture-The -Woman-Red-unwitting-symbol-unrest.html.

119. "Turks Tango in Their Gas Masks as They Defy Orders of Prime Minister and Carry On with Protests," *Daily Mail*, 8 June 2013, http://www.dailymail.co.uk/news /article-2337922/Turkey-protests-Anti-government-demonstrations-continue-despite -Recep-Tayyip-Erdogans-orders.html. See images at https://s-media-cache-ako.pinimg .com/736x/0c/0f/15/0cof15feea7c6874651b1edb72b459cb.jpg; http://jiyan.org/wp -content/uploads/2013/12/foto1.jpg; http://animalnewyork.com/2013/occupygezi -resistance-goes-mainstream-in-istanbul/occupy-gezi-jw-44/.

120. Butler, "Bodies in Alliance and Politics of the Street."

121. Butler, "Bodies in Alliance and Politics of the Street."

122. Hafez, "Bodies That Protest," 27.

BIBLIOGRAPHY

Abdel Aal, Ghada. *I Want to Get Married! One Wannabe Bride's Misadventures with Handsome Houdinis, Technicolor Grooms, Morality Police, and Other Mr. Not Quite Rights*. Translated by Nora El Tahawy. Austin: University of Texas Press, 2010.

Acar, Feride. "Türkiye'de Kadınların İnsan Hakları: Uluslararası Standartlar, Hukuk ve Sivil Toplum" (Human Rights of Women in Turkey: International Standards, Law and Civil Society). In *Kadın Hakları Uluslararası Hukuk ve Uygulama* (International Law of Women's Rights and Its Implementation), edited by Gökçiçek Ayata, Sevinç Eryılmaz Dilek, and Bertil Emrah Oder, 13–22. Istanbul: Istanbul Bilgi Üniversitesi Yayınları, 2010.

Adler, Amy. "Performance Anxiety: Medusa, Sex, and the First Amendment." *Yale Journal of the Law and Humanities* 21, no. 2 (2009): 224–50.

Ahmed, Leila. "Feminism and Feminist Movements in the Middle East, a Preliminary Exploration: Turkey, Egypt, Algeria, People's Democratic Republic of Yemen." In *Arabian and Islamic Studies*, edited by Robin Bidwell and G. Rex Smith, 155–71. London: Longman, 1983.

Alami Mchichi, Houria. *Genre et politique au Maroc: Les enjeux de l'egalité hommes-femmes entre islamisme et modernisme*. Paris: L'Harmattan, 2002.

al-ʿAlas, Asmahan Aqlan. *Awdaʿ al-marʾa al-yamaniyya fi zul al-idara al-britaniyya li ʿadan min 1937–1967* (The Situation of Yemeni Women during the Time of British Administration in Aden 1937–1967). Aden, Yemen: Aden University Printing and Publishing House, 2005.

Alexanian, Janet A. "Publicly Intimate Online: Iranian Web Logs in Southern California." *Comparative Studies of South Asia, Africa, and the Middle East* 26, no. 2 (2006): 134–45.

Alhadar, Ibrahim, and Michael McCahill. "The Use of Surveillance Cameras in a Riyadh Shopping Mall: Protecting Profits or Protecting Morality?" *Theoretical Criminology* 15, no. 3 (2011): 315–30.

al-Ali, Nadje. "Gendering the Arab Spring." *Middle East Journal of Culture and Communication* 5, no. 1 (2012): 26–31.

al-Ali, Nadje, and Nicola Pratt. *What Kind of Liberation? Women and the Occupation of Iraq*. Berkeley: University of California Press, 2009.

Allen, John. *Lost Geographies of Power*. Oxford: Blackwell, 2003.

AlSayyad, Nezar. "The Virtual Square: Urban Space, Media, and the Egyptian Uprising." *Harvard International Review* (Summer 2012): 58–63.

Amar, Paul. "Middle East Masculinity Studies: Discourses of 'Men in Crisis,' Industries of Gender in Revolution." *Journal of Middle East Women's Studies* 7, no. 3 (2011): 36–70.

———. *The Security Archipelago: Human-Security States, Sexuality Politics, and the End of Neoliberalism*. Durham, NC: Duke University Press, 2013.

———. "Turning the Gendered Politics of the Security State Inside Out?" *International Journal of Politics* 13, no. 3 (2011): 299–328.

Amir-Ebrahimi, Masserat. "Transgression in Narration: The Lives of Iranian Women in Cyberspace." *Journal of Middle East Women's Studies* 4, no. 3 (2008): 89–118.

Aouragh, Miriyam. "Framing the Internet in the Arab Revolutions: Myth Meets Modernity." *Cinema Journal* 52, no. 1 (2012): 148–56.

al-ʿAqil, H. M. *Qadiyyat al-janub wa haqaʾiq nahb mumtalakat dawla jumhuriyyat al-yaman al-dimuqratiyya al-shaʿbiyya, al-juzʾu al-awwal, al-tabaʿa al-thaniyya* ("The Southern Cause and the Truth about the Plundering of the People's Democratic Republic of Yemen State Property, Part 1"). 2nd edition. Cairo: Al-Markaz al-ʿArabi li Khidmat al-Sahafa wal-Nashr "Majid," 2012.

Arendt, Hannah. *The Human Condition*. 2nd edition. Chicago: University of Chicago Press, 1998.

Asbar Center for Studies, Research and Communications. "Uses of the Internet in the Saudi Society." Accessed 22 June 2015. http://web.archive.org/web/2015062619 2904/http://www.asbar.com/en/studies-researches/social-research-studies/350 .article.htm.

Augé, Marc. *Non-places: Introduction to an Anthropology of Supermodernity*. London: Verso, 1995.

Baber, Zaheer. "'Race,' Religion and Riots: The 'Racialization' of Communal Identity and Conflict in India." *Sociology* 38, no. 4 (2004): 701–18.

Bakhtin, Mikhail. *The Dialogic Imagination*. Translated by Michael Holquist. Austin: University of Texas Press, 1981.

———. *The Dialogic Imagination: Four Essays*. Austin: University of Texas Press, 1992.

Bamyeh, Mohammed A. "The Arab Revolutions and the Making of a New Patriotism." *Orient: German Journal for Politics, Economics and Culture of the Middle East* 52, no. 3 (July 2011): 6–10.

Bangstad, Sindre. "Contesting Secularism/s: Secularism and Islam in the Work of Talal Asad." *Anthropological Theory* 9, no. 2 (2009): 188–208.

Ba-Obaid, Mohamed, and Catherine Bijleveld. "Violence against Women in Yemen: Official Statistics and an Exploratory Survey." *International Review of Victimology* 9 (2002): 331–47.

Barthes, Roland. *Camera Lucida*. Translated by Richard Howard. New York: Hill and Wang, 1981.

———. *Pleasure of the Text.* Translated by Richard Howard. New York: Farrar, Straus and Giroux, 1973.

Bartky, Sandra Lee. "Foucault, Femininity and the Modernization of Patriarchal Power." In *Writing on the Body: Female Embodiment and Feminist Theory*, edited by Katie Conboy, Nadia Medina, and Sarah Stanbury, 129–54. New York: Columbia University Press, 1997.

Bartu, Ayfer. "Rethinking Heritage Politics in a Global Context: A View from Istanbul." In *Hybrid Urbanism: On the Identity Discourse and the Built Environment*, edited by Nezar AlSayyad, 131–55. Westport, CT: Praeger, 2001.

———. "Who Owns the Old Quarters? Rewriting Histories in a Global Era." In *Istanbul: Between the Global and the Local*, edited by Çağlar Keyder, 31–46. Lanham, MD: Rowman and Littlefield, 1997.

Bassam, Rehab. *Arrz bil-laban li-shakhsayn* (Rice Pudding for Two). Cairo: Dar al-Shuruq, 2008.

Bayat, Asef. "The Arab Spring and Its Surprises." *Development and Change* 44, no. 3 (2013): 587–601.

———. *Life as Politics: How Ordinary People Change the Middle East.* Stanford, CA: Stanford University Press, 2006.

———. *Making Islam Democratic: Social Movements and the Post-Islamist Turn.* Stanford, CA: Stanford University Press, 2007.

———. "A New Arab Street in Post-Islamist Times." *Foreign Policy*, 26 January 2011.

Baydar, Gülsüm. "Embodied Spaces of Resistance." *Women's Studies International Forum* 50 (May–June 2015): 11–19.

Bell, David. "Pleasure and Danger: The Paradoxical Spaces of Sexual Citizenship." *Political Geography* 14, no. 2 (1995): 139–53.

Bell, Vikki. "On Speech, Race and Melancholia: An Interview with Judith Butler." *Theory, Culture and Society* (April 1999): 163–74.

Benhabib, Seyla. "The Pariah and Her Shadow: Hannah Arendt's Biography of Rahel Varnhagen." *Political Theory* 23, no. 1 (1995): 5–24.

Bennani-Chraïbi, Soumia. *Soumis et rebelles, les jeunes au Maroc.* Paris: CNRS, Éditions Méditerranée, 1994.

Bennett, Andy. "Music, Media and Urban Mythscapes: A Study of the 'Canterbury Sound.'" *Media, Culture and Society* 24, no. 1 (2002): 88–100.

Berger, John. *Ways of Seeing.* New York: Penguin, 1972.

Berlant, Lauren. "Intimacy: A Special Issue." *Critical Inquiry* 24, no. 2 (1998): 281–88.

———. *The Queen of America Goes to Washington City.* Durham, NC: Duke University Press, 1997.

Berlant, Lauren, and Jay Prosser. "Life Writing and Intimate Publics: A Conversation with Lauren Berlant." *Biography* 34, no. 1 (2011): 180–87.

Beşpınar, Fatma Umut. "Women and Gender." In *Turkey and the Politics of National Identity: Social, Economic and Cultural Transformation*, edited by Shane Brennan and Marc Herzog, 118–44. London: I. B. Tauris, 2014.

Bhabha, Homi. *The Location of Culture.* London: Routledge, 1994.

———. "Remembering Fanon: What Does the Black Man Want?" *New Formations* 1 (Spring 1987): 118–24.

Biekart, Kees, and Alan Fowler. "Transforming Activisms 2010+: Exploring Ways and Waves." *Development and Change* 44, no. 3 (2013): 527–46.

Bondi, Liz, and Joyce Davidson. "Situating Gender." In *A Companion to Feminist Geography*, edited by Lise Nelson and Joni Seager, 15–31. Malden, MA: Blackwell, 2005.

Bourdieu, Pierre. *La Domination Masculine*. Paris: Editions du Seuil, 1998.

———. "Social Space and Symbolic Power." *Sociological Theory* 7, no. 1 (1989): 14–25.

Bourqia, Rahma, Mohammed El Ayadi, Mokhtar El Harrass, and Hassan Rachik. *Les jeunes et les valeurs religieuses*. Casablanca: Eddif and CODESRIA, 2000.

Bouzid, Nouri. *Man of Ashes*. Seattle: Arab Film Distribution, 1986. VHS.

Brown, Wendy. *States of Injury: Power and Freedom in Late Modernity*. Princeton, NJ: Princeton University Press, 1995.

Brynen, Rex, Bahgat Korany, and Paul Noble. *Political Liberalization and Democratization in the Arab World: Theoretical Perspectives*. Vol. 1. Boulder: Lynne Rienner, 1995.

Butler, Judith. "Bodies in Alliance and Politics of the Street." European Institute for Progressive Cultural Policies. Last modified September 2011. http://www.eipcp.net/transversal/1011/butler/en.

———. *Precarious Life: The Powers of Mourning and Violence*. New York: Verso, 2006.

Butler, Judith, and Athena Athanasiou. *Dispossession: The Performative in the Political*. Cambridge: Polity, 2013.

Carapico, Sheila. "Demonstrators, Dialogues, Drones and Dialectics." *Middle East Report* 269 (2013): 21–24.

———. "No Exit: Yemen's Existential Crisis." In *The Arab Revolts: Dispatches on Militant Democracy in the Middle East*, edited by David McMurray and Amanda Ufheil-Somers, 120–27. Bloomington: Indiana University Press, 2013.

Clifford, James. "Spatial Practices: Fieldwork, Travel, and the Disciplining of Anthropology." In *Anthropological Locations: Boundaries and Grounds of a Field Science*, edited by Akhil Gupta and James Ferguson, 185–222. Berkeley: University of California Press, 1997.

Communication and Information Technology Commission. "Internet in Saudi Arabia." Accessed 22 June 2015. http://www.internet.sa/en/?s=internet+in+saudi+arabia&x=0&y=0.

Convention on the Elimination of All Forms of Discrimination against Women. "Declarations, Reservations, and Objections to CEDAW." UN Women. Accessed 22 June 2015. http://www.un.org/womenwatch/daw/cedaw/reservations-country.htm.

Dabashi, Hamid. *The Arab Spring: The End of Postcolonialism*. London: Zed Books, 2012.

Dahlgren, Susanne. *Contesting Realities: The Public Sphere and Morality in Southern Yemen*. New York: Syracuse University Press, 2010.

———. "Morphologies of Social Flows: Segregation, Time, and the Public Sphere." In *Gendering Urban Space in the Middle East, South Asia, and Africa*, edited by Martina Rieker and Kamran Asdar Ali, 45–70. New York: Palgrave Macmillan, 2008.

———. "Readjusting Women's Too Many Rights: The State, the Public Voice, and Women's Rights in South Yemen." In *Feminist Activism, Women's Rights and Legal Reform*, edited by Mulki al-Sharmani, 48–72. New York: Zed Books, 2014.

———. "Segregation, Illegitimate Encounters, and Contextual Moralities: Sexualities in the Changing Public Sphere in Aden." *Hawwa: Journal of Women in the Middle East and the Islamic World* 4, no. 2 (2006): 214–36.

———. "The Southern Movement in Yemen." *ISIM Review* 22 (Autumn 2008): 50–51.

———. "Welfare and Modernity: Three Concepts for the 'Advanced Woman.'" In *Interpreting Welfare and Relief in the Middle East*, edited by Nefissa Naguib and Inger Marie Okkenhaug, 129–48. Leiden: Brill, 2008.

Dean, Jodi. "Cybersalons and Civil Society: Rethinking the Public Sphere in Transnational Technoculture." *Public Culture* 13, no. 2 (2001): 243–65.

de Certeau, Michel. *The Practice of Everyday Life*. Translated by Steven Rendall. Berkeley: University of California Press, 1984.

Deleuze, Gilles, and Félix Guattari. *A Thousand Plateaus: Capitalism and Schizophrenia*. Translated by Brian Massumi. Minneapolis: University of Minnesota Press, 1987.

Diamond, Larry. "Liberation Technology." *Journal of Democracy* 21, no. 3 (2010): 69–83.

Dikeç, Mustafa. "Space as a Mode of Political Thinking." *Geoforum* 43, no. 4 (2012): 669–76.

Dinshaw, Carolyn. *Getting Medieval: Sexualities and Communities, Pre- and Postmodern*. Durham, NC: Duke University Press, 1999.

———. *How Soon Is Now? Medieval Texts, Amateur Readers, and the Queerness of Time*. Durham, NC: Duke University Press, 2012.

Dixon, Deborah, and Sallie Marston. "Introduction: Feminist Engagements with Geopolitics." *Gender, Place and Culture* 18, no. 4 (2011): 445–53.

Djebar, Assia. *Fantasia: An Algerian Cavalcade*. Translated by Dorothy S. Blair. Portsmouth, NH: Heinemann, 1993.

Donadey, Anne. *Recasting Postcolonialism: Women Writing between Worlds*. Portsmouth, NH: Heinemann, 2001.

Doostdar, Alireza. "The Vulgar Spirit of Blogging: On Language, Culture, and Power in Persian Weblogestan." *American Anthropologist* 106, no. 4 (2001): 651–62.

Douglas, J. Leigh. *The Free Yemeni Movement 1935–1962*. Beirut: American University of Beirut, 1987.

Doumato, Eleanor Abdella. "Gender, Monarchy, and National Identity in Saudi Arabia." *British Journal of Middle Eastern Studies* 19, no. 1 (1992): 31–47.

———. "Saudi Arabia." In *Women's Rights in the Middle East and North Africa: Progress amid Resistance*, edited by Sanja Kelly and Julia Breslin, 425–57. New York: Freedom House, Rowman and Littlefield, 2010.

———. "Women in Civic and Political Life: Reform under Authoritarian Regimes." In *Political Change in the Arab Gulf States: Stuck in Transition*, edited by Mary Ann

Tetreault, Gwenn Okruhlik, and Andrzej Kapiszewski, 193–223. Boulder: Lynne Rienner, 2011.

Dowler, Lorraine, and Joanne Sharp. "A Feminist Geopolitics?" *Space and Polity* 5, no. 3 (2001): 165–76.

Eckoldt, Kai, Marc Hassenzahl, Matthias Laschke, and Martin Knobel. "Alternatives: Exploring the Car's Design Space from an Experience-Oriented Perspective." Proceedings of the 6th International Conference on Designing Pleasurable Products and Interfaces, 156–64. New York: Association for Computing Machinery, 2013.

Ehsani, Kaveh. "Radical Democratic Politics and Public Space." *International Journal of Middle East Studies* 46, no. 1 (2014): 159–62.

Eileraas, Karina. "Sex(t)ing Revolution, Femen-izing the Public Square: Aliaa Magda ElMahdy, Nude Protest, and Transnational Feminist Body Politics." *Signs: Journal of Women in Culture and Society* 40, no. 1 (2014): 40–52.

Elinso, Alexander. "Darija and Changing Writing Practices in Morocco." *International Journal of Middle East Studies* 45, no. 4 (2013): 715–30.

Elnaggar, Ayman. "Towards Gender Equal Access to ICT." *Information Technology for Development* 14, no. 4 (2008): 280–93.

Elsadda, Hoda. "Arab Women Bloggers: The Emergence of Literary Counterpublics." *Middle East Journal of Culture and Communication* 3, no. 3 (2010): 312–32.

Eltahawi, Mona. "Why Do They Hate Us? The Real War on Women Is in the Middle East." *Foreign Policy*, 23 April 2012.

England, Kim V. L. "Getting Personal: Reflexivity, Positionality, and Feminist Research." *Professional Geographer* 46, no. 1 (1994): 241–385.

Enloe, Cynthia. *Bananas, Beaches and Bases: Making Feminist Sense of International Politics.* Berkeley: University of California Press, 1990.

Ennaji, Moha. "Multiculturalism, Gender and Political Participation in Morocco." *Diogenes* 57, no. 1 (2010): 46–56.

Errazouki, Samia. "Working-Class Women Revolt: Gendered Political Economy in Morocco." *Journal of North African Studies* 19, no. 2 (2014): 259–67.

Eslen-Ziya, Hande. "Türk Ceza Kanunu Değişiminde Kadın Aktivistler: Bir Lobicilik Hikayesi" (The Role of Women Activists in Changing Turkey's Penal Code: A Story of Lobbying). *Sosyoloji Araştırmaları Dergisi* 15 (2012): 120–49.

Fahmi, Wael Salah. "Bloggers' Street Movement and the Right to the City: (Re)Claiming Cairo's Real and Virtual 'Spaces of Freedom.'" *Environment and Urbanization* 21, no. 1 (2009): 89–107.

Ferguson, James, and Akhil Gupta. "Spatializing States: Toward an Ethnography of Neoliberal Governmentality." *American Ethnologist* 29, no. 4 (2004): 981–1002.

Fluri, Jennifer. "Armored Peacocks and Proxy Bodies: Gender Geopolitics in Aid/Development Spaces of Afghanistan." *Gender, Place and Culture* 18, no. 4 (2011): 519–36.

Foley, Sean. "All I Want Is Equality with Girls: Gender and Social Change in the Twenty-First Century Gulf." *Middle East Review of International Affairs* 14, no. 1 (2010): 21–37.

Foucault, Michel. *Discipline and Punish: The Birth of the Modern Prison*. Translated by Alan Sheridan. New York: Vintage Books, 1977.

Foucault, Michel, and Jay Moskowitz. "Of Other Spaces." *Diacritics* 16, no. 1 (1986): 22–27.

Fraser, Nancy. "Rethinking the Public Sphere: A Contribution to the Critique of Actually Existing Democracy." In *Civil Society and Democracy: A Reader*, edited by Carolyn M. Elliott, 83–105. New Delhi: Oxford University Press, 2003.

———. "Rethinking the Public Sphere: A Contribution to the Critique of Actually Existing Democracy." *Social Text*, no. 25/26 (1990): 56–80.

Fuccaro, Nelida. *Histories of City and State in the Persian Gulf: Manama since 1800*. Cambridge: Cambridge University Press, 2009.

———. "Understanding the Urban History of Bahrain." *Critique: Critical Middle Eastern Studies* 9, no. 17 (2000): 49–81.

Fuchs, Christian, Kees Boersma, Anders Albrechtslund, and Marisol Sandoval. *Internet and Surveillance: The Challenges of Web 2.0 and Social Media*. New York: Routledge, 2012.

Galán, Susana. "'Today I Have Seen Angels in Shape of Humans': An Emotional History of the Egyptian Revolution through the Narratives of Female Personal Bloggers." *Journal of International Women's Studies* 13, no. 5 (2012): 17–30.

Gardner, Andrew M. *City of Strangers: Gulf Migration and the Indian Community in Bahrain*. Ithaca: Cornell University Press, 2010.

Gauch, Suzanne. *Liberating Shahrazad: Feminism, Postcolonialism, and Islam*. Minneapolis: University of Minnesota Press, 2007.

Genz, Stéphanie. "Third Way/ve: The Politics of Postfeminism." *Feminist Theory* 7, no. 3 (2006): 333–53.

Gershon, Ilana. *The Breakup 2.0: Disconnecting over New Media*. Ithaca: Cornell University Press, 2010.

al-Ghamidi, S. F. *Structure of the Tribe and Urbanization in Saudi Arabia*. Jeddah: Al-Shrooq Press, 1981.

Ghannam, Farha. *Remaking the Modern: Space, Relocation, and the Politics of Identity in a Global Cairo*. Berkeley: University of California Press, 2002.

Ghonim, Wael. *Revolution 2.0: How the Power of the People Is Greater Than the People in Power. A Memoir*. New York: Mariner Books, 2013.

Graciet, Catherine, and Eric Laurent. *Le Roi predateur: Main basse sur le Maroc*. Paris: Seuil, 2012.

Gramsci, Antonio. *Selections from the Prison Notebooks of Antonio Gramsci*. Edited and translated by Quintin Hoare and Geoffrey Nowell Smith. London: Lawrence and Wishart, 1971.

———. *The Southern Question*. Toronto: Guernica Editions, 2005.

Greenfield, Lauren. *Thin*. Documentary. Santa Monica, CA: HBO, 2006.

Grewal, Inderpal. *Transnational America: Feminisms, Diasporas, Neoliberalisms*. Durham, NC: Duke University Press, 2005.

Gupta, Akhil, and James Ferguson. "Spatializing States: Toward an Ethnography of Neoliberal Governmentality." In *Anthropologies of Modernity: Foucault, Govern-*

mentality, and Life Politics, edited by Jonathan Xavier Inda, 105–32. Malden, MA: Blackwell, 2005.

Habermas, Jürgen. *The Structural Transformation of the Public Sphere.* Cambridge, MA: MIT Press, 1991.

Haddad, Joumana. "Look Me in the Eyes . . . I Said the Eyes." *Now Media,* 28 December 2012. https://now.mmedia.me/lb/en/jspot/look_me_in_the_eyes_i_said_the_eyes.

Haddad, Saleem, and Joshua Rogers. "Public Protest and Visions for Change: Voices from within Yemen's Peaceful Youth Movement (Al-Haraka Al-Shababiya Al-Silmiya)." Paper presented at BRISMES Annual Conference, London, 26–28 March 2012.

Hafez, Sherine. "Bodies That Protest: The Girl in the Blue Bra, Sexuality, and State Violence in Revolutionary Egypt." *Signs: Journal of Women in Culture and Society* 40, no. 1 (2014): 20–28.

———. "The Revolution Shall Not Pass through Women's Bodies: Egypt, Uprising and Gender Politics." *Journal of North African Studies* 19, no. 2 (2014): 172–85.

Hakim, Catherine. "Erotic Capital." *European Sociological Review* 26, no. 5 (2010): 499–518.

Halberstam, Judith. "Imagined Violence, Queer Violence: Representation, Rage and Resistance." *Social Text* 37 (Winter 1993): 187–201.

Halliday, Fred. "The Third Inter-Yemeni War and Its Consequences." *Asian Affairs* 26, no. 2 (1995): 131–40.

Hanafi, Sari. "The Arab Revolutions: The Emergence of a New Political Subjectivity." *Contemporary Arab Affairs* 5, no. 2 (2012): 198–213.

Hansen, Henny Harald. "Investigations in a Shiʿa Village in Bahrain." PhD diss., National Museum of Denmark, 1968.

Haraway, Donna. *Simians, Cyborgs, and Women: The Reinvention of Nature.* New York: Routledge, 1991.

———. "Situated Knowledges: The Science Question in Feminism and the Privilege of Partial Perspective." *Feminist Studies* 14, no. 3 (1988): 575–99.

Harlow, Barbara. Introduction to *The Colonial Harem,* by Malek Alloula. Translated by Myrna and Wlad Godzich, ix–xxii. Minneapolis: University of Minnesota Press, 1986.

———. *Resistance Literature.* New York: Routledge, 1987.

Harmanşah, Ömür. "Urban Utopias and How They Fell Apart: The Political Ecology of *Gezi Parkı.*" In *The Making of a Protest Movement in Turkey: #occupygezi,* edited by Umut Özkırımlı, 121–33. Basingstoke, UK: Palgrave Macmillan, 2014.

Harvey, David. "Class Relations, Social Justice and the Politics of Difference." In *Place and the Politics of Identity,* edited by M. Keith and S. Pile, 41–66. London: Routledge, 1993.

———. *Rebel Cities: From the Right to the City to the Urban Revolution.* London: Verso, 2013.

Hasso, Frances S. *Consuming Desires: Family Crisis and the State in the Middle East.* Stanford, CA: Stanford University Press, 2011.

Hayes, Jarrod. *Queer Nations: Marginal Sexualities in the Maghreb*. Chicago: University of Chicago Press, 2000.

Heinze, Marie-Christine. "On 'Gun Culture' and 'Civil Statehood' in Yemen." *Journal of Arabian Studies* 4, no. 1 (2014): 70–95.

Herrera, Linda. *Revolution in the Age of Social Media: The Egyptian Popular Insurrection and the Internet*. London: Verso, 2014.

Herzog, Hanna. "Mixed Cities as a Place of Choice: The Palestinian Women's Perspective." In *Mixed Towns, Trapped Communities: Historical Narratives, Spatial Dynamics, Gender Relations and Cultural Encounters in Palestinian-Israeli Towns*, edited by Dan Rabinowitz and Daniel Monterescu, 243–57. Burlington, VT: Ashgate, 2007.

Hill Collins, Patricia. *Black Feminist Thought: Knowledge, Consciousness, and the Politics of Empowerment*. Boston: Unwin Hyman, 1990.

hooks, bell. *Black Looks: Race and Representation*. Boston: South End, 1992.

Howard, Philip N., and Muzammil M. Hussain. *Democracy's Fourth Wave? Digital Media and the Arab Spring*. New York: Oxford University Press, 2013.

Hudson, Ray. "Regions and Place: Music, Identity, and Place." *Progress in Human Geography* 30, no. 5 (2006): 626–34.

Hyndman, Jennifer. "Mind the Gap: Bridging Feminist and Political Geography through Geopolitics." *Political Geography* 23, no. 3 (2004): 307–22.

Icaza, Rosalba, and Rolando Vázquez. "Social Struggles as Epistemic Struggles." *Development and Change* 44, no. 3 (2013): 683–704.

Irigaray, Luce. *This Sex Which Is Not One*. Translated by Catherine Porter. Ithaca: Cornell University Press, 1985.

Isin, Engin F. "Engaging, Being, Political." *Political Geography* 24, no. 3 (2005): 373–87.

Ismael, Tareq Y., and Jacqueline S. Ismael. *The People's Democratic Republic of Yemen: Politics, Economics and Society*. London: Frances Pinter, 1986.

Ismail, Salwa. "Urban Subalterns in the Arab Revolutions: Cairo and Damascus in Comparative Perspective." *Comparative Studies in Society and History* 55, no. 4 (2013): 865–94.

el-Issawi, Fatima. "The Arab Spring and the Challenge of Minority Rights: Will the Arab Revolutions Overcome the Legacy of the Past?" *European View* 10, no. 2 (2011): 249–58.

Joffé, E. G. H., M. J. Hachemi, and E. W. Watkins, eds. *Yemen Today: Crisis and Solutions. Proceedings of a Two-Day Conference Held at the School of Oriental and African Studies, University of London, November 25th and 26th, 1995*. London: Caravel, 1997.

Joffé, George. "Introduction: Yemen and the Contemporary Middle East." In *Yemen Today: Crisis and Solutions. Proceedings of a Two-Day Conference Held at the School of Oriental and African Studies, University of London, November 25th and 26th, 1995*, edited by E. G. H. Joffé, M. J. Hachemi, and E. W. Watkins. London: Caravel, 1997.

Jones, Sandy Russell. "God's Law or State's Law: Authority and Islamic Family Law Reform in Bahrain." PhD diss., University of Pennsylvania, 2010.

Kandaswamy, Priya. "Gendering Racial Formation." In *Racial Formation in the Twenty-First Century*, edited by Daniel Martinez HoSang, Oneka LaBennett, and Laura Pulido, 23–43. Berkeley: University of California Press, 2012.

Karaman, Ozan. "Urban Neoliberalism with Islamic Characteristics." *Urban Studies* 50, no. 16 (2013): 3412–27.

Kärrholm, Mattias. "Interstitial Space and the Transformation of Retail Building Types." In *Urban Interstices: The Aesthetics and the Politics of the In-Between*, edited by Andrea Mubi Brighenti, 135–52. Farnham, UK: Ashgate, 2013.

Katz, Cindi. "On the Grounds of Globalization: A Topography for Feminist Political Engagement." *Signs: Journal of Women in Culture and Society* 26, no. 4 (2001): 1213–34.

Kedourie, Elie. "'Civil Politics' in the Middle East." *American Scholar* 57, no. 1 (1988): 107–10.

Kelly, Sanja. "Hard-Won Progress and a Long Road Ahead: Women's Rights in the Middle East and North Africa." In *Women's Rights in the Middle East and North Africa: Progress amid Resistance*, edited by Sanja Kelly and Julia Breslin, 1–14. New York: Freedom House, Rowman and Littlefield, 2010.

Khalaf, Abdulhadi. "Double Efforts to Contain Women's Mobility in Bahrain" (Arabic). *As-Safir*, 10 October 2012, http://arabi.assafir.com/article.asp?aid=344.

Khalaf, Amal. "The Many Afterlives of Lulu: The Story of Bahrain's Pearl Roundabout." *Ibraaz*, 20 February 2013. http://www.ibraaz.org/essays/56.

———. "Squaring the Circle: Bahrain's Pearl Roundabout." "The Arab Uprisings of 2011," special issue, *Middle East Critique* 22, no. 3 (2013): 265–80.

Khosrokhavar, Farhad. *The New Arab Revolutions That Shook the World*. Boulder: Paradigm, 2012.

Khuri, Fuad I. *Tribe and State in Bahrain: The Transformation of Social and Political Authority in an Arab State*. Chicago: University of Chicago Press, 1980.

Kies, Samantha Mallory. "Matriarchy, the Colonial Situation, and the Women's War of 1929 in Southeastern Nigeria." MA thesis, Eastern Michigan University, 2013.

Kilbourne, Jean. "'The More You Subtract, the More You Add': Cutting Girls Down to Size." In *Gender, Race and Class in Media*, 2nd edition, edited by Gail Dines and Jean Humez, 258–67. Thousand Oaks, CA: Sage, 2003.

Kofman, Eleonore, and Linda Peak. "Into the 1990s: A Gendered Agenda for Political Geography." *Political Geography Quarterly* 9, no. 4 (1990): 313–36.

Konda. "Gezi Report: Public Perception of the 'Gezi Protests' and Who Were the People at Gezi Park." 5 June 2014. http://konda.com.tr/en/raporlar/KONDA _Gezi_Report.pdf.

Kongar, Emre, and Aykut Küçükkaya. *Gezi Direnişi* (Gezi Resistance). Istanbul: Cumhuriyet, 2013.

Koning, Anouk de. "Gender, Public Space and Social Segregation in Cairo: Of Taxi Drivers, Prostitutes and Professional Women." *Antipode: A Radical Journal of Geography* 41, no. 3 (2009): 533–56.

Koskela, Hille. "Urban Space in Plural: Elastic, Tamed, Suppressed." In *A Companion to Feminist Geography*, edited by Lise Nelson and Joni Seager, 257–70. Malden, MA: Blackwell, 2005.

Kotnik, Toni. "The Mirrored Public: Architecture and Gender Relationship in Yemen." *Space and Culture* 8, no. 4 (2005): 472–83.

Kraidy, Marwan M. "The Revolutionary Body Politic: Preliminary Thoughts on a Neglected Medium in the Arab Uprisings." *Middle East Journal of Culture and Communication* 5, no. 1 (2012): 66–74.

Langohr, Vickie. "Women's Rights Movements during Political Transitions: Activism against Public Sexual Violence in Egypt." *International Journal of Middle East Studies* 47, no. 1 (2015): 131–35.

Lefebvre, Henri. *The Production of Space*. 1974. Oxford: Blackwell, 1991.

———. *Writings on Cities*. Translated by Eleonore Koffman and Elizabeth Lebas. Oxford: Blackwell, 1996.

Leonard, Karen. "South Asian Workers in the Gulf: Jockeying for Places." In *Globalization under Construction: Governmentality, Law, and Identity*, edited by Richard Warren Perry and Bill Maurer, 129–70. Minneapolis: University of Minnesota Press, 2003.

Le Renard, Amélie. "'Only for Women': Women, the State, and Reform in Saudi Arabia." *Middle East Journal* 6, no. 4 (2008): 610–29.

———. "Young Urban Saudi Women's Transgressions of Official Rules and the Production of a New Social Group." *Journal of Middle East Women's Studies* 9, no. 3 (2013): 108–35.

Lévesque, Luc. "Trajectories of Interstitial Landscapeness: A Conceptual Framework for Territorial Imagination and Action." In *Urban Interstices: The Aesthetics and the Politics of the In-Between*, edited by Andrea Mubi Brighenti, 21–64. Farnham, UK: Ashgate, 2013.

Lobo, Sunila, and Silvia Elaluf-Calderwood. "The BlackBerry Veil: Mobile Use and Privacy Practices by Young Female Saudis." *Journal of Islamic Marketing* 3, no. 2 (2012): 190–206.

Longhurst, Robyn. *Bodies: Exploring Fluid Boundaries*. London: Routledge, 2000.

———. "The Geography Closest In—The Body . . . the Politics of Pregnability." *Australian Geographical Studies* 32, no. 2 (1994): 214–23.

Louër, Laurence. *Shiism and Politics in the Middle East*. Translated by John King. London: C. Hurst, 2012.

Lynch, Marc. "Blogging the New Arab Public." *Arab Media and Society*, February 2007. http://www.arabmediasociety.com/articles/downloads/20070312155027_AMS1_Marc_Lynch.pdf.

Maghraoui, Driss. "Constitutional Reforms in Morocco: Between Consensus and Subaltern Politics." *Journal of North African Studies* 16, no. 4 (2011): 679–99.

Makdisi, Ussama. *The Culture of Sectarianism: Community, History, and Violence in Nineteenth-Century Ottoman Lebanon*. Berkeley: University of California Press, 2000.

al-Marshad, ʿAbbas Mirza, and ʿAbdulhadi al-Khawaja. *Political Organizations and Societies in Bahrain: A Descriptive Human Rights Study* (Arabic). Manama, Bahrain: Faradis, 2008.

Marston, Sallie. "The Social Construction of Scale." *Progress in Human Geography* 24, no. 2 (2000): 219–42.

———. "Who Are 'the People'? Gender, Citizenship and the Making of the American Nation." *Environment and Planning D: Society and Space* 8, no. 4 (1990): 449–58.

Massey, Doreen. *For Space*. London: Sage, 2005.

———. "Politics and Space/Time." In *Place and the Politics of Identity*, edited by Michael Keith and Steve Pile, 141–61. London: Routledge, 1993.

Massumi, Brian. *Parables for the Virtual: Movement, Affect, Sensation*. Durham, NC: Duke University Press, 2002.

McDowell, Linda. *Gender, Identity and Place: Understanding Feminist Geographies*. Minneapolis: University of Minnesota Press, 1999.

Mchich, Houria Alami. *Genre et politique au Maroc: Les enjeux de l'egalité hommes-femmes entre Islamisme et modernisme* (Gender and Politics in Morocco: The Stakes of Male-Female Equality between Islamism and Modernism). Paris: L'Harmattan, 2002.

Meijer, Roel. "Reform in Saudi Arabia: The Gender-Segregation Debate." *Middle East Policy* 17, no. 4 (2010): 80–100.

Mejias, Ulises A. "Liberation Technology and the Arab Spring: From Utopia to Atopia and Beyond." *Fibreculture Journal* 20 (June 2012). http://twenty.fibreculture journal.org/2012/06/20/fcj-147-liberation-technology-and-the-arab-spring-from-utopia-to-atopia-and-beyond/.

Mermier, Franck. "Le mouvement sudiste." In *Yémen, le tournant révolutionnaire*, edited by L. Bonnefoy, F. Mermier, and M. Poirier, 41–65. Sanaʿa: CEFAS-Éditions Karthala, 2012.

Mernissi, Fatima. *Beyond the Veil: Male-Female Dynamics in Modern Muslim Society*. Bloomington: Indiana University Press, 1987.

———. *Scheherazade Goes West: Different Cultures, Different Harems*. New York: Washington Square Press, 2001.

Mills, Amy. "Critical Place Studies and Middle East Histories: Power, Politics, and Social Change." *History Compass* 10, no. 10 (2012): 778–88.

Mirzoeff, Nicholas. *Bodyscape: Art, Modernity and the Ideal Figure*. New York: Routledge, 1995.

Mitchell, Don. "Feminism and Cultural Change: Geographies of Gender." In *Cultural Geography: A Critical Introduction*, 199–229. Malden, MA: Blackwell, 2000.

———. *The Right to the City: Social Justice and the Fight for Public Space*. New York: Guilford, 2003.

Mitra, Ananda. "Voices of the Marginalized on the Internet: Examples from a Website for Women of South Asia." *Journal of Communication* 54, no. 3 (2004): 492–510.

Molyneux, Maxine. "Women and Revolution in the People's Democratic Republic of Yemen." *Feminist Review*, no. 1 (1979): 5–20.

Morse, Margaret. *Virtualities: Television, Media Art, and Cyberculture.* Bloomington: Indiana University Press, 1998.

Morton, Adam David. *Unravelling Gramsci: Hegemony and Passive Revolution in the Global Economy.* London: Pluto, 2007.

Mouffe, Chantal. "Deliberative Democracy or Agonistic Pluralism." Institute for Advanced Studies, Vienna. December 2002. http://www.ihs.ac.at/publications/pol /pw_72.pdf.

———. *On the Political.* London: Routledge, 1995.

———. *The Return of the Political.* New York: Verso, 2005.

Mourad, Sara. "The Naked Body of Alia: Gender, Citizenship, and the Egyptian Body Politic." *Journal of Communication Inquiry* 38, no. 1 (2014): 62–78.

Mubi Brighenti, Andrea. Introduction to *Urban Interstices: The Aesthetics and the Politics of the In-Between,* edited by Andrea Mubi Brighenti, xv–xxiii. Farnham, UK: Ashgate, 2013.

Mulvey, Laura. "Visual Pleasure and Narrative Cinema." *Screen* 16, no. 3 (1975): 6–18.

Muñoz, José E. *Disidentifications: Queers of Color and the Performance of Politics.* Minneapolis: University of Minnesota Press, 1999.

Naji, Ahmed. *Al-Mudawwanat min al-Bust ila al-Twit* (Blogs from Posting to Tweeting). Cairo: Arab Network for Human Rights Information, 2010.

Nakamura, Lisa. *Cybertypes: Race, Ethnicity, and Identity on the Internet.* New York: Routledge, 2002.

Nast, Heidi, and Steve Pile, eds. *Places through the Body.* London: Routledge, 1998.

Neti, Leila. "Blood and Dirt: Politics of Women's Protest in Armagh Prison, Northern Ireland." In *Violence and the Body: Race, Gender, and the State,* edited by Arturo Aldama, 77–93. Bloomington: Indiana University Press, 2003.

Nora, Pierre. "Between Memory and History: *Les Lieux de mémoire.*" *Representations* 26 (Spring 1989): 7–24.

Norton, Augustus Richard. Introduction to *Civil Society in the Middle East,* vol. 1, edited by Augustus Richard Norton, 1–25. Leiden: Brill, 2005.

Nouraie-Simone, Fereshteh. "Wings of Freedom: Iranian Women, Identity, and Cyberspace." In *On Shifting Ground: Muslim Women in the Global Era,* edited by Fereshteh Nouraie-Simone, 61–79. New York: Feminist Press at the City University of New York, 2005.

Omi, Michael, and Howard Winant. "Once More, with Feeling: Reflections on Racial Formation." "Special Topic: Comparative Racialization," PMLA 123, no. 5 (2008): 1565–72.

Omi, Michael, and Howard Winant. *Racial Formation in the United States: From the 1960s to the 1990s.* 2nd edition. New York: Routledge, 1994.

Al Omran, Ahmed. "'A Historical Moment': The Saudi Women Challenging a Government by Driving." NPR, 19 June 2011. http://www.npr.org/blogs/thetwo-way /2011/06/19/137271964/a-historical-moment-the-saudi-women-challenging-a -government-by-driving.

Öniş, Ziya. "Sharing Power: Turkey's Democratization Challenge in the Age of the AKP Hegemony." *Insight Turkey* 15 (2013): 103–22.

————. "The Triumph of Conservative Globalism: The Political Economy of the AKP Era." *Turkish Studies* 13, no. 2 (2012): 135–52.

Otterman, Sharon. "Publicizing the Private: Egyptian Women Bloggers Speak Out." *Arab Media and Society* 1 (February 2007): 1–17.

Ó Tuathail, Gearóid. *Critical Geopolitics: The Politics of Writing Global Space*. London: Routledge, 1996.

Ousmanova, Almira. "Flashmob—The Divide between Art and Politics in Belarus." *Art Margins Online*, 15 July 2010. http://www.artmargins.com/index.php/2-articles /588-flashmob-divide-between-art-politics-belarus.

Özbudun, Ergun. "AKP at the Crossroads: Erdoğan's Majoritarian Drift." *South European Society and Politics* 19, no. 2 (2014): 155–67.

Paluch, Marta. *Yemeni Voices: Women Tell Their Stories*. Sanaʻa: British Council, 2001.

Pandya, Sophia. *Muslim Women and Islamic Resurgence: Religion, Education, and Identity Politics in Bahrain*. London: I. B. Tauris, 2012.

————. "Women's Shiʻi Maʼatim in Bahrain." *Journal of Middle East Women's Studies* 6, no. 2 (2010): 31–58.

Parmar, Pratibha. *A Place of Rage*. Documentary. London: Women Make Movies, 1991.

Peirce, Leslie P. *The Imperial Harem: Women and Sovereignty in the Ottoman Empire*. Oxford: Oxford University Press, 1993.

Philippopoulos-Mihalopoulos, Andreas. "Spatial Justice in the Lawscape." In *Urban Interstices: The Aesthetics and the Politics of the In-Between*, edited by Andrea Mubi Brighenti, 87–102. Farnham, UK: Ashgate, 2013.

Pratt, Geraldine, and Susan Hanson. "Geography and the Construction of Difference." *Gender, Place and Culture: A Journal of Feminist Geography* 1, no. 1 (1994): 5–29.

Princess Tam Tam. Directed by Edmond T. Greville. New York: Kino on Video International, 1935.

al-Rabiʻi, Fadhl ʻAbdulla. *Fashl mashruʻ al-wahda bayna jumhuriyya al-yaman al-dimuqratiyya al-shaʻbiyya wal-jumhuriyya al-ʻarabiyya al-yamaniyya: Madkhal li fahm qadiyya al-janub wal haraka al-silmiyya* (Failure of the Unity between the PDRY and the Yemen Arab Republic: An Introduction to Understanding the Southern Cause and the Peaceful Movement). N.p.: Madar, 2013.

Rancière, Jacques. *Dissensus: On Politics and Aesthetics*. Translated by Steven Corcoran. London: Continuum, 2010.

————. *The Nights of Labor: The Workers' Dream in Nineteenth Century France*. Translated by Rana Dasgupta. Philadelphia: Temple University Press, 1989.

————. "Politics and Aesthetics: An Interview." *Angelaki: Journal of the Theoretical Humanities* 8, no. 2 (2003): 191–211.

————. *The Politics of Aesthetics: The Distribution of the Sensible*. Translated by Gabriel Rockhill. London: Continuum, 2004.

————. "Ten Theses on Politics." *Theory and Event* 5, no. 3 (2001): 1–18. Online only. http://muse.jhu.edu/journals/theory_and_event/v005/5.3ranciere.html.

———. "The Thinking of Dissensus: Politics and Aesthetics." In *Reading Rancière: Critical Dissensus*, edited by Paul Bowman and Richard Stamp, 1–17. London: Continuum, 2011.

al-Rasheed, Madawi. *Contesting the Saudi State: Islamic Voices from a New Generation.* New York: Cambridge University Press, 2006.

———. *A Most Masculine State: Gender, Politics, and Religion in Saudi Arabia.* New York: Cambridge University Press, 2013.

Renan, Ernest. *Études d'histoire religieuse.* 1857. Saint-Armand: Gallimard, 1992.

———. *Qu'est-ce qu'une nation?* Paris: Presses-Pocket, 1992.

Rheingold, Howard. *Smart Mobs: The Next Social Revolution.* Cambridge, MA: Perseus, 2002.

Rifaat, Yasmine. "Blogging the Body: The Case of Egypt." *Surfacing* 1, no. 1 (2008): 52–71.

Rogers, Joshua, Hannah Wright, Saleem Haddad, Marwa Baabad, and Basma Gaber. "'It's Dangerous to Be the First': Security Barriers to Women's Public Participation in Egypt, Libya and Yemen." Saferworld, October 2013. http://www.saferworld.org.uk/downloads/pubdocs/its-dangerous-to-be-the-first–web.pdf.

Rooney, Caroline. "'In Less Than Five Years': Rehab Bassam Interviewed by Caroline Rooney, Dar Al-Shorouk, Nasr City, Cairo, April 2010." "Egyptian Literary Culture and Egyptian Modernity," special issue, *Journal of Postcolonial Writing* 47, no. 4 (2011): 467–76.

Rose, Gillian. *Feminism and Geography: The Limits of Geographical Knowledge.* Cambridge: Polity, 1993.

———. *Visual Methodologies: An Introduction to Researching with Visual Materials.* 3rd edition. London: Sage, 2012.

Rose, Nikolas. *Powers of Freedom: Reframing Political Thought.* Cambridge: Cambridge University Press, 1999.

Sadiqi, Fatima, and Moha Ennaji. "The Feminization of Public Space: Women's Activism, the Family Law, and Social Change in Morocco." *Journal of Middle East Women's Studies* 2, no. 2 (2006): 86–114.

Al Saggaf, Yeslam. "The Effect of Online Community on Offline Community in Saudi Arabia." *Electronic Journal on Information Systems in Developing Countries* 16, no. 2 (2004): 1–16.

Salazar Parreñas, Rhacel. *Servants of Globalization: Women, Migration, and Domestic Work.* Stanford, CA: Stanford University Press, 2001.

Saldana-Portillo, Maria Josefina. *The Revolutionary Imagination in the Americas and the Age of Development.* Durham, NC: Duke University Press, 2006.

Salime, Zakia. "Arab Revolutions: Legible, Illegible Bodies." *Comparative Studies of South Asia, Africa and the Middle East* 35, no. 3 (2015): 525–38.

———. *Between Feminism and Islam: Human Rights and Shari'a Law in Morocco.* Minneapolis: University of Minnesota Press, 2011.

———. "I Vote, I Sing: The Rise of Aesthetic Citizenship in Morocco." *International Journal of Middle East Studies* 47, no. 1 (2015): 136–39.

―――. "New Feminism as Personal Revolutions: Microrebellious Bodies." *Signs: Journal of Women in Culture and Society* 40, no. 1 (2014): 14–20.

―――. "Securing the Market, Pacifying Civil Society, Empowering Women: The Middle East Partnership Initiative." *Sociological Forum* 25, no. 4 (2010): 725–45.

al-Saqqaf, Abu Bakr. "Equal Citizenship: The Big Absence." In *Yemen Today: Crisis and Solutions. Proceedings of a Two-Day Conference Held at the School of Oriental and African Studies, University of London, November 25th and 26th, 1995,* edited by E. G. H. Joffé, M. J. Hachemi, and E. W. Watkins, 127–30. London: Caravel, 1997.

Schaap, Andrew. "Enacting the Right to Have Rights: Jacques Rancière's Critique of Hannah Arendt." *European Journal of Political Theory* 10, no. 1 (2011): 22–45.

Sebbar, Leila. *Sherazade: Missing, Aged 17, Dark Curly Hair, Green Eyes.* Translated by Dorothy S. Blair. London: Quartet Books, 1991.

Sebbar, Leila, and Jean-Michel Belorgey. *Femmes d'Afrique du Nord: Cartes postales (1885–1930).* Saint-Pourcain-sur-Sioule: Bleu autour, 2002.

Secor, Anna J. "Toward a Feminist Counter-Geopolitics: Gender, Space and Islamist Politics in Istanbul." *Space and Polity* 5, no. 3 (2001): 191–211.

―――. "The Veil and Urban Space in Istanbul: Women's Dress, Mobility and Islamic Knowledge." *Gender, Place and Culture: A Journal of Feminist Geography* 9, no. 1 (2002): 5–22.

Sghaier, Amira Aleya. *Bourguiba: Le despote.* Tunis: Maghreb International Presse et Editions, 2011.

Sghiri, Malek. "Greetings to the Dawn: Living through the Bittersweet Revolution (Tunisia)." In *Dairies of an Unfinished Revolution,* edited by Layla Al-Zubaidi, Matthew Cassel, and Nemonie Craven Roderick, translated by Robin Moger and Georgina Collins, 9–47. New York: Penguin Books, 2013.

Shabout, Nada. "Whose Space Is It?" *International Journal of Middle East Studies* 46, no. 1 (2014): 163–65.

Shah, Nishant. "Citizen Action in the Time of the Network." *Development and Change* 44, no. 3 (2013): 665–81.

Sharpley-Whiting, Denean T. *Pimps Up, Ho's Down: Hip Hop's Hold on Young Black Women.* New York: New York University Press, 2007.

Sheller, Mimi. "Automotive Emotions: Feeling the Car." *Theory, Culture and Society* 21, nos. 4–5 (2004): 221–42.

Sheller, Mimi, and John Urry. "Mobile Transformations of 'Public' and 'Private' Life." *Theory, Culture, and Society* 20, no. 3 (2003): 107–25.

Singh, Nikhil. "Racial Formation in an Age of Permanent War." In *Racial Formation in the Twenty-First Century,* edited by Daniel Martinez HoSang, Oneka LaBennett, and Laura Pulido, 276–301. Berkeley: University of California Press, 2012.

Skalli, Loubna H. "Communicating Gender in the Public Sphere: Women and Information Technologies in the MENA." *Journal of Middle East Women's Studies* 2, no. 2 (2006): 35–59.

―――. "Youth Media and the Politics of Change in North Africa: Negotiating Identities, Spaces and Power." *Middle East Journal of Culture and Communication* 6, no. 1 (2013): 1–10.

Smith, Sara. "Intimate Geopolitics: Religion, Marriage, and Reproductive Bodies in Leh, Ladakh." *Annals of the Association of American Geographers* 102, no. 6 (2012): 1511–28.

———. "She Says to Herself, 'I Have No Future': Love, Fate, and Territory in Leh District, India." *Gender, Place and Culture* 18, no. 4 (2011): 455–76.

Sontag, Susan. *On Photography.* New York: Farrar, Straus and Giroux, 1977.

Sowards, Stacey K., and Valerie R. Renegar. "The Rhetorical Functions of Consciousness-Raising in Third Wave Feminism." *Communication Studies* 55, no. 4 (2004): 535–52.

Spivak, Gayatri. "French Feminism in an International Frame." *Yale French Studies,* no. 62 (1981): 154–84.

Staeheli, Lynn, and Eleonore Kofman. "Mapping Gender, Making Politics: Towards Feminist Political Geographies." In *Mapping Women, Making Politics: Feminist Perspectives on Political Geography,* edited by Eleonore Kofman and Lynn Staeheli, 1–13. New York: Routledge, 2004.

Staeheli, Lynn, and Don Mitchell. "Spaces of Public and Private: Locating Politics." In *Spaces of Democracy: Geographical Perspectives on Citizenship, Participation, and Representation,* edited by Clive Barnett and Murray Low, 147–60. London: Sage, 2004.

Steg, Linda. "Car Use: Lust and Must. Instrumental, Symbolic and Affective Motives for Car Use." *Transportation Research Part A* 39, nos. 2–3 (2005): 147–62.

Stoler, Ann Laura. "Intimidations of Empire: Predicaments of the Tactile and Unseen." In *Haunted by Empire: Geographies of Intimacy in North American History,* edited by Ann Laura Stoler, 1–22. Durham, NC: Duke University Press, 2006.

Strobl, Staci. "From Colonial Policing to Community Policing in Bahrain: The Historical Persistence of Sectarianism." *International Journal of Comparative and Applied Criminal Justice* 35, no. 1 (2011): 19–37.

———. "The Women's Police Directorate in Bahrain: An Ethnographic Exploration of Gender Segregation and the Likelihood of Future Integration." *International Criminal Justice Review* 18, no. 1 (2008): 39–58.

Swanson, Nathan. "Embodying Tahrir: Bodies and Geopolitics in the 2011 Egyptian Uprising." *Area,* 16 December 2014. doi: 10.1111/area.12163.

Tanke, Joseph J. *Jacques Rancière: An Introduction, Philosophy, Politics, Aesthetics.* London: Continuum, 2011.

Taş, Tuğba, and Oğuzhan Taş. "Resistance on the Walls, Reclaiming Public Space: Street Art in Times of Political Turmoil in Turkey." *Interactions: Studies in Communication and Culture* 5, no. 3 (2014): 327–49.

Taussig, Michael. *The Nervous System.* New York: Routledge, 1992.

Taylor, Charles. "Modern Social Imaginaries." *Public Culture* 14, no. 1 (2002): 91–124.

———. *Modern Social Imaginaries.* Durham, NC: Duke University Press, 2003.

———. "To Follow a Rule . . ." In *Bourdieu: Critical Perspectives,* edited by Craig Calhoun, Edward LiPuma, and Moishe Postone, 29–44. Cambridge: Polity, 1993.

Teitelbaum, Joshua. "Dueling for Daʿwa: State vs. Society on the Saudi Internet." *Middle East Journal* 56, no. 2 (2002): 222–39.

Thiollet, Hélène. "The Ambivalence of Immigration Policy in Saudi Arabia: Public and Private Actors in Migration Management." In *Migrant Labor in the Gulf: Working Group Summary Report*, edited by Center for International and Regional Studies, 23–24. Doha: Georgetown University, School of Foreign Service in Qatar, 2011. https://repository.library.georgetown.edu/bitstream/handle/10822/558543/CIRSSummaryReport2MigrantLaborintheGulf2011.pdf?sequence=5.

Toprak, Binnaz, Iran Bozam, Tan Murgul, and Nedim Sener. *Being Different in Turkey: Religion, Conservatism and Otherization*. Istanbul: Bogazici University, Open Society Foundation, 2009.

Tozi, Mohamed. *Al-Malakiyya wal-Islam al-Siyasi* (The Kingdom and Political Islam). Casablanca: Le Fennec, 1999.

Tuğal, Cihan. *Passive Revolution: Absorbing the Islamic Challenge to Capitalism*. Stanford, CA: Stanford University Press, 2009.

Turam, Berna. *Gaining Freedoms: Claiming Space in Istanbul and Berlin*. Stanford, CA: Stanford University Press, 2015.

Turkle, Sherry. *Alone Together: Why We Expect More from Technology and Less from Each Other*. New York: Basic Books, 2011.

Urry, John. "Inhabiting the Car." *Sociological Review* 54, no. s1 (2006): 17–31.

Vom Bruck, Gabriele. "A House Turned Inside Out: Inhabiting Space in a Yemeni City." *Journal of Material Culture* 2, no. 2 (1997): 139–72.

Warner, Michael. "Publics and Counterpublics." *Public Culture* 14, no. 1 (2002): 49–90.

Wedeen, Lisa. "The Politics of Deliberation: *Qāt* Chews as Public Sphere in Yemen." *Public Culture* 19, no. 1 (2007): 59–84.

Weitzer, Ronald, and Charis E. Kubrin. "Misogyny in Rap Music: A Content Analysis of Prevalence and Meanings." *Men and Masculinities* 12, no. 1 (2009): 3–29.

Weyman, George. "Personal Blogging in Egypt: Pushing Social Boundaries or Reinforcing Them?" *Arab Media and Society*, no. 3 (Fall 2007). http://www.arabmediasociety.com/topics/index.php?t_article=164.

———. "Speaking the Unspeakable: Personal Blogs in Egypt." *Arab Media and Society*, no. 3 (Fall 2007). http://www.arabmediasociety.com/?article=425.

Wheeler, Deborah L. "Blessings and Curses: Women and the Internet Revolution in the Arab World." In *Women and Media in the Middle East: Power through Self-Expression*, edited by Naomi Sakr, 138–61. London: I. B. Tauris, 2004.

———. "Empowerment Zones? Women, Internet Cafés, and Life Transformations in Egypt." *Information Technologies and International Development* 4, no. 2 (2007): 89–104.

Women National Committee. "Status of Woman in Yemen." 1996. Accessed 11 June 2014. http://www.yemen-women.org/.

Woodhull, Winifred. *Transfigurations of the Maghreb: Feminism, Decolonization, and Literatures*. Minneapolis: University of Minnesota Press, 1993.

Yadav, Stacey Philbrick. "Tawakkul Karman as Cause and Effect." In *The Arab Revolts: Dispatches on Militant Democracy in the Middle East*, edited by David McMurray and Amanda Ufheil-Somers, 152–56. Bloomington: Indiana University Press, 2013.

Yadav, Stacey Philbrick, and Sheila Carapico. "The Breakdown of the GCC Initiative." *Middle East Report* 273 (December 2014): 2–6.

Yazbek, Samar. Introduction to *Diaries of an Unfinished Revolution: Voices from Tunisia to Damascus*, edited by Layla Al-Zubaidi, Matthew Cassel, and Nemonie Craven Roderick, translated by Robin Moger and Georgina Collins, 1–7. New York: Penguin Books, 2013.

Young, Iris Marion. "Polity and Group Difference: A Critique of the Ideal of Universal Citizenship." *Ethics* 99, no. 2 (1989): 250–74.

Yuce, Serpil, Nitin Agarwal, and Rolf T. Wigand. "Mapping Cyber-Collective Action among Female Muslim Bloggers for the Women to Drive Movement." *Lecture Notes in Computer Science* 7812 (2013): 331–40.

Zayzafoon Ben Youssef, Lamia. "Is It the End of State Feminism? Tunisian Women during and after the Revolution." In *The Arab Revolutions in Context: Civil Society and Democracy in a Changing Middle East*, edited by Benjamin Isakhan, Fethi Mansouri, and Sharam Akbarzadeh, 41–62. Carlton: Melbourne University Publishing, 2012.

———. *The Production of the Muslim Woman: Negotiating Text, History, and Ideology.* Lanham, MD: Lexington Books, 2005.

Zerilli, Linda M. G. *Feminism and the Abyss of Freedom.* Chicago: University of Chicago Press, 2005.

Zoepf, Katherine. "Shopgirls." *New Yorker*, 23 December 2013. http://www.newyorker.com/reporting/2013/12/23/131223fa_fact_zoepf.

CONTRIBUTORS

LAMIA BENYOUSSEF is an assistant professor in the Department of Modern Foreign Languages at Birmingham Southern College. She has a PhD in English from Michigan State University. Her areas of specialization are postcoloniality, feminist theory, Arab studies, and African literature, with a specific emphasis on the Maghreb. She is the author of *The Production of the Muslim Woman: Negotiating Text, History and Ideology* (2005) and a number of journal articles.

SUSANNE DAHLGREN studied anthropology at the University of Edinburgh, the London School of Economics and Political Science, and the University of Helsinki. Her book, *Contesting Realities: The Public Sphere and Morality in Southern Yemen,* was published in 2010. After a postdoctorate at the Helsinki Collegium for Advanced Studies she served as the Academy of Finland research fellow at the University of Helsinki. Currently she is a senior lecturer at the University of Tampere and an academic scholar in the National University of Singapore. She has written numerous articles on ethnography of law and moralities, sexuality, and urban space. With Samuli Schielke she coedited the volume "Moral Ambiguities and Muslim Lives" of *Contemporary Islam* (2013), and she edited two volumes of the journal *Hawwa* on Middle Eastern family studies.

KARINA EILERAAS is a visiting assistant professor of gender studies at the University of Southern California. She was the first graduate of the women's studies PhD program at UCLA. Her areas of interest include sexual violence, fantasy, film, performance studies, and visual culture and sexuality, revolution, exile, and women's memoir and artistic practice in the Middle East and North Africa. She has published numerous journal articles, book chapters, and the book *Between Image and Identity: Transnational Fantasy, Trauma, and Feminist Misrecognition* (2007).

SUSANA GALÁN is a PhD candidate in women's and gender studies at Rutgers University. She has coedited a Comparative Perspective Symposium, "Gendered Bodies in the Protest Sphere," for *Signs: Journal of Women in Culture and Society*, where she also worked as a graduate research assistant. Her dissertation focuses on autonomous practices of self-defense and community intervention against public sexual violence in Egypt and their impact on gendered urban dynamics after the 2011 revolution. More broadly she is interested in exploring the potentials, limitations, and paradoxes of online sites and privatized urban developments as spaces for experimentation with and enactment of alternative, dissonant, and subversive gendered performances.

BANU GÖKARIKSEL is an associate professor of geography with a joint appointment in global studies at the University of North Carolina, Chapel Hill, and an adjunct appointment at Duke Women's Studies. She is an editor of the *Journal of Middle East Women's Studies* (2015–18). She works on the politics of everyday life and questions of religion, secularism, and gender with a focus on bodies and urban space in Turkey. She collaborated with Anna Secor on a project funded by the National Science Foundation that examines the production and consumption of veiling fashion. Her current project with Secor analyzes the renewed role of religion in the public sphere of Turkey (also funded by the NSF). She has contributed articles to a number of scholarly journals and chapters to several edited books and coedited a special issue of the *Journal of Middle East Women's Studies* on Muslim women, consumer capitalism, and the Islamic culture industry.

FRANCES S. HASSO is an associate professor in the Program in Gender, Sexuality and Feminist Studies, holds a secondary appointment in the Sociology Department, and is an affiliate faculty member in the Middle East Studies Center at Duke University. She is an editor of the *Journal of Middle East Women's Studies* (2015–18) and the author of *Consuming Desires: Family Crisis and the State in the Middle East* (2011) and *Resistance, Repression and Gender Politics in Occupied Palestine and Jordan* (2005). She has published a number of book chapters and journal articles, most recently "Civil and the Limits of Politics in Revolutionary Egypt," in *Comparative Studies of South Asia, Africa and the Middle East* (2015).

SONALI PAHWA is an assistant professor of theater arts and dance at the University of Minnesota. An anthropologist of theater and performance in the Arab world, she has researched youth theater and self-help performance in pre-revolution Egypt and street performance at Egyptian protests and festivals. A new project on women's digital lives in Egypt brings the lens of performance to blogs, vlogs, YouTube channels, and video games. Her theoretical interests include affect theory, gender performance, materiality, and virtuality.

ZAKIA SALIME is an associate professor of sociology and women's and gender studies at Rutgers University. She is the author of *Between Feminism and Islam: Human Rights and Sharia Law in Morocco* (2011). Her work covers the areas of gender and globalization, culture, social movements, youth cultural politics, and the political economy of the "war on terror." Her current project investigates the Soulaliyyates movement, a nationwide grassroots mobilization for land rights led by rural women in contemporary Morocco. She explores communal land privatization and the disruptive voices of rural women and their agency as they negotiate competing notions of value, belonging, development, and rights.

INDEX

Note: page numbers in *italics* refer to illustrations.

Baber, Zaheer, 106–7

backstage politics, 154

Bahrain: demographics and differential access to resources and jobs in, 109–10, 132n24; Economic Vision 2030 and Northern Town campaign, 109; gender culture in, 105, 110–12; global and regional networks in, 129; Iranian revolution, impact of, 112; Al Khalifa regime, 109; National Action Charter (2000), 113; National Democratic Action Society, 115; regime surveillance in, 108; sectarianism in, 106–10; women's rights and codification of family law in, 112–13. *See also* Pearl Revolution

Bahrain Online (Multaqa bahrayn), 114

Bahrain Shield videos, 126–27, *127*

Balti, 59, 60–61

Banoub, Amanda, 202

Barthes, Roland, 200

Bassam, Rehab, 28, 30

Bayat, Asef, 6, 150

Belaid, Chokri, 52, 72, 78n41

Ben Ali, Zine al Abidine, 51, 57, 62, 65, 72, 75n5, 140

Bendir Man, 59, 76n19

Ben Jaafar, Mustapha, 51–52

Bennett, Andy, 75n4

Ben Slama, Raja, 76n18

Ben Youssef, Nejib, 53

Berger, John, 204–5

Berlant, Lauren, 31, 84

Bhabha, Homi, 149, 199

al-Bidh, Ali Salim, 93–94

blogs, Egyptian women's: Abdel Aal's *I Want to Get Married*, 28; affective performance and subject formation in digital persona, 32–36; autobiographical blogs, 25–26; citizenship, space for reframing performance of, 45; civil society activism vs. sentimental politics and, 40–43; debate repertoires, development of, 39–40; discursive authority and, 33; disidentification and, 27, 44–45; Eman and *Lasto Adri* (I Don't Know), 29, 30–31, 32–34, 36–37, 44–45; Fatma, 32, 34–36, 39; intimate body politics and, 226; intimate publics, digital home, and, 29–32; *Kalam Banat* (Girls' Talk), 29–30; "Kolena Laila" network (We Are All Laila), 36–39,

41, 44; Maha, 39, 40–41, 42; Mona's *Maat's Bits & Pieces*, 25, 41–43; as performative, 26; the personal, political, and gendered in blog genres, 27–29; as personal blogs, 27; post-revolution trends, 44–45; prerevolution blogs, 28; Shahinaz Abdel Salam, 44–45; "We Are Sorry" post (Sara), 37–38. *See also* nude activism of Aliaa Magda Elmahdy

blogs, Saudi Arabian women's, 169–72, 177–85

blogs and blogosphere: autobiographical blogs, 25–26; civil society activism vs., 40–43; gender as marker of genre (Egypt), 27–28, 29; as incubator of civil society, 41; new political space, blog networks as, 36–40; publication of (Egypt), 28; women's activism, role in, 8–9

bodies and embodiment: as artistic representation of being, 208; artists disrupting normative social order with, 198; audiovisual Islamist mythscapes and, 62–63; Bahrain's Pearl Revolution and, 105, 119–25; body as material space of multiple dimensions, 4; centrality of gender and sexuality in revolutions revealed by, 247–48; destruction of, as microrebellion, 227; dualisms destabilized by, 250n17; erotic capital and, 205; feminist geopolitics and, 225; *fitna* (disorder or chaos), women's bodies as source of, 169, 208; Freeze for Freedom, 158–59, *159*; Haraway's cyborg, 198; intimate body politics, 223, 225–27; investment and disinvestment, 213; language of the body, finding, 196; male hypervisibility and female invisibility, 140; as modalities of power, 247; Morocco's Feb20 Movement and, 144, 149, 152; naming of body parts in public forum, 158; ownership of one's body, 210, 212; political claims made by, 247; potency of embodied expression, 198–99; public sites of violence, bodies as, 235; public spaces redefined through, 243–44; sexual turn in Morocco's Feb20 Movement and, 155–58; as sites of ideological reproduction and resistance, 242; solidaristic modes of resistance and, 153; space as corporeal practice, 90; space-body nexus, 4, 144; spatial body politics (overview), 9–12; spatial strategies, embodied (overview), 11; stripping as staged act of formal destruction, 199; "throwntogetherness" and, 243; Tunisian secularist mythscapes and, 65–70. *See also* intimacy; nude activism of Aliaa Magda Elmahdy; sartorial practices

Bondi, Liz, 14

Bouazizi, Mohamed, 12, 51, 58, 227

Boughalbi, Amina, *145*, 145–46, 149

Bourdieu, Pierre, 22n42

Bouslama, Rabia, 156

Brahmi, Mbarka, 72–73

Brahmi, Muhammad, 52, 72–73

Brown, Wendy, 7

Buali, Sheyma, 109

Burden, Chris, 205

Butler, Judith, 213, 247

call to prayer, feminist version of, 212

Cansever, Emine, 238, *238*

cartoons, Tunisian, 66, *71*, 71–72

chaos, 15–17

citizenship: aesthetic, in Morocco, 149; in Bahrain, 109, 131n12; differentiated, in Morocco, 149; Egyptian women's blogs and reframing of performance of, 46; sexy or diva, in Elmahdy's nude activism, 204; Tunisian Revolution and, 58

civilpolitics, 81, 95, 96–97. *See also* Southern Yemen, gender relations and civil-politics in

civil society activism and blog politics, 40–43

civil state, defined, 99n5

class: *akhdam* social group (Yemen), 91, 102n39; in Bahrain, 110; Morocco's Feb20 Movement and, 156; "riffraff" and, in Tunisian parody, 69; Southern Yemen revolution and, 91, 92–93

Clifford, James, 90

clothing. *See* sartorial practices

Conquest of the Clock (Tunisia), 64–65, 226

counterpublics, 31

Cut Piece (Ono), 205

"cyber-niqabs," 76n18

Dabashi, Hamid, 7, 199

Darija language, 147–49, 163n27

Davidson, Joyce, 14

decentralization trends, 11–12

democratic centralism, 11, 22n34

digital home, 30–31

digital persona, 32–36

digital publics, Egyptian women's blogs and, 29

digital revolution and conflict, 8, 113. *See also* blogs and blogosphere

Dinshaw, Carolyn, 65

disidentification, 9, 17, 27, 44–45, 197, 204, 213–14, 225

dissensus, 9, 119, 139, 144, 158, 245

al-Dosari, Hala, 171, 177–78

Doumato, Eleanor, 169, 171, 182

driving rights. *See* Women2Drive campaign, Saudi Arabia

eating together as protest, 257n113

Egypt: classed and gendered space in Cairo, 13; disappearances in, 50n49; feminism in, 200–201; private and public space in Cairo, 12; "revolution of the body" (*thawrat al-jasad*), 12; *sitt al-banat* ("the girl in the blue bra") assault, 42, 223, 234–35; Ultras soccer fans in, 14

Egyptian women's blogs. *See* blogs, Egyptian women's; nude activism of Aliaa Magda Elmahdy

El Général, 59, 76n19

Elmahdy, Aliaa. *See* nude activism of Aliaa Magda Elmahdy

Elsadda, Hoda, 9

Eltahawy, Mona, 202

emasculation, 53, 55

English language, use of, 35

Enloe, Cynthia, 205

Ennahda Party, Tunisia, 51–52, 66, 68–69, 73, 74n1

Ennaji, Moha, 13

Erdoğan, Recep Tayyip, 228, 229, 230, 232, 236, 239, 240

Errazouki, Samia, 156

Essebsi, Beji Caid, 52

Eyck, Aldo van, 167

al-Ezab, Rasha, 41–42

Facebook: Bahrain Online (Multaqa bahrayn), 114; Elmahdy's nude activism and,

El Saadawi, Nawal, 206

Sadiqi, Fatima, 13

al-Saffar, Rula, 125

Sahat al-iʿtisam (Sit-in Square), Aden, 103n46

Said, Khaled, 43, 46. See also *We Are All Khaled Said* Facebook page

Salafism, 52, 62–65, 152, 154, 196–97

Saleh, ʿAli ʿAbdullah, 23n59, 82–83, 100n13, 103n40

Salih, Zahra Abdullah, 97

Salime, Zakia, 175

Salman, Ali, 125

sartorial practices: *ʿAbaya* (full black cloak), 120, 169; in Bahrain, 111, 120, 121, *121*; drag performance, Tunisian national identity presented as, 55–56; *hijab* (headscarf), 35, 121; invisibility and, 101n29; *niqab* (face veil), 66–67, 87–88, 169, 172; in Saudi Arabia, 169, 172, 181; *Sefsari*, 72; in Southern Yemen, 87–88, 90–91; in Tunisia, 66–67, 72

Saudi Arabia (KSA): gender regime in, 168–72; Internet access and surveillance in, 174–75, 189n49; oil revenue in, 168; religious police (*mutawwiʿin*), 169, 170, 171, 181, 182; shopping malls in, 181–82, 192n86; walking in, 182–83; women's blogs in, 169–72, 177–85; women's suffrage in, 185, 194n115. *See also* Women2Drive campaign, Saudi Arabia

Saudi Nail Polish Girl, 180, 182

Saudi Stepford Wife, 169, 177–78, 182–83, 184

"Sawt al-marʾa ʿawra" (The voice of women is defective), 16

"Sawt al-marʾa thawra" (The voice of women is a revolution), 16–17, 24n63

sect-sex-police nexus in Bahrain, 107, 125–28

secularism, 54, 60, 65–70, 75n6, 141, 142–43

Sefsari, 72

sentimental politics, 36, 42–43

sexual abuse and assault, 41–42, 125, 156–57, 201

sexual harassment in public spaces, 26, 36–39, 95, 111, 156, 197, 208

sexuality and sexualization: asynchrony and, 65; Bahrain's Pearl Revolution and, 125, 128; body revealing centrality of, 247–48; Elmahdy's nude activism and, 196, 208, 213; headscarf-wearing mother with baby story (Turkey) and, 236; LGBTQ, 174, 230, 240; Morocco's Feb20 Movement, sexual turn in, 155–58; naming of body parts and, 158; national identity and, 74; nudity, agency expressed by, 199–200; purity narratives and, 74; refusal to postpone addressing, 205–6; sect-sex-police nexus in Bahrain, 107, 125–28; sex as terror, 201; slingshot auntie image (Turkey) and, 238; Taksim Gezi Park protests, Istanbul, and, 233–35, 242; Tunisian narratives and, 65, 70; virginity and virginity tests, 12, 155, 197, 208, 210, 227

Sghiri, Malek, 11

Shabakat al-tadamun maʿ al-shuʿub (Network of Solidarity with the Peoples), 140

al-Shabib, Hussain, 111–12, 121

Shabout, Nadia, 159

Shamsir, Radhia, 85

al-Sharif, Manal, 170, 172, 182–83, 189n37

Shawqi, Nida, 93

al-Shehabi, Alaʾa, 113–14, 119–20, 127–28

Al Shmasi, Azza, 172, 173

shopping malls in Saudi Arabia, 181–82, 192n86

Silueta Series (Mendieta), 205

al-Sisi, Abdel Fattah, 44

sitt al-banat ("the girl in the blue bra"), Egypt, 42, 223, 234–35

Skalli, Loubna, 175

sleeping in public, 245

slingshot auntie (*sapanlı teyze*) image (Turkey), 237–38, *238*

SlutWalk, 156, 164n50

Smith, Sara, 225

Sontag, Susan, 231

Southern Revolution. *See* Southern Yemen, gender relations and civil politics in

Southern Yemen, gender relations and civil politics in: al-ʿAidrus Revolution Square, 91–92, *92*; competing narratives from Sanaʿa and the South, 83–84; establishment of Southern Movement, 98n2; gendered spatiality and intimacy, political history of, 84–88; informal activities and projects, 81; intimate politics in revolutionary Aden, 88–97; Khormaksar Revolution Square, 95–97, *96*, 103n46; Midan Revo-

Yassine, Sheikh Abdessalam, 143
Yazbek, Samar, 7
Yemen: Ansar Allah Houthi movement, 83,
97; civil war, 84–85; gendered spatiality in, 84–88; Hadhramaut, 91, 102n38;
Islah Party, 83, 92, 103n42; mixed-gender
activism in, 11; National Committee of
Women, 87, 101n27; political history of, 80,
82–84, 100n13; private and public space in,
12–13; regime violence against citizens, 97,
103n48. *See also* Aden, Southern Yemen;
Southern Yemen, gender relations and
civilpolitics in
Yemeni Socialist Party, 80, 94, 99n9, 100n20
Yemeni Youth Revolution, 82
YouTube, 119, 126–27, *127*, 173

Zaʿbar, Ahmed ʿUmar, 69–70
Zerilli, Linda, 9
Zitane, Naima, 158